'*A Global Law of Diversity* marks a milestone in the studies on territorial and cultural pluralism. It provides a methodological framework to analyse and further develop the instruments to cope with growing complexity in contemporary societies.'

Prof. Francesco Palermo, *University of Verona and Eurac Research Bolzano/Bozen*

'In *A Global Law of Diversity*, Alessi breaks new grounds for the study of diversity accommodation in a perspective of constitutionalism. Drawing on global sources of law-making and by boldly infusing non-codified models, he presents a new conceptual framework. Anyone ready to question the status quo of legal theory will find this ground-breaking volume rewarding.'

Prof. Tove H. Malloy, *Europa-Universität Flensburg*

'This excellent work of comparative legal research integrates the equality paradigm with a comprehensive "law of diversity" to overcome the State-bias in majority-minority relations. *A Global Law of Diversity* is a valuable contribution to the exploration of the constitutional foundations of truly inclusive societies. Necessary, because in countertendency to the current political trends in many countries.'

Prof. Jens Woelk, *University of Trento*

A Global Law of Diversity

This book provides a global perspective on the accommodation of diversity within constitutional traditions, considering the most innovative approaches and legal instruments of the Global North and Global South. This field of study, traditionally dominated by a Global North approach based on majority-minority and rights-based discourse, is undergoing significant development. The work thus assesses the appropriateness of the existing mainstream theoretical tools and concepts – in particular minority and minority-related concepts as well as rights discourse – to grasp the ongoing evolution of this field of law. A reconsideration of the traditional conceptual categories and the introduction of the concept "Law of Diversity" is proposed as a theoretical framework to grasp the ongoing developments in this area. Among the models studied, those that are referred to as emergent models for the accommodation of diversity in the Global North appear to be particularly in need of theoretical recognition. To this end, the theory of federalism is used to serve a rather unexplored theoretical function. Federal theory is put forward as a theoretical instrument to frame and explain the emergent instruments for the accommodation of diversity, as well as provide practical solutions for their development. The book will be of interest to researchers, academics, and policy-makers working in the areas of comparative constitutional law, minority and indigenous rights law, and federal studies.

Nicolò Paolo Alessi is a post-doctoral researcher in Comparative Public Law at the World Trade Institute and the Institute of Political Science of the University of Bern. His main research interests are Italian and comparative constitutional law, diversity accommodation, minority rights, gender governance, climate governance, and federalism. He is also an expert on the Aosta Valley's legal system.

Routledge Advances in Minority Studies

Series Editors Stavroula Pipyrou is a Senior Lecturer in Social Anthropology at the University of St Andrews, UK, and Founding Director of the cross-disciplinary Centre for Minorities Research (CMR). She has published widely on minority politics, governance, and civil society in Italy and Greece.

Kyriaki Topidi is Head of the Research Cluster on Culture and Diversity and a Senior Researcher at the European Centre for Minority Issues, Germany. Her research interests focus on diversity management, minority protection rights and mechanisms, with a special interest in religion, and human rights law. She has published extensively on these and related areas.

Routledge Advances in Minority Studies (RAMS) provides a platform for outstanding state-of-the-art research on interdisciplinary and intersectional understandings of minorities, globally. Monographs and edited volumes in the series advance scholarly and practitioner insights from Anthropology, Law, Politics, Sociology, History and beyond. The series foregrounds pluralism and diversity of both authors and subjects of study, with a particular focus on emerging fields and marginalized voices.

Under the editorial supervision of Dr Stavroula Pipyrou and Dr Kyriaki Topidi, the series will be a primary source for students, scholars and practitioners in minority studies while presenting authors with a valuable means to reach a wide and growing readership.

Titles in the series:

Minority Rights and Social Change
Norms, Actors and Strategies
Edited by Kyriaki Topidi and Eugenia Relaño Pastor

Minorities at War
Cultural Identity and Resilience in Ukraine
Edited by Elmira Muratova and Nadia Zasanska

A Global Law of Diversity
Evolving Models and Concepts
Nicolò Paolo Alessi

For more information about this series, please visit: https://www.routledge.com/Routledge-Advances-in-Minority-Studies/book-series/RAIMS

A Global Law of Diversity

Evolving Models and Concepts

Nicolò Paolo Alessi

Routledge
Taylor & Francis Group
LONDON AND NEW YORK

First published 2025
by Routledge
4 Park Square, Milton Park, Abingdon, Oxon OX14 4RN

and by Routledge
605 Third Avenue, New York, NY 10158

Routledge is an imprint of the Taylor & Francis Group, an informa business

The Open Access publication of this book has been published with the support of the Swiss National Science Foundation.

British Library Cataloguing-in-Publication Data
A catalogue record for this book is available from the British Library

Library of Congress Cataloging-in-Publication Data
Names: Alessi, Nicolò Paolo, author.
Title: A global law of diversity : evolving models and concepts / Nicolò Paolo Alessi.
Description: Abingdon, Oxon [UK] ; New York, NY : Routledge, 2024. | Series: Routledge advances in minority studies | Includes bibliographical references and index.
Identifiers: LCCN 2024030575 (print) | LCCN 2024030576 (ebook) | ISBN 9781032795850 (hardback) | ISBN 9781032797199 (paperback) | ISBN 9781003493518 (ebook)
Subjects: LCSH: Minorities—Legal status, laws, etc. | Cultural pluralism. | Culture and law.
Classification: LCC K3242 .A947 2024 (print) | LCC K3242 (ebook) | DDC 342.08/7—dc23/eng/20240714
LC record available at https://lccn.loc.gov/2024030575
LC ebook record available at https://lccn.loc.gov/2024030576

ISBN: 978-1-032-79585-0 (hbk)
ISBN: 978-1-032-79719-9 (pbk)
ISBN: 978-1-003-49351-8 (ebk)

DOI: 10.4324/9781003493518

Typeset in Galliard
by Apex CoVantage, LLC

To my wonderful wife Kerstin, who simply makes everything brighter.
To Itala and Edoardo, loving grandparents that I miss every day.
To Raffaella, Nicola, Gaia, Mattia, and Marta, for always being there when it counts.

Contents

Foreword

Minority studies have been deeply engaged in the past few decades in understanding how national and ethnic minority (or minoritized) groups develop their identities as recognizable subjects in need of legal protection. From multiculturalist and interculturalist frames to the pursuit of policy aims such as social cohesion and diversity governance, states and their constitutional settings have been challenged by the quest to embed intersectionally factors of vulnerability of traditional and new minority groups in frames of both anti-discrimination laws as well as within more distinct minority protection regimes. Minority protection, in the meantime, has made an important transition: it is less considered as a separate competence within the centralized state's strict realm but rather a transversal objective that attracts a variety of actors and stakeholders. As such, more complex solutions compatible with life within culturally super-diverse societies are being considered and, in some cases, developed.

The role of law in these circumstances can be two-fold: to operate as a conflict-resolution tool and/or to adopt a more inclusive function fostering pluralism.[1] Indeed, comparative studies of contemporary European constitutional texts suggest that there is an increase observed in the total number of grounds of discrimination recognized.[2] But do these provisions adequately capture the socio-legal dynamics and processes at play that prevent minority groups from achieving substantive, meaningful equality in opportunities? True, constitutions are limited framework documents, but they are still ones that may change and evolve. Social and political contexts differ tremendously and yet remain united in their struggles to respond adequately to cultural diversity. The challenge in these circumstances is to devise instruments that correspond more closely to the needs of minority groups, striking a balance

1 Palermo, Francesco and Woelk, Jens, "From Minority Protection to a Law of Diversity? Reflections on the Evolution of Minority Rights", 3 *European Yearbook of Minority Issues 2003/4* (2005), 5–13.

2 Ruiz Vieytez, Eduardo J., "Constitutions, Minorities and Superdiversity", 19 *The Age of Human Rights Journal* (2022), 187–203.

between equality and difference, autonomy and inclusion. Through proportionality, efficiency, and sustainability assessments, the law thus can attempt to become inclusive in its construction and outlook.

Within these processes, cultural pluralism has occupied constitutional spaces within individual state frameworks in multiple ways. The main instrument to defend cultural pluralist approaches has been built around the idea of equality. The idea of equality has been, nevertheless, criticized as falling short of delivering an adequate standard of fairness to minorities and disadvantaged groups. Will Kymlicka, Charles Taylor, Bhikhu Parekh, or Iris Marion Young, to name some of the proponents of such criticism, have advocated for a long time the idea that states should actively engage with ethno-cultural differences of minority groups through special recognition or exemption regimes. Moving in this direction while grounded in multidisciplinarity, the *Law of Diversity* reflects on the fundamental query of what constitutes the rule and what the exception is in each context where different groups co-exist.

The *Law of Diversity* has been defined as "the body of law that has been and is being developed to deal with the issues involved in accommodating the differences represented by diverse groups within a pluralistic society".[3] It is based on the assumption that as societies evolve in their composition and needs, so does the law governing the diversity within them. So far, the design and implementation of legal norms have been largely based on the categorisation of people into groups, although it is becoming increasingly clear that minority group members experience both the development of their identities but also discrimination in more individualized terms. Alongside language, ethnicity, religion, or nationality, the *Law of Diversity*, as a direct response to the need to consider broader matrices of disadvantage, is additionally turning to gender, political opinions and convictions, or socio-economic status, to name a few examples to devise anti-discrimination legal processes and guarantees. Within these processes, methodological and analytical tools such as legal pluralism, federalism, and intersectionality, to name a few, are being considered as tools likely to capture the multiple and complex ways in which our societies are diversifying. The challenge then becomes to devise adequate legal indicators that allow fair and equitable outcomes in diversity management. What remains nevertheless constant in these various constellations is the observable involvement of a wider number of actors – beyond states – when shaping the normative principles and practical legal solutions used to accommodate differences.

In the study of such complex legal solutions, comparative law must take account of the cultural aspects that guide and determine a society's approach to the *Law of Diversity*. In this task, the law must also be approached as a cultural phenomenon, including within its 'soft law' components. The cultural embeddedness of solutions is, in any case, not foreign to comparative public

3 Palermo, Francesco, "Accommodating Differences: The Present and Future of the Law of Diversity", 30 *Vermont Law Review* (2006), 431–442, at 431.

law methodology. Neither are asymmetry, pluralism, and negotiation as identifiable features in the process of understanding and assessing differences across legal systems and cultures. Still, what becomes particularly remarkable is how legal instruments in the field of diversity "become outdated with increasing speed".[4] This speed of social change is spearheaded by non-state actors, including the minority groups themselves or private entities,[5] making evolution not only inevitable but also faster and harder for states and their legal systems to follow.

Unsurprisingly, public tasks and diversity governance functions are therefore characterized today by a tendency of polycentric diffusion. Devolved and decentralized options have proliferated in managing diversity at the state level. At the same time, given the exponential growth of 'diversities' and the proliferation of grounds for the protection of difference, the regulatory framing of difference is being embedded in law and policy-making more and more horizontally, in mainstreaming terms. As policies of diversity move closer to local authorities, by virtue of decentralization forces and arrangements, the complexity of the *Law of Diversity* becomes also noticeable. The richness of tools devised for the protection and promotion of diversity is testimony to such complexity but also to the versatility of solutions within which minority groups strive to exist and make themselves heard.

Ultimately, the current dynamics of diversification indicate that the *Law of Diversity* will not lose any of its grip when it comes to combatting discriminatory and segregating trends in society. More than that, it can assist the legal discipline in acknowledging and embedding the impact of cross-membership of certain groups within societies. Such a function for law is invaluable, especially in a considerable number of circumstances where difference tends to become the rule and equality the exception.

Dr. habil. Kyriaki Topidi
European Centre for Minority Issues

4 Palermo, Accommodating Differences . . . , 436.
5 Consider, for instance, the pressure applied by digitalization and technological evolution processes on minority cultural diversity and protection mechanisms.

Acknowledgments

I would like to thank Professor Francesco Palermo, to whom I am profoundly grateful for being the first person who believed in me and my research project and for giving me the opportunity to work on it.

A special thanks go to all the people who, in different ways, contributed to this achievement: Eva Maria Belser, Lidia Bonifati, my friends and colleagues at Eurac Research in Bolzano/Bozen (and, above all, Greta Klotz, Martina Trettel and Alice Valdesalici), all the Professor and colleagues that helped me enrich my work through their suggestions and comments.

Among them, I would like to express my sincere gratitude to Kyriaki Topidi, who generously endorsed the inclusion of this book in this Routledge series.

Introduction

From minorities to diversity: a global inquiry

Diversity and constitutionalism: an introduction

This book aims to provide a general overview of the global trends related to the accommodation of diversity within the constitutional tradition. Based on this, it will then offer some theoretical considerations that aim to support the introduction of a renewed conceptual framework to recognize and validate the most innovative models for diversity accommodation and possibly foster their development.

The evolution of how the law approaches the many forms of societal diversity is inextricably intertwined with the trends of constitutionalism on the whole and its demarche towards the continuous implementation of its structural principles as a legal and political doctrine.

First, modern liberal constitutionalism has implemented some foundational (and, at the time, revolutionary) content – especially the legal entrenchment of rights and the principle of equality. Constitutionalism and democracy have broadened the scope of their application and determined a rise in sensitivity to many forms of diversity.

Secondly, the democratic evolution of constitutionalism has structurally favored the increasing legal recognition of diversity since it has provided stable channels for the expression of societal pluralism. In other words, recognizing the enforceability of rights as a basis of contemporary democracy means that claims for the protection or promotion of differential conditions find a relatively steady, concrete, and reliable mode of expression and, thus, a specific target for political mobilization.[1] More generally, the expansion of democracy, together with its peaceful and pluralist content, encourages the expression of diversity through both political activism at different levels and civil associationism and implies the inclusion of broader sectors of society in decision-making processes.[2] As a consequence, the structural promotion of pluralism has led

1 Kymlicka, Will, "Multiculturalism and Minority Rights: West and East", 14(4) *Journal on Ethnopolitics and Minority Issues in Europe* (JEMIE) (2015), 4–25, at 9–11.

2 Kymlicka, Multiculturalism . . ., 9–11.

DOI: 10.4324/9781003493518-1

to increased legal prominence of diversity (naturally to various extents and in many forms, based on the different countries' traditions).

In other words, the liberal contents of constitutions have been conducive to the growing legal relevance of diversity, which today holds a significant place in several constitutional systems and expresses, to different extents, liberal-democratic constitutionalism's counter-majoritarian and, especially, pluralist rationale.[3]

Following the process of decolonization, Global North constitutionalism has become a worldwide doctrine that has expanded as a consequence of (military or economic) imposition or the prestige of its democratic contents.[4] Nevertheless, in parallel, other visions of constitutionalism have gradually emerged and enriched the global constitutional discourse. Consequently, comparative constitutional lawyers are increasingly encouraged not to address constitutionalism as a unitary category but to consider the varieties of constitutional traditions that have developed in different areas of the world.[5]

As in constitutional theory in general, the Global North has had an epistemological, theoretical, and practical hegemonic role as concerns the study of the models for the legal and constitutional accommodation of diversity. Accordingly, the models and theoretical reconstructions stemming from this tradition have essentially dominated academic and political milieus as well as international law developments.

From a practical legal perspective, the protection of diversity has traditionally assumed two main shapes in the Global North, at both domestic and international levels.

On the one hand, several dimensions of diversity have increasingly been addressed by non-discrimination legal instruments in a bid to implement the principle of equality, in its various manifestations.[6]

3 Ruiz Vieytez, Eduardo J., "Diversity, Immigration and Minorities Within a Human Rights Framework", in Ruiz Vieytez, Eduardo J. and Dunbar, Robert (eds.), *Human Rights and Diversity: New Challenges for Plural Societies* (University of Deusto, Bilbao, 2007), 20–33, at 25, referred to rights as "exceptions to the numerical rule of the majority", and, at 29–30, he indicated that "the whole idea of human rights, constitutes a corrective or a limit to the numerical rule of the majority".

4 Glenn, Patrick, *Legal Traditions of the World: Sustainable Diversity in Law* (Oxford University Press, Oxford, 2004), 273–274.

5 On this, see Dowdle, Michael W. and Wilkinson, Michael A., "On the Limits of Constitutional Liberalism: In Search of Constitutional Reflexivity", in Dowdle, Michael W. and Wilkinson, Michael A. (eds.), *Constitutionalism Beyond Liberalism* (Cambridge University Press, Cambridge, 2017), 17–37.

6 Because, as will be seen, the present work is not specifically focused on the theoretical framing of the concept of equality (right or principle), nor on the theoretical differences between equality and non-discrimination, these issues will not be addressed extensively. In general, while in the literature equality has been described as a value, a principle, and a right, it will here mainly be referred to as the principle of equality.

On the other, when further legal measures to protect and promote diversity have been put in place, they have generally taken a specific shape and structure, i.e., they have been framed in terms of the rights of people belonging to some selected cultural, linguistic, religious or ethnic minorities[7] having a varying collective dimension.[8] In fact, what the historical developments show is that some factors of diversity have been prominently addressed (and protected beyond non-discrimination) by law, namely, cultural, linguistic, religious, or ethnic features, strong identifiers of persons and groups, and, in particular, very powerful grounds for political (elite) mobilization.[9] As a result, a specific corpus of human rights has been established in international law – namely, minority and indigenous peoples' rights law – in parallel to the general framework of human rights law. This is variously implemented by state legal systems, especially in Europe.

Notably, the wealth of legal and political literature that has been devoted to this topic, albeit from various perspectives,[10] as well as state responses and international law, have mainly relied on this basic distinction. The analysis of the legal responses to diversity is, therefore, rooted in two distinct branches of study that, in practice, have hardly communicated. Accordingly, non-discrimination legal instruments have been studied and applied as wide-ranging measures potentially protecting an indefinite number of differential conditions, while further legal instruments have generally been framed in terms of minority and indigenous rights, with their application connected to some legally selected addressees having specific ethno-cultural features.

The present seems to offer new challenges and avenues for this field of study, both within and outside the Global North tradition.

The first goal of the work – after having described the varying treatment of diversity within liberal and liberal-democratic constitutionalism in Chapters 1 and 2 – will be to offer an exhaustive account of the most recent and innovative tendencies in this area of law.

7 Hereinafter, they will be referred to as "national minorities"; when the legal models and provisions analyzed in what follows show a wider reach than national minorities, "non-majority groups" or "non-dominant groups" will be used.

8 The very concept of autonomy is also often framed in terms of a collective right; for instance, see Jakubowski, Andrzej, *Cultural Rights as Collective Rights: An International Law Perspective* (Brill-Nijhoff, Leiden, 2016).

9 On the role of ethnic politics and minority elites in shaping minority rights, see Brubaker, Roger, *Nationalism Reframed: Nationhood and the National Question in the New Europe* (Cambridge University Press, Cambridge, 1996); May, Stephen, Modood, Tariq and Squires, Judith (eds.), *Ethnicity, Nationalism, and Minority Rights* (Cambridge University Press, Cambridge, 2004).

10 On this, see Heinze, Eric, "The Construction and Contingency of the Minority Concept", in Fottrell, Deirdre and Bowring, Bill (eds.), *Minority and Groups Rights in the New Millennium* (Martinus Nijhoff, The Hague, 1999), 25–74.

A snapshot of the trends and innovations in the Global North: between macro- and micro-perspectives

In the Global North, migration flows and globalization have undoubtedly determined new claims and challenges for the accommodation of differences in what have been defined as diverse and divided societies[11] and shaped the continuously increasing social and political sensitivity to human diversity in democratic settings in several parts of the world. Consequently, Western democratic legal systems are confronted – albeit with variations from country to country – with increasing demands for recognition and accommodation. These have come from several, more or less cohesive groups expressing various kinds of diversity, making variable requests. For instance, among them, one can identify the so-called new minorities – constituted of people with migratory backgrounds – and a composite ensemble of other societal groups, such as people with disabilities, women, the LGBTQ+ community, and the elderly, to name just a few.

These trends are putting under stress the consolidated categories and approach of minority and indigenous peoples' rights law.

This is all the more evident if one draws attention to the international level. Since the nineties, the international community has worked to rapidly construct a minority (and indigenous peoples) rights framework following the explosion of ethnic tension after the end of the Cold War. Such a system – which relies on the theoretical assumptions sketched previously and a generally defensive approach to the survival of minorities – successfully contributed to overcoming that phase of emergency.[12] The international system had, in fact, a strong influence on state legal systems and a profound impact on constitutional developments regarding minority rights, especially on the European continent. However, after overcoming the emergency, international law has faced notable difficulties both in its conditioning

11 On the concepts of diverse and divided societies, see, among others, Choudry, Sujit, "Bridging Comparative Politics and Comparative Law: Constitutional Design in Divided Societies", in Choudry, Sujit (ed.), *Constitutional Design for Divided Societies: Integration or Accommodation?* (Oxford University Press, Oxford, 2008), 3–40, at 4–5: "whether through conquest, colonization, slavery or immigration, it is hard to imagine a state today that is not diverse in one or more of these dimensions. The age of the ethno-culturally homogeneous state, if there ever was one, is long over"; diverse societies are be distinguished from the so-called divided societies for in the latter diversity is the origin of cleavages that have a political and social salience: Choudry, Bridging Comparative Politics . . . , 4–5: "a divided society is not merely a society which is ethnically, linguistically, religiously, or culturally diverse. . . . Rather, what marks a divided society is that these differences are politically salient – that is, they are persistent markers of political identity and bases for political mobilization".

12 Palermo, Francesco, "Current and Future Challenges for International Minority Protection", 10 *European Yearbook of Minority Issues* (2011), 21–36, at 22–25.

function[13] and in addressing the challenges that the implementation of a consolidated system for the accommodation of diversity poses beyond the basic guarantee of survival for non-majority groups.[14] In particular, the security approach to minority and indigenous rights – relying on exclusive identity framings and "hard" forms of protection – proved ineffective when it came to providing solutions for the peaceful integration of diversity in contemporary societies.[15]

Against this background, this work aims to illustrate that Global North legal systems are evolving in response to the described trends, offering solutions designed to manage a complex and fluid society where individuals can find themselves members of several more or less cohesive groups.

Consequently, legal sources at both domestic and international levels show signs of an emergent approach that understands and legally addresses diversity as a general phenomenon – the management of which requires the dynamic and proportionate employment of a wide set of legal instruments, regardless of the recipients' type of differential condition and legal status.[16] Along with non-discrimination – a basic and essential form of guarantee for every individual – and minority and indigenous peoples' rights, other legal approaches and tools are emerging.

In this sense, in recent decades, European international law has attempted to develop a renovated perspective in a bid to overcome the structural limits of its defensive approach. Accordingly, it has progressively shifted the focus from minority (and indigenous) rights to the concepts of diversity accommodation and integration of diverse societies – where diversity is a general, complex, and dynamic societal phenomenon – with a view to extending the scope of minority rights and revitalizing their function in response to the contemporary challenges.

Along with international developments and their various implementations, further and "less orthodox" forms of accommodation have also emerged in the Global North. The latter are meant to accommodate diversity beyond non-discrimination and diverge, to different degrees, from the traditional structure of minority and indigenous rights, primarily focusing on governance rather than rights.

13 Palermo, Francesco, "'The Borders of My Language Mean the Borders of My World'. Language Rights and Their Evolving Significance for Minority Rights and Integration of Societies", in Ulasiuk, Iryna, Hadîrcă, Laurenţiu and Romans, William (eds.), *Language Policy and Conflict Prevention* (Brill-Nijhoff, Leiden-Boston, 2018), 135–154, at 141, underlined "the emergence of a new 'statism'" in this area – due to several factors, such as the terrorist threat and the global financial crisis – which "considerably reduced the role of the international community in this field, pushed minority issues back into the domestic arena, limited the impact of conditionality and, in overall terms, put the minority question much lower on the priority scale of both States and international community".

14 Palermo, Current and Future Challenges . . . , 28–31 referred to a phase of "monitoring fatigue" of the international bodies.

15 Palermo, The Borders . . . , 141.

16 On this, see Ruiz Vieytez, Diversity, Immigration and Minorities . . . , 20–33; Palermo, Francesco, "Legal Solutions to Complex Societies. The Law of Diversity", in Ruiz Vieytez and Dunbar (eds.), Human Rights and Diversity . . . , 63–82.

Specific attention will be drawn in Chapter 4 to these instruments and their evolutive potential. Non-territorial autonomy (especially in its functional dimension), legal pluralism, and participatory democracy will be considered the main emergent categories of models of the "Law of Diversity" in the Global North. They can all be seen as legal instruments for the accommodation of diversity that depart from the traditional structure or paradigm underlying the traditional models and seem particularly suited to managing diverse societal settings as they resonate with their fluidity and complexity.

The described developments ultimately strive for greater inclusion and manifold accommodation of many forms of diversities in constitutional settings beyond the basic guarantee of non-discrimination. They adapt to forms that are, to various extents, different from the traditional structure of minority protection mechanisms, especially as they all imply a strong emphasis on an active role for interested non-majority groups. Furthermore, they encourage the relativization of legal classifications in this area based on minority-related concepts, according to which groups that are legally recognized as minorities enjoy positive protection or promotion through individual or collective rights. In this sense, the emergent legal instruments for the accommodation of diversity appear to be of particular interest as they show a double tendency of flexibilization, namely in terms of their structure and recipients, compared to the other categories of instruments. This double tendency indicates the decreasing significance of rigid classifications when it comes to the promotion of forms of diversity beyond those protected by minority and indigenous peoples' rights law.

The inclusion of the Global South: methodological issues and its theoretical and practical contribution

The Global North perspective does not exhaust the issue of innovative developments in the contemporary accommodation of diversity. Rather, it is worth adding another layer of analysis that stems from a Global South standpoint.

To be clear, the expression Global South will here be employed to describe the area of the world comprising Latin America, Africa and Central,[17] Middle East, South and Southeast Asia, as opposed to the Global North, including North America, most of Europe, and certain parts of Oceania and East and Southeast Asia. As illustrated by Hirschl, this global representation of

17 Central Asia covers the territory of five countries: Kazakhstan, Kyrgyzstan, Tajikistan, Turkmenistan and Uzbekistan, which gained independence following the collapse of the Soviet Union in 1991. Their inclusion among the Global South countries is debated, for they are, as observed by Levander, Caroline and Mignolo, Walter, "Introduction: The Global South and World Dis/Order", 5(1) *The Global South* (2011), 1–11, "neither in the South nor in the North but that somehow are "marginal" in relation to the global north". This condition of marginality allows for including them in the Global South, as indicated by Dzhuraev, Shairbek, "How Southern is Central Asia?", 31(2) *Newsletter of APSA Comparative Politics Section* (2021), 97–105.

the world – which was created by the former West German Chancellor Willy Brandt[18] – has substituted the pejorative terminology of "first world" versus "third world", and nowadays sits alongside the notions of "developed world" and "developing world" to describe the global socioeconomic and political divide between these two groups of countries.[19]

As far as comparative constitutional legal studies are concerned, the Global South-Global North terminology seems to add a new perspective to the established Western-Non-Western dichotomy. This standpoint is strictly tied to recognizing the equal theoretical dignity of different constitutional traditions and the need to overcome the existing methodological biases in favor of countries in the Global North in mainstream comparative constitutional studies.[20]

The inclusion of Global South traditions in the present analysis endorses this renovated approach to public law comparison, which is intended to relativize the concept of constitutionalism and attempts to reduce the centrality of the Global North point of view in comparative legal inquiry.

Specifically, the method of comparison that is followed here has been labeled as "decolonial comparative law".[21] Advocates of decolonial thought assert that what is referred to as mainstream comparative law has been long marked by the centrality of a Global North point of view. In particular, they argue that this discipline has been built on some core Eurocentric assumptions that have consistently affected its developments, namely, a focus on legislation,[22] methodological nationalism,[23] assumed homogeneity within, and

18 The so-called Brandt line is a visual depiction that divides the economic (rich) Global North and (poor) Global South; see Brandt, Willy, *North-South: A Programme for Survival: Report of the Independent Commission on International Development Issues* (Pan, London, 1980); on the continuing relevance of this visualization, see Lees, Nicolas, "The Brandt Line after Forty Years: The More North–South Relations Change, the More They Stay the Same?", 47(1) *Review of International Studies* (2021), 85–106.

19 Hirschl, Ran, *Comparative Matters: The Renaissance of Comparative Constitutional Law* (Oxford University Press, Oxford, 2014), 207.

20 Hirschl, Comparative Matters . . . , 207–223, refers to this strand of literature as the "Global South critique" to the "World Series syndrome" of comparative constitutional law; the latter refers to the methodological and normative preference for a concrete set of values and the constitutional models stemming from the Global North that characterize the mainstream comparative constitutional literature.

21 On this, and for further references, see Salaymeh, Lena and Michaels, Ralf, "Decolonial Comparative Law: A Conceptual Beginning", 22(1) *Max Planck Institute for Comparative and International Private Law Research Paper Series* (2022), 166–188.

22 Salaymeh and Michaels, Decolonial Comparative Law . . . , 171, observed that "Mainstream comparative law emerges from comparative legislation, with both positivist and anti-positivist strands sharing this heritage. Such a focus makes comparison with normative traditions or with systems that are not based on such legal rules difficult, if not impossible".

23 Which means that according to Salaymeh and Michaels, Decolonial Comparative Law . . . , 171: "The central object of modern comparative law is frequently the *national unit*" (italic of the authors) and "Non-state laws are often ignored. When non-state law is not ignored, it is often either reduced to the law of states – for example, Islamic law as the state law of Muslim-majority states – or construed like state law to fit the discipline's paradigms".

relative heterogeneity between, different legal systems,[24] and an implied superiority of the Global North.[25] Comparative legal studies have been wedded to those assumptions since their origin, leading to a hierarchization of legal systems and, most importantly, systems of thought and legal epistemologies that survived after colonization.[26] As a result, the Global South's epistemic approach to law as well as its theoretical and practical contributions, have been marked as inadequate or antiquated,[27] and comparison has been tied to the Global North. This is visible in two respects. First, its legal categories and concepts – conceived of as universally acceptable notions in a specific (Western) meaning – have been the lens through which comparative studies have been conducted; second, the Global North has constituted the benchmark against which other legal systems have been measured and, sometimes, ranked or classified.[28]

By arguing that the end of colonialism has not ended coloniality,[29] decolonial comparatists challenge the mainstream comparative standpoint, suggesting a method that understands the Global North tradition as part of a broad landscape of epistemological and political possibilities[30] (even within the Global North itself)[31] and delinks comparison from Eurocentrism.[32]

24 As stated by Salaymeh and Michaels, Decolonial Comparative Law . . . , 172, this leads to a "difficulty . . . in accounting for legal orders in ways that include necessary ambivalences and internal insuperable frictions".

25 Salaymeh and Michaels, Decolonial Comparative Law . . . , 172.

26 In fact, as stated by Reiter, Bernd, "Introduction", in Reiter, Bernd (eds.), *Constructing the Pluriverse: The Geopolitics of Knowledge* (Duke University Press, Durham-London, 2018), 1–15, at 4: "European colonization has destroyed not only people and their cultures, but also their diverse knowledge systems. Genocide thus went hand in hand with "epistemicide"; for further references, see Salaymeh and Michaels, Decolonial Comparative Law . . . , 179–180.

27 Salaymeh and Michaels, Decolonial Comparative Law . . . , 179.

28 Salaymeh and Michaels, Decolonial Comparative Law . . . , 172.

29 Which has been defined as, in the words of Walsh, Catherine, "Development as Buen Vivir: Institutional Arrangements and (De)Colonial Entanglements", in Reiter, Constructing the Pluriverse . . . , 184–196, at 184: "a matrix of global power that has hierarchically classified populations, their knowledge, and cosmological life systems according to a Eurocentric standard".

30 Boaventura de Sousa, Santos, *Epistemologies of the South: Justice against Epistemicide* (Routledge, London-New York, 2014), 44.

31 In fact, it has been affirmed that even the approach to the Global North should be the object of this reconsideration of the methodology of comparison, with a view to taking into account smaller, suppressed, or marginalized traditions and epistemologies within it; in this sense, see Santos, Epistemologies . . . , 44.

32 On this, see Mignolo, Walter D., "Delinking: The Rhetoric of Modernity, the Logic of Coloniality and the Grammar of Decoloniality", 21(2–3) *Cultural Studies* (2007), 449–514; *Id.*, "Geopolitics of Sensing and Knowing: On (De)Coloniality, Border Thinking and Epistemic Disobedience", 14(3) *Postcolonial Studies* (2011), 273–283, at 276: "Delinking means that you do not accept the options that are available to you"; see also Salaymeh and Michaels, Decolonial Comparative Law . . . , 179: "Delinking results in imagining alternatives that the status quo in the global North views as impossible".

In particular, as far as constitutional comparative law is concerned, such an approach involves delving into alternatives to Global North models and institutions, focusing on their decolonial functions, and refusing the superiority of a specific tradition. In other words, it is about openness to alternative solutions, different and plural conceptions of law and governance, and a more balanced comparison between the Global North and Global South models. Put simply, decolonial comparative law is, therefore, "a tool for discovering new legal options"[33] freed from pre-assumptions. This is supposed to enrich scientific observations and foster communication among legal systems that is not uni-directional, which implies – rather than spreading Global North institutions in the Global South or classifying the Global South by Eurocentric criteria – recognizing their equal dignity.

Along similar lines is a plural conceptualization of constitutionalism, which is advocated by a recent strand of constitutional literature. This resonates with and actualizes Tully's thought[34] – and is well represented by two recent publications, namely "*Constitutionalism Beyond Liberalism*" and "*The Global South and Comparative Constitutional Law*".[35]

According to the editors of these books, there is a need to open up constitutionalism, which requires that one refuses the structural coupling with liberalism that has marked the development of constitutional thought as well as the evolution of the discipline of comparative constitutional law. This process is capable of leading the comparative scholar to not only appreciate a wealth of constitutional experiences that are alternative or complementary to the ones exclusively based on a liberal paradigm but also possibly learn from them. This facilitates an evolution of liberal-democratic constitutionalism itself in response to the emergent needs of contemporary societies.[36] A comparison that includes constitutional orders that in many respects differ from those of the Global North is not necessarily new in comparative studies.[37] What is innovative here is the fact that equal standing is explicitly given to very different

33 Salaymeh and Michaels, Decolonial Comparative Law . . . , 186.

34 The reference here is to Tully, James, *Strange Multiplicity: Constitutionalism in an Age of Diversity* (Cambridge University Press, Cambridge, 1995) and his proposed reconceptualization of constitutionalism as a plural concept embracing a vast array of constitutional experiences; for more on Tully's account, see Chapter 1; for further theoretical references, see Hirschl, Comparative Matters . . . , 205–223.

35 Dowdle and Wilkinson (eds.), Constitutionalism Beyond Liberalism . . . ; Dann, Philipp, Riegner, Michael and Bönnemann, Maxim (eds.), *The Global South and Comparative Constitutional Law* (Oxford University Press, Oxford, 2020).

36 On this, see Dowdle, Michael W. and Wilkinson, Michael, "Introduction and Overview", in Dowdle and Wilkinson (eds.), Constitutionalism Beyond Liberalism . . . , 1–14.

37 Even though, as observed by Hirschl, Comparative Matters . . . , 211–212, the accounts dealing with Global South countries in comparative studies mainly refer to a "handful of 'usual suspect' settings that are mainly of the Western, liberal-democratic breed".

experiences of constitutionalism and also accorded to them when it comes to their contribution to theory and practice.[38]

Put differently, the proposed view is meant to expand the appreciation of the "human possibilities of constitutionalism"[39] and, consequently, enrich its theoretical content, a process that may help liberal constitutionalism address its own limits.[40] Constitutionalism is thus described as a "complex, uneven, and ever-changing historical discourse – it is 'bricolage' rather than blueprint, 'layered narrative' rather than grand narrative", of which the Global North vision "is a significant voice" in a "pluralist and diverse" tradition that does not have a linear and universal path of progression.[41]

For the sake of the present work, what is specifically interesting as regards the described approaches is that both finally foster a renovated idea of comparison from which a presumed hierarchization of concepts and experiences is avoided insofar as possible. They both lay the groundwork for a renewed consideration of constitutional orders and their models that acknowledges the possibility of bi-directional exchange or influence which does not consider their differences as a hindrance to this. The existence of different constitutional principles and organizations, as well as different epistemologies, is not thought to create an obstacle to profitable comparison when freed from the assumed hierarchization of legal systems.

38 In this sense, Dann, Philipp, Riegner, Michael and Bönnemann, Maxim, "The Southern Turn in Comparative Constitutional Law: An Introduction", in Dann, Riegner, and Bönnemann (eds.), The Global South . . . , 1–38, at 32, refers to epistemic equality, which implies according " 'equal dignity' to all constitutional discourses in North and South".

39 The expression is employed by the editors of Dowdle and Wilkinson (eds.), Constitutionalism Beyond Liberalism . . . , in the abstract of the book and is arguably intended to underline the intrinsic dynamicity of constitutionalism as a political and legal theory, considering the different contexts in which it develops.

40 The basic insight that one can draw from Dowdle and Wilkinson (eds.), Introduction and Overview . . . , 1–14 is that solely framing constitutionalism as a theory of limited government does not do justice to the varied materializations of this principle, which in some parts of the world is much more of an enabling than a restrictive concept; it must also be recalled that the description of the constitution and constitutionalism as enabling forces have been already proposed by Holmes, Stephen, "Constitutions and Constitutionalism", in Rosenfeld, Michel and Sajó András (eds.), *The Oxford Handbook of Comparative Constitutional Law* (Oxford University Press, Oxford, 2012), 189–217, with regard to the Global North (and especially US) experiences; as regards the limits of liberal constitutionalism, Dowdle, Michael W. and Wilkinson, Michael, On the Limits . . . , 21–27, have made reference to three blind spots, i.e. three areas that mainstream constitutionalism theory does not seem able to account for: a. the fact that liberal constitutionalism, besides being a theory for the limitation of power, plays a significant role in the dynamic state-building processes; b. such a vision does not appear to satisfactorily account for the phenomena of evolutionary change and revolutionary rupture, as it presumes that knowledge of the possibilities of constitutionalism and its future is already complete; c. liberal constitutionalism theory does not allow for clear visualization of the constitution's interdependence from its surrounding social and economic environments, which is most often taken for granted and not problematized.

41 Dowdle and Wilkinson, On the Limits . . . , 31.

More specifically, these perspectives provide the theoretical groundwork for considering the legal traditions and tools of the Global South from a completely different angle, which is essentially the opposite to the one that is generally adopted in comparative legal studies. That is to say, by not presuming the superiority of the Global North, it is possible to consider the potential for active contribution by Global South countries to the general evolution of constitutional models, institutions, and theory. Following the described approach thereby acknowledges that mainstream constitutional models and theories may be fruitfully complemented and enriched by often overlooked traditions and experiences.[42]

And, importantly, it is in the field of diversity accommodation that the Global South may provide some particularly valuable insights, given its "colonial legal heritage and long history of ethnic and religious diversity" that have shaped its legal systems, which appear to be "better equipped for dealing creatively with today's dilemmas of multiculturalism and diversity than most Western countries that adhere to stricter legal uniformity".[43] In this sense, of much interest are forms of legal pluralism and the accommodation of indigenous peoples' diversity in several constitutional settings in the Global South.

While such manifestations of diversity accommodation in regions of the Global South have significant connections with minority and indigenous rights law, the concepts related to the latter are not consolidated in those areas of the world. Accordingly, it would probably be misleading to frame them through minority and indigenous rights-related notions, as this approach

42 This is specifically proposed by Dann, Riegner, and Bönnemann, The Southern Turn . . . , 31: "The Global South thus acquires a double meaning: it is not only a concept that captures a constitutional distinct *experience*, but also an epistemic, methodological, and institutional *approach* to doing comparative law. This double understanding also promises new insights for constitutional law in the Global North" because constitutional issues that are particularly salient for the Global South "may equally be present in the Global North and deserve closer attention there. Besides the entangled nature of the North and the South means that one cannot be understood without the other. Finally, the complementary notion of the Global North may . . . be useful in rethinking the distinctive constitutional experience of Euro-America in a global framework"; see also Dann, Riegner and Bönnemann, The Southern Turn . . . , 33, where the authors affirm the need for multi-perspectivity in comparative constitutional law, which means that "there is no one privileged standpoint for comparison, and the comparatist must adopt multiple perspectives. This implies . . . a decentring of Euro-American perspectives – not only by addition of new materials, but by provincializing its theoretical approach with respect to the scope of their claims to validity and applicability; by engaging in inter-contextual dialogue; by decentring the thematic focus or agenda setting in order to go beyond constellations of the Euro-Atlantic world".

43 Hirschl, Comparative Matters . . . , 211, making reference to Menski, Werner, *Comparative Law in a Global Context: The Legal Systems of Asia and Africa* (Cambridge University Press, Cambridge, 2009), 202; also, see Menski, Werner, "Beyond Europe", in Örücü, Esin, and Nelken, David (eds.), *Comparative Law: A Handbook* (Hart, Oxford-Portland, 2007), 189–216, who illustrated the contribution that Global South countries may make to the development of this area of law in theory and practice through two case-studies from Indian law.

would most likely lead to them being – albeit unconsciously – assessed against the Global North standards. This also risks implying a hierarchization of models. Following the previously mentioned perspective, this work instead aims to make those models speak – as much as possible – for themselves. It, therefore, seeks to include them in a wide scientific observation that is meant to add to the discourse on diversity accommodation by enlarging the analysis beyond the most debated issues and themes.

In particular, two regions of the world will specifically be addressed in Chapter 3, namely, South America and Southeast Asia, as they are thought to reflect comprehensive constitutional traditions that complement the mainstream liberal-democratic approach to constitutionalism and diversity accommodation through the introduction of innovative constitutional concepts and approaches.

The theoretical aims of the study

The description of the innovative perspectives related to diversity accommodation in the Global North and Global South – which will underscore the changes and evolutions this area of law is experiencing – will represent the first step of the study. Afterward, a more analytical and theoretical part will follow.

Starting from the comprehensive observations provided in Chapters 1–4, the second part of the work will be devoted to assessing the appropriateness of the existing "mainstream" theoretical tools and concepts – in particular minority and minority-related concepts as well as the rights discourse – to grasp the ongoing evolution of this field of law. In Chapter 5, an argument will be advanced in support of a reconsideration of the traditional conceptual categories and the introduction of the concept "Law of Diversity" as a novel theoretical standpoint.

It seems that the mainstream theoretical approach to the issue of the accommodation of diversity, based on the rather neat distinction between the addressees of the legal measures and, particularly, the centrality of minority and indigenous peoples' rights discourse, while still absolutely useful, is somewhat a limited standpoint to grasp the ongoing evolution occurring in this field. Interestingly, it has been noted that this approach may act as a veritable epistemological constraint in this area of research.[44] This is also true in the sense that the rights discourse originates and is still particularly tied to the Global North's legal approach to the issue of the management of diversity.

The present work aims to address this theoretical hurdle. Accordingly, it intends, based on the richness of contemporary legal responses to diversity, to demonstrate that the minority and indigenous peoples' rights discourse can be considered a limiting standpoint. It, therefore, proposes an alternative framing that one could rely on for a comprehensive understanding of this evolving area of law.

44 On this, see especially Chapter 5.

Such an endeavor appears necessary to provide the conceptual tools for these evolutions to be understood, as well as to foster their further development. It is, in fact, among the lawyer's main tasks to observe the development of models and approaches and to propose, when necessary, new and appropriate interpretations of the legal phenomenon.[45]

A reconsideration of the traditional theoretical approach toward these issues has already been suggested by a few scholars whose accounts represent the starting point for the presented theoretical proposition.[46] Therefore, after having described the evolution of the role of diversity and its management in constitutionalism and the different paradigms that underpin the various approaches within the constitutional tradition, a revisited version of Palermo and Woelk's expression "Law of Diversity" will be put forward as a renovated category of analysis in this area of research.

The concept "Law of Diversity" will be advanced to comprehensively describe the wealth of legal instruments that are sensitive to the numerous factors that differentiate human beings (also referred to as models for the accommodation of diversity) originating from various constitutional traditions. This perspective, therefore, departs from the mainstream theoretical framing, aiming to offer a platform that connects consolidated and innovative instruments for the accommodation of diversity.

Notably, it will be illustrated that, among the models studied in this work, those emerging in the Global North – analyzed in Chapter 4 – appear to be the most in need of theoretical recognition, validation, and explanation. To this end, in Chapter 6, it will be argued that the theory of federalism may serve a rather unexplored theoretical (or, as will be defined, meta-theoretical) function. A review of modern and contemporary accounts of the concept of federalism will be proposed in a bid to prove that federal theory may be a very useful theoretical instrument to understand the functioning of emergent models for the accommodation of diversity and provide solutions for their development. The latter represents the second main theoretical goal of the study.

Overview of the chapters

The present work can be imagined as an incremental path in that the first four chapters provide an exhaustive picture of the state of the art of the area of

45 On the lawyer's role in grasping the evolution of legal categories, and, in particular, the concept of equality, Palermo, Francesco and Nicolini, Matteo, "La Semantica delle Differenze e le Regole Diseguali: dall'Egualitarismo nel Diritto all'Eccezione Culturale", in VV.AA., *Studi in Onore di Maurizio Pedrazza Gorlero*, Vol. 1 (ESI, Naples, 2014), 513–549.

46 Especially by Palermo, Legal Solutions to Complex Societies . . . , 70; *Id.*, "Accommodating Differences: The Present and Future of the Law of Diversity", 30(3) *Vermont Law Review* (2006), 431–442; also, see Palermo, Francesco and Woelk, Jens, "From Minority Protection to a Law of Diversity? Reflections on the Evolution of Minority Rights", 3 *European Yearbook of Minority Issues* (2003–2004), 5–13; Heinze, The Construction . . . . , 25–74.

interest and set the stage for the theoretical proposals contained in the last two chapters. Accordingly, the study will be structured as follows.

Chapter 1 offers a historical account of the treatment of diversity within the realms of liberal and liberal-democratic constitutionalism. The analysis will show that, along with the growing importance of democracy and pluralism in constitutional settings and international law, diversity has increasingly been taken into account and protected by various indirect and direct legal means.

Chapter 2 contains an analytical overview of the legal instruments for the accommodation of diversity stemming from liberal and liberal-democratic constitutionalism. The chapter will provide a general description of the models, supported by several examples.

In Chapter 3, the book approaches the issue of emergent trends concerning the accommodation of diversity and delves into what is referred to as macro-perspectives. The latter are constitutional and international law (thus, indirectly constitutional) developments in this field that have regional significance. In particular, two Global South regions will first be examined, namely, South America and Southeast Asia, since both constitute comprehensive approaches that are alternative or complementary to the liberal-democratic one. Secondly, the European continent will be addressed, with its soft law regulations advancing a considerable revision of their previous approaches to diversity accommodation.

Chapter 4 will specifically delve into the emergent models for the accommodation of diversity in the Global North, thus adopting a micro-perspective. These tools are of particular interest in that they appear to significantly diverge from the traditional structure of minority and indigenous peoples' rights law and mechanisms and require theoretical recognition and validation. In a nutshell, all the instruments – grouped in three categories: governance forms of autonomy, participatory democracy, and legal pluralism – appear to be forms of variously institutionalized and governance-like self-management.

Based on the foregoing, Chapter 5 will propose the introduction of the notion of the "Law of Diversity" as the theoretical tool to capture recent evolutions and connect them with the traditional corpus of minority and indigenous peoples' rights law. The theoretical proposal will be preceded by an analysis of the varying (and increasingly significant) position of diversity as the source of differential treatment in the constitutional tradition. This will highlight that diversity is a derogation from the constitutional order within liberal constitutionalism, an exception in liberal-democratic constitutionalism, and a rule within what is labeled plural constitutionalism. An assessment of the structure of the various instruments for the accommodation of diversity described – made through the concept of paradigm – will be the final theoretical premise that leads to the introduction of the "Law of Diversity" as a new theoretical framework in this area of law. This will be fundamental to unveiling the key elements that inform the legal tools that correspond to different constitutional epochs and stages of refinement. The end of the chapter will then be devoted to proposing a classification of the instruments for the accommodation of diversity based on the new conceptual framework.

Finally, Chapter 6 will connect federalism and the "Law of Diversity" by proposing the former as a potentially useful explanatory tool to understand better the emergent instruments of the latter. This will be based on a thorough analysis of federal thought, an exploration of the possible analytical function of federalism as a frame of understanding for phenomena – like the innovative models for the accommodation of diversity – that imply the diffusion of power through governance means and a justification of the theoretical potential of federal theory to understand their functioning and provide solutions for their further development.

Methodological issues

Lastly, a few final methodological notes seem necessary.

The study conducted here intends to present the most recent and innovative tendencies related to the treatment of diversity in the constitutional tradition. It does so not only for descriptive reasons but also to demonstrate that this area needs to be theoretically grounded in updated conceptual tools. As such, the goal is to propose innovations in general theory through legal comparison.

The methodological approach to comparison most conducive to this goal does not imply a pre-determined set of countries described as case studies. Instead, the primary focus will be on a general description of constitutional traditions and instruments, which will be further explained through the provision of examples of model legal systems. Model legal systems are thought to be the countries where a specific model a. has been first introduced, b. has been applied in a way that has served as a model for other countries or that could serve this function potentially, or c. has been regulated and carried out in an original way, unique to that country.[47]

Together with a dynamic set of countries, which varies depending on the analyzed issue, a global perspective will be essential to achieving the theoretical aim of the study. This would be hindered by the *a priori* definition of a set of countries or regions of the world to compare.

In addition, the book does not provide a systematic analysis of paradigmatic case law in the areas of minority rights and diversity accommodation, but it refers to it when describing the evolution of diversity accommodation. The

47 Following the method used by Palermo, Francesco and Kössler, Karl, *Comparative Federalism. Constitutional Arrangements and Case Law* (Hart Publishing, Oxford-Portland, 2019) and Palermo, Francesco and Woelk, Jens, *Diritto costituzionale comparato dei gruppi e delle minoranze* (CEDAM, Padova, 2021).

aim of the book is not to unveil the concrete content of minority rights and other diversity accommodation instruments in their application. Conversely, it aims to provide a comprehensive description of their evolution that highlights the existence of innovations taking place in different parts of the world and the need to take them into consideration. Based on this, the work intends to advance theoretical innovations to grasp the evolution of this area of law. In other words, the historical and comparative analysis in Chapters 1–4 is meant to offer an up-to-date state of the art as well as be the basis upon which innovative theoretical perspectives are built. This double aim of the publication implies that a balance should be kept between these two parts of the work and that the descriptive part focuses on the aspects that are more functional to the analytical and theoretical ones.

Lastly, the work will deal with hard and soft law regulations, especially when analyzing the emergent macro-perspectives in Chapter 3. Specifically in this area of law, international soft law has proved, at least in some epochs and constitutional settings, very influential. Furthermore, one must not underestimate the very significant role soft law may still play in the regulation of diversity. It is a persuasive mechanism that may successfully complement rigid hard law systems. International soft law can be an instrument to update outdated approaches to the issue of diversity – as has been the case in the European region. It has wide leeway and faces fewer political hurdles than hard law due to the soft status of the acts established by expert bodies. At a domestic level, the existence of (constitutional) soft law – on this, see, for instance, the case of Singapore – may help reinforce the content of hard domestic regulations by encouraging their application through persuasion rather than punishment. For these reasons, the role of soft law at the international and domestic levels cannot be overlooked when it comes to this field of study.

Bibliography

Boaventura de Sousa, Santos, *Epistemologies of the South: Justice against Epistemicide* (Routledge, London-New York, 2014)

Brandt, Willy, *North-South: A Programme for Survival: Report of the Independent Commission on International Development Issues* (Pan, London, 1980)

Brubaker, Roger, *Nationalism Reframed: Nationhood and the National Question in the New Europe* (Cambridge University Press, Cambridge, 1996)

Choudry, Sujit, "Bridging Comparative Politics and Comparative Law: Constitutional Design in Divided Societies", in Choudry, Sujit (ed.), *Constitutional Design for Divided Societies: Integration or Accommodation?* (Oxford University Press, Oxford, 2008), 3–40

Dann, Philipp, Riegner, Michael and Bönnemann, Maxim (eds.), *The Global South and Comparative Constitutional Law* (Oxford University Press, Oxford, 2020)

Dann, Philipp, Riegner, Michael and Bönnemann, Maxim, "The Southern Turn in Comparative Constitutional Law: An Introduction", in Dann, Philipp, Riegner, Michael and Bönnemann, Maxim (eds.), *The Global South and Comparative Constitutional Law* (Oxford University Press, Oxford, 2020), 1–38

Dowdle, Michael W. and Wilkinson, Michael A., "Introduction and Overview", in Dowdle, Michael W. and Wilkinson, Michael (eds.), *Constitutionalism Beyond Liberalism* (Cambridge University Press, Cambridge, 2017), 1–14

Dowdle, Michael W. and Wilkinson, Michael A., "On the Limits of Constitutional Liberalism: In Search of Constitutional Reflexivity", in Dowdle, Michael W. and Wilkinson, Michael (eds.), *Constitutionalism Beyond Liberalism* (Cambridge University Press, Cambridge, 2017), 17–37

Glenn, Patrick, *Legal Traditions of the World: Sustainable Diversity in Law* (Oxford University Press, Oxford, 2007)

Heinze, Eric, "The Construction and Contingency of the Minority Concept", in Fottrell, Deirdre and Bowring, Bill (eds.), *Minority and Group Rights in the New Millennium* (Martinus Nijhoff, Leiden-Boston, 1999), 25–74

Hirschl, Ran, *Comparative Matters: The Renaissance of Comparative Constitutional Law* (Oxford University Press, Oxford, 2014)

Holmes, Stephen, "Constitution and Constitutionalism", in Rosenfeld, Michel and Sajó, András (eds.), *The Oxford Handbook of Comparative Constitutional Law* (Oxford University Press, Oxford, 2012), 189–217

Jakubowski, Andrzej, *Cultural Rights as Collective Rights: An International Law Perspective* (Brill-Nijhoff, Leiden-Boston, 2016)

Kymlicka, Will, "Multiculturalism and Minority Rights: West and East", 14(4) *Journal on Ethnopolitics and Minority Issues in Europe* (JEMIE) (2015), 4–25

Lees, Nicolas, "The Brandt Line after Forty Years: The More North–South Relations Change, the More They Stay the Same?", 47(1) *Review of International Studies* (2021), 85–106

May, Stephen, Modood, Tariq and Squires, Judith (eds.), *Ethnicity, Nationalism, and Minority Rights* (Cambridge University Press, Cambridge, 2004)

Menski, Werner, "Beyond Europe", in Örücü, Esin and Nelken, David (eds.), *Comparative Law: A Handbook* (Hart Publishing, Oxford-Portland, 2007), 189–216

Menski, Werner, *Comparative Law in a Global Context: The Legal Systems of Asia and Africa* (Cambridge University Press, Cambridge, 2009)

Mignolo, Walter D., "Delinking: The Rhetoric of Modernity, the Logic of Coloniality and the Grammar of Decoloniality", 21(2–3) *Cultural Studies* (2007), 449–514

Mignolo, Walter D., "Geopolitics of Sensing and Knowing: On (De)Coloniality, Border Thinking and Epistemic Disobedience", 14(3) *Postcolonial Studies* (2011), 273–283

Palermo, Francesco, "Accommodating Differences: The Present and Future of the Law of Diversity", 30(3) *Vermont Law Review* (2006), 431–442

Palermo, Francesco, "Legal Solutions to Complex Societies: The Law of Diversity", in Ruiz Vieytez, Eduardo J. and Dunbar, Robert (eds.), *Human Rights and Diversity: New Challenges for Plural Societies* (University of Deusto, Bilbao, 2007), 63–82

Palermo, Francesco, "Current and Future Challenges for International Minority Protection", 10 *European Yearbook of Minority Issues* (2011), 21–36

Palermo, Francesco, "'The Borders of My Language Mean the Borders of My World': Language Rights and Their Evolving Significance for Minority Rights and Integration of Societies", in Ulasiuk, Iryna, Hadîrcă, Laurențiu and Romans, William (eds.), *Language Policy and Conflict Prevention* (Brill-Nijhoff, Leiden-Boston, 2018), 135–154

Palermo, Francesco and Kössler, Karl, *Comparative Federalism: Constitutional Arrangements and Case Law* (Hart Publishing, Oxford-Portland, 2019)

Palermo, Francesco and Nicolini, Matteo, "La semantica delle differenze e le regole diseguali: dall'egualitarismo nel diritto all'eccezione culturale", in VV.AA., *Studi in onore di Maurizio Pedrazza Gorlero*, Vol. 1 (ESI, Naples, 2014), 513–549

Palermo, Francesco and Woelk, Jens, "From Minority Protection to a Law of Diversity? Reflections on the Evolution of Minority Rights", 3 *European Yearbook of Minority Issues* (2003–2004), 5–13

Palermo, Francesco and Woelk, Jens, *Diritto costituzionale comparato dei gruppi e delle minoranze* (CEDAM, Padua, 2021)
Reiter, Bernd, "Introduction", in Reiter, Bernd (eds.), *Constructing the Pluriverse: The Geopolitics of Knowledge* (Duke University Press, Durham-London, 2018), 1–15
Ruiz Vieytez, Eduardo J., "Diversity, Immigration and Minorities within a Human Rights Framework", in Ruiz Vieytez, Eduardo J. and Dunbar, Robert (eds.), *Human Rights and Diversity: New Challenges for Plural Societies* (University of Deusto, Bilbao, 2007), 20–33
Salaymeh, Lena and Michaels, Ralf, "Decolonial Comparative Law: A Conceptual Beginning", 22(1) *Max Planck Institute for Comparative and International Private Law Research Paper Series* (2022), 166–188
Tully, James, *Strange Multiplicity: Constitutionalism in an Age of Diversity* (Cambridge University Press, Cambridge, 1995)
Walsh, Catherine, "Development as Buen Vivir: Institutional Arrangements and (De) Colonial Entanglements", in Reiter, Bernd, "Introduction", in Reiter, Bernd (eds.), *Constructing the Pluriverse: The Geopolitics of Knowledge* (Duke University Press, Durham-London, 2018), 184–196

1 The growing significance of diversity for constitutionalism

Liberal constitutionalism and the centrality of equality

The emerging nation-states: equality, citizenship, and majority rule

As illustrated by Palermo and Woelk,[1] while contemporary liberal democratic constitutionalism is increasingly concerned with the accommodation of diversity, liberal constitutionalism was traditionally characterized by the guarantee of equality.

The principle of equality is generally described as the conquest of the French and American revolutions and, more generally, the building block of modern (Global North's) constitutionalism,[2] sitting in direct opposition to the hierarchical social and political systems of the Middle Ages.[3] According to this principle, all citizens of new-born modern states – i.e., originally a part of the population corresponding to the (new) bourgeoisie – are equal in freedom before the law, irrespective of their differences.[4]

The liberal revolutions brought about the implementation of liberal constitutionalism's political and legal theories, reliant on the development of a system of (constitutional or fundamental) rights where diversity was not specifically taken into account as legally significant. By contrast, equality (in freedom) was the central concern, the key to untying the bourgeois society from medieval

1 Palermo, Francesco and Woelk, Jens, *Diritto costituzionale comparato dei gruppi e delle minoranze* (CEDAM, Padua, 2021), 3.

2 Naturally, the principle of equality features British constitutionalism too, and has developed in a way that is unique to that country, i.e., through the constant dialogue, internally, between common law and statutory law (or judiciary and parliament), and, externally, between the UK's legal system and the international human rights law system; on this, see Buratti, Andrea, *Western Constitutionalism: History, Institutions, Comparative Law* (Springer-Giappichelli, Cham-Turin, 2019), 28; on the difficulties in developing a theoretical account of the principle of equality in the UK, see Jowel, Jeffrey, "Is Equality a Constitutional Principle?", 47(2) *Current Legal Problems* (1994), 1–18.

3 The latter revolutions represent the outcome of a process which began gradually and unevenly during the Renaissance: on this, see Minow, Martha, *Making All the Difference: Inclusion, Exclusion and American Law* (Cornell University Press, Ithaca-London, 1990), 123.

4 On this, see Grimm, Dieter, *Constitutionalism: Past, Present, and Future* (Oxford University Press, Oxford, 2016), 65–70.

DOI: 10.4324/9781003493518-2

structures[5] and legitimizing its supremacy in the social order.[6] In other words, diversity, i.e., being part of different social groups, had no legal relevance and was a. a past condition to be avoided for the sake of the establishment or consolidation of a particular social setting and b. a denied condition within the dominant social group: in other words, the freedoms recognized by the constitutional system implied by definition non-discrimination.[7]

Citizenship was the cornerstone of the emerging state organizations and the gateway to formal equality. Indeed, citizenship became the condition allowing one to enjoy a status of equal protection and entitlement to rights provided by the legal system. Although citizenship could be based either on an ethnic or a civic model of membership,[8] either way, it implied the idea of a specific and rather culturally (and racially) homogeneous (national) community with shared characteristics and values. Such a community corresponded to the class whose interests the liberal state was meant to protect and empower: in other words, the principle of equality, though it had a universal tone from the outset, basically applied to a limited group of citizens[9] and guaranteed the equal enjoyment of only their basic rights.[10]

5 Or, as Tully, James, Strange Multiplicity . . . , 66–67, put it, to impose a new order over the "ancient constitution", which was seen by the modern theorists as an irregular assemblage of laws, customs, and institutions that led to the eruption of wars.

6 Although, according to Buratti, Western Constitutionalism . . . , 66–67, some differences are observable between the European and the Anglo-American traditions, related to hegemony of bourgeoisie and the attendant legitimizing use of constitutionalism; on the differences between American and European constitutionalism as regards this point, see also Grimm, Constitutionalism . . . , 83; on the double function of constitutionalism as a doctrine restraining but also legitimizing power, see Holmes, Stephen, "Constitution and Constitutionalism", in Rosenfeld, Michel and Sajó, András (eds.), *The Oxford Handbook of Comparative Constitutional Law* (Oxford University Press, Oxford, 2012), 189–217, at 192.

7 Frankerberg, Günther, *Comparative Constitutional Studies: Between Magic and Deceit* (Edward Elgar, Cheltenham-Northampton, 2018), 245; on this, also see Belser, Eva Maria, "Concluding Remarks", in Belser, Eva Maria, Bächler, Thea, Egli, Sandra and Zünd, Lawrence (eds.), *The Principle of Equality in Diverse States: Reconciling Autonomy with Equal Rights and Opportunities* (Brill-Nijhoff, Leiden-Boston, 2021), 415–428, at 415: "the classic nation-state was structured around the idea of a shared homogeneous national identity which was more often than not constructed, orchestrated top-down and enforced by assimilation policies".

8 On this, see Marko, Joseph, Marko-Stöckl, Edith, Harzl, Benedikt and Unger, Hedwig, "The Historical and Sociological Foundations: State Formation and Nation Building in Europe and the Construction of the Identitarian Nation-cum-State Paradigm", in Marko, Joseph and Constantin, Sergiu, (eds.), *Human and Minority Rights Protection by Multiple Diversity Governance: History, Law, Ideology and Politics in European Perspective* (Routledge, London-New York, 2019), 33–95, at 53–71; Marko, Joseph, "Effective Participation of National Minorities in Public Affairs in Light of National Case Law", 16(4) *International Journal on Minority and Group Rights* (2009), 621–649, at 622.

9 Exclusions were not limited to "cultural" identity markers but applied (and, in part, still apply) to gender, age, people with disabilities, etc.

10 Naturally, the process of democratization would eventually determine the gradual extension of rights to more categories of recipients, starting with civil and political rights in what has been defined as the process of "generalization of rights" by Fariello, Sara, "I diritti fondamentali nella società multiculturale: il contributo della sociologia del diritto", in Baldini, Vincenzo (ed.), *Multiculturalismo* (CEDAM, Padua, 2012), 267–276, at 268.

The correspondent of the equality principle in decision-making processes is the decision by the majority. Majority rule has been theorized as the basis of the new legal order stemming from the liberal revolutions;[11] besides that, the connection between equality and the principle of majority is basically intuitive: the majoritarian decision may indeed be conceived of as the counterpart of individual equality in the enjoyment of political rights.[12]

Equality, citizenship, and majority rule can thus be seen as the basic elements of the modern state, which was the privileged playing field of the theories of liberal constitutionalism.[13]

The influence of these original elements of constitutional theory cannot be overestimated: the basic tenets of liberal constitutionalism still play a fundamental role in shaping political theorists' and constitutional lawyers' – and, consequently, political actors' – approaches to the theme of diversity.

This is highlighted by J. Tully in his "*Strange Multiplicity. Constitutionalism in an Age of Diversity*".[14] The Canadian philosopher and political scientist illustrated that theorists of modern liberal constitutionalism – whose theses were embedded in the constitutional documents of the time – have contributed to creating a number of "conventions of constitutionalism" that have, to various extents, affected its evolution up to today, as they have been internalized by the scientific community and practitioners as sort of a common language. In keeping with his view, seven features of modern constitutionalism have served either to assimilate (cultural) diversity or to exclude it from the very core elements of the emerging constitutional order.

11 On this, see Palermo and Woelk, Diritto costituzionale comparato . . . , 383–385; the principle of majority, like the principle of equality, has been referred to as one of the "legal mythologies" of modernity by Grossi, Paolo, *Mitologie giuridiche della modernità* (Giuffrè, Milan, 2nd ed., 2005).

12 Palermo, Francesco, and Nicolini, Matteo, "La semantica delle differenze e le regole diseguali: dall'egualitarismo nel diritto all'eccezione culturale", in VV.AA., *Studi in onore di Maurizio Pedrazza Gorlero*, Vol. 1 (ESI, Naples, 2014), 513–549, at 516.

13 See Ridola, Paolo, "Preistoria, origini e vicende del costituzionalismo", in Carrozza, Paolo, Di Giovine, Alfonso and Ferrari, Giuseppe F. (eds.), *Diritto costituzionale comparato* (Laterza, Rome-Bari, 2019), 737–774; on the relationships between constitutionalism and state, see Tierney, Stephen, *The Federal Contract: A Constitutional Theory of Federalism* (Oxford University Press, Oxford, 2022), 291–292: the author suggested that, in general, and also in the contemporary epoch, the state is the most natural and fruitful stage where constitutionalism can operate; furthermore, the author indicated that constitutionalism must not be seen as just instrumental to the legitimation of the state: "While the state has often been taken to be the dominant political structure of modernity and the constitution its instrumental bulwark, . . . when viewed through the relationship between political power and legal authority, the opposite is more true. The state provides a bounded space within which constitutionalism can operate safely and securely as the fundamental validation of legitimate political authority".

14 Tully, James, *Strange Multiplicity: Constitutionalism in an Age of Diversity* (Cambridge University Press, Cambridge, 1995).

First, the concept of popular sovereignty which, albeit interpreted in several ways, has generally entailed a society of equal and undifferentiated individuals.[15]

Second, the idea that the modern constitutions set out to serve a modern society that is by nature closed and uniform as a result of its socio-economic development.[16]

Third, the centrality of uniformity as a solution to the (negatively framed) irregularity of the Middle Age's 'ancient constitution',[17] which was thought to be the main cause of the wars plaguing Europe during the seventeenth century.[18]

Fourth is the determinist view of the socio-economic evolution of societies, the progress of which inevitably leads to undermining social pluralism in favor of convergence toward "uniform manners and institutions".[19]

Fifth is the conflation of a specific set of European institutions with the universal model of constitutional institutions.[20]

Sixth is the framing of modern states' communities in national terms, albeit in different ways.[21]

15 Tully, Strange Multiplicity . . . , 63–64; liberal concepts and theories applied, to a certain extent, differently in federations; this is the case with the concept of sovereignty; at the same time, the federal systems born in this epoch were strongly embedded in a liberal political culture, which, in turn, reinforced the theoretical elision of federalism and liberalism (and successively democratic liberalism) that still today characterizes the approach of a significant part of federal literature. As a consequence, it seems possible to affirm that the concept of sovereignty, even if divided and more complex in the case of a federal legal order, implied the idea of a common, even if in some parts variable, "ideal" legal reality of citizenship, at least for what concerns the focus of our work. In other terms, besides possible diversities that federal countries recognized, the basic idea of citizenship was based on a set of common, uncontested elements (such as being white, male, wealthy, etc.). On this, and on the fact that the elision of federalism and liberalism in the US system has then conditioned the evolution of federal studies, mostly marked by the superposition between political science normative theories and constitutional theory and by the idea of federalism being a model of government conducive to liberal values, see Tierney, Stephen, "Federalism and Constitutional Theory", in Jacobsohn, Gary and Schor, Miguel (eds.), *Comparative Constitutional Theory* (Edward Elgar Publishing, Cheltenham, 2018), 45–65; for a comprehensive study on federalism based on a constitutional theory perspective, see Tierney, The Federal Contract . . .; furthermore, with specific regard to the US system, according to Tully, Strange Multiplicity . . . , 91–98, the idea of a people composed of equals with common culture and very similar manners, which was the final holder of national sovereignty and represented in the federal institutions, was one of the main arguments of the victorious federalist side (expressed in the *Federalist Papers*) during the debates that finally led to the adoption of the Constitution.

16 Tully, Strange Multiplicity . . . , 65–66; hence, for instance, indigenous communities in several countries were seen as less developed societies and consequently excluded, dominated, assimilated, or, worse, exterminated.

17 On this, see Fioravanti, Maurizio, "Il principio di eguaglianza nella storia del costituzionalismo moderno", 2(4) *Contemporanea* (1999), 609–630.

18 Tully, Strange Multiplicity . . . , 66–67.

19 Ibid., 66.

20 Ibid., 67–68.

21 Ibid., 68.

Seventh, the belief that the existence of a specific type of constitution modeled on the liberal pattern is the precondition (and not a part) of democracy.[22]

Since the very beginning, these conventional features of modern constitutionalism have consistently affected the place of diversity in constitutional thought and practice. They have created a legal "ideal reality"[23] characterized by (internal) neutrality and (external) universalism that has unquestionably been a significant point of reference in the evolution of constitutionalism. On the one hand, this implies that the new constitutional principles were meant to apply to a whole state community as if it was uniform (while actually applying to the uniform part of the society), taking "some types of people as the norm".[24] On the other, the fact that constitutionalism was thought to be the expression of the most civilized and developed stage of human evolution – while also bringing forward concepts with an unquestionably universal tone – meant it was considered to be *per se* superior to other non-Western forms of political organization and thus worthy of diffusion or imposition.[25] Put differently, the Eurocentric and imperialist perspective of liberal constitutionalism would characterize its successive evolution by implying the idea of an existing hierarchy among legal orders. In turn, this standpoint would also condition the development of scholarship for a long time. This has meant that the Global South's models of organization have been overlooked or considered inferior and less worthy of scientific interest.[26]

Recognition of the legal significance of diversity through treaty mechanisms and federalism

Treaty mechanisms to manage some forms of diversity

Nevertheless, several examples of accommodation emerged in various parts of the world from the sixteenth century on. These entailed recognition of diversity as

22 Ibid., 69–70.

23 See Gaudreault-DesBiens, Jean-F., "Introduction to Part II", in Foblets, Marie-Claire, Gaudreault-DesBiens, Jean-F. and Dundes Relteln, Alison (eds.), *Cultural Diversity and the Law: State Responses Around the World* (Bruylant and Yvon-Blais, Bruxelles and Montréal, 2010), 367–380, at 377.

24 As affirmed by Minow, Making All the Difference . . . , 152.

25 Of course, the aim of this summary is not to apply the contemporary categories to such an approach to diversity issues and judge it accordingly; it must, indeed, be recognized that liberal constitutionalism has unquestionably brought remarkable improvements to the lives of an increasing number of people.

26 With this limiting the observer's standpoint on constitutional phenomena and, importantly, possibly interesting cases of diversity accommodation occurring in Global South's countries; on what has been called the "epistemic hierarchy" that has characterized comparative constitutional studies, see Dann, Philipp, Riegner, Michael and Bönnemann, Maxim, "The Southern Turn in Comparative Constitutional Law: An Introduction", in Dann, Philipp, Riegner, Michael and Bönnemann, Maxim (eds.), *The Global South and Comparative Constitutional Law* (Oxford University Press, Oxford, 2020), 1–38, at 4.

a condition that justified the differential treatment of some groups not based on exclusion.[27] Apart from a few cases of domestic accommodation on the European continent,[28] it was generally through treaty mechanisms that such legal safeguards were put in place. That was the case with the treaties between the European colonizers and indigenous peoples in New Zealand, Canada, and the US as well as those signed in Europe during the second half of the nineteenth century.

Those examples show that diversity was, to some extent, taken into account by liberal constitutionalism but occupied an outer position and was managed through various forms of treaties or treaty-like instruments.

A limited degree of diversity in state structures through federalism in the liberal epoch

A second way diversity was legally taken into consideration was through the employment of federalism in countries that embraced it as an essential and constitutive element of their constitutional order from the outset. In fact, federalism inherently implies the recognition and management of different degrees and forms of diversity within a polity[29] and a non-unitarian conception of internal sovereignty.[30]

Two examples of this are the US and Switzerland. However, only the latter presents the features of a real exception to the general overview presented here. Indeed, to a certain extent, it is a precursor to the successive models for the accommodation of diversity – yet has kept its peculiarities that characterize it as somewhat *unicum*.

The path toward greater equality and the consolidation of the concepts of minority and indigenous peoples at the international and domestic levels

The second stage of evolution in the path towards diversity within constitutionalism was the outcome of different dynamics occurring in national and international jurisdictions during the twentieth century.

27 On the "two tracks" of legal rules, one for "normal" people and one for a residual category of individuals not corresponding to the former category, see Minow, Making All the Difference . . . , 121–145.

28 As observed by Pizzorusso, Alessandro, *Minoranze e maggioranze* (Einaudi, Milan, 1997), 168, Article 19 of the Austrian Constitution of 1867, Article 23 of the Belgian Constitution of 1831 and Article 116 of the Swiss Constitution of 1874 contained some provisions aimed at safeguarding some rights of communities in their societies (especially their linguistic rights); it should nevertheless be observed that the three countries' features (Austria was part of the so-called "Dual monarchy" with Hungary from 1867) were significantly different from those typical of the nation states emerging at that time for several reasons.

29 For an in-depth analysis of the concept of federalism employed in this work, see Chapter 6.

30 On the liberal monist assumptions that have, to a large degree, conditioned the debate on sovereignty within federal theory, see Tierney, The Federal Contract . . . , 83–99.

All the developments were marked and conditioned by several transversal phenomena.

The first was the slow but generalized process of democratization, which largely resulted in merging liberal constitutionalism with democracy and its ethical underpinnings, especially after the tragedies of the world wars. As a result, the democratic element has gradually become the new fundamental core component for countries that adhere to constitutionalism.[31] The democratic turn of constitutionalism brought about the centrality of democratic pluralism, of which cultural, religious, ethnic, and linguistic pluralism constitute fundamental elements. Furthermore, democratization, which goes along with the extension of the right to vote and participate in public life, allowed an increasing number of issues to enter decision-making processes, be taken into account, and become legally relevant.

The second is the concomitant constitutionalization of international law and internationalization of constitutional law, which has had the same impact on this field as human rights in general.[32] This trend marked minority rights law even before the emergence of international human rights law.[33] As a matter of fact, international law has increasingly regulated constitutional matters that were previously completely within a state's jurisdiction, and, in turn, states have accepted and constitutionally provided for stronger ties between their legal systems and international law (albeit to different extents). As will be described in what follows, the developments at the international and national levels have affected each other and mainly determined the evolution of human rights concepts in two respects, both linked to the idea of the further and effective enforcement of the principle of equality. First, the reach of human rights has been continuously extended and thus applied to an increasing number of people; second, the very meaning of equality concepts has fundamentally changed and been enriched.

31 See Schütze, Robert, "Constitutionalism(s)", in Masterman, Roger and Schütze, Robert (eds.), *The Cambridge Companion to Comparative Constitutional Law* (Cambridge University Press, Cambridge, 2019), 40–66; Buratti, Western Constitutionalism . . . , 92–114; Fioravanti, Il principio di eguaglianza . . . , 628–629.

32 With specific regard to how this trend has affected minority rights law, see Palermo, Francesco, "Current and Future Challenges for International Minority Protection", 10 *European Yearbook of Minority Issues* (2011), 21–36, at 22–25; Kymlicka, Will, "The Internationalization of Minority Rights", in Choudry, Sujit (ed.), *Constitutional Design for Divided Societies: Integration or Accommodation?*, (Oxford University Press, Oxford, 2008), 111–140; more in general, on this phenomenon, see De Wet, Erika, "The Constitutionalization of Public International Law", in Rosenfeld and Sajó, (eds.), The Oxford Handbook . . . , 1209–1230; Chang, Wen-Chen and Yeh, Jiunn-Rong, "Internationalization of Constitutional Law", in Rosenfeld and Sajó (eds.), The Oxford Handbook . . . , 1166–1184; Bartole, Sergio, *The Internationalisation of Constitutional Law: A View from the Venice Commission* (Hart Publishing, Oxford-New York, 2020).

33 See Thornberry, Patrick, "Is There a Phoenix in the Ashes? International Law and Minority Rights", 15(3) *Texas International Law Journal* (1980), 421–458, at 425–438.

A third factor corresponds to the political significance of nationalist theoretical categories and political agendas, which, to a greater or lesser extent, have conditioned the relationships between the international and domestic spheres in this field, as well as national approaches to societal diversity.[34]

The complex dynamics resulting from the interaction of these factors and trends are the *fil rouge* connecting all the developments that will be listed further on.

The emergence of diversity/1: the interwar period, the international minority rights system, its demise, and experiments of non-territorial autonomy

Whereas the interwar period saw the described practice of adopting treaties devoted to safeguarding national minorities continue,[35] at the same time, an attempt to create a general minority rights protection mechanism under the auspices of the League of Nations was put in operation. Security concerns mainly accounted for this project: the protection of national minorities was a tool to avoid the risk of geopolitical tensions that could escalate to war.

The system derived from the practical unavailability of Woodrow Wilson's self-determination doctrine, which aimed to recompose states and nations in order to avoid new global conflicts.[36] The minority regime thus arose from the nationalistic political thought – dominant and uncontested at that time – which underpinned the model of the modern state[37] and, notably, was a corollary of its concrete unfeasibility.[38]

34 On the concept of nationalism and its connection to the European continent's history (and for further references), see Brubaker, Roger, *Nationalism reframed: Nationhood and the National Question in the New Europe* (Cambridge University Press, Cambridge, 1996); on the relationships between nationalism and minority rights from a political science's standpoint, see May, Stephen, Modood, Tariq and Squires, Judith (eds.), *Ethnicity, Nationalism, and Minority Rights* (Cambridge University Press, Cambridge, 2004); for an account aimed at reconnecting political theory (including the one related to nationalism), history and law in the field of minority rights, see Barth, William K., *On Cultural Rights: The Equality of Nations and the Minority Legal Tradition* (Martinus Nijhoff Publishers, Leiden-Boston, 2008); see also Anderson, Benedict, *Imagined Communities: Reflections on the Origins and Spread of Nationalism* (Verso, London-New York, 2006).

35 Thornberry, Is There a Phoenix . . . , 430–431; on the role of bilateral treaties, see Bloed, Arie and van Dijk, Pieter (eds.), *Protection of Minority Rights Through Bilateral Treaties: The Case of Central and Eastern Europe* (Kluwer Law International, The Hague, 1999); Medda-Windischer, Roberta, "Protection of National Minorities through Bilateral Agreements in South Eastern Europe", 1 *European Yearbook of Minority Issues* (2001–2002), 535–556.

36 Barth, On Cultural Rights . . . , 49.

37 Pizzorusso, Alessandro, "Articolo 6", in Branca, Giuseppe (ed.), *Commentario della Costituzione* (Zanichelli-Il Foro Italiano, Bologna-Rome, 1975), 296–321, at 296–297; Pizzorusso, Minoranze . . . , 168.

38 Thornberry, Is There a Phoenix . . . , 429; interestingly, Arato, Andrew and Cohen, Jean L., "Introduction: Forms of Pluralism and Democratic Constitutionalism", in Arato, Andrew, Cohen, Jean L. and von Busekist, Astrid (eds.), *Forms of Pluralism and Democratic Constitutionalism* (Columbia University Press, New York-Chichester, 2018), 1–30, at 2, have described minority rights as a by-product of the nation-state model.

It must be noted that the League's covenant did not include any specific minority provision. The absence of general rules confirms the mentioned security-based and paternalistic approach toward minority issues that had characterized the epoch prior to WWI.[39] In other words, the international multilateral protection regime was guaranteed by the institutions of the new-born League but stemmed from specific agreements binding few states and not the great powers (except for Germany).[40]

As indicated by Thornberry, the system was built upon the following international documents: a. five special minorities treaties binding Poland, the Serbo-Croat-Slovene State, Romania, Greece, and Czechoslovakia; b. special minorities clauses in the treaties of peace with four of the defeated Central Powers – Austria, Bulgaria, Hungary, and Turkey; c. five general declarations on their admission to the League by Albania, Lithuania, Latvia, Estonia, and Iraq; d. a special declaration made by Finland in relation to the Åland Islands, after Finland had been admitted to the League; and e. treaties relating to the territories of Danzig, Upper Silesia and Memel.[41]

Besides those documents, obligated states incorporated the treaty provisions at the state level[42] or bound themselves to respect their internal minorities through unilateral declarations when acceding to the League.[43] This led to a closer interconnection between the international and domestic jurisdictions.

Furthermore, a petition procedure and an international court[44] were created to implement and interpret the treaties, respectively. Notably, the former was not at the disposal of minority groups and their members, who were entitled to file petitions for informational purposes only. Only states could submit a formal complaint before the League's authorities.

Several flaws marked the model built by the League of Nations, not least the fact that "what could not be achieved by persuasion and mediation could not

39 See Barth, On Cultural Rights . . . , 61: "The primary purpose of the minority treaty petition system was to avoid the outbreak of war between states by removing the protection of minorities from the jurisdiction of individual states to the collectivity of all states".

40 Thornberry, Is There a Phoenix . . . , 430.

41 Ibid., 429–430.

42 By recognizing the international provisions' supremacy over state sources of law contrasting with them.

43 For instance, USSR, Finland, Belgium, and Spain; on this, see Palermo and Woelk, Jens, Diritto costituzionale comparato . . . , 81.

44 The Permanent Court of International Justice (PCIJ) has addressed minority issues on some occasions, such as the cases *Advisory Opinion on Certain Questions Relating to Settlers of German Origin in the Territory ceded by Germany to Poland*, Advisory Opinion of September 10th, 1923, Ser. B., Fasc. No. 6, 5–43, *Access to German Minority Schools in Upper Silesia*, Advisory Opinion of May 15th, 1931, Ser. A./B., Fasc. No. 40, 4–21, Interpretation *of the Statute of the Memel Territory*, Judgement of August 11th, 1932, Ser. A./B., Fasc. No. 50, 294–340 and *Minority Schools in Albania*, Advisory Opinion April 6th,1935, Ser. A./B., Fasc. No. 64, 4–23.

be achieved at all".[45] Hence, although it helped work out some specific minority questions – such as, for instance, that concerning the Åland Islands[46] – the system was doomed to fail.

Nevertheless, it represented an important experience for several reasons. First, it was an attempt to create an international multilateral mechanism of minority protection based on the direct role of the League of Nations as a guarantor, a model that was never subsequently replicated in this shape. Second, the treaties that created that system listed a set of minority rights that became a point of reference for successive instruments – such as the right to life, liberty, and freedom of religion, detailed non-discrimination and equality rights, as well as providing for the use of minority languages in some sectors of public life.[47] Third, such a system led to the establishment of a working model of territorial autonomy as an instrument for minority protection, which has undoubtedly been a source of inspiration to other successive experiences.

Besides the system of the League of Nations, the interwar period witnessed another emergence of diversity within the tradition of constitutionalism that originated from state practice. This was the establishment of non-territorial or cultural autonomy regimes in the Baltic states of Estonia, Latvia, and Lithuania in the 1920s and 1930s, based on the theories of the Austro-Marxist Renner and Bauer.[48] Cultural autonomy was characterized by the creation of public institutions representing minority communities on

45 Thornberry, Is There a Phoenix . . . , 436.

46 On this, see Spiliopoulou Åkermark, Sia (ed.), *The Åland Example and Its Components: Relevance for International Conflict Resolution* (Åland Islands Peace Institute, Mariehamn, 2011); other less successful experiences of autonomy granted to some territories (and the minorities residing there) in this period are the creation of the Free City of Danzig and the Memel Territory.

47 See Henrard, Kristin and Dunbar, Robert, "Introduction", in Henrard, Kristin and Dunbar, Robert (eds.), *Synergies in Minority Protection: European and International Law Perspectives* (Cambridge University Press, Cambridge-New York, 2008), 1–19, at 2; the PCIJ played an important role too: for instance, see the considerations on the equality principle in *Advisory Opinion on Certain Questions. . .* , and in *Minority Schools in Albania . . .* which already brought forward a substantive conception of the principle beyond its formal characterization.

48 Renner, Karl, "State and Nation", in Nimni, Ephraim (ed.), *National Cultural Autonomy and its Contemporary Critics* (Routledge, London-New York, 1899/2005), 15–48; Bauer, Otto, *The Question of Nationalities and Social Democracy* (University of Minnesota Press, Minneapolis, 2000), translated by O'Donnell, Joseph, originally published as Bauer, Otto, *Die Nationalitiitenfrage und die Sozialdemokratie* (Verlag der Wiener Volksbuchhandlung, Vienna, 1924); on the three cases of NTA during the interwar period, see, for instance, Germane, Maria, "Paul Schiemann, Max Laserson and Cultural Autonomy: A Case Study from Interwar Latvia", in Nimni, Ephraim, Osipov, Alexander and Smith, David J. (eds.), *The Challenge of Non-Territorial Autonomy: Theory and Practice* (Peter Lang, Oxford, 2013), 101–115; Smith, David J., "Estonia: A Model for Interwar Europe?", 15(1) *Ethnopolitics* (2015), 89–104; Gringauz, Samuel, "Jewish National Autonomy in Lithuania (1918–1925)", 14(3) *Jewish Social Studies* (1952), 225–246.

a personal rather than territorial basis, and they were assigned the power to manage the minorities' educational and cultural affairs. These models allowed some of the national minorities existing in those states to concretely enjoy a form of self-government in a shape that was considered to be less threatening than territorial autonomy and more practical in cases of minorities scattered in the state territories.[49]

The emergence of diversity/2: the extension of rights in the domestic and international domains and diversity protection through non-discrimination

A second way diversity has emerged in the constitutional tradition is related to the implementation of the principle of equality in constitutional settings and at the international level. If rights had already been partially extended in the name of equality from the mid-nineteenth century onwards, it was the aftermath of WWII that concretely affirmed their universal vocation in constitutions and treaties. The universality of rights is built upon the idea that every human being, regardless of his or her specific status, has inherent dignity and that human dignity is to be protected from infringements.[50]

In continental Europe, the tragedies of WWII showed that liberal constitutions were "short of legal antibodies" to prevent the political systems they ruled from turning into totalitarian regimes. This led to the establishment of thick constitutions and the consolidation of constitutional rigidity and supremacy theories, which in turn have allowed for a wider reach and enforceability of rights and equality provisions through constitutional review of legislation in several legal systems.[51] In practice, constitutional rigidification and supremacy have put human rights and constitutional values like the principle of equality in a much stronger legal position, with specific regard given to their status as supreme principles of the legal system that guide and condition the lawmakers' activity.[52]

In the US, where the supremacy of the Constitution represented one of the foundations of the legal system born after the revolution,[53] the evolution of the constitutional order toward a greater expansion of the equality principle

49 For further references, see the paragraph dedicated to non-territorial autonomy.

50 On the concept of human dignity, see Cohn, Margit and Grimm, Dieter, " 'Human Dignity' as a Constitutional Doctrine", in Tushnet, Mark, Fleiner, Thomas and Saunders, Cheryl (eds.), *Routledge Handbook of Constitutional Law* (Routledge, London-New York, 2013), 193–203.

51 On this, see Pizzorusso, Minoranze . . . , 82.

52 The UK moved in the same direction while keeping the peculiarities connected to the specificities of its system, based on the coexistence of common law and statutory law and on the principle of parliamentary sovereignty; this, for instance, has meant that control over public actions is addressed to the government rather than against parliament; for a historical comparative constitutional account, see Ridola, Preistoria, origini e vicende . . . , 737–774.

53 As definitively affirmed in the ruling *Marshall v Madison* of 1804; on this, see, Schütze, Constitutionalism(s). . . , 40–66, at 49–50.

began earlier while at the same time keeping its specificities. Although the Constitution maintained its liberal structure, the XIV and XV amendments provided the legal basis for equality to be enforced. Despite this, the process of their application has been slow. It has moved through several phases based upon leading Supreme Court decisions and generally relied upon incremental refinement of its content by the judiciary.[54]

What both traditions share is the trend toward greater enforcement and the extension of the principle of "equality of the law" during the second half of the twentieth century. Such a tendency gained further momentum from the introduction and operation of non-discriminatory clauses in constitutions.[55] In other words, while liberal equality was equal to legality and thus discretionarily implemented by the legislatures, liberal-democratic equality also became a constitutional cornerstone value stemming from the Constitution, with direct enforceability even against the lawmaker activity in most constitutional legal systems.[56] The latter trend was reinforced by the parallel enshrinement of non-discrimination clauses in several international human rights documents during the second half of the twentieth century. The interconnectedness between state and international legal systems became, albeit to different extents, an essential feature of this season of constitutionalism and, consequently, of minority rights law.[57]

Furthermore, it must be noted that the concept of equality in its non-discriminatory dimension was consistently enriched at both international and national levels during this phase. Indeed, it has been acknowledged that societal discrimination took place even in the absence of directly discriminatory legal provisions, with this requiring that, in some cases, the adoption of specific measures – generally known as affirmative actions or, in international law, special measures[58] – to overcome these forms of unequal treatments and

54 As indicated by Palermo and Woelk, Diritto costituzionale comparato . . . , 283–310, the implementation of equality in the US can arguably be described as tied to the concept of formal equality, non-discrimination, and narrow-tailored affirmative action as its most recognizable elements.

55 In this sense, Seibert-Fohr, Anja, 'The Rise of Equality in International Law and its Pitfalls: Learning from Comparative Constitutional Law', in Tushnet, Mark (ed.), *Comparative Constitutional Law: Volume III: Freedom of Expression and Religion, and Equality* (Edgar Elgar, Cheltenham-Northampton, 2017), 477–515, at 494–495.

56 The direct enforceability against the lawmaker is the feature that, according to Khaitan, Tarunabh, "Discrimination", in *Max Planck Encyclopedia of Comparative Constitutional Law* (Oxford University Press, Oxford, 2017), available at the following link: https://papers.ssrn.com/sol3/papers.cfm?abstract_id=3277053, accounts for the conceptual distinction between equality and non-discrimination.

57 Khaitan Discrimination . . .

58 On non-discrimination in international law, see Bossuyt, Marc, "Comprehensive Examination of Thematic Issues relating to Racial Discrimination: The Concept and Practice of Affirmative Action", in Castellino, Joshua (ed.), *Global Minority Rights* (Routledge, London-New York, 2016), 333–356.

achieve what is generally referred to as substantive equality or full and effective equality.[59] Given their rationale, such legal instruments are supposed to be temporary and only last as long as is necessary to redress the type of inequality they are countering.[60]

Therefore, in the aftermath of WWII, the interwar period's idea of "internationalizing the rights of troublesome groups was replaced by the concept of universal human rights on a non-discriminatory basis".[61] However, it can be said that (at least the formal) universal affirmation of the equality principle gave diversity legal – albeit negative – recognition. As a matter of fact, diversity acquired general legal acknowledgment as a manifold personal condition that cannot be grounds for unjustified differential legal treatment. Of course, this is a dimension of diversity that is very much related to the principle of formal equality, as well as to the tradition and the ratio underlying it. In other words, it can be seen as the natural outcome of the encounter between constitutionalism and democracy, which resulted in broadening the recipients of rights once addressed only to some categories of persons. This also explains why, today, non-discrimination categories are numerous and tend to be considered unlimited, whereas diversity as a condition allowing for differential rules – including

59 "Affirmative actions" may be considered as a general category that includes several forms of regulations that are intended to redress societal inequality; their theoretical framing has been tied to various interpretations of the principle of equality, and among them, as described by Fredman, Sandra, "Substantive Equality Revisited", 14(3) *International Journal of Constitutional Law* (2016), 712–738, the most common are equality of results, equality of opportunity, and dignity. The author then proposed a renovated unitary theorization of the principle of substantive equality based on four dimensions: redressing disadvantage; addressing stigma, stereotyping, prejudice, and violence; enhancing voice and participation; and accommodating difference and achieving structural change; for a further general overview on affirmative actions in the national and international legal orders, see Sabbagh, Daniel, "Affirmative Action", in Rosenfeld and Sajó (eds.), The Oxford Handbook . . . , 1124–1141; see also Cottroll, Robert J. and Davis, Megan, "Affirmative Action", in Tushnet, Fleiner, and Saunders (eds.), Routledge Handbook . . . , 325–336; the expression "full and effective equality" is generally used when referring to the guarantee of non-discrimination in favor of national minorities, and is stated in Article 4, para. 2 of the Framework Convention for the Protection of National Minorities: "The Parties undertake to adopt, where necessary, adequate measures in order to promote, in all areas of economic, social, political and cultural life, full and effective equality between persons belonging to a national minority and those belonging to the majority. In this respect, they shall take due account of the specific conditions of the persons belonging to national minorities".

60 Bossuyt, Comprehensive Examination . . . , 351, indeed observed that "The requirement of 'limited duration' of special measures has been continually stressed in international law"; however, Sabbagh, Affirmative Action . . . , 1127, maintained that affirmative actions "in democratic societies where benefits, once given, cannot easily be withdrawn, as a practical matter affirmative action tends to become permanent", presenting some examples such as India, Malaysia, and Pakistan to support his argument.

61 Thornberry, Is There a Phoenix . . . , 438–439.

the recognition and promotion of a differential status[62] – is still frequently conceived of as an exception.[63]

Besides the recognition of diversity due to the expansion of the equality principle, the international legal framework built at the very outset of WWII – which also witnessed the continued use of bilateral treaties for specific situations[64] – gradually showed a certain sensitivity to the existence and worth of diversity, originally framed in terms of national minorities and subsequently of indigenous peoples.[65] Albeit initially based upon general and non-minority-specific instruments, which established the foundations of international human rights law,[66] it nonetheless did so by addressing some conditions of diversity directly – for instance, by embedding a specific provision into non-minority-specific treaties – or indirectly – generally by regulating issues that may particularly affect them. All these developments moved in the same direction, giving initial legal significance to some diversities, i.e., those linked to membership in cultural, linguistic, or ethnic groups.

Several international non-minority-specific instruments issued at the global or regional level may be read as according indirect protection to national minorities and other non-majority groups such as indigenous peoples. Among them, some main examples can be pinpointed.

This was, firstly, the case with the United Nations Convention for the Prevention and Punishment of the Crime of Genocide of 1948 (Genocide Convention) and the Statute of the International Criminal Court of Rome,

62 This is the element that seems to differentiate non-discrimination instruments from further legal instruments for the accommodation of diversity, which do not aim to rebalance unequal structural conditions but to promote diversity as a condition worthy of differential treatment; on this, see Capotorti, Francesco, *Study on the Rights of Persons Belonging to Ethnic, Religious and Linguistic Minorities* (New York, 1977) (UN Doc. E/CN.4/sub.2/384/Rev.1, UN sales Nr. E.78.XIV.1)/Geneva UN Center for Human Rights, UN Doc E/CN.4/sub.2/384/Add.1–7, 1–114, at 40–41; this will be further made clear in the following sections, where a synthetical classification of the instruments used for the accommodation of diversity will be provided.

63 Heinze, Eric, "The Construction and Contingency of the Minority Concept", in Fottrell, Deirdre and Bowring, Bill (eds.), *Minority and Group Rights in the New Millennium* (Martinus Nijhoff, Leiden-Boston, 1999), 25–74, at 33.

64 For instance, the De Gasperi-Gruber treaty of 1946 (included in the Paris Peace Treaty of 1947) provided for safeguards in favor of the German-speaking minority of South Tyrol (Italy), the London Memorandum of Understanding of 1954, and the Osimo Treaty of 1963 constitute the international framework for the protection of the Slovene minority in Italy.

65 It must be noted that the same considerations apply to indigenous peoples, which on several occasions were addressed by UN treaty bodies and afforded protection under the aforementioned non-minority-specific instruments from the end of the twentieth century; for more on this, see the section devoted to indigenous peoples.

66 The expression non-minority-specific instruments is used to describe treaties and institutions that do not exclusively deal with national minorities; the definition is borrowed from Henrard, Kristin and Dunbar, Robert, "Introduction", in Henrard and Dunbar (eds.), Synergies in Minority Protection . . . , 1–19.

which defined the concept of crimes against humanity. While both instruments have been referred to as non-minority-specific as their potential reach goes beyond national minorities, their provisions nonetheless resonate deeply with minority protection.[67] Indeed, Article 2 of the Genocide Convention states that "genocide means any of the following acts committed with intent to destroy, in whole or in part, a national, ethnical, racial or religious group" and Article 7 of the Rome Statute includes among the behaviors that constitute a crime against humanity:

> Persecution against any identifiable group or collectivity on political, racial, national, ethnic, cultural, religious, gender as defined in paragraph 3, or other grounds that are universally recognized as impermissible under international law, in connection with any act referred to in this paragraph or any crime within the jurisdiction of the Court.

Their application to non-majority groups is specified by several leading rulings and resolutions of the General Assembly of the United Nations.[68] Hence, the two international acts and the attendant implementations, which entrenched the very basic right to existence and survival of non-majority groups in international law, can arguably be viewed as the first building block of what will be called the Law of Diversity.

By contrast, the UNESCO Convention Against Discrimination in Education (CADE) of 1960 embeds an express – albeit rather weak – provision concerning national minorities. This is reflected in Article 5, which provides for the right of their members to carry on their own schools and educational activities as well as the use or teaching of their own language insofar as some conditions are respected.[69]

In 1966, the United Nations General Assembly adopted the so-called 'twin human rights covenants', The International Covenant on Economic,

67 In the following pages, "minority" is to be read as a general term encompassing national, cultural, linguistic, ethnic, or religious minorities and other non-dominant or non-majority groups; these latter terms will also be used as general expressions for national minorities, indigenous peoples, and other non-recognized groups in a minority condition.

68 On this, see Schabas, William A., "Developments Relating to Minorities in the Law on Genocide", in Henrard and Dunbar (eds.), Synergies in Minority Protection . . . , 189–212.

69 Specifically, the exercise of the rights shall not prevent "the members of these minorities from understanding the culture and language of the community as a whole and from participating in its activities, or which prejudices national sovereignty", the standard of education shall not be "lower than the general standard laid down or approved by the competent authorities" and the attendance at such schools shall be optional; for a thorough analysis, see Coomans, Fons, "UNESCO's Convention Against Discrimination in Education", in Henrard and Dunbar (eds.), Synergies in Minority Protection . . . , 297–313; another important UNESCO document is the UNESCO Universal Declaration on Cultural Diversity: on this, see Burri, Mira, "The UNESCO Convention on Cultural Diversity: An Appraisal Five Years after its Entry into Force", 20(4) *International Journal of Cultural Property* (2013), 357–380.

Social and Cultural Rights (ICESCR), and the International Covenant on Civil and Political Rights (ICCPR). The former has an indirect application to non-majority groups. Its general rights provisions focus on equality and non-discrimination, providing gateways for (mainly) national minorities and indigenous peoples to be fairly included among its recipients.[70]

The latter, besides containing various non-discrimination provisions, also represented the first international document embedding an explicit general article (Article 27) devoted to the protection of diversity, framed in terms of the rights of individuals belonging to national minorities.[71] Although the content of Article 27 ICCPR is rather vague and expressed in negative terms, this provision has nonetheless constituted the basis for the development of remarkable standard-setting (soft) jurisprudence by the United Nations Human Rights Committee[72] that has extended its reach and made it a fundamental point of reference as regards minority and indigenous peoples' rights. The latter article also provided the main inspiration for the Declaration on the Rights of Persons Belonging to National or Ethnic, Religious and Linguistic Minorities of 1992, which will be analyzed further on.

70 On this, see Amor, María and Estébanez, Martín, "The United Nations International Covenant on Economic, Social and Cultural Rights", in Henrard and Dunbar (eds.), Synergies in Minority Protection . . . , 213–247.

71 Article 27, ICCPR: "In those States in which ethnic, religious or linguistic minorities exist, persons belonging to such minorities shall not be denied the right, in community with the other members of their group, to enjoy their own culture, to profess and practice their own religion, or to use their own language"; other provisions apply indirectly to groups and minorities and are interdependent from Article 27, such as the ones dealing with the rights of participation (Article 25), the right of peoples to self-determination (Article 1), the freedom of expression (Article 19), the right to privacy and family life (Article 17), and non-discrimination (Article 26); far less incisive is Article 15 ICESR, which only provides for a general right to participate in public life.

72 The HRC has been established by Article 28 of the ICCPR and is assigned the task of monitoring state compliance with the treaty; in particular, Article 40 ICCPR provides for a mandatory reporting procedure and Article 41–42 ICCPR establish an inter-state complaint procedure; furthermore, the first Optional Protocol to the ICCPR foresees an optional procedure for individual complaints; on this, Scheinin, Martin, "The United Nations International Covenant on Civil and Political Rights: Article 27 and Other Provisions", in Henrard and Dunbar (eds.), Synergies in Minority Protection . . . , 23–46; on its soft jurisprudence and the results it wielded in the field of minority rights, see Strydom, Hennie, "International Treaty-based Protection of Minorities: Select Cases of the UN Human Rights Committee", in De Villiers, Bertus, Marko, Joseph, Palermo, Francesco and Constantin, Sergiu (eds.), *Litigating the Rights of Minorities and Indigenous Peoples in Domestic and International Courts* (Brill-Nijhoff, Leiden-Boston, 2021), 219–238; Nowak, Manfred, *UN Covenant on Civil and Political Rights: CCPR Commentary* (N.P. Engel, Strasbourg, 2nd ed., 2005); Joseph, Sarah, *International Covenant on Civil and Political Rights: Cases, Materials and Commentary* (Oxford University Press, Oxford, 2nd ed., 2004); Hanski, Raija and Scheinin, Martin, *Leading Cases of the Human Rights Committee* (Åbo Akademi University, Turku, 2nd ed., 2007).

Furthermore, both treaties explicitly affirmed the peoples' right to self-determination with the very same wording.[73] The reach and the recipients of these provisions, as with other international documents, are still contentious theoretical issues.[74]

Another international non-minority-specific treaty that lays down provisions covering the rights of non-majority groups is the United Nations International Convention on the Elimination of All Forms of Racial Discrimination (ICERD) – entered into force in 1969 – although the wording used to define racial discrimination does not specifically include religion and language among the grounds of discrimination.[75] Nevertheless, according to Garvalov, this has not prevented the monitoring body (the Committee on the Elimination of Racial Discrimination, CERD/C) from addressing minority issues several

73 Other sources of international soft and hard law deal with the right of self-determination, such as the Universal Declaration of Human Rights (Article 1(2) and Article 55), the Declaration on the Granting of Independence to Colonial Countries and Peoples of 1960 and the 1970 Declaration on Principles of International Law concerning Friendly Relations and Cooperation among States in accordance with the Charter of the United Nations; in addition, self-determination has been addressed in other international treaties concerning indigenous peoples that will be indicated in what follows.

74 Whether minorities and other non-dominant groups may be included in the notion of people was not clarified in the documents; nevertheless, it must be noted that the concept of external self-determination *stricto sensu* – leading to secession – has subsequently been spelled out, and its application restricted to specific cases. This has been done by international bodies and some leading decisions of domestic courts, such as the Supreme Court of Canada; on this, see Thornberry, Is There a Phoenix . . . , 452–453, who observed that the external dimension of self-determination leading to possible secession has been strictly narrowed down to self-determination for decolonization purposes; the Canadian Supreme Court's Opinion *Reference Re: Secession* of 1995 has provided a thorough analysis of the conditions that can lead to secession in Canada which have been an important point of reference for the soft jurisprudence of the Human Rights Committee of the United Nations: on this, see Scheinin, The United Nations International Covenant . . . , 23–46; also, see Kymlicka, Will, "Theorizing Indigenous Rights", in Kymlicka, Will (ed.), *Politics in the Vernacular: Nationalism, Multiculturalism, and Citizenship* (Oxford University Press, Oxford, 2001), 120–132, at 123, who observed that the scope of self-determination "has been drastically restricted in international law" and "limited by what is called the 'salt-water thesis': peoples who are subject to colonization from overseas have the right to independence, but national minorities within a (territorially contiguous) state do not have a right to independence"; according to Göcke, Katja, "Indigenous Peoples in International Law", in Hauser-Schäublin, Brigitta (eds.), *Adat and Indigeneity in Indonesia: Culture and Entitlements between Heteronomy and Self-Ascription* (Göttingen University Press, Göttingen, 2013), 17–29, at 27: "A right to external self-determination is only permissible in absolutely exceptional cases, in particular when there are widespread and systematic human rights violations or a total exclusion of a certain group from the decision-making process"; on indigenous peoples' self-determination, see the dedicated section further on.

75 Article 1(1), ICERD: "In this Convention, the term 'racial discrimination' shall mean any distinction, exclusion, restriction or preference based on race, colour, descent, or national or ethnic origin which has the purpose or effect of nullifying or impairing the recognition, enjoyment or exercise, on an equal footing, of human rights and fundamental freedoms in the political, economic, social, cultural or any other field of public life".

times.[76] Moreover, it must be noted that the Convention explicitly encourages the states "to ensure the adequate development and protection of certain racial groups and individuals belonging to them".[77]

Not dissimilarly, the UN Convention on the Elimination of All Forms of Discrimination against Women (CEDAW) of 1979 has been considered to play a significant role in protecting minority women's rights as well as pointing to their particular condition of intersectionality, which highlights that they can be victims of multiple types of discrimination.[78]

Reference to national minorities, as well as to ethnic and indigenous backgrounds, is made in the United Nations Convention on the Rights of the Child (CRC) of 1989, too.[79] Article 30 CRC – reproducing Article 27 ICCPR almost exactly – lays down a non-discrimination guarantee in favor of child members of minorities and includes children with indigenous origins in the list of the provision's recipients.

At the regional-international level, it is generally maintained that the European Convention on Human Rights (ECHR) has concretely contributed to diversity protection in its area of influence. In several cases, the European Court of Human Rights (ECtHR) has interpreted the Convention's provisions so as to apply them to members of national minorities, even if not always coherently and substantially.[80] Other regional international sources and

76 Garvalov, Ivan, "The United Nations International Convention on the Elimination of All Forms of Racial Discrimination", in Henrard and Dunbar (eds.), Synergies in Minority Protection . . . , 249–277.

77 Articles 1.2 and 2.2 of the Convention.

78 For references to the CEDAW committee's opinions on this issue, see Campbell, Meghan, "Cedaw and Women's Intersecting Identities: A Pioneering New Approach to Intersectional Discrimination", 11(2) *Revista Direito GV* (2015), 479–503.

79 On this, see Doek, Jaap E., "The United Nations Convention on the Rights of the Child and Children Belonging to Minority Groups", in Henrard and Dunbar (eds.), Synergies in Minority Protection . . . , 278–296.

80 As observed by Palermo and Woelk, Diritto costituzionale comparato . . . , 91, the Court has progressively devoted attention to members of minorities and groups, and several rulings have been issued in this regard, among them, for instance, *D.H. and others v Czech Republic*, 2007–57325/00 and *Oršuš and others v Croatia*, 2010–15766/03 on scholastic segregation of Rom pupils in Czech Republic and Croatia, *Tasev v North Macedonia*, 2019–9825/13 on self-identification of minority members; the court's activity has been described by Henrard Kristin, "A Patchwork of 'Successful' and 'Missed' Synergies in the Jurisprudence of the ECHR", in Henrard and Dunbar (eds.), Synergies in Minority Protection . . . , 314–364, at 315, as follows: "While the Court seems increasingly aware of the especially vulnerable position of minorities, and adopts important theoretical approaches with considerable potential for minority protection, the actual protection flowing from the case law is far from consistently positive. The developments that can be identified are not linear and do not point in one specific direction"; similarly, Geoff, Gilbert, "The Burgeoning Minority Rights Jurisprudence of the European Court of Human Rights", 24(3) *Human Rights Quarterly* (2002), 736–780; Peroni, Lourdes, "Minorities before the European Court of Human Rights", in Boulden, Jane and Kymlicka, Will (eds.), *International Approaches to Governing Ethnic Diversity* (Oxford University Press, Oxford, 2015), 25–50; the latter author examined how the notion of democratic pluralism has impacted on several cases related to minorities brought before the Court.

mechanisms have not had the same impact on the protection of the rights of national minorities. In this regard, it must be underlined that the minority rights discourse, beyond the concept of non-discrimination, is much related to the European area (and a Global North approach). In other areas of the world, the framing of diversity questions has followed different paths, tied more to the idea of peoplehood and decolonization or indigenous rights.

As for indigenous peoples' rights and their indirect protection through non-minority-specific instruments, the most active regional actors have been in the Americas and, to a lesser extent, the African continent.[81] In particular, it is maintained that the Inter-American Commission on Human Rights (IACHR) and the Inter-American Court of Human Rights (I/A Court HR) have produced pioneering jurisprudence related to indigenous peoples based on the general provisions of the American Convention on Human Rights (ACHR) – even before a specific (non-binding) instrument was adopted in 2016 in that area – which tied indigenous rights to the general framework of human rights law.[82]

81 In this regard, despite theoretical and political hurdles as regards the definition of the category of indigenous people in the African countries' traditions, since the 2000s the African Commission on Human and Peoples' Rights (ACHPR) has promoted indigenous peoples' rights with its soft jurisprudence (on this see Pentassuglia, Gaetano. "Towards a Jurisprudential Articulation of Indigenous Land Rights", 22(1) *European Journal of International Law* (2011), 165–202) and, mainly, through the establishment of the Working Group on Indigenous Populations/Communities in Africa, which published the "Report of the African Commission's Working Group of Experts on Indigenous Populations/Communities. Submitted in accordance with the 'Resolution on the Rights of Indigenous Populations/Communities in Africa', Adopted by the African Commission on Human and Peoples' Rights at Its 28th Ordinary Session" in 2005; also, the ACHPR had a fundamental role in the success of the UNDRIP negotiations and overcoming the concerns coming from several African countries; it did so by releasing an Advisory Opinion on the UNDRIP that still exerts major influence over this field: on this, see Kipuri, Naomi, "The UN Declaration on the Rights of Indigenous People in the African Context", in Charters, Claire and Stavenhagen Rodolfo (eds.), *Making the Declaration Work: The United Nations Declaration on the Rights of Indigenous Peoples* (IWGIA, Copenhagen, 2009), 252–262; as for the African Court on Human and Peoples' Rights (ACtHPR), it pronounced its first judgment on indigenous peoples' rights in 2017: for more on this, see Tramontana, Enzamaria, "The Contribution of the African Court on Human and Peoples' Rights to the Protection of Indigenous Peoples' Rights", 6 *federalismi.it* (2018), 1–19.

82 According to Anaya, James S. and Rodríguez-Piñero, Luis, "The Making of the United Nations Declaration on the Rights of Indigenous Peoples", in Hohmann, Jessie and Weller, Marc (eds.), *The UN Declaration on the Rights of Indigenous Peoples: A Commentary* (Oxford University Press, Oxford, 2018), 38–62, the watershed in the process of recognition of indigenous peoples' demands has been the *Awan Tingni case*: (*Awas Tingni Mayagna (Sumo) Indigenous Community v Nicaragua*, Judgment 31 August 2001, IACtHR Series C No 79 (2001)); also, on this, Pasqualucci, Jo M., "The Evolution of International Indigenous Rights in the Inter-American Human Rights System", 6(2) *Human Rights Law Review* (2006), 281–322; Mariadaga Cuneo, Isabel, "The Rights of Indigenous People and the Inter-American Human Rights System", 22(1) *Arizona Journal of International and Comparative Law* (2005), 53–64.

The emergence of diversity/3: multiple constitutional ideal-typical models for the accommodation of diversity within the framework of democratic constitutionalism

The international developments described in the previous sections have contributed to creating a common legal framework shared by the countries that adhere to the principles of democratic constitutionalism, marked by the non-discriminatory guarantee of individual human rights. While variously implemented, today, the principle of equality in terms of non-discrimination is generally seen as a common element of the contemporary constitutional tradition – further reinforced by its enshrinement in international law[83] – as well as *a conditio sine qua non* for minority protection.[84] As known, however, there is no corresponding ability to implement the provisions through international mechanisms.[85] Furthermore, though the principle has been interpreted by several international bodies as embedding a positive dimension intended to redress inequalities in the starting position to reach equal opportunities, this does not mean that a state international obligation exists in this regard.[86]

In other words, although the principle of equality in the sense of non-discrimination is central to democratic constitutional systems, the states maintain a large margin of discretion as regards the accommodation of diversity within their borders so long as their regulations abide by the existing minimum international standards. This remained the case even after the surge of (regional) international documents in the 1990s, following the break-up of the USSR and Yugoslavia, as will be described in what follows. In this section, it seems useful to give a snapshot of the main ideal-typical models, as their main distinguishing elements can be traced back to this epoch. It must be taken into account that countries like Switzerland were precursors in this respect and that several others – both within and outside Europe – would thereafter witness the introduction of further forms of accommodation (also) inspired by the most recent international developments in this area.

Against this background, in the second half of the twentieth century, several approaches to diversity issues were developed. Four ideal-typical constitutional

83 Heinze, The Construction . . . , 30, pointed out that not only is the principle of discrimination "anchored in international law", but that there are also "strong arguments in favour of its status of customary law" (for further references, see footnote 24, at 30 of the quoted writing); also according to Castellino, Joshua, "Introduction", in Castellino (ed.), Global Minority Rights . . . , xi–xxiv, at xviii, non-discrimination amounts to a principle of international *jus cogens*.

84 Henrard, Kristin, "Non-Discrimination and Full and Effective Equality", in Weller, Marc (ed.), *Universal Minority Rights: A Commentary on the Jurisprudence of International Courts and Treaty Bodies* (Oxford University Press, Oxford, 2007), 75–147, at 75–76.

85 Apart from the protection against gross violations of human rights, which is generally considered as part of *jus cogens*.

86 See, for broad references on the activity of the HRC and other relevant bodies, Henrard, Non-Discrimination . . . , 112–136; Wheatley, Steven, *Democracy, Minorities and International Law* (Cambridge University Press, Cambridge, 2005), 38–43.

models have been distinguished, three of which can arguably be considered as fostering (at least formally) the basic principles of liberal constitutional democracies.[87]

The first model has been defined as orthodox liberal (or liberal agnostic). The US and France are two paradigmatic examples of this model. The liberal agnostic constitutional approach is reliant on the idea of the correspondence between state and nation and, consequently, of nationality and citizenship. The main focus of liberal agnostic states is individual rights and formal equality, i.e., the guarantee of equal legal treatment at the points of departure without any form of discrimination. In contrast, substantive equality, which implies that the state takes action to remove the social and economic obstacles some categories of people may encounter and that can limit their life opportunities, is not generally promoted. *A fortiori*, rules that aim to provide for differential treatments based on the worth of different conditions *per se* are usually not accepted.

This does not mean that specific measures cannot be taken to this end; nevertheless, they are necessarily put under thorough legitimacy scrutiny. In other words, special measures with regard to some groups are not legitimate unless justified by special needs, generally connected to redressing long-standing inequalities. A case in point is the situation of the black minority in the US. As a result of the long and troubled history and legal treatment of black communities, the judiciary has developed a strict scrutiny test according to which positive discrimination (affirmative action) in favor of these (and other) communities will be considered unlawful unless a compelling public interest is present and proportionate means are used.[88]

The second model has been referred to as promotional. It implies the recognition of diversity as a constitutive element of society and its protection as conducive to the promotion of democratic pluralism. Promotional systems lay down concrete safeguards in favor of some legally selected ethno-linguistic groups whose members are citizens of the country holding a non-majority position. In a way, it is the majority that accepts that guarantees be put in place

87 See Marko, Joseph, "Equality and Difference: Political and Legal Aspects of Ethnic Group Relations", in Matscher, Franz (ed.), *Vienna International Encounter on Some Current Issues Regarding the Situation of National Minorities* (N. P. Engel, Kehl-Strasbourg-Arlington, 1997), 67–97; Toniatti, Roberto, "Minoranze e minoranze protette: modelli costituzionali comparati", in Bonazzi, Tiziano and Dunne, Michael (eds.), *Cittadinanza e diritti nelle società multiculturali* (Il Mulino, Bologna, 1994), 273–283; Palermo and Woelk, Diritto costituzionale comparato . . . , 43–71; what the authors called the repressive model is here excluded as it does not imply the acceptance of the basic foundations of constitutionalism; however, while a repressive model cannot help but lead to repressive outcomes, formally liberal models can lead to similar results, depending on how the formal provisions apply to a given context: every legal system should be assessed in relation to the societal situation it rules, taking into account its effects and its application also by means of judicial and administrative activities.

88 On this, and for further references, see Palermo and Woelk, Diritto costituzionale comparato . . . , 283–310.

for the sake of some minorities, the criteria for the selection being affected by geographical, demographical, historical, and political factors. In general, protection is afforded to communities of citizens that have a long-standing tie with the respective territory.[89]

In this model, specific measures in favor of non-majority groups are deemed lawful unless discrimination is proven. This is the opposite of liberal agnostic models. Legal protections may include varying forms of autonomy, linguistic and educational rights, religious rights, exemptions, and political rights.

Italy is commonly described as an example of a promotional legal system, specifically targeting linguistic minorities. The general national system for the protection of linguistic minorities has its main reference in Article 6 of the Constitution, according to which: "The Republic safeguards linguistic minorities through appropriate measures". The state is the only authority endowed with the power to establish which minorities are to be legally protected. Only in 1999, a general law (no. 482/1999) on linguistic minorities was approved by the Parliament. The law has identified and recognized a limited number of historical linguistic minorities (12), defined the general criteria (territorial, linguistic, and historical) for their recognition, and set out a series of promotional measures. Moreover, asymmetrical territorial arrangements have been created (also) for minority protection purposes, with this allowing for a greater degree of autonomy for some territorially located linguistic groups.[90]

The third approach has been labeled as multinational. The main characterizing element of multinational systems resides in the fact that they are entirely organized according to the principle of 'institutional equality' of two or more groups, i.e., the ones that are legally considered as the constitutive communities of the attendant state or regional society.[91] In other words, there is no such thing as a majority that grants differential legal treatments to some non-majority groups. Rather, all groups have (almost) equal standing and representation in the state structures, and their members enjoy the same rights. The agreement of groups and their collaboration are basic tenets of these systems, which make use of power-sharing, i.e., "those rules that, in addition to defining how decisions will be made by groups within the polity, allocate decision-making rights, including access to state resources, among

89 In this work legal systems that embed protection for indigenous peoples are included in this ideal-typical model since they follow similar assumptions.

90 On the Italian regional system and the role of identity politics in the so-called special regions created (also) for minority protection, see Alessi, Nicolò P. and Palermo, Francesco, "Intergovernmental Relations and Identity Politics in Italy", in Fessha, Yonatan T., Kössler, Karl and Palermo, Francesco (eds.), *Intergovernmental Relations in Divided Societies* (Palgrave Macmillan, Cham, 2022), 183–218.

91 Multinational systems may indeed be present at a regional level only, like in the case of South Tyrol in Italy or Northern Ireland in the UK.

collectivities competing for power".[92] The concrete ways that power-sharing is put into practice are various, but they all basically imply a consensual method of government and the participation of all the constituent communities in the state (or regional) institutions, a logic that largely limits the application of the majority principle. Power-sharing institutions and mechanisms entail a (proportional or equal) representation of groups in the common executive, parliamentary, judicial and administrative branches, veto powers, cultural rights, and (territorial or non-territorial) autonomy for the groups.

Power-sharing institutions are present in consolidated democracies but are also increasingly resorted to in emerging democratic settings as tools for conflict resolution.[93] Bosnia-Herzegovina is a much-studied case where power-sharing is in place, as it clearly shows the potential and the limits of the model.[94] Consolidated multinational models can be found in Switzerland,[95] Belgium, and Canada or, at a subnational level, South Tyrol and Northern Ireland.

It should be stressed that the ideal-typical models while displaying different degrees of sensitivity to diversity, move within the same tradition and are based on the same conceptual and legal categories. The first model is tied to the liberal idea of neutrality and is based on the creation of an ideal legal reality of equals composing the nation. At the same time, it (formally) prevents diversity from being a ground of discrimination, following the developments of contemporary liberal-democratic constitutionalism. The promotional model

92 On this, see Hartzell, Caroline and Hoddie, Matthew, "Institutionalizing Peace: Power-Sharing and Post-Civil War Conflict Management", 47(2) *American Journal of Political Science* (2003), 318–332, at 320; power-sharing is often associated to consociationalism, a more specific term used as an analytical and normative category and coined as early as the 1960s by Arend Lijphart, whose most known descriptions of the model can be found in Lijphart Arend, *Democracy in Plural Societies: A Comparative Exploration* (Yale University Press, New Haven-London, 1977) and in *Id., Patterns of Democracy: Government Forms and Performance in Thirty-Six Countries* (Yale University Press, New Haven-London, 2012).

93 For an overview and further references, see Keil, Soeren and McCulloch, Allison (eds.), *Power-Sharing in Europe: Past Practice, Present Cases, and Future Directions* (Palgrave Macmillan, Cham, 2021) and in part of the Introduction.

94 On Bosnia and Herzegovina, see Benedizione, Ludovica and Scotti, Valentina R. (eds.), *Twenty Years after Dayton: The Constitutional Transition of Bosnia and Herzegovina* (Luiss University Press, Rome, 2016); Keil, Soeren, *Multinational Federalism in Bosnia and Herzegovina* (Routledge, London, 2016).

95 However, once more, Switzerland must be recognized as a peculiar example: while it is characterized by the existence of power-sharing mechanisms, it has been underlined that the Swiss country cannot be labeled as multinational but multilingual and mono-national, as there is no linguistic (nor religious) community that claims to be a national community; in other terms, the societal cleavages existing in Switzerland cross-cut each other, and none of them has gained such political salience as to become the main factor of identification in internal "national" communities; on this, see Dardanelli, Paolo, "Multi-Lingual but Mono-National: Exploring and Explaining Switzerland's Exceptionalism", in Caminal, Miquel and Requejo, Ferran (eds.), *Federalism, Plurinationality, and Democratic Constitutionalism: Theory and Cases* (Routledge, London-New York, 2011), 295–323.

recognizes the fact that a society may be composed of some groups that are, for various reasons, deemed worth protection, with this implying a form of accommodation that goes further than the minimum international standards in place until the 1990s. If this perspective weakens the tenet of correspondence between one state and one nation, it aims to protect at the same time selected groups that generally have national-like characteristics. Compared to the others, the multinational system makes diversity a structural element of the state organization, informing all aspects of public life, but similarly frames diversity in terms of specifically selected groups having national features.

The emergence of diversity/4: minority and indigenous peoples' rights law

New developments related to the condition of diversity in constitutionalism followed the end of the Cold War and the ensuing disruption of the USSR and Yugoslavia. The tragedies of the wars and ethnic conflicts in Europe and many other parts of the world showed how strong nationalistic ideas still were, what their radicalization could lead to, and how the human rights law system was ineffective in preventing them. As a consequence, (ethnic) diversity was once more brought to the forefront – principally as a potential threat to peace and security all around the world, with this asking for new political and legal responses.

Against this backdrop, in this epoch, Europe became the center of a new season of international law regarding diversity in terms of minorities. This led to the creation of a corpus of international minority rights law and other minority-specific institutions and mechanisms. In turn, the international developments had significant consequences for several domestic jurisdictions, especially in Southeast Europe, which witnessed a surge in minority rights provisions at various levels.[96] In other words, the double dynamic of constitutionalization of international law and internationalization of constitutional law reached its peak – at least in this area of the world – as minority rights were no longer supposed to be entirely at state discretion.[97]

The first minority-specific international act came from the universal international legal system. This was the United Nations Declaration on the Rights of Persons Belonging to National or Ethnic, Religious and Linguistic Minorities (Declaration on Minorities) of 1992,[98] which implemented the content of Article 27 ICCPR. Following this renewed focus on minorities, the posts of

96 On the evolution of minority rights in East Europe and the influence of international bodies as well as the EU, see Rechel, Bernd (ed.), *Minority Rights in Central and Eastern Europe* (Routledge, London-New York, 2009).

97 Palermo, Francesco, "The Protection of Minorities in International Law: Recent Developments and Trends", in VV.AA., *Les minorités: un défi pour les États: actes du colloque international (22 et 23 mai 2011)* (Académie Royale de Belgique, Bruxelles, 2012), 165–185, at 169.

98 Resolution no. 47/135, 18 December 1992.

High Commissioner on Human Rights[99] and Special Rapporteur on Minority Issues[100] were established, and a Forum on minority issues was created within the Human Rights Council.[101]

Further and significant international developments took place on the European continent, reflecting three different dimensions of state cooperation.

The first layer of European cooperation that played a remarkable role was the Conference on Security and Cooperation in Europe – then the Organisation for Security and Cooperation in Europe (OSCE) – which was mostly driven by geopolitical security concerns. In 1992, the organization appointed a High Commissioner on National Minorities (HCNM), who was assigned the tasks of monitoring the developments concerning minority rights in the OSCE area, intervening diplomatically in situations of crisis or conflict, gathering best practices, and providing recommendations. The activity of the HCNM remains highly relevant, both diplomatically and advisorily.[102]

The second and stricter level of cooperation is the one within the framework of the Council of Europe, which has produced the most advanced international instruments for the accommodation of diversity in the form of individual minority rights. Besides the ECHR – to which Protocol 12 on positive measures to prevent non-discrimination was added (albeit not signed) by several states – in 1995, the Council of Europe adopted the Framework Convention on National Minorities, which entered into force in 1998. It is the first legally binding multilateral treaty on minorities, and it lays down the most comprehensive set of minority rights and guarantees that arguably touch upon all aspects of their possible accommodation.

The treaty embeds program-type provisions aimed at promoting minority protection in the form of obligations that signatory states undertake to put in place in their jurisdictions at the moment of ratifying the act.[103] Also, while neither a petition system nor jurisdictional mechanisms have been adopted, a monitoring system is in place based on the activity of the Advisory Committee on the Framework Convention (ACFC). The FCNM addresses issues such as the right of "persons belonging to minorities" to self-identification, language, identity, education, religion, association, cross-border contacts, and

99 Resolution no. 48/141, 20 December 1993.

100 The mandate of the Special Rapporteur on minority issues was established by resolution 2005/79 of the Commission on Human Rights, on 21 April 2005.

101 Human Rights Council resolution no. 6/15, 28 September 2007, renewed by resolution no. 19/23, 23 March 2012; this body has taken over the tasks of the Human Rights Commission.

102 Interestingly, Jackson-Preece, Jennifer, "The High Commissioner on National Minorities as a Normative Actor", 12(3) *Journal on Ethnopolitics and Minority Issues in Europe* (2013), 77–82, defined the HCNM as a veritable "normative actor"; this has been all the more so in the last decades, as the HCNM has issued very important documents characterized by a significant change of perspective on the accommodation of diversity; on this, see Chapter 3.

103 According to Article 20 FCNM, the states must "specify the territory or territories for whose international relations it is responsible to which this framework Convention shall apply".

participation. Interestingly, it also firmly states that minority rights are "part of the international system for human rights protection". This holds notable symbolic meaning in the global rights discourse.

Furthermore, in 1992, the Council of Europe approved the European Charter for Regional or Minority Languages (ECRML), which entered into force the same year as the FCNM. The international treaty cannot be strictly defined as a minority rights instrument as it focuses on the survival of languages more than the rights of the respective communities. Nevertheless, it goes without saying that this document adds another guarantee for minority-related practices. The ECRML is designed as an "à la carte" set of provisions chosen by the signing states and a monitoring system carried out by the Committee of Experts of the European Charter for Regional or Minority Languages. More precisely, states indicate the measures they are going to implement in their jurisdictions and the recipient languages to which they will apply.

The European Union is the third geopolitical area whose activity covers – albeit to a lesser extent – diversity and minority accommodation. Indeed, despite being the most advanced model of supranational integration, the EU is not entitled to any specific competencies on minority protection. Notwithstanding that, minorities and their rights are taken into account at the treaty level, and they benefit from the non-discrimination regulations enacted by the European institutions and implemented by the Court of Justice.

Article 2 TEU affirms that the "respect for human rights, including the rights of persons belonging to minorities", is a value of the EU and part of the *acquis communautaire*. Moreover, Article 21 of the Charter of Fundamental Rights of the European Union (CFA) provides for the guarantee of non-discrimination while Article 22 states that "The Union shall respect cultural, religious and linguistic diversity".

Importantly, Article 19 TFEU entrenches a specific EU competence to take action "to combat discrimination based on sex, racial or ethnic origin, religion or belief, disability, age or sexual orientation". This article has been the legal basis upon which European legislation on non-discrimination has been put forward, mainly based on the Council Directive 2000/43/EC of 29 June 2000, implementing the principle of equal treatment between persons irrespective of racial or ethnic origin and Council Directive 2007/78/EC, establishing a general framework for equal treatment in employment and occupation. Other treaty provisions further address diversity, albeit to varying extents.[104] The summarized legal bases have given the EU Court of Justice

104 Such as Article 13 TFEU, requiring the EU to respect cultural traditions and regional heritages in its activity; also, see Article 167, para. 4 TFEU, which states that: "The Union shall take cultural aspects into account in its action under other provisions of the Treaties, in particular in order to respect and to promote the diversity of its cultures".

the opportunity to judge cases related to diversity accommodation on several occasions.[105]

Finally, in 1993, the Copenhagen criteria – the political criteria candidate states need to fulfil to be eligible for European accession – were adopted, among which the protection of national minorities is included.[106]

Hence, the EU legal framework has, to a certain extent, provided another – peculiar – source of legal recognition of diversity on the European continent. Interestingly, and moving away from a purely legal standpoint, recent research has also demonstrated how the very process of Europeanization has had a (complex and) broad impact on minority communities in Europe by enabling processes of bottom-up empowerment, too.[107]

Indigeneity as a distinct category of diversity object of specific arrangements

Indigenous peoples are another category of non-majority group that has witnessed a steady growth of interest and regulation as a result of worldwide movements for the recognition and protection of their styles of life.

As is well known, after centuries of exclusion and assimilation in several parts of the world, indigenous peoples' demands for recognition arose during

105 For a description of most ECJ cases related to minority protection, see Marko and Constantin (eds.), Human and Minority Rights . . .; also, see Palermo and Woelk, Diritto costituzionale comparato . . . , 109–114: among the most significant cases, one can identify three related to South Tyrol's complex power-sharing system, which show that the ECJ has sometimes examined state regulations dealing with the accommodation of diversity to verify their compatibility with European law: *Bickel and Franz* (ECJ, case C-274/96, judgement of 24 November 1998, ECR 1998 I-07637), *Angonese v Cassa di Risparmio di Bolzano S.p.A.* (ECJ, case C-281/99, judgement of 6 June 2000, ECR 2000 I-04139) and *Kamberaj v Istituto per l'Edilizia sociale della Provincia autonoma di Bolzano (IPES), Giunta della Provincia autonoma di Bolzano, Provincia autonoma di Bolzano* (ECJ, case C-571/10, judgement of 24 April 2012, in *Digital Reports* of the ECJ); moreover, the Court has scrutinized affirmative actions several times: among others, see *Eckhard Kalanke v Freie Hansestadt Bremen* (ECJ, case C-450/93, judgement of 17 October 1995, ECR 1995 I-03051), *Helmut Marschall v Land Nordrhein Westfalen* (ECJ, case C-409/95, judgement of 11 November 1997, ECR 1997 I-06363), *Georg Badeck et al.* (ECJ, case C-158/97, judgement of 28 march 2000, ECR 2000 I-01875), *Abrahamson and Andersen* (ECJ, case C-407/98, judgement of 6 July 2000, ECR 2000 I-05539); on the ECJ's role in the implementation of the European legal framework on non-discrimination, see also Kochenov, Dimitry, "The European Union's Troublesome Minority Protection: A Bird's Eye View", in Boulden and Kymlicka (eds.), International Approaches . . . , 79–101.

106 These criteria only monitor applicant states and not states that were already members of the EU.

107 On this, Crepaz, Katharina, *The Impact of Europeanization on Minority Communities* (Springer, Cham, 2016); on the concept of bottom-up empowerment, see Chapters 4 and 5.

the 1970s[108] and determined a spike of interest within the international community.[109] Consequently, as shown, they were first increasingly taken into account as recipients of non-minority-specific human rights treaties and general standards[110]; secondly, distinct international acts and mechanisms addressing them directly were adopted.[111]

The first international documents dealing with indigenous peoples were issued by the International Labour Organization (ILO), whose attention was drawn to the situation of those communities at the beginning of the twentieth century. After two decades of studies and works on these issues, which mainly concerned the working conditions of indigenous communities, the ILO adopted at its 40th session the Convention on the Protection and Integration of Indigenous and Other Tribal and Semi-Tribal Populations in Independent Countries, No. 107 of 1957 (ILO 107) and the Indigenous and Tribal Populations Recommendation (Recommendation No. 104). Though

108 Several conditions accounted for the described trend, which are outlined by Niezen, Ronald, *The Origins of Indigenism: Human Rights and the Politics of Identity* (University of California Press, Berkeley-Los Angeles-London, 2003), 40–42, can be summarized as follows: the establishment of a minority-friendly human rights system; the reinforcement of anti-colonial legal discourses; the fact that assimilationist policies did not lead to the elimination of indigenous peoples; the emergence of an "indigenous middle class".

109 What is particularly interesting in regard to the indigenous peoples is that they have developed many transnational forms of cooperation and reciprocal support, which seems to be a distinguishing feature of indigenous movements; it must be underlined that prior to the Seventies (i.e., from the second half of the nineteenth century), the international community had taken into consideration indigenous peoples, but it had done so on the basis of the so-called 'trusteeship doctrine' and the idea of the inherent superiority of European countries: on this, see Anaya and Rodríguez-Piñero, The Making . . . , 39–41.

110 This is the case with several treaties pertaining to environmental, biodiversity, and sustainable development issues adopted in the 1990s, as well as the CRC of 1989 (Article 30), which contain provisions targeting indigenous peoples; furthermore, some UN treaty monitoring bodies explicitly included them within the reach of non-minority-specific instruments: for instance, the HRC's General Comment no. 23 of 1994, para. 3.2. , on Article 27 ICCPR affirmed that: "The enjoyment of the rights to which article 27 relates does not prejudice the sovereignty and territorial integrity of a State party. At the same time, one or other aspect of the rights of individuals protected under that article – for example, to enjoy a particular culture – may consist in a way of life which is closely associated with territory and use of its resources. This may particularly be true of members of indigenous communities constituting a minority". The committee then confirmed its interpretation when adjudicating subsequent complaints lodged by indigenous groups and held the provision regarding self-determination applies to indigenous peoples; similarly, the ICERD's General Recommendation no. 23 of 1997, para. 1, stated that: "the Committee has consistently affirmed that discrimination against indigenous peoples falls under the scope of the Convention and that all appropriate means must be taken to combat and eliminate such discrimination" and called upon state parties to ensure the equal enjoyment of rights by indigenous peoples; on this, see Anaya and Rodríguez-Piñero, The Making . . . , 45–48.

111 For a thorough analysis of the international legal framework, see Anaya, James S., *International Human Rights and Indigenous People* (Aspen Publishers, New York, 2009).

the ILO 107 was still focused on an assimilationist model;[112] subsequent international instruments marked a move toward the recognition of the rights of indigenous peoples, stressing their collective dimension.

An important role in this change of perspective was played by the UN Working Group on Indigenous Populations (WGIP), which was created in 1982. This body's work laid the foundations for the two "big breaks"[113] as regards indigenous peoples' rights, namely the ILO's Indigenous and Tribal Peoples Convention of 1989 (ILO 169) and the United Nations Declaration on the Rights of Indigenous Peoples (UNDRIP) of 2007.[114]

The ILO 169 is the first convention addressing indigenous communities as "peoples" and the only binding international act when it comes to indigenous peoples' rights.[115] It sets out provisions aimed at guaranteeing non-discrimination and protecting indigenous peoples' (work-related and non-work-related) rights and cultures. This includes positive actions, as well as further measures specifically tailored to these groups, such as the right to prior consultation and land rights.

The UNDRIP is the most detailed set of provisions related to indigenous peoples at the international level. Its non-binding character has not prevented it from becoming a fundamental point of reference for indigenous peoples' rights. Moreover, it should be noted that several provisions – for instance, those on equality, non-discrimination, and self-determination – resonate with already existing binding standards and principles of international law.

The Declaration expands on and adds a new layer of protection to what had previously been foreseen by the ILO 169. To sum up, its main contents deal with equality and non-discrimination, cultural integrity rights exercised in a collective dimension; self-determination, autonomy, participation, consultation, and consent; rights to lands, resources, and territories, as well as determining social and economic development; rights to redress and compensation for past injustices.

To conclude the description of the global dimension of indigenous peoples' rights, it should be noted that the mentioned documents are complemented by the action of three UN-specific mechanisms: the United Nations Permanent Forum on Indigenous Issues (UNPFII), a subsidiary body of the Economic and Social Council; the Expert Mechanism on the Rights of Indigenous Peoples, a five-member expert advisory body of the Human Rights Council;

112 Bens, Jonas, *The Indigenous Paradox: Rights, Sovereignty, and Culture in the Americas* (University of Pennsylvania Press, Philadelphia, 2020), 13.

113 Expression borrowed from Bens, The Indigenous Paradox . . . , 13.

114 As observed by Anaya and Rodríguez-Piñero, The Making . . . , 42, prior to them, an extensive study on indigenous peoples was commissioned by the UN Economic and Social Council, which resulted in a series of reports by Special Rapporteur José Martinez Cobo that were issued from 1981 to 1983.

115 At the moment, ratified by only 24 countries (source: https://www.ilo.org/dyn/normlex/en/f?p=NORMLEXPUB:11300:::NO:11300:P11300_INSTRUMENT_ID:312314:NO, last access: 3 June 2024).

and the Special Rapporteur on the rights of indigenous peoples, one of the special procedures of the Human Rights Council.

At the regional-international level, the most remarkable progress has taken place in the Americas. The Inter-American Court of Human Rights has significantly contributed to human rights standards related to indigenous peoples. In addition, in 2016, the American Declaration on the Rights of Indigenous Peoples was adopted. Not only does the Declaration recall several UNDRIP principles, but it also touches upon further issues not addressed by other international documents, thereby reflecting a notable commitment of the American continent to indigenous peoples' issues.[116]

The international legal framework on indigenous peoples' rights has been developing in parallel to advancements in domestic jurisdictions in several parts of the world and affecting them to various extents.[117] This is especially true of Scandinavian countries, Australia and New Zealand, and the states of the American continent. It is generally maintained that the South American legal systems provide some of the most advanced forms of national recognition and guarantees to indigenous peoples, which in some cases go so far as to include them in the very foundational components of the constitutional systems (at least on paper).[118] As will be shown further on, the Canadian model also seems to have developed very promising instruments to accommodate diversity in general and indigenous peoples' demands in particular.

Bibliography

Alessi, Nicolò P. and Palermo, Francesco, "Intergovernmental Relations and Identity Politics in Italy", in Fessha, Yonatan T., Kössler, Karl and Palermo, Francesco (eds.), *Intergovernmental Relations in Divided Societies* (Palgrave Macmillan, Cham, 2022), 183–218

116 On this, see Errico, Stefania, "The American Declaration on the Rights of Indigenous Peoples", 21(7) *ASIL Insights* (2017), available at: https://www.asil.org/insights/volume/21/issue/7/american-declaration-rights-indigenous-peoples.

117 As indicated by Bankes, Nigel, "Themes and Reflections: A Perspective from Canada", in Allard, Christina and Funderud Skogvang, Susann (eds.), *Indigenous Rights in Scandinavia: Autonomous Sami Law* (Routledge, London-New York, 2016), 9–22, at 9–13, international jurisdiction affects European (Scandinavian) countries to a larger extent, as their legal systems allow for a greater interminglement of international and domestic law in this and other areas compared to other constitutional traditions.

118 As outlined by the UN Report on indigenous peoples' rights in South America *Guaranteeing Indigenous People's Rights in Latin America: Progress in the Past Decade and Remaining Challenges* (United Nations, Santiago, 2014), 12–15, many constitutional reforms were adopted in South America to include indigenous peoples' rights in the constitutional framework; on the difficulties concerning the implementation of the latter reforms, see Martínez Espinoza, Manuel Ignacio, "Reconocimiento sin implementación: un balance sobre los derechos de los pueblos indígenas en América Latina", 60(224) *Revista Mexicana de Ciencias Políticas y Sociales* (2015), 251–278; for more on this, see Chapter 3.

Amor, María and Estébanez, Martín, "The United Nations International Covenant on Economic, Social and Cultural Rights", in Henrard, Kristin and Dunbar, Robert (eds.), *Synergies in Minority Protection: European and International Law Perspectives* (Cambridge University Press, Cambridge-New York, 2008), 213–247

Anaya, James S., *International Human Rights and Indigenous People* (Aspen Publishers, New York, 2009)

Anaya, James S. and Rodríguez-Piñero, Luis, "The Making of the United Nations Declaration on the Rights of Indigenous Peoples", in Hohmann, Jessie and Weller, Marc (eds.), *The UN Declaration on the Rights of Indigenous Peoples: A Commentary* (Oxford University Press, Oxford, 2018), 38–62

Anderson, Benedict, *Imagined Communities: Reflections on the Origins and Spread of Nationalism* (Verso, London-New-York, 2006)

Arato, Andrew and Cohen, Jean L., "Introduction: Forms of Pluralism and Democratic Constitutionalism", in Arato, Andrew, Cohen, Jean L. and von Busekist, Astrid (eds.), *Forms of Pluralism and Democratic Constitutionalism* (Columbia University Press, New York-Chichester, 2018), 1–30

Bankes, Nigel, "Themes and Reflections: A Perspective from Canada", in Allard, Christina and Funderud Skogvang, Susann (eds.), *Indigenous Rights in Scandinavia: Autonomous Sami Law* (Routledge, London-New-York, 2016), 9–22

Barth, William K., *On Cultural Rights: The Equality of Nations and the Minority Legal Tradition* (Martinus Nijhoff Publishers, Leiden-Boston, 2008)

Bartole, Sergio, *The Internationalisation of Constitutional Law: A View from the Venice Commission* (Hart Publishing, Oxford-New York, 2020)

Bauer, Otto, *The Question of Nationalities and Social Democracy* (University of Minnesota Press, Minneapolis, 2000), translated by O'Donnell, Joseph, originally published as Bauer, Otto, *Die Nationalitiitenfrage und die Sozialdemokratie* (Verlag der Wiener Volksbuchhandlung, Vienna, 1924)

Belser, Eva Maria, "Concluding Remarks", in Belser, Eva Maria, Bächler, Thea, Egli, Sandra and Zünd, Lawrence (eds.), *The Principle of Equality in Diverse States: Reconciling Autonomy with Equal Rights and Opportunities* (Brill-Nijhoff, Leiden-Boston, 2021), 415–428

Benedizione, Ludovica and Scotti, Valentina R. (eds.), *Twenty Years after Dayton: The Constitutional Transition of Bosnia and Herzegovina* (Luiss University Press, Rome, 2016)

Bens, Jonas, *The Indigenous Paradox: Rights, Sovereignty, and Culture in the Americas* (University of Pennsylvania Press, Philadelphia, 2020)

Bloed, Arie and van Dijk, Pieter (eds.), *Protection of Minority Rights Through Bilateral Treaties: The Case of Central and Eastern Europe* (Kluwer Law International, The Hague, 1999)

Bossuyt, Marc, "Comprehensive Examination of Thematic Issues Relating to Racial Discrimination: The Concept and Practice of Affirmative Action", in Castellino, Joshua (ed.), *Global Minority Rights* (Routledge, London-New York, 2016), 333–356

Brubaker, Roger, *Nationalism reframed: Nationhood and the National Question in the New Europe* (Cambridge University Press, Cambridge, 1996)

Buratti, Andrea, *Western Constitutionalism: History, Institutions, Comparative Law* (Springer-Giappichelli, Cham-Turin, 2019)

Burri, Mira, "The UNESCO Convention on Cultural Diversity: An Appraisal Five Years after Its Entry into Force", 20(4) *International Journal of Cultural Property* (2013), 357–380

Campbell, Meghan, "Cedaw and Women's Intersecting Identities: A Pioneering New Approach to Intersectional Discrimination", 11(2) *Revista Direito GV* (2015), 479–503

Capotorti, Francesco, *Study on the Rights of Persons Belonging to Ethnic, Religious and Linguistic Minorities* (United Nations, New York, 1977) (UN Doc. E/CN.4/sub.2/384/Rev.1, UN sales Nr. E.78.XIV.1) / Geneva UN Center for Human Rights, UN Doc E/CN.4/sub.2/384/Add.1–7, 1–114

Castellino, Joshua, "Introduction", in Castellino, Joshua (ed.), *Global Minority Rights* (Routledge, London-New York, 2016), xi–xxiv

Chang, Wen-Chen and Yeh, Jiunn-Rong, "Internationalization of Constitutional Law", in Rosenfeld, Michel and Sajó, András (eds.), *The Oxford Handbook of Comparative Constitutional Law* (Oxford University Press, Oxford, 2012), 1166–1184

Cohn, Margit and Grimm, Dieter, "'Human Dignity' as a Constitutional Doctrine", in Tushnet, Mark, Fleiner, Thomas and Saunders, Cheryl (eds.), *Routledge Handbook of Constitutional Law* (Routledge, London-New York, 2013), 193–203

Coomans, Fons, "UNESCO's Convention Against Discrimination in Education", in Henrard, Kristin and Dunbar, Robert (eds.), *Synergies in Minority Protection: European and International Law Perspectives* (Cambridge University Press, Cambridge-New York, 2008), 297–313

Cottroll, Robert J. and Davis, Megan, "Affirmative Action", in Tushnet, Mark, Fleiner, Thomas and Saunders, Cheryl (eds.), *Routledge Handbook of Constitutional Law* (Routledge, London-New York, 2013), 325–336

Crepaz, Katharina, *The Impact of Europeanization on Minority Communities* (Springer, Cham, 2016)

Dann, Philipp, Riegner, Michael and Bönnemann, Maxim, "The Southern Turn in Comparative Constitutional Law: An Introduction", in Dann, Philipp, Riegner, Michael and Bönnemann, Maxim (eds.), *The Global South and Comparative Constitutional Law* (Oxford University Press, Oxford, 2020), 1–38

Dardanelli, Paolo, "Multi-Lingual But Mono-National: Exploring and Explaining Switzerland's Exceptionalism", in Caminal, Miquel and Requejo, Ferran (eds.), *Federalism, Plurinationality, and Democratic Constitutionalism: Theory and Cases* (Routledge, London-New York, 2011), 295–323

De Wet, Erika, "The Constitutionalization of Public International Law", in Rosenfeld, Michel and Sajó, András (eds.), *The Oxford Handbook of Comparative Constitutional Law* (Oxford University Press, Oxford, 2012), 1209–1230

Doek, Jaap E., "The United Nations Convention on the Rights of the Child and Children Belonging to Minority Groups", in Henrard, Kristin and Dunbar, Robert (eds.), *Synergies in Minority Protection: European and International Law Perspectives* (Cambridge University Press, Cambridge-New York, 2008), 278–296

Errico, Stefania, "The American Declaration on the Rights of Indigenous Peoples", 21(7) *ASIL Insights* (2017), at https://www.asil.org/insights/volume/21/issue/7/american-declaration-rights-indigenous-peoples

Fariello, Sara, "I diritti fondamentali nella società multiculturale: il contributo della sociologia del diritto", in Baldini, Vincenzo (ed.), *Multiculturalismo* (CEDAM, Padua, 2012), 267–276

Fioravanti, Maurizio, "Il principio di eguaglianza nella storia del costituzionalismo moderno", 2(4) *Contemporanea* (1999), 609–630

Frankerberg, Günther, *Comparative Constitutional Studies: Between Magic and Deceit* (Edward Elgar, Cheltenham-Northampton, 2018)

Fredman, Sandra, "Substantive Equality Revisited", 14(3) *International Journal of Constitutional Law* (2016), 712–738

Garvalov, Ivan, "The United Nations International Convention on the Elimination of All Forms of Racial Discrimination", in Henrard, Kristin and Dunbar, Robert (eds.), *Synergies in Minority Protection: European and International Law Perspectives* (Cambridge University Press, Cambridge-New York, 2008), 249–277

Gaudreault-DesBiens, Jean-F., "Introduction to Part II", in Foblets, Marie-Claire, Gaudreault-DesBiens, Jean-F. and Dundes Relteln, Alison (eds.), *Cultural Diversity and the Law: State Responses Around the World* (Bruylant and Yvon-Blais, Bruxelles-Montréal, 2010), 367–380

Geoff, Gilbert, "The Burgeoning Minority Rights Jurisprudence of the European Court of Human Rights", 24(3) *Human Rights Quarterly* (2002), 736–780

Germane, Maria, "Paul Schiemann, Max Laserson and Cultural Autonomy: A Case Study from Interwar Latvia", in Nimni, Ephraim, Osipov, Alexander and Smith, David J. (eds.), *The Challenge of Non-Territorial Autonomy: Theory and Practice* (Peter Lang, Oxford, 2013), 101–115

Göcke, Katja, "Indigenous Peoples in International Law", in Hauser-Schäublin, Brigitta (eds.), *Adat and Indigeneity in Indonesia: Culture and Entitlements between Heteronomy and Self-Ascription* (Göttingen University Press, Göttingen, 2013), 17–29

Grimm, Dieter, *Constitutionalism: Past, Present, and Future* (Oxford University Press, Oxford, 2016)

Gringauz, Samuel, "Jewish National Autonomy in Lithuania (1918–1925)", 14(3) *Jewish Social Studies* (1952), 225–246

Grossi, Paolo, *Mitologie giuridiche della modernità* (Giuffrè, Milan, 2nd ed., 2005)

Hanski, Raija and Scheinin, Martin, *Leading Cases of the Human Rights Committee* (Åbo Akademi University, Turku, 2nd ed., 2007)

Hartzell, Caroline and Hoddie, Matthew, "Institutionalizing Peace: Power-Sharing and Post-Civil War Conflict Management", 47(2) *American Journal of Political Science* (2003), 318–332

Heinze, Eric, "The Construction and Contingency of the Minority Concept", in Fottrell, Deirdre and Bowring, Bill (eds.), *Minority and Group Rights in the New Millennium* (Martinus Nijhoff, Leiden-Boston, 1999), 25–74

Henrard, Kristin, "A Patchwork of 'Successful' and 'Missed' Synergies in the Jurisprudence of the ECHR", in Henrard, Kristin and Dunbar, Robert (eds.), *Synergies in Minority Protection: European and International Law Perspectives* (Cambridge University Press, Cambridge-New York, 2008), 314–364

Henrard, Kristin, "Non-Discrimination and Full and Effective Equality", in Weller, Marc (ed.), *Universal Minority Rights: A Commentary on the Jurisprudence of International Courts and Treaty Bodies* (Oxford University Press, Oxford, 2007), 75–147

Henrard, Kristin and Dunbar, Robert, "Introduction", in Henrard, Kristin and Dunbar, Robert (eds.), *Synergies in Minority Protection: European and International Law Perspectives* (Cambridge University Press, Cambridge-New York, 2008), 1–19

Holmes, Stephen, "Constitution and Constitutionalism", in Rosenfeld, Michel and Sajó, András (eds.), *The Oxford Handbook of Comparative Constitutional Law* (Oxford University Press, Oxford, 2012), 189–217

Jackson-Preece, Jennifer, "The High Commissioner on National Minorities as a Normative Actor", 12(3) *Journal on Ethnopolitics and Minority Issues in Europe* (2013), 77–82

Joseph, Sarah, *International Covenant on Civil and Political Rights: Cases, Materials and Commentary* (Oxford University Press, Oxford, 2nd ed., 2004)

Jowel, Jeffrey, "Is Equality a Constitutional Principle?", 47(2) *Current Legal Problems* (1994), 1–18

Keil, Soeren, *Multinational Federalism in Bosnia and Herzegovina* (Routledge, London, 2016)

Keil, Soeren and McCulloch, Allison (eds.), *Power-Sharing in Europe: Past Practice, Present Cases, and Future Directions* (Palgrave Macmillan, Cham, 2021)

Khaitan, Tarunabh, "Discrimination", in *Max Planck Encyclopedia of Comparative Constitutional Law* (Oxford University Press, Oxford, 2017), at https://papers.ssrn.com/sol3/papers.cfm?abstract_id=3277053

Kipuri, Naomi, "The UN Declaration on the Rights of Indigenous People in the African Context", in Charters, Claire and Stavenhagen, Rodolfo (eds.), *Making the Declaration Work: The United Nations Declaration on the Rights of Indigenous Peoples* (IWGIA, Copenhagen, 2009), 252–262

Kochenov, Dimitry, "The European Union's Troublesome Minority Protection: A Bird's Eye View", in Boulden, Jane and Kymlicka, Will (eds.), *International Approaches to Governing Ethnic Diversity* (Oxford University Press, Oxford, 2015), 79–101

Kymlicka, Will, "The Internationalization of Minority Rights", in Choudry, Sujit (ed.), *Constitutional Design for Divided Societies: Integration or Accommodation?* (Oxford University Press, Oxford, 2008), 111–140

Kymlicka, Will, "Theorizing Indigenous Rights", in Kymlicka, Will (ed.), *Politics in the Vernacular: Nationalism, Multiculturalism, and Citizenship* (Oxford University Press, Oxford, 2001), 120–132

Lijphart, Arend, *Democracy in Plural Societies: A Comparative Exploration* (Yale University Press, New Haven-London, 1977)

Lijphart, Arend, *Patterns of Democracy: Government Forms and Performance in Thirty-Six Countries* (Yale University Press, New Haven-London, 2012)

Mariadaga Cuneo, Isabel, "The Rights of Indigenous People and the Inter-American Human Rights System", 22(1) *Arizona Journal of International and Comparative Law* (2005), 53–64

Marko, Joseph, "Effective Participation of National Minorities in Public Affairs in Light of National Case Law", 16(4) *International Journal on Minority and Group Rights* (2009), 621–649

Marko, Joseph, "Equality and Difference: Political and Legal Aspects of Ethnic Group Relations", in Matscher, Franz (ed.), *Vienna International Encounter on Some Current Issues Regarding the Situation of National Minorities* (N. P. Engel, Kehl-Strasbourg-Arlington, 1997), 67–97

Marko, Joseph, Marko-Stöckl, Edith, Harzl, Benedikt and Unger, Hedwig, "The Historical and Sociological Foundations: State Formation and Nation Building in Europe and the Construction of the Identitarian Nation-cum-State Paradigm", in Marko, Joseph and Constantin, Sergiu (eds.), *Human and Minority Rights Protection by Multiple Diversity Governance: History, Law, Ideology and Politics in European Perspective* (Routledge, London-New York, 2019), 33–95

May, Stephen, Modood, Tariq and Squires, Judith (eds.), *Ethnicity, Nationalism, and Minority Rights* (Cambridge University Press, Cambridge, 2004)

Medda-Windischer, Roberta, "Protection of National Minorities through Bilateral Agreements in South Eastern Europe", 1 *European Yearbook of Minority Issues* (2001–2002), 535–556

Minow, Martha, *Making All the Difference: Inclusion, Exclusion and American Law* (Cornell University Press, Ithaca-London, 1990)

Niezen, Ronald, *The Origins of Indigenism: Human Rights and the Politics of Identity* (University of California Press, Berkeley-Los Angeles-London, 2003)

Nowak, Manfred, *UN Covenant on Civil and Political Rights: CCPR Commentary* (N.P. Engel, Strasbourg, 2nd ed., 2005)

Palermo, Francesco, "Current and Future Challenges for International Minority Protection", 10 *European Yearbook of Minority Issues* (2011), 21–36

Palermo, Francesco, "The Protection of Minorities in International Law: Recent Developments and Trends", in VV.AA., *Les minorités: un défi pour les États: actes du colloque international (22 et 23 mai 2011)* (Académie Royale de Belgique, Bruxelles, 2012), 165–185

Palermo, Francesco and Nicolini, Matteo, "La semantica delle differenze e le regole diseguali: dall'egualitarismo nel diritto all'eccezione culturale", in VV.AA., *Studi in onore di Maurizio Pedrazza Gorlero*, vol. 1 (ESI, Naples, 2014), 513–549

Palermo, Francesco and Woelk, Jens, *Diritto costituzionale comparato dei gruppi e delle minoranze* (CEDAM, Padua, 2021)

Pasqualucci, Jo M., "The Evolution of International Indigenous Rights in the Inter-American Human Rights System", 6(2) *Human Rights Law Review* (2006), 281–322

Pentassuglia, Gaetano. "Towards a Jurisprudential Articulation of Indigenous Land Rights", 22(1) *European Journal of International Law* (2011), 165–202

Peroni, Lourdes, "Minorities before the European Court of Human Rights", in Boulden, Jane and Kymlicka, Will (eds.), *International Approaches to Governing Ethnic Diversity* (Oxford University Press, Oxford, 2015), 25–50

Pizzorusso, Alessandro, "Articolo 6", in Branca, Giuseppe (ed.), *Commentario della Costituzione* (Zanichelli-Il Foro Italiano, Bologna-Rome, 1975), 296–321

Pizzorusso, Alessandro, *Minoranze e maggioranze* (Einaudi, Milan, 1997)

Rechel, Bernd (ed.), *Minority Rights in Central and Eastern Europe* (Routledge, London-New York, 2009)

Renner, Karl, "State and Nation", in Nimni, Ephraim (ed.), *National Cultural Autonomy and Its Contemporary Critics* (Routledge, London-New York, 1899/2005)

Ridola, Paolo, "Preistoria, origini e vicende del costituzionalismo", in Carrozza, Paolo, Di Giovine, Alfonso and Ferrari, Giuseppe F. (eds.), *Diritto costituzionale comparato* (Laterza, Rome-Bari, 2019), 737–774

Sabbagh, Daniel, "Affirmative Action", in Rosenfeld, Michel and Sajó, András (eds.), *The Oxford Handbook of Comparative Constitutional Law* (Oxford University Press, Oxford, 2012), 1124–1141

Schabas, William A., "Developments Relating to Minorities in the Law on Genocide", in Henrard, Kristin and Dunbar, Robert (eds.), *Synergies in Minority Protection: European and International Law Perspectives* (Cambridge University Press, Cambridge-New York, 2008), 189–212

Scheinin, Martin, "The United Nations International Covenant on Civil and Political Rights: Article 27 and Other Provisions", in Henrard, Kristin and Dunbar, Robert (eds.), *Synergies in Minority Protection: European and International Law Perspectives* (Cambridge University Press, Cambridge-New York, 2008), 23–46

Schütze, Robert, "Constitutionalism(s)", in Masterman, Roger and Schütze, Robert (eds.), *The Cambridge Companion to Comparative Constitutional Law* (Cambridge University Press, Cambridge, 2019), 40–66

Seibert-Fohr, Anja, "The Rise of Equality in International Law and Its Pitfalls: Learning from Comparative Constitutional Law", in Tushnet, Mark (ed.), *Comparative Constitutional Law: Volume III: Freedom of Expression and Religion, and Equality* (Edgar Elgar, Cheltenham-Northampton, 2017), 477–515

Smith, David J., "Estonia: A Model for Interwar Europe?", 15(1) *Ethnopolitics* (2015), 89–104

Spiliopoulou Åkermark, Sia (ed.), *The Åland Example and Its Components: Relevance for International Conflict Resolution* (Åland Islands Peace Institute, Marieham, 2011)

Strydom, Hennie, "International Treaty-based Protection of Minorities: Select Cases of the UN Human Rights Committee", in De Villiers, Bertus, Marko, Joseph, Palermo, Francesco and Constantin, Sergiu (eds.), *Litigating the Rights of Minorities and Indigenous Peoples in Domestic and International Courts* (Brill-Nijhoff, Leiden-Boston, 2021), 219–238

Thornberry, Patrick, "Is There a Phoenix in the Ashes? International Law and Minority Rights", 15(3) *Texas International Law Journal* (1980), 421–458

Tierney, Stephen, "Federalism and Constitutional Theory", in Jacobsohn, Gary and Schor, Miguel (eds.), *Comparative Constitutional Theory* (Edward Elgar Publishing, Cheltenham, 2018), 45–65

Tierney, Stephen, *The Federal Contract: A Constitutional Theory of Federalism* (Oxford University Press, Oxford, 2022)

Toniatti, Roberto, "Minoranze e minoranze protette: modelli costituzionali comparati", in Bonazzi, Tiziano and Dunne, Michael (eds.), *Cittadinanza e diritti nelle società multiculturali* (Il Mulino, Bologna, 1994), 273–283

Tramontana, Enzamaria, "The Contribution of the African Court on Human and Peoples' Rights to the Protection of Indigenous Peoples' Rights", 6 *federalismi.it* (2018), 1–19

Tully, James, *Strange Multiplicity: Constitutionalism in an Age of Diversity* (Cambridge University Press, Cambridge, 1995)

Wheatley, Steven, *Democracy, Minorities and International Law* (Cambridge University Press, Cambridge, 2005)

2 Models for the accommodation of diversity from liberal and democratic constitutionalism

The present chapter will provide a description of the models for the accommodation of diversity stemming from the evolution of constitutionalism described previously. Such classification is designed to give as clear a picture as possible of the state of the art of this area of law before going into what is here referred to as innovative or emergent models. In turn, this endeavor lays the groundwork for strengthened comparison among the models, which will allow both the elements they share and points of divergence to emerge. A comparison of the structure, the (even potential) addressees, and the rationale of these models appears particularly useful when analyzing the emergent instruments, as their theoretical framings as tools for the accommodation of diversity are not consolidated. Indeed, as will be demonstrated, one of their main peculiarities is that they diverge from the structure and rationale of liberal-democratic models.

Models for the accommodation of diversity in the liberal epoch and their targets

Treaty mechanisms represent the first models for the accommodation of diversity in the tradition of constitutionalism. Different kinds of treaties were put in place, mainly in the European and North American continents.

In North America, as well as in today's New Zealand, numerous treaties were signed between the European settlers[1] and a large number of indigenous tribes. In particular, this mechanism was used by British colonizers

1 It is, in fact, possible to focus on British policies and regulations since they took over the colonial hegemony in these areas of the world; contrarily, as observed by Tamanaha, Brian Z., *Legal Pluralism Explained: History, Theory, Consequences* (Oxford University Press, Oxford, 2021), 108, the case of Australia shows some differences, since "Aborigines were hunter-gatherers who lacked large political structures like chiefdoms that existed elsewhere. Consequently, British colonizers and settlers faced less formidable resistance to their incursions, and did not enter treaties with Aborigines to justify their takings. Invoking the monist law state image, they claimed that Australia was terra nullius and territorium nullius, respectively, unoccupied land with no semblance of civil society, sovereignty, or law".

DOI: 10.4324/9781003493518-3

from their very arrival in those areas. It was a model of Aboriginal-European relationship management based on reciprocal recognition, respect, and equal standing of the two parties. Interestingly, according to Tully, this experience shows that the seeds for the pluralization of modern constitutionalism's concepts, as well as the recognition and accommodation of diversity within this tradition, were already there in the very foundational elements of this political and legal doctrine.[2] As a matter of fact, at the very first stage of negotiations between the Crown and indigenous peoples, the former was able to mold the supposedly uniform categories and concepts of modern constitutionalism and represent Aboriginal populations through concepts like nations and republics, recognizing their rights and self-government.[3] It must also be noted that even if a system of treaties based on the described principles was in place, the prevailing approach among the founding leaders was that

> Indian tribes . . . would inevitably fall under the sway of civilization. The "dying race" thesis was a factor in these early territorial disputes with Indian tribes and suggested that tribal connection to land, whatever their precise legal nature, represented only a temporary impediment to the national expansion.[4]

Furthermore, the situation described previously did not last for long: the nation-state model subsequently consolidated in this area as treaty mechanisms were rapidly outplayed by the growing monopolizing attitude of the newly formed states.[5] From the end of the eighteenth century, the treaty model was gradually frustrated either through the enactment of regulations that subjected the indigenous peoples to the control of the colonizers or the

2 Tully, James, *Strange Multiplicity: Constitutionalism in an Age of Diversity* (Cambridge University Press, Cambridge, 1995), 100, observed that "Rather than forcing citizens and institutions to fit the uniform of modern constitutionalism, the language of constitutionalism has been shaped to fit the cultural diversity of citizens and institutions in practice"; his work is focused on the North American continent, but the same considerations can arguably apply to the case of New Zealand, given that the settlers were also British and followed the same ideas, at least at the very beginning; as for the latter, the document framing British-First Nations relationships was the treaty of Waitangi of 1840, which failed to prevent conflict as early as the 1860s; on this, see Brookfield, Frederic M. (Jock), *Waitangi and Indigenous Rights: Revolution, Law and Legitimation* (Auckland University Press, Auckland, 2006).

3 See Tully, Strange Multiplicity . . . , 121; also, see Hueglin, Thomas O., "Exploring Concepts of Treaty Federalism A Comparative Perspective", *Paper Prepared as Part of the Research Program of the Royal Commission on Aboriginal Peoples* (1994), available at https://publications.gc.ca/site/eng/9.829489/publication.html.

4 Duthu, Bruce, *American Indians and the Law* (Viking Penguins, New York, 2008), 66.

5 For instance, as regards Canada, see Hueglin, Exploring Concepts . . . ; for what concerns the US, see Tully, Strange Multiplicity . . . , 94, observed that: "Once a constitution modelled on the theories of Paine and the Federalist papers was established in 1787, it provided a 'license for empire' over the Aboriginal territories as the United States expanded westward".

use of treaties with the same goal.[6] Indigenous peoples were thus not considered in the calculations of the original constitutional design; they were not regarded as full citizens, and the arrangements for their governance did not have to conform to any constitutional rights or principles.[7] In other words, control and paternalism rapidly became the principal goals of policies related to indigenous peoples.[8]

Besides these experiences, as early as the nineteenth century, several international treaties aimed at protecting some national minority groups were signed in Europe.

These represented the first steps toward the construction of an international system for the protection of minorities.[9] Although some early formulations of minority rights as religious freedoms had arisen in the seventeenth and eighteenth centuries,[10] the two main examples of this first stage of international minority protection are to be found in the treaties approved during the Congresses of Vienna (1815)[11] and Berlin (1878).[12]

6 Tully, Strange Multiplicity . . . , 94.

7 Ghai, Yash, "Decentralization and the Accommodation of Ethnic Diversity", in Young, Crawford (ed.), *Ethnic Diversity and Public Policy* (Palgrave, Basingstoke-New York, 1998), 31–71, at 37.

8 Ghai, Decentralization . . . , 37; also, see Asch, Michael, *Home and Native Land: Aboriginal Rights and the Canadian Constitution* (University of British Columbia Press, Vancouver, 1993); Bish, Robert L. and Cassidy, Frank, *Indian Government: Its Meaning in Practice* (The Institute for Research of Public Policy, Halifax, 1989); Hanks, Peter and Keon-Cohen, Bryan (eds.), *Aboriginals and the Law* (Allena and Unwin, Sidney, 1994); Lyons, Oren and Mohawk, John (eds.), *Exiled in the Land of the Free: Democracy, Indian Nations, and the US Constitution* (Clear Light Publishers, Santa Fe, 1992); Pevar, Stephen, *The Rights of Indians and Tribes* (Southern Illinois University Press, Carbondale and Edwardsville, 1992).

9 Palermo, Francesco and Woelk, Jens, *Diritto costituzionale comparato dei gruppi e delle minoranze* (CEDAM, Padua, 2021), 77.

10 On this, see Jackson-Preece, Jennifer, "Minority Rights in Europe: From Westphalia to Helsinki", 23 *Review of International Studies* (1997), 75–92, at 76; the author recalled that the first type of legally significant minority groups were religious minorities, given that "religious affiliation was the most important dividing line between different communities in Europe at this time"; similarly, Cavaggion, Giovanni, *Diritti culturali e modello costituzionale di integrazione* (Giappichelli, Turin, 2018), 13.

11 See, Thornberry, Patrick, "Is There a Phoenix in the Ashes? International Law and Minority Rights", 15(3) *Texas International Law Journal* (1980), 421–458, at 426: "the treaty recognised three minorities as worthy of protection: Belgians, Savoyards and Poles, the latter receiving protection based more upon nationality than religion"; furthermore, Poles were entitled to have political institutions and representation (however, those provisions been infringed have many times).

12 The outcome of the latter was a number of treaties that accorded protection to certain national minority rights in several newly formed states, especially in the Balkan area; interestingly, Jackson-Preece, Minority Rights in Europe . . . , 80, stated that those treaties were "dictated preconditions for the new nation-states' membership in international society", and an expression of a "practice of imposed and indeed paternalistic minority obligations" put in place by the Great Powers with regard to states that were seen as "backward, if not intrinsically inferior".

These both understood minorities as groups in national rather than religious terms, following the general evolution of that time, where religion gave way to national features as the central elements defining the political communities in Western countries.[13] Consequently, groups deemed worthy of protection were "national" minorities marked by the following characteristics: a. they possessed linguistic, ethnic, or cultural characteristics that differentiated them from the majority of their country's population; b. they lived in a numerical minoritarian condition; c. they were generally but not always culturally linked to a kin state that usually bordered the country where they lived;[14] d. they were (or were supposed to become) citizens of the state where they resided.[15]

The treaties generally provided for equal treatment in favor of the mentioned communities, which, as a result of the readjustments of national borders defined by the Treaties, ended up being transferred from the sovereignty of one state to that of another.[16]

Interestingly, Jackson-Preece drew attention to the fact that "this older discourse on minorities was not articulated in the language of 'rights' but that of 'guarantees'",[17] the latter being "state obligations either voluntarily assumed as a gesture of goodwill toward a particular group or state (usually kin-state of the minority in question) or externally imposed upon new or weak states by the powers in the interests of international peace and stability".[18] Therefore, minority guarantees concerned weaker states and were frequently dictated by the Great Powers, which were generally not willing to bind themselves to the very same provisions.

Although the liberal epoch of constitutionalism was marked by the centrality of equality, the models that were developed are nonetheless of much interest. Firstly, notwithstanding their flaws (from a liberal-democratic standpoint),

13 On this, Jackson-Preece, Minority Rights in Europe . . . , 78; this, of course, does not mean that the religious element was not taken into account as one of the most important dimensions of minority protection at that time.

14 This was not always the case; a first exception to this model is the Jewish community, which cannot be strictly defined as a national community nor enjoyed the support of a kin state; yet notably, the Romanian Jewish community was one of the beneficiaries of para. 44 of the Treaty of Berlin, which stated that the non-Christian communities should be recognized as full citizens and granted equal treatment; a second exception is the Polish community, which was granted, at least on paper, the right to be represented in the national institutions of Russia, Austria and Prussia by the Treaty of Vienna.

15 In fact, as stated by Jackson-Preece, Minority Rights in Europe . . . , 79: "At this time, . . . there was a . . . change in the content of minority rights which reflected new understandings of sovereignty as ultimately vested in the people rather than the prince: hence the new impetus for incorporating into the body politic minority communities or outsiders acquired through territorial readjustments".

16 Jackson-Preece, Minority Rights in Europe . . . , 79.

17 Jackson-Preece, Jennifer, *Minority Rights: Between Diversity and Community* (Polity, Cambridge-Malden, 2005), 13.

18 Ibid., 13–14.

the employment of treaty or treaty-like tools allowing some degree of self-government and/or rights, as well as (partially) federal territorial structures to accommodate diversity, is still an important way to deal with this issue. Secondly, the logic of agreement, covenant, and consent underlying those models for the accommodation of diversity has become an element marking, as a matrix, several instruments for the accommodation of diversity that have subsequently been developed.

Regarding the use of federal structures for the accommodation of diversity, two main models may be analyzed to examine the extent to which the federal principle provided solutions for accommodating diversity in the liberal epoch: the US and Switzerland. The latter only appears to show some distinguishing features as compared to the general treatment of diversity during this period.

While the US federal system has always allowed for a degree of recognition of diversity as it acknowledged from its very outset the public salience of territorial diversities – i.e., the existence of different state communities in the federal structure – and a degree of social variation along religious and political lines, it is arguable that such recognition did not touch upon the core tenets of formal equality. Rather, it referred to differences occurring within the same social group in the framework of a rather homogeneous dominant cultural identity.[19] The recognition and accommodation of other forms of diversity beyond the dominant one – and, especially, the recognition of the rights of African Americans – therefore followed a rather long, complex, and uneven path.

By contrast, the Swiss federal system that emerged after the short civil war in 1847 was fundamentally multicultural, a union of the people of the cantons, and homes of different linguistic and religious groups that agreed to coexist under a common federal constitutional framework.[20] Here, it is evident that diversity has been a core element of the constitutional order since the Constitution of 1848 was adopted. However, it must also be noted that federal organization in the liberal epoch was based upon a rather rigid dual federalism where the central government had very limited power to

19 On this, see Glazer, Nathan, "Federalism and Ethnicity: The Experience of the United States", 7(4) *Publius* (1977), 71–87; Cavaggion, Diritti culturali . . . , 114; also, see Tully, Strange Multiplicity . . . , 93: "The authors of the Federalist papers present a constitutional theory similar to Paine's. John Jay observes in the second paper . . . that the American people are culturally homogeneous by ancestry and war. . . . It follows in the next seven papers that a uniform federation with a sovereign federal government is the appropriate form of constitution. Any form of confederation that recognises constitutive differences and aspects of co-ordinate sovereignty among the states will lead inevitably to internal dissension and disunity, and so to weakness in the face of the republic's enemies. Hence, the federalist constitution is identified with a '*united America*' and the anti-federalists with a '*disunited* America'".

20 For an in-depth analysis of the Swiss constitutional system from an internal and comparative perspective, see Linder, Wolf and Mueller, Sean, *Swiss Democracy: Possible Solutions to Conflict in Multicultural Societies* (Palgrave Macmillan, Cham, 2021).

condition the cantons' autonomy;[21] the latter were mainly internally homogeneous religion and language-wise, and the management of diversity within their borders was based on liberal categories similar to other countries in the same epoch.[22]

Albeit an exception to the previous discourse, to a certain extent, this case also shares with it a common core aspect, namely the fact that it created a system that includes and recognizes diversity based on a (confederal and then federal) agreement. In a way, this confirms the centrality of the treaty or covenant model to the accommodation of diversity in this epoch.

An overview of the models for the accommodation of diversity stemming from the democratic turn of constitutionalism

The outcome of the evolution of the models for the accommodation of diversity in democratic constitutionalism is a *corpus* of law that includes respect for equality and non-discrimination as a common basic guarantee, as well as a body of rights and instruments that go beyond it. In the following sections, an outline of these will be proposed, which will primarily engage with international and constitutional provisions.[23]

21 On this, see Dardanelli, Paolo and Mueller, Sean, "Dynamic De/Centralisation in Switzerland, 1848–2010", 49(1) *Publius* (2017), 138–165.

22 Ghai, Decentralization . . . , 33, indeed defined Switzerland as only a partial exception to how federalism was employed in the liberal epoch; also, see Linder and Mueller, Swiss Democracy . . . , 31–39; the authors have described how the religious cleavage had a significant weigh in the early stages of the Swiss Confederation, leading to societal segmentation and several forms of discrimination against the Catholic minorities in Protestant or mixed cantons; the management of linguistic and cultural diversity in Switzerland has never become a source of tension – except the case of Jura – and has always been based on the use of federalism as a tool to accommodate differences, where cantons are entitled to a very large degree of autonomy in these matters; moreover, the fact that the latter were and are generally linguistically homogeneous is one of the main factors that has favored the successful management of linguistic diversity through federalism; accordingly, a system of power-sharing (also) guarantees the representation of all four linguistic minorities and the consequent protection of their rights at the federal level; in addition, according to Article 70, para. 2 of the Swiss constitution, the subunits are obliged to respect the traditional distribution of languages and take into account the linguistic minorities that live within their borders; it must be taken into account that out of 26 cantons, only three of them traditionally hosting minorities are bilingual (Bern, Fribourg, Valais) and one trilingual (Graubünden); on this, and especially on the challenges that today the Swiss system faces with respect of new diversities (beyond those that have been the core of the Swiss Confederal compact), see Belser, Eva Maria, "Accommodating National Minorities in Federal Switzerland: Old Concepts Meet New Realities", in Gagnon, Alain-G. and Burgess, Michael (eds.), *Revisiting Unity and Diversity in Federal Countries: Changing Concepts, Reform Proposals and New Institutional Realities* (Brill-Nijhoff, Leiden-Boston, 2018), 79–111.

23 When appropriate, statutory measures will be taken into account, especially in cases where no constitutional guarantee is retrievable or when the constitutional provisions are of a programmatic character.

International law as the source of a general right to existence and survival

The very first dimension of diversity protection that followed from the evolution of international law after WWII was the firm defense of the right to existence and survival of non-majority groups.[24] Such a right represents a foundational element of human and minority rights law as it counters gross violations of human rights such as genocide, ethnic cleansing, and other abhorrent crimes against any kind of identifiable societal group. Notably, the right to existence and survival has a broad scope of application that does not seem limited to particular groups.[25]

From a legal vantage point, three categories of illegal practice are targeted: genocide,[26] crimes against humanity,[27] and war crimes.[28] Conversely, the notion of ethnic cleansing – which was first used to describe the ethnic policies adopted during the Yugoslav wars and has become a concept widely used in international law literature[29] – is not the subject of specific legal provisions, but criminal acts corresponding to this can be subsumed under the three other categories of crimes.[30]

Equality and non-discrimination as essential guarantees (also) for minorities

The concept of equality has been considerably enriched within the tradition of democratic constitutionalism compared to the limited and rather elitist notion marking the liberal epoch. Nowadays, this principle is entrenched in most constitutions of the world, together with non-discriminatory provisions.

According to Bryde and Stein,[31] it is possible to classify three basic constitutional patterns: constitutions containing only general equality provisions;[32]

24 Unfortunately, this has not prevented several crimes against national minorities from taking place, like the genocides of Srebrenica (1995) and Rwanda (1994); on this, see Marko, Joseph, Unger, Hedwig, Medda-Windisher, Roberta, Tomaselli, Alexandra and Ferraro, Filippo, "Against Annihilation: The Right to Existence", in Marko, Joseph and Constantin, Sergiu (eds.), *Human and Minority Rights Protection by Multiple Diversity Governance: History, Law, Ideology and Politics in European Perspective* (Routledge, London-New York, 2019), 178–226.

25 While genocide includes a series of acts committed with intent to destroy, in whole or in part, a national, ethnical, racial, or religious group (Article 2 UN Genocide Convention), the notion of crimes against humanity includes "persecution against any identifiable group or collectivity on political, racial, national, ethnic, cultural, religious, gender . . . , or other grounds that are universally recognized as impermissible under international law . . .".

26 See Article 2 of the UN Genocide Convention of 1948.

27 See Article 7 of the Rome Statute of the International Criminal Court.

28 See Article 8 of the Rome Statute of the International Criminal Court.

29 For instance, see Cigar, Norman L., *Genocide in Bosnia: The Policy of "Ethnic Cleansing"* (Texas A&M University Press, College Station, 1995).

30 On this, see Marko, Unger, Medda-Windischer, Tomaselli and Ferraro, Against Annihilation . . ., 178–226.

31 Bryde, Brun-O. and Stein, Micheal A., "General Provisions Dealing with Equality", in Tushnet, Mark, Fleiner, Thomas and Saunders, Cheryl (eds.), *Routledge Handbook of Constitutional Law* (Routledge, London-New York, 2013), 287–300, at 288–289.

32 Besides the well-known cases of France and the US, Argentina, Brazil, China, Greece, Luxembourg, Morocco, and Vietnam fit into this category as well.

constitutions with only non-discrimination provisions;[33] and constitutions including equality provisions and either general discrimination prohibitions or discrimination provisions based on particular characteristics.[34] Apart from the letter of the constitutional provisions, it must be recognized that the actual meaning of equality and non-discrimination mostly results from the constitutional or supreme courts' hermeneutical activity in any given legal system and, especially in civil law countries, the existence of antidiscrimination regulations implementing constitutional principles. In any case, what is possible to observe is a general tendency to expand the protected grounds of discrimination, while the extent to which affirmative actions are admitted varies significantly from country to country.[35]

Importantly, equality and non-discrimination represent the very first form of (negative) recognition of conditions of diversity as well as a *conditio sine qua non* for diversity accommodation. Equality provisions and non-discrimination measures are basic guarantees for every individual, including members of non-majority groups, without which the implementation of further instruments for the accommodation of diversity would be impossible and senseless. Members of non-majority groups thus benefit to different extents from this general form of protection, which permits them to exercise some basic rights without being discriminated against on the grounds of their differential status. In other words, such basic rights are general rights that acquire specific and differentiated contents if they refer to members of minorities.

For instance, the general guarantee of freedom of speech, when applied to members of minorities, implies recognition of the right to employ their own mother tongue in the private sphere without any sort of discrimination or the right to use surname and family names in minority language. Moreover, essential political rights for minorities are the right to vote and stand as a candidate under the same conditions as the rest of the population. As regards religion, freedom of worship may be considered to be part of this basic set of rights.

At the same time, albeit fundamental, equality and non-discrimination are aimed at promoting equal treatment or temporarily redressing existing societal

33 An example is Sweden.

34 This has become the most widespread model after the Second World War; constitutions containing a general equality provision and a general non-discrimination provision (this is the case with Afghanistan, Belarus, Belgium, Costa Rica, Latvia, Lebanon, Paraguay, Poland, and Romania) are less common than those containing a general equality provision and identity-specific non-discrimination protection (Albania, Algeria, Bahrain, Canada, Eritrea, Estonia, Germany, Iraq, Italy, Kenya, Lithuania, Madagascar, Namibia, Nepal, Netherlands, Oman, Qatar, Serbia, South Korea, Switzerland, Turkey, Timor Leste).

35 On the general tendency of expansion of the list of protected grounds and the fundamental activity of the judges in this respect, see Khaitan, Tarunabh, "Discrimination", in *Max Planck Encyclopedia of Comparative Constitutional Law* (Oxford University Press, Oxford, 2017), available at the following link: https://papers.ssrn.com/sol3/papers.cfm?abstract_id=3277053.

inequalities through special measures. Hence, they are meant to grant that law is equally enforced – prohibiting any form of direct or indirect discrimination and achieving a legal system where a common and uniform set of rules applies to everyone. In other words, equality and non-discrimination take minority status as one of the disadvantages to be redressed. This feature distinguishes the latter legal instruments from minority rights and mechanisms, which are conversely intended to provide differential treatments in favor of people belonging to some non-majority groups, mainly to preserve and promote their conditions of diversity.[36]

Minority rights and instruments

The (non-)definition of national minority, the prevalence of the state dimension, and the centrality of a European standpoint

Minority rights are doubtlessly the most long-standing and consolidated *corpus* of legal instruments for the accommodation of diversity within the tradition of constitutionalism. However, it must be noted that the minority rights discourse has been predominantly tied to the European geo-political space, while the use of minority rights in other regions of the world is more theoretically contentious and uneven in terms of its application, even though it is common in scholarship to frame diversity issues in these areas through minority concepts.[37]

The goal of minority rights law is to preserve and promote the differential conditions of some groups through particular rules and rights that differ from and add to the general ones. As synthesized by Spiliopoulou Åkermark, minority rights serve four basic functions that justify their establishment: peace and security, effective protection of human rights based on the value of human dignity, protection of cultures and cultural diversity, and democratic participation and political pluralism.[38]

Among the most contentious issues related to minority rights is their scope of application. Despite many attempts in the literature and international

36 The distinction between the two categories was clearly described by Capotorti, Francesco, *Study on the Rights of Persons Belonging to Ethnic, Religious and Linguistic Minorities* (United Nations, New York, 1977) (UN Doc. E/CN.4/sub.2/384/Rev.1, UN sales Nr. E.78. XIV.1)/Geneva UN Center for Human Rights, UN Doc E/CN.4/sub.2/384/Add.1–7, 1–114, at 40–41.

37 On this, see Castellino, Joshua, "Introduction", in Castellino, Joshua (ed.), *Global Minority Rights* (Routledge, London-New York, 2016), xi–xxiv.

38 Spiliopoulou Åkermark, Sia, "Shifts in the Multiple Justifications of Minority Protection", in Malloy, Tove H. and Marko, Joseph (eds.), *Minority Governance in and Beyond Europe: Celebrating 10 Years of the European Yearbook of Minority Issues* (Brill-Nijhoff, Leiden, 2014), 106–134.

studies,[39] no universal definition of what a minority is exists (nor would it be, for many authors, desirable).[40] In this sense, some indications can be drawn from a contextual analysis of international and state law, which illustrates the current state of the art regarding the definitional issue.[41]

From an international law standpoint, it is possible to notice that the legal sources refer to either the concept of "ethnic, religious or linguistic minorities" or of "national minority". The former notion is employed in the UN documents and their supervisory bodies' activities, whereas the latter is linked

39 One of the most influential definitions of national minority was provided by the then Special Rapporteur of the UN Sub-Commission on Prevention of Discrimination and Protection of Minorities Francesco Capotorti in 1979, according to whom a national minority is: "a group numerically inferior to the rest of the population of a state, in a non-dominant position, whose members – being nationals of the state – possess ethnic, religious or linguistic characteristics differing from the rest of the population and show, if only implicitly, a sense of solidarity directed toward preserving their culture, traditions, religion or language"; according to Jackson-Preece, Jennifer, "Beyond the (Non) Definition of Minority", *ECMI Issue Brief* (18 February 2014), available at https://www.ecmi.de/publications/issue-briefs/national-minority-capital-introducing-the-new-concept, five models of framing minorities emerge from analysis of international sources, national legal frameworks, and literature: the first is marked by definitions similar to Capotorti's, based on a list of objective, subjective and power-relations criteria; the second derives from the legal frameworks of states and sees minorities as autochthonous groups; the third, while recognizing a relative relevance to some predefined objective criteria, stresses the importance of individual self-identification as a fundamental premise for the recognition of the existence of a minority; the fourth does not provide a definition of the minority but ties it to some defining adjectives (ethnic, religious, linguistic) or names specific vulnerable groups; the fifth, typically adopted by international organizations, argues for the prevalence of facts over definitions, in the sense that the recognition of the existence of a minority is linked to its concrete condition rather than normative descriptions; on the definitional issue, see also Pejic, Jelena, "Minority Rights in International Law", 19(3) *Human Rights Quarterly* (1997), 666–685; Ramaga, Philip V., "The Group Concept in Minority Protection", 15(3) *Human Rights Quarterly* (1993), 575–588; Rodley, Nigel S., "Conceptual Problems in the Protection of Minorities: International Legal Developments", 17(1) *Human Rights Quarterly* (1995), 48–71; Packer, John, "On the Definition of Minorities", in Packer, John and Myntti, Kristian (eds.), *The Protection of Ethnic and Linguistic Minorities in Europe* (Åbo Akademi, Institute of Human Rights, Åbo, 1993), 23–65.

40 According to Palermo and Woelk, Diritto costituzionale comparato . . . , 14, it is impossible to find a universal (international) definition that includes all the different situations; furthermore, a universal definition would lead to a rigid classification that cannot cope with specific cases; for this reason, Jackson-Preece, Beyond the (Non) Definition . . ., 3–19, argued for a contextual use of definitions, in order to avoid rigid and reified notions of minorities; *contra*, Spiliopoulou Åkermark, Sia, *Justifications of Minority Protection in International Law* (Kluwer Law International, London-The Hague, Boston, 1997), 87, stated that a legal definition of a minority at the international level would be useful to get "certainty, clarity and foreseeability in a legal system".

41 Given the legal perspective endorsed in this chapter and its final theoretical aim, the main focus will thus be on the model of a minority that emerges from the analysis of (hard and soft) legal sources (with some references to case law and soft jurisprudence of international bodies) and will not engage (or will engage to a lesser extent) with the scholarly (political science's) debates that are normally marked by normative aims.

to the European international law dimension.[42] All the international documents are marked by a major focus on rights and instruments rather than on the addressees and thus do not recognize any specific minority.[43] At the same time, the supervisory bodies' activity has undoubtedly shown support for an inclusive reading of the concept of minority and a consequent extension of the scope of minority rights.[44] In this sense, UN and European international bodies have explicitly stated that national, ethnic, religious, and linguistic minorities of both citizens and non-citizens fall under their scope of application, although some differences in treatment between different groups depending on their permanence in the territory of the country may be justified.[45] In other words, those minorities that in literature have been referred to as traditional or old minorities – those composed of citizens, autochthonous people, or persons residing in a state territory for an unspecified but long period of time – are supposed to have stronger entitlements than the so-called new minorities – formed of people with a migratory background.

Conversely, the state dimension shows a much narrower approach to the issue of minority rights. Where forms of protection and promotion of diversity in the shape of minority rights are present, their application is usually limited

42 Both Article 27 of the ICCPR and the Declaration on Minorities of 1992 indeed refer to the notion of ethnic, religious or linguistic minorities; the HCNM Guidelines, the FCNM instead make reference to the concept of national minorities, but they also underline the wide scope of the notion (especially the guidelines); further indications on the wide conception of the notion of minority come from the General Commentary n. 23 of the HRC, and the commentaries of the ACFC; it must be noted that recently a working definition of minority has been elaborated by the Special Rapporteur on Minority Issues in his report transmitted to the General Assembly of the UN in 2019 (UN General Assembly, "Effective promotion of the Declaration on the Rights of Persons Belonging to National or Ethnic, Religious and Linguistic Minorities, Report of the Special Rapporteur on Minority Issues", 2019, A/74/160, available at https://undocs.org/A/74/160): "An ethnic, religious or linguistic minority is any group of persons which constitutes less than half of the population in the entire territory of a State whose members share common characteristics of culture, religion or language, or a combination of any of these. A person can freely belong to an ethnic, religious or linguistic minority without any requirement of citizenship, residence, official recognition or any other status".

43 In a way, an exception is to be found in the European Charter of Regional and Minority Languages, which explicitly excludes the languages of immigrant communities from its application.

44 Which follows the open approach endorsed by the PCIJ already in 1930: see the advisory opinion of 31 July 1930, *Greco-Bulgarian Communities*, Ser. B, Fasc. No. 17, 3–36, at 21–22.

45 See UN Human Rights Committee (HRC), *CCPR General Comment No. 23: Article 27 (Rights of Minorities)*, 8 April 1994; UN Subcommission on the Promotion and Protection of Human Rights, Working Group on Minorities, *Commentary of the Working Group on Minorities to the United Nations Declaration on the Rights of Persons belonging to National or Ethnic, Religious and Linguistic Minorities*, 2004; ACFC, *Thematic Commentary No. 4: The Framework Convention: A Key Tool to Managing Diversity through Minority Rights*, 27 May 2016; OSCE HCNM, *The Ljubljana Guidelines on Integration of Diverse Societies* (OSCE HCNM, The Hague, 2012).

to what in the literature has been referred to as old minorities or traditional minorities, albeit under different labels. Accordingly, only some minorities composed of citizens or autochthonous minorities have access to particular rights and instruments for their protection and promotion.

This is a matter of political choice that reflects the overall approach different countries take toward the management of their internal diversity, which often varies. This can be due to either the constitutional or legal recognition of several selected minorities[46] and/or the submission of declarations and reservations at the time of the ratification of international documents to delimit their application.[47]

Thus, while the international dimension plays an important guiding role in particular as regards the innovative developments of this area of law (at least in some areas of the world), such a legal framework does not go so far as to limit the state margin of appreciation when it comes to the management of their internal diversity. As a result, the picture that emerges from the previous paragraphs is that states retain considerable leeway in deciding which group is entitled to further forms of protection beyond non-discrimination and employ the legal notion of minority as an exclusive status that stems from various types of legal recognition and entitles such parties to forms of protection and promotion.

Conversely, what both dimensions share is the basic idea of what the essential elements that constitute a minority are.

The condition of non-dominance, the sense of internal solidarity, the will to preserve the cultural distinctiveness of the groups and the (individual and collective) self-recognition as a minority can all be drawn from the most influential international definitions as identifying criteria. Bearing in mind the aim of this work, however, of greatest interest is that the legal sources focus on the

46 For instance, in Italy, constitutional recognition is given to linguistic minorities (Article 6 Const.), while state law n. 482/1999 – implementing the constitutional provision – specifies that the beneficiaries of minority rights are linguistic minority groups that have historically resided in the country's territory; other countries of South-Eastern Europe, like Hungary and Croatia, have followed a similar model.

47 This is the case with the application of the FCNM: declarations are used to define the beneficiaries of the Convention; this could be done by establishing some criteria minorities must meet (Austria, Estonia, Latvia, Luxembourg CHECK, Poland, and Switzerland), providing a specific list of minorities to which the measures apply (Albania, Denmark, Germany, the Netherlands, Norway, Sweden, the Slovak Republic, Slovenia, and North Macedonia), or stating that minorities are not present in the states territories (Liechtenstein, Luxembourg, and San Marino); reservations are general limitations of the application of the Convention, and have been made by Belgium and Malta; Sweden similarly identifies minorities as those groups that fulfil several criteria, among which having "historic or long bond with Sweden"; Netherlands stated in a FCNM country report that national minorities are framed as "those groups of citizens who are traditionally resident within the territory of the State and who live in their traditional/ancestral settlement areas, but who differ from the majority population through their own language, culture and history – i.e. have an identity of their own – and who wish to preserve that identity".

existence of one or more objective "national" markers – such as language, religion, and ethnicity – that permanently and uniquely connotate the protected minority and represent the condition of diversity that allows for the establishment of protective arrangements.

Another common pattern is the framing of diversity accommodation beyond non-discrimination in terms of minority-majority relations: this means that all the questions concerning the management of diversity are tied to membership of (stable) minority groups as opposed to some dominant majorities.

The previous considerations refer to the consolidated approach that emerges from the international and national legal systems; it must also be taken into account that the most recent European international documents show a different perspective that sees minority rights as a flexible set of instruments for the accommodation of diversity. That will be analyzed in the subsequent sections of this chapter, together with the instruments that appear to follow this approach.

The next sections will delve into some macro-categories of minority rights that one can derive from the European region's international documents and, especially, the FCNM, the most detailed international act in this area, drawing on examples from several legal systems.

LINGUISTIC, EDUCATIONAL, RELIGIOUS, AND CULTURAL RIGHTS

This category of rights embeds all the legal measures that protect and promote the expression of minority cultural diversity.

Linguistic rights beyond the guarantee of non-discrimination in the enjoyment of the right to free speech – which implies the right to use the minority language in the private sphere[48] – arise in at least three dimensions, namely the official recognition of languages, the use of minority languages with public authorities and their use in education.[49]

The official recognition of languages may be accorded at a national or sub-national level and implies that the official languages are used for governmental purposes – i.e., legislation and administration – as well as in the provision of public services[50] and the communication with speakers of minority

48 It must anyhow be noted that some "hard cases" can emerge where the exercise of the rights could interfere with some public interest or the rights of other individuals; this is, for instance, the case with the exclusive use of a minority language in shop signs, the exercise of which might be in tension with the right of all consumers to understand shop signs; for examples, see Palermo and Woelk, Diritto costituzionale comparato . . . , 197–198.

49 As observed by Dersso, Solomon and Palermo, Francesco, "Minority Rights", in Tushnet, Fleiner and Saunders (eds.), Routledge Handbook . . . , 159–175, at 167–170; other important dimensions that will not be specifically addressed are the use of the minority languages in media and toponymy.

50 Of course, the variations in terms of implementation are numerous: the use of a minority language with public authorities may be limited to some sectors, such as in the communication with public administration, or extended as to imply the establishment of a bi- (or pluri-) lingual trial.

languages.[51] The official recognition of languages may also be tied to a specific territory, which does not always correspond to a sub-national territorial unit.[52]

In other cases, the right to use a minority language in the public sphere does not originate from its general official recognition as one of the national or sub-national languages, but it is authorized upon request of the (officially recognized) minorities in areas where speakers of minority languages are found in significant numbers.[53]

One of the most critical dimensions of language rights is related to education. In this respect, one may find different models: besides the general right to learn one's mother tongue (which can be a minority language), the right to receive instruction in minority languages largely depends on state options concerning the regulation of languages, as sketched before.

In countries or sub-national entities where more than one official language is recognized, the public educational system is organized so as to provide education in all the official languages. This may be achieved by: a. creating a complete bi-plurilingual educational system where all schools use the official languages equally in their activities; b. following the principle of separatism, which engenders the institution of different schools for the different linguistic groups (where generally the other official language(s) is(are) also taught as a second language(s)); c. establishing public minority schools alongside majority ones in areas where this is reasonably feasible. Options a. and b. are, of course, more practicable where there are a limited number of officially recognized languages, while where there are numerous official languages, states or sub-national entities resort to option c.[54]

Where the exercise of language rights in the public area depends upon activation from the interested communities, it is generally provided that such a language be taught and/or used as a vehicular language – at least to a certain extent – in the schools of the respective territories.

When it comes to other minority cultural rights, it is possible to distinguish between (individual) rights that are accorded to people generally but acquire a special meaning when exercised by a member of a minority[55] – which fall under the protection provided by the principles of equality and non-discrimination – and particular additional rights, which often have an evident collective dimension. In any case, the attribution of further rights is always bound to a sort of legal

51 This is the case with South Africa, Switzerland, Canada, Singapore and Belgium.

52 In those cases, what is called the territorial principle in the regulation of languages is applied; Switzerland and Belgium (German linguistic community) are two examples.

53 As in Italy and Sweden.

54 Like in the case of South Africa.

55 On this, see Cavaggion, Diritti culturali . . . ; Kymlicka, Will, *Multicultural Citizenship: A Liberal Theory of Minority Rights* (Clarendon, Oxford, 1995), who referred to them as polyethnic rights.

recognition of the cultural, linguistic, religious, and ethnic minority (which can also be judicial, especially in common law systems).[56]

The former category refers to the right of minorities to freely enjoy their culture, customs, and religion and to form or participate in private cultural, linguistic, and religious associations.

The latter includes forms of protection and promotion of cultures and religious beliefs.

As for religious minorities,[57] specific additional measures of accommodation mainly follow from public recognition of a denomination. This most commonly takes the shape of an agreement between the state and the denomination that sets out the legal framework of their relationship and the public relevance of the latter.[58] Specific additional religious guarantees invest the right to manifest such religion or belief in worship, observance, practice, and teaching, which may also imply the right to establish worship buildings and religious schools.[59]

Furthermore, related to the enjoyment of religious (and cultural) rights are exemption rights, which are in several cases derived from judicial decisions based on the technique known as "reasonable accommodation".[60]

Finally, when it comes to cultural rights, one of their main manifestations is the recognition of religious personal law or customary law, which implies that judges must consider it while deciding cases on some specific matters or that the competencies over those matters are directly delegated to some minority courts.[61]

56 In the case of religious rights, this recognition addresses the denomination representing the religious minority.

57 Ferrari, Daniele, *Legal Code of Religious Minority Rights: Sources in International and European Law* (Routledge, London-New York, 2022), 8, outlined that it is not uncommon that religious minorities be framed in terms of ethnic minorities and enjoy minority rights beyond the strictly religious ones (such as political and participation rights).

58 Palermo and Woelk, Diritto costituzionale comparato . . . , 245–257.

59 Angeletti, Silvia, "Religious Minorities' Rights in International Law: Acknowledging Intersectionality, Enhancing Synergy", 12 *Religions* (2021), 691–711, at 703.

60 Two paradigmatic examples may be drawn from Canada and South Africa; the first is the Supreme Court of Canada's ruling *Multani v Commission scolaire Margherite-Bourgeoys*, [2006] 1 S.C.R. 256 which allowed a Sikh student to wear the traditional knife called *kirpan* at school; the second case, *KwaZulu-Natal MEC on Education v Pillay*, [2007] ZACC 21, concerned a student that was prohibited from wearing a nose stud as a manifestation of her Hindi-Tamil culture in her school: the South African constitutional court eventually held the school responsible for discriminating against the student on the grounds of religion and culture; related to exemption rights is also the theme of cultural defense: see Dundes Rendeln, Alison, "The Cultural Defense: Challenging the Monocultural Paradigm", in Foblets, Marie-Claire, Gaudreault-DesBiens, Jean-F. and Dundes Relteln, Alison (eds.), *Cultural Diversity and the Law: State Responses Around the World* (Bruylant-Yvon-Blais, Bruxelles-Montréal, 2010), 791–818.

61 As is the case of India, Ethiopia, Israel, and South Africa; on this, see Ferrari, Silvio, "Religious Rules and Legal Pluralism: An Introduction", in Bottoni, Rossella, Cristofori, Rinaldo and Ferrari, Silvio (eds.), *Religious Rules, State Law, and Normative Pluralism: A Comparative Overview* (Springer, Cham, 2016), 1–25, at 10–18 and the case studies indicated in the book.

POLITICAL RIGHTS AND PARTICIPATION OF MINORITIES

Political participation rights beyond non-discrimination involve several positive measures intended to favor or grant the representation of minorities in governmental and public institutions.

The most common regulations about minority political rights are connected to the representation of minorities in state and sub-national legislative assemblies. State and regional electoral legislation can indeed provide for arrangements that either encourage the presence of minorities in legislative bodies or assure it.[62] Examples of the former are the exemption from the general electoral thresholds (if present) in proportional electoral systems[63] and the creation of constituencies corresponding to the territory where the minority is located in majoritarian systems.[64] Representation of minorities is conversely granted when seats of the assembly are reserved for one or more minorities regardless of the election results.[65]

Representation does not necessarily lead to the effective participation of minorities.[66] To realize this aim, sometimes further arrangements are put in place, such as the introduction of a veto right in favor of the representatives of the minorities in matters that concern their interests.[67] This is in line with the international legal standards that promote the effective participation of minorities, especially when it comes to decisions that touch upon their interests.[68]

Furthermore, minority representation may be foreseen in other public bodies, like executives, the judiciary, and public administration.[69]

62 On this distinction, see Toniatti, Roberto, "La rappresentanza politica delle minoranze linguistiche: i ladini fra rappresentanza 'assicurata' e 'garantita'", 6 *Le Regioni* (1995), 1271–1290 and the decision of the Italian constitutional court no. 261/1995.

63 This is the case, for instance, with the Danish minority candidates in the German Land Schleswig-Holstein.

64 For instance, a specific constituency corresponding with Aosta Valley was created in Italy to allow the region to elect two representatives in the Parliament.

65 Like in the case of Slovenia, where two seats are reserved to the representatives of the Italian and Hungarian communities.

66 On this, see Vertischel, Annelies, *Participation, Representation and Identity: The Right of Persons Belonging to Minorities to Effective Participation in Public Affairs: Content, Justification and Limits* (Intersentia, Antwerp, 2009) and ACFC, Thematic Commentary No. 2, *The Effective Participation of Persons Belonging to National Minorities in Cultural, Social and Economic Life and Public Affairs*, 27 February 2008, ACFC/31DOC(2008)001.

67 For instance, the Slovenian constitution (Article 64) provides for a right of absolute veto for the Italian and Hungarian representatives.

68 For example, see, Article 15 FCNM and Article 2, para. 3 of the 1992 UN Declaration on the Rights of Persons Belonging to National or Ethnic, Religious and Linguistic Minorities.

69 On this, see Marko, Joseph and Constantin, Sergiu, "Against Marginalisation: The Right to Effective Participation", in Marko and Constantin (eds.), Human and Minority Rights . . . , 340–395.

TERRITORIAL AND NON-TERRITORIAL AUTONOMY

Autonomy is the strongest instrument for the accommodation of minorities as it allows them to manage their affairs to different extents.[70] Furthermore, autonomy has been widely endorsed as an instrument for conflict resolution in deeply divided societies.[71] Such a legal tool has often been framed in terms of a right to self-government; however, the limited indications coming from the international documents do not address it in these terms.[72]

The employment of autonomy for minority interests takes different shapes. Territorial autonomy is the most common model one can find in state practice and, in a way, the most intuitive, for it reproduces the nation-state logic in a portion of the state territory. Accordingly, national minorities become regional majorities within the autonomous territory and are entitled to various degrees of autonomy in fields related to the management of the minority's cultural affairs and possibly others concerning the social and economic development of the subnational entity.[73]

70 On autonomy for minority accommodation, see, for instance, Hannum, Hurst, *Autonomy, Sovereignty, and Self-Determination: The Accommodation of Conflicting Rights* (University of Pennsylvania Press, Philadelphia, 1990); Suksi, Markku (ed.), *Autonomy, Applications and Implications* (Kluwer Law International, The Hague, 1998); Légaré, André and Suksi, Markku, "Introduction: Rethinking Forms of Autonomy at the Dawn of the 21st Century", 15(2–3) *International Journal on Minority and Group Rights* (2008), 195–225; Ghai, Yash (ed.), *Autonomy and Ethnicity: Negotiating Competing Claims* (Cambridge University Press, Cambridge, 2000); Skurbaty, Zelim A. (ed.), *Beyond a One-Dimensional State: An Emerging Right to Autonomy?* (Brill-Nijhoff, Leiden-Boston, 2005); Gagnon, Alain-G. and Keating, Michael (eds.), *Political Autonomy and Divided Societies: Imagining Democratic Alternatives in Complex Settings* (Palgrave Macmillan, Cham, 2012).

71 For instance, see Lapidoth, Ruth, *Autonomy: Flexible Solutions to Ethnic Conflicts* (United States Institute of Peace, Washington, DC, 1996); Weller, Marc and Wolff, Stefan (eds.), *Autonomy, Self-Governance and Conflict Resolution: Innovative Approaches to Institutional Design in Divided Societies* (Routledge, London-New York, 2005); Benedikter, Thomas, *Solving Ethnic Conflict through Self-Government: A Short Guide to Autonomy in Europe and South Asia* (Eurac Research, Bolzano-Bozen, 2009); Schulte, Felix, *Peace through Self-Determination: Success and Failure of Territorial Autonomy* (Palgrave Macmillan, Cham, 2020); also, autonomy as a tool for conflict resolution has been studied by federal scholars; on this, see Keil, Soeren and Alber, Elisabeth (eds.), *Federalism as a Tool of Conflict Resolution* (Routledge, London-New York, 2021).

72 See for instance, OSCE HCNM, *The Lund Recommendations on the Effective Participation of National Minorities in Public Life* (OSCE HCNM, The Hague, 1999), which address territorial and non-territorial forms of autonomy but do not frame them as an expression of a right to autonomy; however, autonomy is seen as a means to achieve effective participation of minorities in public life (see the Lund Recommendations and the UN Declaration of 1992, as interpreted by the Commentary provided by the Chairman of the UN Working Group, Asbjorn Eide, UN Doc E/CN.4.SUB.2/AC.5/2001/2 (2 April 2001), paras 38ff).

73 On the different kinds of powers autonomous territories may be entitled to, see Tkacic, Michael, *Characteristics of Forms of Autonomy*, 15(2–3) *International Journal on Minority and Group Rights* (2008), 369–401.

Territorial autonomous arrangements for minorities may be found in centralized, decentralized, regional, and, of course, federal states.[74]

When it comes to the latter, federalism has been shown to be a principle of state organization through which minority protection may be achieved in two main ways. Federal states may be entirely organized on an ethnic basis or instead, as has become increasingly common during the second half of the century, provide for asymmetrical federal or quasi-federal arrangements specifically designed for territorially concentrated minorities.[75]

In literature, autonomy has acquired a specific theoretical meaning with its own distinctive features. From this perspective, it refers to those autonomous arrangements that have a particular position within a (centralized, decentralized, or federal) state system, created to respond to the special needs of a territory and the community residing in it.[76] Indeed, autonomy often implies asymmetrical *ad hoc* arrangements for definite areas of a state that show a condition of diversity, be it cultural or linguistic (and/or geographical too).[77]

Non-territorial forms of autonomy have ancient origins but, in recent times, have witnessed a surge of interest as a tool for minority protection, especially (but not exclusively) in some areas of the world, such as Eastern

74 According to Kymlicka, Will, "Federalism, Nationalism and Multiculturalism", in Karmis, Dimitrios and Norman, Wayne (eds.), *Theories of Federalism: A Reader* (Palgrave Macmillan, London, 2005), 269–292, the degree to which federal organization can be conducive to minority protection depends on two main factors; first, the definition of subnational units' boundaries: if they coincide with the territory where the minorities are located, subnational autonomy can more easily serve minority purposes; second, the degree of autonomy accorded to the subnational entities; on the distinction between ethnic federalism and multinational federalism, see, for instance, Turton, David (ed.), *Ethnic Federalism: The Ethiopian Experience in Comparative Perspective* (James Currey-Ohio University Press-Addis Ababa University Press, Oxford-Athens-Addis Ababa); on the evolution of federal structures for the accommodation of diversity, the emergence of not traditional federal arrangements and the tendency toward of asymmetry in recent federal experiences, see Keil, Soeren and Kropp, Sabine (eds.), *Emerging Federal Structures in the Post-Cold War Era* (Palgrave Macmillan, Cham, 2022).

75 More insights on the connections between federalism and diversity accommodation will be provided in Chapter 6.

76 Ackrén, Maria, *Conditions for Different Autonomy Regimes in the World: A Fuzzy-Set Application* (Åbo Akademi University Press, Åbo, 2009), 20.

77 Suksi, Markku, "Explaining the Robustness and Longevity of the Åland Example in Comparison with Other Autonomy Solutions", 20(1) *International Journal on Minority and Group Rights* (2013), 51–66, at 56–58.

Europe.[78] The concept of non-territorial autonomy as a specific tool to manage ethno-cultural diversity has been suggested by Otto Bauer and Karl Renner as a policy solution for the management of the Augsburg empire's internal diversity. However, earlier examples of non-territorial autonomous arrangements can be traced back, for instance, to the *millet* system established by the Ottoman Empire to manage the coexistence of its religious and ethnic communities.[79]

Despite their differences, the common feature of non-territorial autonomous arrangements is that "the competences are transferred not in relation to a certain specific territory but in relation to a certain community, irrespective of size and place of residence in the State".[80] Accordingly, this legal tool is particularly useful when it comes to the accommodation of minorities who are not territorially located in a specific area of a country.[81]

It is possible to identify two main patterns of non-territorial autonomy: the first engenders the establishment of public bodies that are entitled to (generally administrative) powers to manage cultural matters in the interest of the

78 According to Malloy, Tove H., "Introduction", in Malloy, Tove H., Osipov, Alexander and Vizi, Balázs (eds.), *Managing Diversity through Non-Territorial Autonomy: Assessing Advantages, Deficiencies, and Risks* (Oxford University Press, Oxford, 2015), 1–15, at 2, the literature on NTA is marked by three different approaches: a. nationalism studies: see Bauer, Otto, *The Question of Nationalities and Social Democracy* (University of Minnesota Press, Minneapolis, 2000), translated by O'Donnell, Joseph, originally published as Bauer, Otto, *Die Nationalitiitenfrage und die Sozialdemokratie* (Verlag der Wiener Volksbuchhandlung, Vienna, 1924); Nimni, Ephraim, Osipov, Alexander and Smith, David J. (eds.), *The Challenge of Non-Territorial Autonomy* (Peter Lang, Bern, 2013); b. conflict studies: see Coakley, John, "Approaches to the Resolution of Ethnic Conflict: The Strategy of Non-Territorial Autonomy", 15(3) *International Political Science Review* (1994), 297–314; Roach, Stephen C., *Cultural Autonomy, Minority Rights, and Globalization* (Ashgate, Burlington, 2005); and c. diversity management: see Gál, Kinga (ed.), *Minority Governance in Europe* (Open Society Institute, Budapest, 2002); Légaré and Suksi, Introduction . . .; Smith, David J. and Cordell, Karl (eds.), *Cultural Autonomy in Contemporary Europe* (Routledge, London-New York, 2008); Prina, Federica, "Nonterritorial Autonomy and Minority (Dis)Empowerment: Past, Present, and Future", 48(3) *Nationalities Papers* (2020), 425–434, at 427, also pointed out that a distinction can be made in the literature on NTA, "between studies that analyze NTA and NCA mechanisms in a broad sense and those whose focus is the original (Renner and Bauer's) model and its potential adaptation to contemporary society".

79 As Barkey, Karen and Gavrilis, George, "The Ottoman Millet System: Non-Territorial Autonomy and its Contemporary Legacy", 15(1) *Ethnopolitics* (2016), 24–42, have observed, the *millet* system was in place from 1453 to the nineteenth century.

80 Henrard, Kristin, "Participation, Representation and Autonomy in the Lund Recommendations and Their Reflections in the Supervision of the FCNM and Several Human Rights Conventions", 12(2–3) *International Journal on Minority and Group Rights* (2005), 133–168, at 141.

81 Besides being more attractive to states, as it seems less threatening than territorial autonomy, which is (wrongly) seen as reinforcing minority claims and as a step toward secession; this is especially the case in the post-communist world: on this, see Palermo, Francesco, "Central, Eastern and South-Eastern Europe and Territorial Autonomy: Are They Really Incompatible?", in Gagnon, Alain-G. and Keating, Michael (eds.), Political Autonomy . . . , 81–97.

minority, directly run some minority services such as public minority schools (receiving public funds), and have consultative functions as regards legal bills and policies that concern the minority.[82]

The second category includes a manifold number of private entities and other less institutionalized autonomous arrangements that serve minority interests and are sometimes recognized by the state or delegated to exercise public functions in areas of concern for the minority. For instance, private minority schools have been framed as non-territorial arrangements.[83] The latter will be specifically addressed in the section dedicated to emergent perspectives on the accommodation of diversity.

Indigenous peoples' rights law: some distinctive aspects

Indigenous peoples' rights law is also faced with significant definitional hurdles. As with minority rights law, a universal definition of indigenous people is not provided at the international level. Nevertheless, what is observable is that Indigenous peoples have widely been framed from a scholarly and legal perspective as possessing different features to minority groups.[84] Consequently, they have followed two parallel and separate paths in the international and, to a certain extent, domestic legal systems, the former maintaining a status of 'people' which does not apply to the latter.[85]

82 Examples are the Sami parliaments in Finland, Sweden and Norway, the minority councils in Croatia, Estonia, Hungary, Serbia and Slovenia; for an overview, see Malloy, Osipov and Vizi (eds.), Managing Diversity . . .; Nimni, Osipov and Smith (eds.), The Challenge . . .

83 As will be seen, in this respect, states and sub-national entities may simply authorize such activity – by specifying that the (widely recognized) guarantee to establish private schools applies to minorities too – or even provide forms of (mostly financial) support for it.

84 On the path of increasing relevance of indigenous peoples in international law, see Anaya, James S., *Indigenous Peoples in International Law* (Oxford University Press, Oxford, 2000) and *Id.*, *International Human Rights and Indigenous People* (Aspen Publishers, New York, 2009); also, see Niezen, Ronald, *The Origins of Indigenism: Human Rights and the Politics of Identity* (University of California Press, Berkeley-Los Angeles-London, 2003), 29–52; on the differences between the categories of minority, people and indigenous people in international law and their attendant legal statuses, see the thorough analysis conducted by Castellino, Joshua and Doyle, Cathal, "Who Are 'Indigenous Peoples'? An Examination of Concepts Concerning Group Membership in the UNDRIP", in Hohmann, Jessie and Weller, Marc (eds.), *The UN Declaration on the Rights of Indigenous Peoples: A Commentary* (Oxford University Press, Oxford, 2018), 7–37; also, on definitional issues, see Thornberry, Patrick, *Indigenous Peoples and Human Rights* (Manchester University Press, Manchester, 2002), 109–155.

85 This is highlighted by Kymlicka, Will, "The Internationalization of Minority Rights", in Castellino (ed.), Global Minority Rights . . . , 35–66, who described that such a scholarly categorization was (and still is to a certain extent) based on the assumption that the two groups have rather different needs and demands, thus requiring different legal responses; however, while the latter categorization is still valid from a legal perspective, one can find convergence on the instruments used to protect and empower minority and indigenous groups; moreover, the classification comes from a Global North (Western) approach to these issues, for, as observed by Kymlicka, The Internationalization . . . , 12; on the applicability of the concept of indigenous peoples in Asian settings, see Kingsbury, Benedict, "Indigenous Peoples in International Law: A Constructivist Approach to the Asian Controversy", 92(3) *American Journal of International Law* (1998), 414–457.

While a convergence of their instruments – at least at the international level – is apparent (and often encouraged[86]) nowadays, the evolutionary trajectories of their legal treatment started in different periods and from opposite sides. As described by Kymlicka, minority groups are widely thought to be "contenders but losers in the process of European state formation",[87] while, on the other, indigenous peoples "were entirely isolated from that process until very recently".[88] Furthermore, it is generally assumed that the two types of community differ in terms of lifestyles and have suffered different forms of injustice; indigenous peoples are being characterized by a situation of special vulnerability and, consequently, a more urgent need for accommodation through forms of self-determination and collective rights given the brutal exclusion and isolation they suffered.[89] All this seems to have decisively determined a shift in their international regulation and theoretical framing that still holds legal significance today.

Accordingly, the main criteria to define indigenous peoples that one can derive from the international documents and, especially, the influential definitions provided by the international supervisory bodies[90] are: a. historical continuity with pre-invasion and/or pre-colonial societies that developed on their territories; b. social, cultural, and political distinctiveness; c. non-dominance; d. a determination to preserve, develop, and transmit to future generations their ancestral territories and identity as people according to their own cultural patterns, social institutions, and legal systems; e. a strong link to territories and surrounding natural resources.[91]

86 For instance, Thornberry, Indigenous Peoples . . . , 341–407 and 623–685, underlined the usefulness of minority international instruments for indigenous peoples.

87 Kymlicka, Will, "Theorizing Indigenous Rights", in Kymlicka, Will (ed.), *Politics in the Vernacular: Nationalism, Multiculturalism, and Citizenship* (Oxford University Press, Oxford, 2001), 120–132, at 122.

88 Kymlicka Theorizing Indigenous Rights . . . , 122.

89 Kymlicka, The Internationalization . . . , 10; the link between indigenous peoples and the concept of self-determination is described by Castellino and Doyle, Who Are 'Indigenous Peoples'. . . , 7–37, as being one of the main reasons that distinguish them from minorities from a theoretical and legal standpoint.

90 The then Special Rapporteur José R. Martínez Cobo's working definition of Indigenous People, in the final report of his *Study of the Problem of Discrimination against Indigenous Populations*, available at the following link: https://www.un.org/esa/socdev/unpfii/documents/MCS_xxi_xxii_e.pdf is still the main point of reference in this field: "Indigenous communities, people and nations are those which, having a historical continuity with pre-invasion and pre-colonial societies that developed on their territories, conider themselves distinct from the other sectors of the societies now prevailing in those territories, or part of them. They form at present non-dominant sectors of society and are determined to preserve, develop and transmit to future generations their ancestral territories, and their ethnic identity, as the basis of their continued existence as peoples, in accordance with their own cultural patterns, social institutions and legal systems".

91 On this, see also the Fact Sheet no. 9, Rev. 2 of the High Commissioner for Human Rights of 2013, *Indigenous Peoples and the United Nations Human Rights System*, available at the following link: https://www.ohchr.org/sites/default/files/Documents/Publications/fs9Rev.2.pdf.

What emerges is that indigenous peoples are also mainly framed in national or cultural terms and identified as non-dominant groups compared to a country's majority.

When it comes to the legal instruments for the accommodation of indigenous peoples' rights, it is possible to say that they, to a large extent, resonate and overlap with minority rights law. Additionally, the recognition of their rights originates from state legal recognition, which can take different shapes.

Nevertheless, indigenous peoples' rights maintain some specificities, besides the fact that in several cases, they are still, to different extents, based on the use of various forms of treaties and agreements.[92] What differentiates them is that a. indigenous peoples' rights law, albeit based upon a right-based approach like minority rights law, strongly affirms a collective dimension of indigenous entitlements; b. a major focus is put on the recognition of forms of autonomous development and decision-making concerning indigenous peoples' lifestyles and traditional territories.[93] In other words, "the provisions regarding indigenous peoples seek to allocate legal authority to these peoples, enabling them to make their own decisions, especially concerning their lands and natural resources".[94] Accordingly, specific regard is given to the right to autonomy, the right to own and use lands, the recognition of customary law, and the right to free, prior, and informed consent.[95]

Bibliography

Ackrén, Maria, *Conditions for Different Autonomy Regimes in the World: A Fuzzy-Set Application* (Åbo Akademi University Press, Åbo, 2009)

Anaya, James S., *Indigenous Peoples in International Law* (Oxford University Press, Oxford, 2000)

92 This is the case with Canada, the US, New Zealand, and Australia, which were the countries that initially did not support the UNDRIP; specific recognition of the significance of the treaty model of accommodation is given in Article 37 of the UNDRIP: "Indigenous peoples have the right to the recognition, observance and enforcement of treaties, agreements and other constructive arrangements concluded with States or their successors and to have States honour and respect such treaties, agreements and other constructive arrangements".

93 See Marko, Joseph, Marko-Stöckl, Edith, Harzl, Benedikt and Unger, Hedwig, "The Historical-Sociological Foundations: State Formation and Nation Building in Europe and the Construction of the Identitarian Nation-Cum-State Paradigm", in Marko and Constantin (eds.), Human and Minority Rights Protection . . . , 33–95, at 83.

94 Marko, Marko-Stöckl, Harzl and Unger, The Historical-Sociological Foundations . . . , 83; also, see the ILO Convention n. 169, Article 7, 8 and 13–19 and UNDRIP, Article 4, 23, 35–41.

95 On the peculiar aspects of indigenous peoples' rights law, besides the literature quoted previously, see, for instance, Xanthaki, Alexandra, *Indigenous Rights and United Nations Standards: Self-Determination, Culture and Land* (Cambridge University Press, Cambridge, 2007); on the contents of the UNDRIP, see Hohmann and Weller (eds.), The UN Declaration . . . ; on the right to free, prior, and informed consent at the international and domestic levels, see Young, Stephen, *Indigenous Peoples, Consent and Rights: Troubling Subjects* (Routledge, London-New York, 2020).

Anaya, James S., *International Human Rights and Indigenous People* (Aspen Publishers, New York, 2009)
Angeletti, Silvia, "Religious Minorities' Rights in International Law: Acknowledging Intersectionality, Enhancing Synergy", 12 *Religions* (2021), 691–711
Asch, Michael, *Home and Native Land: Aboriginal Rights and the Canadian Constitution* (University of British Columbia Press, Vancouver, 1993)
Barkey, Karen and Gavrilis, George, "The Ottoman Millet System: Non-Territorial Autonomy and its Contemporary Legacy", 15(1) *Ethnopolitics* (2016), 24–42
Bauer, Otto, *The Question of Nationalities and Social Democracy* (University of Minnesota Press, Minneapolis, 2000), translated by O'Donnell, Joseph, originally published as Bauer, Otto, *Die Nationalitiitenfrage und die Sozialdemokratie* (Verlag der Wiener Volksbuchhandlung, Vienna, 1924)
Belser, Eva Maria, "Accommodating National Minorities in Federal Switzerland: Old Concepts Meet New Realities", in Gagnon, Alain-G. and Burgess, Michael (eds.), *Revisiting Unity and Diversity in Federal Countries: Changing Concepts, Reform Proposals and New Institutional Realities* (Brill-Nijhoff, Leiden-Boston, 2018), 79–111
Benedikter, Thomas, *Solving Ethnic Conflict through Self-Government: A Short Guide to Autonomy in Europe and South Asia* (Eurac Research, Bolzano-Bozen, 2009)
Bish, Robert L. and Cassidy, Frank, *Indian Government: Its Meaning in Practice* (The Institute for Research of Public Policy, Halifax, 1989)
Brookfield, Frederic M. (Jock), *Waitangi and Indigenous Rights: Revolution, Law and Legitimation* (Auckland University Press, Auckland, 2006)
Bryde, Brun-O. and Stein, Micheal A., "General Provisions Dealing with Equality", in Tushnet, Mark, Fleiner, Thomas and Saunders, Cheryl (eds.), *Routledge Handbook of Constitutional Law* (Routledge, London-New York, 2013), 287–300
Capotorti, Francesco, *Study on the Rights of Persons Belonging to Ethnic, Religious and Linguistic Minorities* (United Nations, New York, 1977) (UN Doc. E/CN.4/sub.2/384/Rev.1, UN sales Nr. E.78.XIV.1) / Geneva UN Center for Human Rights, UN Doc E/CN.4/sub.2/384/Add.1–7, 1–114
Castellino, Joshua, "Introduction", in Castellino, Joshua (ed.), *Global Minority Rights* (Routledge, London-New York, 2016), xi–xxiv
Castellino, Joshua and Doyle, Cathal, "Who Are 'Indigenous Peoples'? An Examination of Concepts Concerning Group Membership in the UNDRIP", in Hohmann, Jessie and Weller, Marc (eds.), *The UN Declaration on the Rights of Indigenous Peoples: A Commentary* (Oxford University Press, Oxford, 2018), 7–37
Cavaggion, Giovanni, *Diritti culturali e modello costituzionale di integrazione* (Giappichelli, Turin, 2018)
Cigar, Norman L., *Genocide in Bosnia: The Policy of "Ethnic Cleansing"* (Texas A&M University Press, College Station, 1995)
Coakley, John, "Approaches to the Resolution of Ethnic Conflict: The Strategy of Non-Territorial Autonomy", 15(3) *International Political Science Review* (1994), 297–314
Dardanelli, Paolo and Mueller, Sean, "Dynamic De/Centralisation in Switzerland, 1848–2010", 49(1) *Publius* (2017), 138–165
Dersso, Solomon and Palermo, Francesco, "Minority Rights", in Tushnet, Mark, Fleiner, Thomas and Saunders, Cheryl (eds.), *Routledge Handbook of Constitutional Law* (Routledge, London-New York, 2013), 159–175
Dundes Rendeln, Alison, "The Cultural Defense: Challenging the Monocultural Paradigm", in Foblets, Marie-Claire, Gaudreault-DesBiens, Jean-F. and Dundes Relteln, Alison (eds.), *Cultural Diversity and the Law: State Responses Around the World* (Bruylant-Yvon-Blais, Bruxelles-Montréal, 2010), 791–818
Duthu, Bruce, *American Indians and the Law* (Viking Penguins, New York, 2008)

Ferrari, Daniele, *Legal Code of Religious Minority Rights: Sources in International and European Law* (Routledge, London-New-York, 2022)

Ferrari, Silvio, "Religious Rules and Legal Pluralism: An Introduction", in Bottoni, Rossella, Cristofori, Rinaldo and Ferrari, Silvio (eds.), *Religious Rules, State Law, and Normative Pluralism: A Comparative Overview* (Springer, Cham, 2016), 1–25

Gagnon, Alain-G. and Keating, Michael (eds.), *Political Autonomy and Divided Societies: Imagining Democratic Alternatives in Complex Settings* (Palgrave Macmillan, Cham, 2012)

Gál, Kinga (ed.), *Minority Governance in Europe* (Open Society Institute, Budapest, 2002)

Ghai, Yash (ed.), *Autonomy and Ethnicity: Negotiating Competing Claims* (Cambridge University Press, Cambridge, 2000)

Ghai, Yash, "Decentralization and the Accommodation of Ethnic Diversity", in Young, Crawford (ed.), *Ethnic Diversity and Public Policy* (Palgrave, Basingstoke-New York, 1998), 31–71

Glazer, Nathan, "Federalism and Ethnicity: The Experience of the United States", 7(4) *Publius* (1977), 71–87

Hanks, Peter and Keon-Cohen, Bryan (eds.), *Aboriginals and the Law* (Allena and Unwin, Sidney, 1994)

Hannum, Hurst, *Autonomy, Sovereignty, and Self-Determination: The Accommodation of Conflicting Rights* (University of Pennsylvania Press, Philadelphia, 1990)

Henrard, Kristin, "Participation, Representation and Autonomy in the Lund Recommendations and their Reflections in the Supervision of the FCNM and Several Human Rights Conventions", 12(2–3) *International Journal on Minority and Group Rights* (2005), 133–168

Hueglin, Thomas O., "Exploring Concepts of Treaty Federalism A Comparative Perspective", *Paper Prepared as Part of the Research Program of the Royal Commission on Aboriginal Peoples* (1994), at https://publications.gc.ca/site/eng/9.829489/publication.html

Jackson-Preece, Jennifer, "Beyond the (Non) Definition of Minority", *ECMI Issue Brief* (18 February 2014), at https://www.ecmi.de/publications/issue-briefs/national-minority-capital-introducing-the-new-concept

Jackson-Preece, Jennifer, *Minority Rights: Between Diversity and Community* (Polity, Cambridge-Malden, 2005)

Jackson-Preece, Jennifer, "Minority Rights in Europe: From Westphalia to Helsinki", 23 *Review of International Studies* (1997), 75–92

Keil, Soeren and Alber, Elisabeth (eds.), *Federalism as a Tool of Conflict Resolution* (Routledge, London-New York, 2021)

Keil, Soeren and Kropp, Sabine (eds.), *Emerging Federal Structures in the Post-Cold War Era* (Palgrave Macmillan, Cham, 2022)

Khaitan, Tarunabh, "Discrimination", in *Max Planck Encyclopedia of Comparative Constitutional Law* (Oxford University Press, Oxford, 2017), at https://papers.ssrn.com/sol3/papers.cfm?abstract_id=3277053

Kingsbury, Benedict, "Indigenous Peoples in International Law: A Constructivist Approach to the Asian Controversy", 92(3) *American Journal of International Law* (1998), 414–457

Kymlicka, Will, "Federalism, Nationalism and Multiculturalism", in Karmis, Dimitrios and Norman, Wayne (eds.), *Theories of Federalism: A Reader* (Palgrave Macmillan, London, 2005), 269–292

Kymlicka, Will, *Multicultural Citizenship: A Liberal Theory of Minority Rights* (Clarendon, Oxford, 1995)

Kymlicka, Will, "Theorizing Indigenous Rights", in Kymlicka, Will (ed.), *Politics in the Vernacular: Nationalism, Multiculturalism, and Citizenship* (Oxford University Press, Oxford, 2001), 120–132

Lapidoth, Ruth, *Autonomy: Flexible Solutions to Ethnic Conflicts* (United States Institute of Peace, Washington, DC, 1996)

Légaré, André and Suksi, Markku, "Introduction: Rethinking Forms of Autonomy at the Dawn of the 21st Century", 15(2–3) *International Journal on Minority and Group Rights* (2008), 195–225

Linder, Wolf and Mueller, Sean, *Swiss Democracy: Possible Solutions to Conflict in Multicultural Societies* (Palgrave Macmillan, Cham, 2021)

Lyons, Oren and Mohawk, John (eds.), *Exiled in the Land of the Free: Democracy, Indian Nations, and the US Constitution* (Clear Light Publishers, Santa Fe, 1992)

Malloy, Tove H., "Introduction", in Malloy, Tove H., Osipov, Alexander and Vizi, Balázs (eds.), *Managing Diversity Through Non-Territorial Autonomy: Assessing Advantages, Deficiencies, and Risks* (Oxford University Press, Oxford, 2015), 1–15

Marko, Joseph and Constantin, Sergiu, "Against Marginalisation: The Right to Effective Participation", in Marko, Joseph and Constantin, Sergiu (eds.), *Human and Minority Rights Protection by Multiple Diversity Governance: History, Law, Ideology and Politics in European Perspective* (Routledge, London-New York, 2019), 340–395

Marko, Joseph, Marko-Stöckl, Edith, Harzl, Benedikt and Unger, Hedwig, "The Historical and Sociological Foundations: State Formation and Nation Building in Europe and the Construction of the Identitarian Nation-cum-State Paradigm", in Marko, Joseph and Constantin, Sergiu (eds.), *Human and Minority Rights Protection by Multiple Diversity Governance: History, Law, Ideology and Politics in European Perspective* (Routledge, London-New York, 2019), 33–95

Marko, Joseph, Unger, Hedwig, Medda-Windisher, Roberta, Tomaselli, Alexandra and Ferraro, Filippo, "Against Annihilation: The Right to Existence", in Marko, Joseph and Constantin, Sergiu (eds.), *Human and Minority Rights Protection by Multiple Diversity Governance: History, Law, Ideology and Politics in European Perspective* (Routledge, London-New York, 2019), 178–226

Martinez Cobo, José R., *Study of the Problem of Discrimination against Indigenous Populations*, at https://www.un.org/esa/socdev/unpfii/documents/MCS_xxi_xxii_e.pdf

Niezen, Ronald, *The Origins of Indigenism: Human Rights and the Politics of Identity* (University of California Press, Berkeley-Los Angeles-London, 2003)

Nimni, Ephraim, Osipov, Alexander and Smith, David J. (eds.), *The Challenge of Non-Territorial Autonomy* (Peter Lang, Bern, 2013)

Packer, John, "On the Definition of Minorities", in Packer, John and Myntti, Kristian (eds.), *The Protection of Ethnic and Linguistic Minorities in Europe* (Åbo Akademi, Institute of Human Rights, Åbo, 1993), 23–65

Palermo, Francesco, "Central, Eastern and South-Eastern Europe and Territorial Autonomy: Are They Really Incompatible?", in Gagnon, Alain-G. and Keating, Michael (eds.), *Political Autonomy and Divided Societies: Imagining Democratic Alternatives in Complex Settings* (Palgrave Macmillan, Cham, 2012), 81–97

Palermo, Francesco and Woelk, Jens, *Diritto costituzionale comparato dei gruppi e delle minoranze* (CEDAM, Padua, 2021)

Pejic, Jelena, "Minority Rights in International Law", 19(3) *Human Rights Quarterly* (1997), 666–685

Pevar, Stephen, *The Rights of Indians and Tribes* (Southern Illinois University Press, Carbondale-Edwardsville, 1992)

Prina, Federica, "Nonterritorial Autonomy and Minority (Dis)Empowerment: Past, Present, and Future", 48(3) *Nationalities Papers* (2020), 425–434

Ramaga, Philip V., "The Group Concept in Minority Protection", 15(3) *Human Rights Quarterly* (1993), 575–588

Roach, Stephen C., *Cultural Autonomy, Minority Rights, and Globalization* (Ashgate, Burlington, 2005)

Rodley, Nigel S., "Conceptual Problems in the Protection of Minorities: International Legal Developments", 17(1) *Human Rights Quarterly* (1995), 48–71

Schulte, Felix, *Peace through Self-Determination: Success and Failure of Territorial Autonomy* (Palgrave Macmillan, Cham, 2020)

Skurbaty, Zelim A. (ed.), *Beyond a One-Dimensional State: An Emerging Right to Autonomy?* (Brill-Nijhoff, Leiden-Boston, 2005)

Smith, David J. and Cordell, Karl (eds.), *Cultural Autonomy in Contemporary Europe* (Routledge, London-New York, 2008)

Spiliopoulou Åkermark, Sia, *Justifications of Minority Protection in International Law* (Kluwer Law International, London-The Hague-Boston, 1997)

Spiliopoulou Åkermark, Sia, "Shifts in the Multiple Justifications of Minority Protection", in Malloy, Tove H. and Marko, Joseph (eds.), *Minority Governance in and Beyond Europe: Celebrating 10 Years of the European Yearbook of Minority Issues* (Brill-Nijhoff, Leiden, 2014), 106–134

Suksi, Markku (ed.), *Autonomy, Applications and Implications* (Kluwer Law International, The Hague, 1998)

Suksi, Markku, "Explaining the Robustness and Longevity of the Åland Example in Comparison with Other Autonomy Solutions", 20(1) *International Journal on Minority and Group Rights* (2013), 51–66

Tamanaha, Brian Z., *Legal Pluralism Explained: History, Theory, Consequences* (Oxford University Press, Oxford, 2021)

Thornberry, Patrick, *Indigenous Peoples and Human Rights* (Manchester University Press, Manchester, 2002)

Thornberry, Patrick, "Is There a Phoenix in the Ashes? International Law and Minority Rights", 15(3) *Texas International Law Journal* (1980), 421–458

Tkacic, Michael, "Characteristics of Forms of Autonomy", 15(2–3) *International Journal on Minority and Group Rights* (2008), 369–401

Toniatti, Roberto, "La rappresentanza politica delle minoranze linguistiche: i ladini fra rappresentanza 'assicurata' e 'garantita'", 6 *Le Regioni* (1995), 1271–1290

Tully, James, *Strange Multiplicity: Constitutionalism in an Age of Diversity* (Cambridge University Press, Cambridge, 1995)

Turton, David (ed.), *Ethnic Federalism: The Ethiopian Experience in Comparative Perspective* (James Currey-Ohio University Press-Addis Ababa University Press, Oxford-Athens-Addis Ababa, 2006)

Vertischel, Annelies, *Participation, Representation and Identity: The Right of Persons Belonging to Minorities to Effective Participation in Public Affairs: Content, Justification and Limits* (Intersentia, Antwerp, 2009)

Weller, Marc and Wolff, Stefan (eds.), *Autonomy, Self-Governance and Conflict Resolution: Innovative Approaches to Institutional Design in Divided Societies* (Routledge, London-New York, 2005)

Xanthaki, Alexandra, *Indigenous Rights and United Nations Standards: Self-Determination, Culture and Land* (Cambridge University Press, Cambridge, 2007)

Young, Stephen, *Indigenous Peoples, Consent and Rights: Troubling Subjects* (Routledge, London-New-York, 2020)

3 Innovative macro-perspectives of diversity accommodation

The premises for the evolution of the models for the accommodation of diversity

The third and fourth chapters will now set out to investigate recent developments in international and domestic jurisdictions and the consequences they have had in shaping the meaning and accommodation of diversity in contemporary liberal-democratic constitutional settings.

Whereas much research has been conducted as regards the contemporary patterns of diversity accommodation, it seems that this has generally been done by mainly focusing on specific models and without drawing attention to the common aspects they share. Therefore, what appears to be missing in the literature is a comprehensive observation of the phenomenon, which would be able to underline the commonalities of the different emerging models and consider them as part of a general trend occurring in this area. This perspective appears to be theoretically worth endorsement as, by connecting classic and emergent approaches to the regulation of diversity, it lays the groundwork for strengthened communication among models, which, in turn, facilitate their development and reciprocal learning. In addition, this makes one aware that there are forms of accommodation that do not correspond to the models to which the attention is most often drawn.

Specifically, the next chapters aim to show that innovative models and instruments for the accommodation of diversity beyond non-discrimination are emerging (or have long been overlooked). These complement those which are most longstanding and share a common core structure or paradigm. Indeed, all are characterized by their divergence, though to different extents, from the structure or paradigm of the traditional models.

Several conditions have been conducive to such developments.

Firstly, contemporary global dynamics in several parts of the world seem to favor changes to the organization of human life in many respects, which also affect the development of the instruments for the accommodation of diversity. The evolution of human life is developing in an increasingly complex economic and social setting (at least in some parts of the world) mostly owing

DOI: 10.4324/9781003493518-4

to the information revolution.[1] In turn, this has set the stage for renovated forms of economic, social, and legal-constitutional organizations that embed a great deal of complexity and acknowledge various and multifaceted forms of regulation of diversity. The global dynamics related to the information revolution are among the factors that are leading to a shift in legal-constitutional structures, which implies that the straightforward hierarchy of the modern state is progressively complemented by horizontal forms of distribution of power and authority whereby many state and non-state actors play a role in the activities once reserved to the state structures.[2]

If the aforementioned global phenomena related to human organization and its attendant social, economic, and legal-constitutional structures constitute the substratum in which innovations in this field (as in others) often take root, other more specific factors seem to have determined either the emergence of innovative models for the accommodation of diversity or, at least, the growing attention drawn to them.

The first is related to demographic changes, especially in the Global North. In a much more connected world, areas with better conditions of life have experienced considerable flows of immigration. This has been particularly true in central and Southwest Europe, which first witnessed migration flows from East European countries and, subsequently, from several Asian and African states. Without a doubt, the phenomenon of migration has put significant stress on the models for the accommodation of diversity in Europe and in Western countries in general. The need and demand for the accommodation of diversity have surely increased due to new groups claiming legal recognition, protection, or empowerment.

Secondly, several studies from different disciplines have revealed that identity is anything but a static and mono-dimensional concept.[3] Such developments also affect law, as today, a growing consensus on framing identity as dynamic and multi-dimensional in legal sources is observable – including from a non-discrimination standpoint. This has been partially endorsed at the international level and in several legal systems and has implied the recognition of the dynamic features of identity and diversity, as well as the emergence of innovative, practical solutions or the rediscovery of ancient ones recast in a modern light. These experiences and models are underlain by what will be labeled as a plural paradigm.[4] In sum, this perspective leads to the relativization of both the

1 On this, see Ortino, Sergio, *La struttura delle rivoluzioni economiche* (Cacucci, Bari, 2010).

2 See, for instance, Ferrarese, Maria Rosaria, *La governance tra politica e diritto* (Il Mulino, Bologna, 2010); Ost, François and Van de Kerchove, Michel, *De la pyramide au réseau? Pour une théorie dialectique du droit* (Université Saint-Louis, Bruxelles, 2002).

3 On the role of globalization as a force engendering, at least to a certain extent, a rise of plurality and an emphasis upon differences as a result of a heightened level of interconnectedness, see Bhamra, Meena K., *The Challenges of Justice in Diverse Societies: Constitutionalism and Pluralism* (Ashgate, Farnham-Burlington, 2011), 51–52.

4 On the plural paradigm, see Chapter 5.

practical and theoretical monopoly of the most consolidated approach to the management of diversity, denoted by a national(ist) blueprint. In fact, through the use of various means, diversity accommodation has evolved following recognizable common principles and approaches as well as a specific conception of targeted recipients that do not always seem sufficient as exclusive tools to regulate the contemporary diverse reality.

In addition to that, it must be noted that the evolution of constitutionalism in countries considered as being part of the Global South, together with increasing scientific attention towards them, encourages the observer to look at these systems and their legal instruments and include them in comparative analyses. This, in turn, opens up scientific inquiry in this field and, once more, seems to imply a reconsideration of the centrality of a Global North perspective to the issue of diversity management. As a consequence, the models for the accommodation of diversity existing in the Global South countries may be considered emergent in two respects: on the one hand, some of them are innovative in the sense that they have been introduced relatively recently; on the other, and more generally, they are to be considered as innovative since, given that they have been previously overlooked due to the monopoly of a specific standpoint on this topic, they essentially add a new dimension to the general theoretical discourse concerning the accommodation of diversity.

All these factors have, to various degrees, accounted for the emergence of several innovative models for the accommodation of diversity. The following paragraphs will be devoted to the analysis of the emerging macro-developments in this area, providing an overview of the innovative (international and) constitutional frameworks that have endorsed a renovated perspective on the accommodation of diversity.

The chapter will first delve into developments in the Global South, which are meant to enrich the vocabulary of constitutionalism through the creation of constitutional frameworks that include diversity in the very foundations of state structures. This is with the aim of displaying such tools and enlarging the global debate on diversity accommodation by taking into account traditions that are often overlooked by the Global North-driven approach to this topic in international law and academia. In other words, some Global South traditions and legal instruments are presented here as emergent models for the accommodation of diversity in a bid to extend the observation of this area of law and bolster the bilateral exchange between different regions of the world.

Afterward, attention will be drawn to the most innovative macro-perspectives in international soft law adopted in Europe. Notably, the macro-level developments are coupled with micro-level innovations in various parts of the Northern region of the world, which appear to follow (and, sometimes, go beyond) most of the innovative principles outlined in the soft law international regulations and will be dealt with in the next chapter.

All the perspectives presented here differ from the consolidated models stemming from liberal-democratic constitutionalism. As such, they complement it. The former does so from "outside" (to different degrees) in the sense that it introduces concepts, instruments, and practices widely unknown to or unpracticed in the Global North constitutional tradition. The latter does so mainly from "inside", complementing the existing corpus of minority and indigenous peoples' rights law and adapting legal responses to the challenge of diversity in contemporary times.

The methodological approach that will be taken follows the model of dynamic comparison described in the Introduction. Accordingly, the analysis will primarily focus on the innovative perspectives introduced within different constitutional traditions and then provide examples of how those instruments have been employed in model legal systems.

Innovative macro-perspectives

This section is meant to deal with some of the macro developments in the area of diversity accommodation that have occurred in several parts of the world over recent decades. The expression "macro-constitutional perspectives" is here intended to label all the developments that have directly or indirectly (at the international level) concerned the constitutional systems of several countries when it comes to the accommodation of diversity.

Accordingly, the analysis will first address constitutional traditions that comprehensively – or structurally – show a distinct and peculiar approach to the issue of diversity accommodation and add to the liberal-democratic model by including diversity and plurality in the basic structure of the state. Afterward, European developments, which are the result of a new season of soft law regulation, will be analyzed.

A Global South macro-perspective to diversity accommodation: emerging constitutional frameworks and their instruments for the accommodation of diversity

The scope of the analysis: emerging constitutional traditions in the Global South

Following the methodological approach described in the Introduction, the present section revolves around those regions of the Global South where a common tradition has emerged, made up of shared constitutional principles and approaches that, to different extents, diverge from the liberal-democratic tradition and integrate the global discourse on constitutionalism and diversity accommodation. Accordingly, in the next sections, the focus will be on the comprehensive constitutional traditions that characterize some regions of the world and introduce new foundational concepts, especially when it comes to the treatment and position of diversity in a constitutional system.

It must be noted that several countries in the Global South (and Global North) display creative constitutional models and instruments for the accommodation of diversity that resonate with the perspectives analyzed here. For instance, the existence and operation of legal pluralism, which is one of the characteristic elements of both the studied Global South traditions, features in several other legal systems of the world. In countries such as Israel,[5] Lebanon,[6] India,[7] South Africa,[8] Greece,[9] and the UK,[10] legal pluralist arrangements also operate in different – more or less formalized and legally entrenched – forms and with different scopes. Furthermore, several legal systems allow or tolerate a deep inclusion and recognition of diversity through flexible forms of accommodation – which constitutes another founding element of the macro-perspectives analyzed in this section. This is mainly the result of judicial activity, which is increasingly opening up room for cultural practices to be taken into account and recognized in concrete cases.[11]

5 For an overview of the Israeli legal pluralist arrangements for the management of its religious diversity and for further references, see Maoz, Asher, "The Application of Religious Law in a Multi-Religion Nation State: The Israeli Model", in Bottoni, Rossella, Cristofori, Rinaldo and Ferrari, Silvio (eds.), *Religious Rules, State Law, and Normative Pluralism: A Comparative Overview* (Springer, Cham, 2016), 209–227.

6 On the peculiar consociational system of Lebanon structured along religious lines, see Aboultaif, Eduardo W., *Power-Sharing in Lebanon: Consociationalism since 1820* (Routledge, London-New York, 2019).

7 On the complex personal law system in force in India (and other South Asian countries), see Ghosh, Partha S., *The Politics of Personal Law in South Asia: Identity, Nationalism and the Uniform Civil Code* (Routledge, London-New York, 2018); Menski, Werner, "Law, State and Culture: How Countries Accommodate Religious, Cultural and Ethnic Diversity, the British and Indian Experiences", in Foblets, Marie-Claire, Gaudreault-DesBiens, Jean-F. and Dundes Renteln, Alison (eds.), *Cultural Diversity and the Law: State Responses from Around the World* (Bruylant-Yvonne Blais, Bruxelles-Montréal, 2010), 403–446.

8 On the recognition of systems of personal and family law (allowed by Article 15 of the South African constitution), see Coertzen, Pieter, "Religion and the Constitutional Experience of South Africa", in Bottoni, Cristofori and Ferrari (eds.), Religious Rules . . . , 343–355; on the recognition and operation of customary law in South Africa, see Thandabantu, Nhlapo and Chuma, Himonga (eds.), *African Customary Law in South Africa: Post-Apartheid and Living Law Perspectives* (Oxford University Press, Southern Africa, Cape Town, 2014).

9 The Province of Western Thrace in Greece has official Sharia courts that render rulings on family law and inheritance: on this, see Akgönül, Samim, "Le statut personnel des musulmans de Grèce: vestiges ottomans et réalités contemporaines", in Aoun, Marc (ed.), *Les statuts personnels en droit comparé: évolutions récentes et implications pratiques* (Peeters, Leuven, 2009), 279–291; as indicated by Neo, Jacklyn L., "State Legal Pluralism and Religious Courts: Semi-Autonomy and Jurisdictional Allocations in Pluri-Legal Arrangements", in Berman, Paul S. (ed.), *The Oxford Handbook of Global Legal Pluralism* (Oxford University Press, Oxford, 2020), e-book version, 1628–1668, at 1633, the ruling *Molla Sali v Greece* (App. No. 20452/14 (2018)) has called this model into question, and the situation has partially "changed in January 2018 under a new law stating that Greek civil courts have priority in all cases and that recourse to Syariah law in cases of inheritance, divorce, or marriage can only apply if all parties agree"; for an overview of the ECHR jurisprudence concerning religious courts, see Rynkowski, Michael, *Religious Courts in the Jurisprudence of the European Court of Human Rights* (Brill, Leiden-Boston, 2019).

10 For a general overview of the existing "minority legal orders" in the UK, see Malik, Maleiha, *Minority Legal Orders in the UK: Minorities, Pluralism and the Law* (The British Academy, London, 2012); for more on legal pluralism in the UK, with a focus on the most innovative forms of accommodation, see Chapter 4; for a general perspective on legal pluralism in Europe, see Ferrari, Silvio, "Religiously Based Personal Laws and Management of Diversity in Europe", 25 *Law and Business* (2022), 1–15.

11 For a thorough study on the role of the judiciary when it comes to the accommodation of cultural diversity in Global North countries, see Ruggiu, Ilenia, *Culture and the Judiciary: The Anthropologist Judge* (Routledge, London-New York, 2019); for what concerns the Global South, and especially the role of the judiciary in Colombia, India and South Africa, see Bonilla Maldonado, Daniel (ed.), *Constitutionalism of the Global South: The Activist Tribunals of India, South Africa and Colombia* (Cambridge University Press, Cambridge, 2013).

This being said, the cases indicated below represent single models that do not offer findings that can systematically be applied to entire regions.[12] Consequently, they present interesting solutions but not general constitutional patterns.

By contrast, the regions studied below – South America and Southeast Asia – seem to display a common constitutional pattern that makes it possible to consider them as expressing new general regional traditions that integrate the liberal-democratic strand of constitutionalism, and, for this reason, they will be addressed in the next sections.

The South American constitutional perspective

From a macro-constitutional perspective, the South American continent displays some intriguing approaches to the management of diversity, especially concerning the accommodation of indigenous peoples' interests.

In general, most Latin American constitutional orders have paid increasing attention to (cultural) diversity – in particular, in the form of indigeneity – in recent decades. Indeed, since the end of 1980s, the region has witnessed a "multicultural turn", whereby a considerable number of countries have recognized and promoted their internal diversity through constitutional reform.[13]

Besides the few legal systems that do not mention indigenous peoples and their rights in their constitutions,[14] one can observe a vast range of approaches in the degree of protection and empowerment of those communities as well as the type of instruments utilized.

According to Bonilla Maldonado, it is possible to classify Latin American constitutions into two groups based on their approaches to the issue of diversity: Liberal constitutions and radical constitutions. Paradigmatic cases of

12 On the different position of legal pluralism in the European and Asian traditions, see Ferrari, Religiously Based Personal Laws . . . , 5–7.

13 Bonilla Maldonado, Daniel, "Multicultural Constitutions", in Mendes, Conrado H., Gargarella, Roberto and Guidi, Sebastián (eds.), *The Oxford Handbook of Constitutional Law in Latin America* (Oxford University Press, Oxford, 2022), 832–845, at 834; the "multicultural turn" is one of the elements that have marked the most recent evolution of the South American constitutional tradition, which has been labeled as the epoch of "neoconstitutionalism"; on this, see Pozzolo, Susanna, "Neoconstitucionalismo=Neoconstitutionalism", 11 *Eunomía: Revista en Cultura de la Legalidad* (2016), 142–151, who is the author credited with coining this concept; on the different strands of new constitutionalism – progressive neo-constitutionalism and radical neo-constitutionalism – and for further references, see De Domingo Soler, Carlos, "Brief Introduction of Andean Neoconstitutionalism for Europeans: Possibilities and Impossibilities", 9(1) *Ius Humani, Revista de Derecho* (2020), 9–44; Latin American constitutionalism is also related to another feature that is considered to be distinctive to Global South constitutional traditions, i.e., transformative constitutionalism: the concept was firstly employed to describe the South African constitution and was originally defined by Klare, Karl E., "Legal Culture and Transformative Constitutionalism", 14(1) *South African Journal on Human Rights* (1998), 146–188, at 150: "By transformative constitutionalism I mean a long-term project of constitutional enactment, interpretation, and enforcement committed . . . to transforming a country's political and social institutions and power relationships in a democratic, participatory, and egalitarian direction"; see also Langa, Pius, "Transformative Constitutionalism", 17(3) *Stellenbosch Law Review* (2006), 351–360.

14 This is the case with Belize, Chile, Costa Rica, Cuba, the Dominican Republic, Puerto Rico, Suriname, and Uruguay.

liberal constitutions are those of Brazil, Colombia, and Paraguay,[15] while the Bolivian and Ecuadorian (and, to a lesser extent, the Venezuelan) constitutions have been framed as radical constitutions.

While both categories are informed by modern concepts of liberal constitutionalism, the countries falling into the latter show some elements that distance them from this tradition in two respects. First, not only have they recognized (cultural) diversity, but their systems have been entirely designed to include it in their core constitutional structure. Second, and related to that, their constitutions contain some concepts and principles that go beyond the traditional grammar of liberal constitutionalism.[16]

The following paragraph will deal with radical constitutions, which appear to offer the most innovative perspectives regarding diversity accommodation.

BOLIVIA AND ECUADOR: PLURINATIONALITY AND INTERCULTURALISM AS REVOLUTIONARY AND TRANSFORMATIVE CONSTITUTIONAL PRINCIPLES

The constitutions of Bolivia and Ecuador – with the former generally considered the most innovative and implemented case – present some features that complement the traditional contents of liberal-democratic constitutionalism.

To begin with, both constitutional orders have introduced the concept of plurinationality as a fundamental element of their constitutional identities.[17] Besides its symbolic value as a decolonization hallmark,[18] this notion is particularly innovative from a constitutional standpoint in that it is supposed to describe a constitutional order that not only recognizes but is structured to

15 Argentina, Costa Rica, El Salvador, Guatemala, Honduras, Mexico, Nicaragua, Panama, Peru, Paraguay, and Venezuela follow the same model; for an analysis of the different degrees of constitutional recognition of cultural diversity and indigeneity in those countries, see Aguilar, Gonzalo, Lafosse, Sandra, Rojas, Hugo and Steward, Rébecca, "The Constitutional Recognition of Indigenous Peoples in Latin America", 2(2) *Pace International Law Review Online Companion* (2010), 44–96.

16 On this, see Bonilla Maldonado, Multicultural Constitutions . . . , 834–845.

17 In particular, the plurinational character of the Bolivian state – already stated in the Preamble – is explicitly affirmed in Article 1, and its content is specified by Article 98, first period: "Cultural diversity constitutes the essential basis of the Pluri-National Communitarian State" (Estado Unitario Social de Derecho Plurinacional Comunitario); see, also, Article 30, para. II, no. 5, which affirms the rights of indigenous peoples and that their institutions are part of the general structure of the State; the Ecuadorian constitution is evidently marked by the principle of plurinationality (precisely, the term used is plurinationalism), even though it appears only three times in the constitutional text: in Article 6, on the Ecuadorian nationality, described as "a political and legal bond between individuals and the State, without detriment to their belonging to any of the other indigenous nations that coexist in plurinational Ecuador"; in Article 257, on indigenous autonomies, which must be "governed by the principles of interculturalism and plurinationalism"; and in Article 380, where it is stated that the state is responsible for protecting the Ecuadorian cultural heritage "that constitute the plurinational, pluricultural and multiethnic identity of Ecuador"; on this, see Tushnet, Mark, "The New 'Bolivarian' Constitutions: A Textual Analysis", in Dixon, Rosalind and Ginsburg, Tom (eds.), *Comparative Constitutional Law in Latin America* (Edward Elgar, Cheltenham-Northampton, 2017), 126–152.

18 On this, see Schavelzon, Salvador, *El nacimiento del Estado plurinacional de Bolivia: etnografía de una asamblea constituyente* (Plural editores, La Paz, 2012), esp. 8, 10 and 53.

institutionally incorporate diversity (in terms of cultural communities).[19] As a result, a renewed conception of the state is put forward. This implies considering it as an entity composed of several communities and legal orders of equal standing under a common constitutional framework. In other words, plurinational constitutionalism envisages a constitutionally endorsed pluralization of legal sources, institutions, and, more generally, governance systems in the same political space that leads to the demise of an exclusively state-centered system of production of legal norms.[20]

Introducing plurinationality as a core constitutional element denotes a clear shift toward a renewed conception of the state that distances itself from the traditional liberal-democratic perspective observable in most Global North countries, as well as the previous approaches to the indigenous question on the South American continent.[21] Despite their differences, the latter, when designing legal tools for the accommodation of diversity, are ultimately informed by liberal categories that strongly accent rights discourse and/or the reproduction of the nation-state model when autonomous arrangements are foreseen.

By contrast, the radical constitutions of South America lay the foundations for state organizations that accord indigenous (and possibly other) communities a position of equal dignity to other groups in the countries and value their active role. An understanding of them as subjects of legal empowerment rather than objects of legal protection is emphasized. This results in constitutional systems that display (partially) inclusive, empowering, and governance-driven features.

These constitutions are (partially) inclusive in that both provide for broad descriptions of their national communities and consequently extend the tools

19 Schilling-Vacaflor Almut and Kuppe, René, "Plurinational Constitutionalism: A New Era of Indigenous-State Relations?", in Nolte, Detlef and Schilling-Vacaflor, Almut (eds.), *New Constitutionalism in Latin America: Promises and Practices* (Routledge, London-New York, 2016), e-book version, 538–574, at 545, have stated that "The reasons for assuming that a new era of indigenous-state relations in Bolivia and Ecuador may be emerging are that the new constitutions establish plurinational states by conceiving of indigenous peoples and institutions as transversal dimensions of the whole state structure".

20 On the concept of plurinationality as a nation-building project and a defining element of a (at least partly) renewed plural conception of the state, see Àvila Santamaria, Ramiro, *El neoconstitucionalismoa andino* (Universidad Andina Simón Bolivar, Sede Ecuador and Huaponi Ediciones, Quito, 2016); Llasag Fernández, Raúl, "Plurinacionalidad: una propuesta constitucional emancipadora", in Ávila Santamaría, Ramiro (ed.), *Neoconstitucionalismo y sociedad* (Ministerio de la Justicia y Derechos Humanos, Quito, 2008), 311–355, at 336–340; Salazar, Daniela, "Ecuador", in Mendes, Gargarella and Guidi (eds.), The Oxford Handbook . . . , 174–202, at 181–182; Walsh, Catherine, "The Plurinational and Intercultural State: Decolonization and State Re-founding in Ecuador", 1 *RUDN Journal of Philosophy* (2012), 103–115.

21 On the previous approaches to governing diversity and indigenous peoples' rights on the American continent, see Ramírez, Silvina and Maisley, Nahuel, "The Protection of the Rights of Indigenous Peoples", in Gonzalez-Bartomeu, Juan F. and Gargarella, Roberto (eds.), *The Latin American Casebook: Courts, Constitutions, and Rights* (Routledge, London-New York, 2016), 189–208, at 189–192.

for the accommodation of diversity to groups besides indigenous peoples, i.e., the communities that have traditionally been targeted by those instruments.

Article 56 of the Ecuadorian constitution affirms that: "Indigenous communities, peoples and nations, the Afro-Ecuadorian people, the back-country people (*montubios*) of the inland coastal region, and communes are part of the single and indivisible Ecuadorian State". In addition, Articles 57–60 protect the rights of those communities and allow them to create self-governing territorial entities for the preservation of their culture.

Bolivia's plurinational and inclusive stance first emerges from Article 3, which states that: "The Bolivian nation is formed by all Bolivians, the native indigenous nations and peoples, and the inter-cultural and Afro-Bolivian communities that, together, constitute the Bolivian people". In addition, Article 5 of the constitution recognizes 37 official languages (Spanish and 36 indigenous peoples' languages) and, according to Article 32, extends its instruments for the accommodation of diversity provided for indigenous peoples (that are listed in Articles 30–31 and further specified in other articles) to the Afro-Bolivian people.[22] Furthermore, several articles of the constitution include other groups, i.e., intercultural or rural communities, among the addressees of protective or empowering measures.[23]

Hence, both constitutions appear to be (partially) inclusive as they extend the reach of the tools for the accommodation of indigenous peoples' needs to other communities (i.e., culturally diverse black communities). This implies an open approach to the concept of diversity and a willingness to recognize and include all the groups that compose the two societies in the constitutional framework. In a way, the Ecuadorian and Bolivian experiences seem to corroborate the relativity of exclusive definitions when it comes to diversity accommodation, as well as the potential "exportability" of models in favor of groups that are not traditional addressees.

22 Article 32, Bolivian constitution: "The Afro-Bolivian people enjoy, in everything corresponding, the economic, social, political and cultural rights that are recognized in the Constitution for the nations and the rural native indigenous peoples".

23 Article 100, para. II, Bolivian constitution: "The State shall protect this wisdom and knowledge through the registration of the intellectual property that safeguards the intangible rights of the nations and rural native indigenous peoples and of the intercultural and Afro-Bolivian communities"; Article 218, para. II, Bolivian constitution: "The Public Defender shall also promote the defense of the rights of the nations and rural native indigenous peoples, of urban and intercultural communities, and of Bolivians who are abroad"; Article 394, para. III, Bolivian constitution: "The State recognizes, protects and guarantees communitarian or collective property, which includes rural native indigenous territory, native, intercultural communities and rural communities . . ."; Article 395, para. I: "The lands that are taken over shall be given to rural native indigenous peoples, intercultural indigenous communities, Afro-Bolivian and rural communities, which do not possess them or have insufficient lands, in accordance with state policy concerned with the ecological and geographic realities, as well as the population, social, cultural and economic necessities".

Besides that, the Ecuadorian and Bolivian constitutions (especially the latter) are empowering and governance-driven in the following terms.

To begin with, territorial autonomy is an important tool that is directly recognized by the analyzed constitutions. Nevertheless, it differentiates itself from the liberal-democratic structure in at least three respects, which contributes to making this tool rather flexible and adaptable to the needs of the relevant communities.

Firstly, autonomous arrangements for indigenous peoples are mainly characterized by a bottom-up dynamic, whereby protected communities are entitled to activate forms of constitutionally guaranteed self-governance at different levels through popular consultations or referenda,[24] even if these may be subject to (stronger or weaker) limits and forms of state control.[25] Moreover, autonomous instruments are varied and flexible in the sense that several paths to autonomy are provided for by the constitutions.[26] Notably,

24 Articles 245 and 257, Ecuadorian constitution, and Article 290, Bolivian constitution.

25 Regarding Bolivia, autonomous indigenous entities can be created only in what is referred to as "ancestral lands", and this is a prerequisite that is under governmental control. This is confirmed by the General Decentralization Law (Article 56, para. I), even if some authors have remarked that it could be possible for indigenous majorities to convert a city they inhabit into an indigenous autonomous community. Moreover, the statutes of the indigenous entities are put under the scrutiny of the *Tribunal Constitucional Pluricultural* (TPC), which must certify their compliance with constitutional law; on this, see Barrios, Franz, "The Bolivian Invention: Plurinationality and Indigenous People within an Unusual Composite State Structure", in Requejo, Ferran and Caminal, Miquel (eds.), *Federalism, Plurinationality and Democratic Constitutionalism: Theory and Cases* (Routledge, London-New York, 2012), e-book version, 436–482, at 451–460; Colque Fernández, Gonzalo, *Autonomías indígenas en las tierras altas* (Instituto Internacional para la Democracia y la Asistencia Electoral (IDEA), La Paz, 2009), 28; Ecuador can be seen as less innovative in this regard, as confirmed by Martínez Novo, Carmen, "Managing Diversity in Postneoliberal Ecuador", 19(1) *The Journal of Latin American and Caribbean Anthropology* (2014), 103–125.

26 As described by Barrios, The Bolivian Invention . . . , 453–454, the constitution (Articles 289–296) and the General Decentralization Law in Bolivia foresee three paths to access autonomy for indigenous peoples (and other protected communities): the first implies the transformation of an indigenous communitarian land (*tierras comunitarias de origen*, TCO), which is legally recognized as a collective land property, into a full-fledged self-governing territory; the second is the conversion of a municipality into an indigenous municipality (which, in Bolivia, is entitled to lawmaking powers); the third is the consolidation of indigenous regions by the aggregation of municipalities; in Ecuador, Article 257 of the constitution states that within "the framework of political-administrative organization, indigenous or Afro-Ecuadorian territorial districts may be formed. These shall have jurisdiction over the respective autonomous territorial government and shall be governed by the principles of interculturalism and plurinationalism, and in accordance with collective rights", and that "parishes, cantons and provinces comprised in their majority by indigenous, Afro-Ecuadorian, coastal back-country (Montubio) or ancestral communities, peoples or nations may take up this special administration system following a referendum passed by at least two-thirds"; interestingly, the Organic Code of Territorial Organization, Autonomy and Decentralization of 2010 has also foreseen different forms of autonomy: besides the conversion of already existing territorial entities (according to Chapter II of the law), the communities that are not able to follow this path can exercise their self-government rights on ancestral lands in accordance with the territorial entity where they reside (Article 97); on this, see Schilling-Vacaflor and Kuppe, Plurinational Constitutionalism . . . , 554–557.

in Bolivia, indigenous autonomy systems may also be created by two or more communities together.[27]

As a result, this territorial organization engenders the creation of unitary composite states based on an asymmetric and dynamic structure that is different from the classic regional and federal ones, thus appearing to introduce a novel element to the territorial organization of states.[28]

Secondly, indigenous autonomy follows its own rules and procedures, which may deviate considerably from those designed by the state for its institutions.[29] For instance, the rules concerning the election or appointment of the indigenous autonomies' governing bodies are defined by the communities themself based on their traditions.[30]

Notably, autonomy is not the only tool of empowerment for indigenous peoples in Bolivia and Ecuador. Both countries have designed (at least at the constitutional level) complex and comprehensive governance systems – which echo the most developed international standards in the area of indigenous rights law – that envisage other guaranteed forms of active participation and self-rule. These manifest as a. communal (property and other) rights over traditionally indigenous territories,[31] b. consent of indigenous peoples when it comes to decisions that affect their interests and, especially, the exploitation of natural resources existing on their traditional lands,[32] and c. forms of legal pluralism in terms of indigenous legal and judicial systems. These mechanisms are set to function regardless of the existence of institutionalized forms of self-government.

As hinted above, a notable manifestation of the plurinational logic of the analyzed South American countries is the constitutional recognition of

27 Article 291, para. II, Bolivian constitution.

28 As affirmed by Barrios, The Bolivian Invention . . . , 449–450.

29 On this, see Article 296 of the Bolivian constitution: "The government of the rural native indigenous autonomies is exercised through their own norms and forms of organization, with the name that corresponds to each town, nation or community, as established in their statutes and subject to the Constitution and the law". This is not explicitly stated by the Ecuadorian constitution; however, this does state that the indigenous governments should be informed by the principles of plurinationalism and interculturalism; the Organic Code of Territorial Organization, Autonomy and Decentralization states that the indigenous government shall be governed according to the customs of the relevant communities (Article 93).

30 This is explicitly stated, for instance, in the Bolivian constitution, in Article 11, para. II, where it is affirmed that democracy is exercised in several forms: direct and participatory (Article 11, para. II, no. 1), representative (Article 11, para. II, no. 2) and communal (Article 11, para. II, no. 3), the last one meaning "by means of the election, designation or nomination of the authorities and representatives pursuant to the norms and procedures of the native indigenous nations and peoples, among others, in accordance with the law".

31 Article 57, para. II, nos. 4 and 5, Ecuadorian constitution and Article 30, para. II, nos. 4 and 6; on this, see Saffon, Maria Paula, "Property and Land", in Mendes, Gargarella and Guidi (eds.), The Oxford Handbook . . . , 578–597.

32 Article 30, para. II, no. 15, Bolivian constitution and Article 57, para. I, no. 7 and Article 57, para. I, no. 6 Ecuadorian constitution; however, the implementation of this right has been rather troublesome; on the Bolivian case, see Tomaselli, Alexandra, *Indigenous Peoples and Their Right to Political Participation* (Nomos, Baden-Baden, 2016), 332–351; on Ecuador, see Vela-Almeida, Diana and Torres, Nataly, "Consultation in Ecuador: Institutional Fragility and Participation in National Extractive Policy", 48(3) *Latin American Perspectives* (2021), 172–191.

indigenous legal and judicial systems. Both constitutions acknowledge the existence of indigenous normative orders as well as the right to practice indigenous law and (partly) directly regulate it.

Once more, Bolivia seems to show a much more comprehensive (and innovative) system.[33] In this country – which is defined by Article 1 as being founded on linguistic, cultural, economic, political, and legal pluralism – indigenous law has the same hierarchical status as ordinary law,[34] and the right to apply indigenous law is affirmed both as a general right and as a right that can be exercised in the indigenous autonomies.[35] Notably, traditional indigenous justice is included in the unitary judicial system as one of its pillars.[36]

In Ecuador, which is referred to by Article 1 as an "*Estado de derechos*",[37] the constitution entitles indigenous peoples to create, develop, and exercise their own laws within their legally recognized or traditionally inhabited territories.[38] Unlike Bolivia, indigenous law does not enjoy equal status with state law. The bodies of indigenous justice are not considered as part of the judicial branch but as special entities.[39]

In both countries, indigenous legal systems must respect the human rights provided for by the constitutions,[40] and the decisions of indigenous judicial entities are to be enforced by all public authorities.[41] In this regard, both constitutions specifically affirm the need to establish mechanisms of coordination among ordinary and indigenous courts.[42] Moreover, indigenous justice can

33 On this, see Barrera, Anna, "Turning Legal Pluralism into State-Sanctioned Law: Assessing the Implications of the New Constitutions and Laws in Bolivia and Ecuador", in Nolte and Schilling-Vacaflor (eds.), New Constitutionalism in Latin America . . . , 575–604.

34 See Bolivian constitution, Article 179, paras. I and II; *Ley del Órgano Judicial* (LOJ), Article 4; *Ley Orgánica de Delimitación Jurisdiccional* (LODJ), Article 3.

35 See Bolivian constitution, Articles 30, para. II, no. 14, 190, para. I, 289, 304, para. I, no. 8.

36 Article 179, Bolivian constitution; see Barrera, Turning Legal Pluralism . . . , 578.

37 For a thorough analysis of the meaning of this expression, and its relationship with the concept of legal pluralism, see Ávila Santamaría, Ramiro, "Ecuador Estado constitucional de derechos y justicia", in Ávila Santamaría, Ramiro (ed.), *La Constitución del 2008 en el contexto andino: análisis desde la doctrina y el derecho comparado* (Ministerio de Justicia y Derechos Humano, Quito, 2008), 19–38.

38 Article 57, para. I, nos. 9–10 and Article 171, Ecuadorian constitution.

39 Barrera, Turning Legal Pluralism . . . , 581–584 and the Organic Law on the Judicial Branch (*Código Orgánico de la Función Judicial*, COFJ) of 2009.

40 Article 191, para. II, Bolivian constitution; Articles 57, no. 10 and 171, Ecuadorian constitution.

41 Article 192, para. I, Bolivian constitution and Article 12 of the LODJ; Articles 76, para. I, no. 7 and 171, Ecuadorian constitution.

42 As seen, in Bolivia, this has been done through the adoption of the LOJ and LODJ; in Ecuador, only few provisions of the COFJ and the *Ley Orgánica de Garantías Jurisdiccionales y Control Constitucióñal* (LOGJCC) address this issue, while different proposals for a Law of Coordination and Cooperation between Indigenous and Ordinary Justice (*Proyecto Ley Orgánica de Coordinación y Cooperación entre la Jurisdicción Indígena y la Jurisdicción Ordinaria*, hereafter PLOCCJIJO) have been drafted, but no specific law on this matter has been approved so far; on this, and on the contents of the drafts, see Vintimilla Saldaña, Jaime, *Ley orgánica de cooperación y coordinación entre la justicia indígena y la jurisdicción ordinaria ecuatoriana: ¿Un mandato constitucional necesario o una norma que limita a los sistemas de justicia indígena?* (Cevallos, Quito, 2012).

only be exercised when personal, material, and territorial conditions are met. Accordingly, those systems are applied only to members of the indigenous peoples,[43] regulate only some matters (generally connected to cultural issues), and their scope is limited to some geographic areas. Consequently, they are not enforceable on a personal basis based on membership in indigenous communities regardless of territory.[44] These delimitations of the scope of indigenous justice have been described as problematic in several respects and have contributed to hindering the implementation of the constitutional provisions, especially in Ecuador.[45]

In addition, the constitutions of Bolivia and Ecuador explicitly value and encourage the principle of interculturalism, which, like plurinationality, is expected to inform their legal systems in their entirety and function as a guiding principle for state organization and activity.[46]

In the analyzed constitutional systems, interculturalism implies a non-exclusivist approach to (cultural) diversity that demands the establishment of measures and policies intended to foster coexistence, communication, and reciprocal understanding among the different components of their diverse societies.[47]

Consequently, the principle urges the inclusion of multiple viewpoints in mainstream institutions. In other words, if plurinationality emphasizes and seeks to promote diversity in unity (and in particular, the plural organization of the state in terms of territorial and legal pluralism), interculturalism fosters

43 Even though the PLOCCJIJO, in its first version, stated that indigenous bodies' jurisdictions would cover cases involving non-indigenous peoples that have committed acts against indigenous peoples in their territories (Articles 18–19).

44 However, the LODJ, Article 5–6, establishes that indigenous jurisdiction can be exercised with regard to acts committed outside the indigenous territories that affect the interest of indigenous peoples.

45 On this, see Barrera, Turning Legal Pluralism . . . , 584–588; Boaventura de Sousa, Santos and Grijalva Jiménez, Agustín (eds.), *Justicia indígena, plurinacionalidad e interculturalidad en Ecuador* (Abya Yala-Fundación Rosa Luxembourg, Quito, 2012); Boaventura de Sousa, Santos and Exeni Rodríguez, José Luis (eds.), *Justicia indígena, plurinacionalidad e interculturalidad en Bolivia* (Abya Yala-Fundación Rosa Luxembourg, Quito, 2012).

46 This is especially the case in the Ecuadorian constitution, where the principle of interculturalism is explicitly affirmed numerous times, specifically, with regard to: the definition of the Ecuadorian state (Article 1), rights to information and communication (Article 16), mainstream and indigenous education (Articles 27, 28, 57, no. 14, 343, 347, no. 9), the management of the healthcare system (Articles 32, 358), democratic participation (Article 95), the national equality councils (Article 156), the electoral branch of government (Article 217), territorial organisation of the state and indigenous autonomy (Articles 249, 257), the achievement of the development system based on the concept of *buen vivír* (Article 275), social rights and their implementation (Article 340), habitat and housing (Article 375), the national system for culture (Article 378), Latin American integration (Article 423, no. 4).

47 On this, see Walsh, Catherine, The Plurinational and Intercultural State . . . , with considerations that can be applied to both countries; for thorough analysis of the concept and its implications, see Boaventura de Sousa and Grijalva Jiménez, (eds.), Justicia indígena, plurinacionalidad e interculturalidad en Ecuador . . . , and Boaventura de Sousa and Exeni Rodríguez, (eds.), Justicia indígena, plurinacionalidad e interculturalidad en Bolivia . . .

unity in diversity.[48] Thus, interculturalism requires the representation of indigenous peoples and other communities in state political bodies, as well as the incorporation of their cultural, legal, economic, and political perspectives in the foundational constitutional structure and other mainstream institutions like the judiciary,[49] healthcare system,[50] and school.[51]

As for the constitutional inclusion of indigenous views, both constitutions do include principles and values stemming from indigenous traditions, like the principles of *Sumka Kawsay* (a good way of living) in Ecuador and *Suma qamaña* (living well) in Bolivia. This implies a specific global approach to social and economic development that shies away from the capitalistic logic of accumulation.[52] Additionally, the introduction of the very same principles of plurinationality and interculturalism stems from the claims of indigenous movements during the constituent process.[53]

Lastly, both principles seem to underpin the substantial democratic innovations that these legal systems provide for, aimed at fostering citizens' – and especially non-majority and marginalized groups' – participation.[54]

48 Grijalva Jiménez, Agustín, "Del presente se inventa el futuro: justicias indígenas y estado en Ecuador", in Boaventura de Sousa and Grijalva Jiménez (eds.), Justicia indígena, plurinacionalidad e interculturalidad en Ecuador . . . , 51–76, esp. at 73–74, where the author highlighted the complementarity between the two concepts.

49 This is done in two ways: by fostering the representation of people with an indigenous background and by providing that ordinary (and constitutional) justice respects indigenous justice as well as takes into account its principles and values; on this, and on the (partial) implementation of interculturalism in the judicial branch, Barrera, Turning Legal Pluralism . . . , 588–591.

50 Article 358, Ecuadorian constitution; Articles 18, 30, para. II, no. 13, 35, para. II, Bolivian constitution.

51 Article 57, para. I, no. 14, Ecuadorian constitution; Articles 30, para. II, no. 12, 77, 78, 79, 80, 90, para. III, 91, 93, 95, 96, Bolivian constitution.

52 On this, see Acosta, Alberto, *El Buen Vivir: Sumak Kawsay, una oportunidad para imaginar otros mundos* (Abya-Yala, Quito, 2012); Pacari, Nina, "Naturaleza y territorio desde la mirada de los pueblos indigenas", in Acosta, Alberto and Martinez, Esperanza (eds.), *Derechos de la naturaleza: el futuro es ahora* (Abya-Yala, Quito, 2009), 129–132; Chassagne, Natasha, *Buen Vivir as an Alternative to Sustainable Development: Lessons from Ecuador* (Routledge, London-New York, 2021); Schavelzon, Salvador, *Plurinacionalidad y Vivir Bien/Buen Vivir: dos conceptos leídos desde Bolivia y Ecuador post-constituyentes* (Abya Yala, Quito, 2019).

53 On this, and for further references, see Merino, Roger, "Reimagining the Nation-State: Indigenous Peoples and the Making of Plurinationalism in Latin America", 31(4) *Leiden Journal of International Law* (2018), 773–792.

54 The presence of fascinating models of democratic innovation is not limited to these two countries on the South American continent; some democratic innovations appear particularly conducive to the emergence of the views of minority groups, such as in Brazil (although this model has been discontinued during Bolsonaro's presidency); on this, see Pogrebinschi, Thamy, "Turning Participation into Representation Innovative Policy Making for Minority Groups in Brazil", in Girouard, Jennifer (ed.), *Varieties of Civic Innovation: Deliberative, Collaborative, Network, and Narrative Approaches* (Vanderbilt University Press, Nashville, 2014), e-book version, 321–365.

Article 11 of the Bolivian Constitution defines Bolivia as a "*participatory*, representative, and communal democracy". Accordingly, plurinational councils of culture, health boards, and urban planning and development councils have been established at the local, regional, and national levels, creating the conditions necessary for citizens and groups to define policy agendas autonomously. Furthermore, management committees composed of self-appointed citizens have also diffused to manage access to water, deliver sanitary services, conduct rural and communal education, and regulate the use of natural resources.[55]

Ecuador's new Constitution puts a strong emphasis on participation and encourages democratic innovation, together with the Social Participation Law of 1997 and the Decentralization and Social Participation Law of 2010. Participatory forms of democracy are structured as a "multilevel policy-making system"[56] of Equality Councils and Citizen Participation and Social Monitoring Councils. At the national level, three main institutions contribute to setting the strategic goals and governmental guidelines of each policy area: the National Council for the Equality of Peoples and Nationalities (*Consejo Nacional para la Igualdad de Pueblos y Nacionalidades*), the Plurinational and Intercultural Citizen Assembly for Good Living (*Asamblea Ciudadana Plurinacional e Intercultural para el Buen Vivir*), and the Plurinational and Intercultural Conference on Food Sovereignty (*Conferencia Plurinacional e Intercultural de Soberanía Alimentaria*).[57]

Of course, the implementation of the two radical Latin American constitutions is far from complete and has suffered several setbacks. In addition, both legal systems provide broad (and, in the case of Bolivia, very broad[58]) measures for the accommodation of diversity that resonate with the more traditional

55 Pogrebinschi, Thamy and Ros, Melisa, "Democratic Innovations in Latin America", in Elstub, Stephen and Escobar, Oliver (eds.), *Handbook of Democratic Innovation and Governance* (Edward Elgar, Cheltenham-Northampton, 2019), 389–403, at 398.

56 Ibid., 398.

57 Ibid., 398.

58 For instance, the Bolivian constitution provides for several channels of indigenous peoples' representation in numerous state bodies at all levels; in fact, two out of seven constitutional judges must self-identify as indigenous (Law 027 of 2010 on the Plurinational Constitutional Tribunal); the new electoral law gave seven seats to indigenous peoples who represent minorities in their respective departments (Article 57, para. II, Law 026 of 2010 on the Electoral Regime); a minimum of two of the seven members of the Supreme Electoral Court (Tribunal Supremo Electoral, TSE), and one of the five members of the Departmental Electoral Tribunal must be of indigenous origin (Articles 12 and 33, para. II, Law 030 of 2010 on the Plurinational Electoral Organ, *Organo Electoral Plurinational*, OEP); for what concerns the Plurinational Legislative Assembly, seven seats are reserved to indigenous representatives: on this, and on the role of indigenous organizations, which can nominate candidates for the reserved indigenous seats according to their customary norms and procedures, see Barié, Cletus Gregor, "Representation of Indigenous Peoples in Times of Progressive Governments: Lessons Learned from Bolivia", 17(2) *Latin American and Caribbean Ethnic Studies* (2022), 167–192.

(liberal) ones,[59] to the point that some authors have underlined the unresolved issue of how to balance the "two souls" (multicultural and pluricultural) of those constitutional orders.[60]

Furthermore, it has been pointed out that although such constitutional systems offer very innovative perspectives on the accommodation of diversity, at the same time, they seem to be conducive to strengthening centralizing and populist forces – traditionally characterized in a macro-regional context by a hyper-presidentialist turn in the forms of government – that may discourage the full realization of their "revolutionary" potential. For instance, the slow and cumbersome path of activation of the autonomous arrangements for indigenous peoples (particularly visible in Ecuador),[61] the operationalization of the right of prior consultation,[62] and the implementation of the systems of indigenous justice testify to such difficulties.

At the same time, it seems worth taking these models into account, as they have advanced innovations in the vocabulary of constitutionalism and offer concepts and solutions that are clearly of interest from a comparative constitutional perspective. This includes the concept of plurinationality, which is the foundation of every aspect of the analyzed constitutional systems and holds revolutionary potential. That is, the potential to create a state structure based on constitutionalism, which breaks down the traditional symbioses between constitutionalism and the nation-state and between law and state law.

Moreover, plurinationality has an inclusive potential – even broader than its actual application – and, complemented by the principle of interculturalism, engenders a non-isolationist and integrationist approach to the issue of diversity accommodation. This echoes the recent European developments that will be described below.

59 Interestingly, both constitutions devote several specific provisions to the protection of the rights of some social groups like the elderly, women (and pregnant women), children, adolescents, and people with disabilities.

60 On this, with considerations that are also applicable to the Ecuadorian case, see Barrantes-Reynolds, Maria-Paula, *Legal Pluralism in the Constitution of Bolivia of 2009: Between Multiculturalism and Plurinationalism* (PhD dissertation, University of Leicester, Leicester, 2016).

61 On this, see Schilling-Vacaflor and Kuppe, Plurinational Constitutionalism . . . , 558–565; Tockman, Jason and Cameron, John, "Indigenous Autonomy and the Contradictions of Plurinationalism in Bolivia", 56(3) *Latin American Politics and Society* (2014), 46–69; Englert, Franziska and Schaub-Englert, Jonathan, "A Fruitless Attempt Towards Plurinationality and Decolonization? Perplexities in the Creation of Indigenous Territorial Autonomies in Bolivia", 52(1) *VRÜ Verfassung und Recht in Übersee* (2019), 67–89; Ortiz Tirado, Pablo, "El laberinto de la autonomía indígena en el Ecuador: las circunscripciones territoriales indígenas en la amazonía central, 2010–2012", 10(1) *Latin American and Caribbean Ethnic Studies* (2015), 60–86.

62 On this, see Wright, Claire and Tomaselli, Alexandra (eds.), *The Prior Consultation of Indigenous Peoples in Latin America: Inside the Implementation Gap* (Routledge, London-New York, 2020); Gargarella, Roberto, "Equality", in Dixon and Ginsburg (eds.), Comparative Constitutional Law . . . , 176–197, at 194–197.

However, unlike the latter region, the South American perspective engenders a strong role for constitutional reform as a method to advance and consolidate new models for the accommodation of diversity – complemented by the activity of constitutional courts.[63] This goes along with a very open and porous relationship between constitutional and international law, as is particularly evident in the jurisprudence of the Inter-American court of human rights.[64] Regardless of the weaknesses related to its limited implementation, the transformational use of the constitution and the revision of the concept of the nation – with all the implications that have been described above – is doubtlessly a method for setting new standards for diversity management that may be of interest even for other parts of the world. This opens the possibility of inverting the traditional direction of circulation of legal models.[65]

The Southeast Asian constitutional perspective: pluralist constitutions focus on interests rather than rights, and legal pluralism

PLURALIST CONSTITUTIONALISM IN SOUTHEAST ASIA AS A NEW LEGITIMATE LAYER IN THE GLOBAL CONSTITUTIONAL DISCOURSE

Another region of much interest to this work is Southeast Asia. This region is here considered to include all the countries that make up the Association of Southeast Asian Nations (ASEAN), i.e., Brunei, Cambodia, Indonesia, Laos, Malaysia, Myanmar, Philippines, Singapore, Thailand, and Vietnam. It is one of the most diverse regions in the world, hosting a vast range of diversity in terms of language, culture, religion, and ideology.

As in other parts of the Global South, the concepts of minority and indigenous peoples are not consolidated in political and legal discourses. The

63 On the transformational role of the constitutional courts of Bolivia and Ecuador, especially as concerns the implementation of the principles of plurinationality and interculturalism, see Boaventura de Sousa, Santos, "Cuando los excluidos tienen derecho: justicia indígena, plurinacionalidad e interculturalidad", in Boaventura de Sousa and Grijalva Jiménez (eds.), Justicia Indígena, Plurinacionalidad e Interculturalidad en Ecuador . . . , 13–50, at 38; Bagni, Silvia, "Il ruolo delle Corti costituzionali tra pluralismo giuridico, plurinazionalità e interculturalità", available at the following link: https://www.robertotoniatti.eu/contributi/il-ruolo-delle-corti-costituzionali-tra-pluralismo-giuridico-plurinazionalita-e-interculturalita.

64 On this, see section III of Von Bogdandy, Armin, Ferrer Mac-Gregor, Eduardo, Antoniazzi Morales, Mariela, Piovesan Flávia and Soley, Ximena (eds.), *Transformative Constitutionalism in Latin America: The Emergence of a New Ius Commune* (Oxford University Press, Oxford, 2017), 279–408; on the successes and the setbacks of the Inter-American system of human rights, see Huneeus, Alexandra, "The Limits of Inter-American Constitutionalism", in Dixon and Ginsburg (eds.), Comparative Constitutional Law . . . , 300–324.

65 On this, see Pegoraro, Lucio, "Comparare l'America Latina (e in America Latina): introduzione critica", in Bagni, Silvia e Baldin, Serena (eds.), *Latinoamérica: viaggio nel costituzionalismo comparato dalla Patagonia al Río Grande* (Giappichelli, Turin, 2022), 3–15; see also Toniatti, Roberto, "Il paradigma costituzionale dell'inclusione della diversità culturale in Europa e in America Latina: premesse per una ricerca comparata sui rispettivi modelli", (6) *The Pluralist Papers* (2015), available at the following link: http://www.jupls.eu/images/JPs_WP6_RT__paradigma_costituzionale_dellinclusione_culturale.pdf.

position of non-dominant groups, therefore, shifts between different classifications depending on the options available in any given country. In general, as is to be expected, the more the countries have endorsed a liberal-democratic constitutional structure and participated in UN mechanisms, the more those concepts appear to be present and employed both legally and politically.[66]

However, regardless of their proximity to liberal-democratic constitutional discourse and concepts, the Southeast Asian countries have been considered to express a tradition that has many peculiar traits when compared to the Global North. Observers should, therefore, be urged to shy away from simplistic comparisons based on concepts mostly stemming from a Western standpoint. The Southeast Asian regional approach to diversity issues appears to offer an intriguing perspective that relies on a comprehensive constitutional tradition that has developed its own recognizable features. Notably, this may add to the existing discourse over diversity accommodation, as it embeds and fosters the employment of instruments such as legal pluralism that, while also present to a limited extent in Global North countries, are often overlooked and understudied by scholars and certainly not framed as general theoretical models in this area of study.

If the constitutions of Latin America appear to show a deep inclusion of diversity in the structure of the state through the pluralization of liberal-democratic constitutional concepts – which, in turn, engenders a pluralization of legal epistemologies in mainstream institutions and the recognition of a plurality of legal authorities – Southeast Asian constitutions have been recently referred to as pluralist for their common tendency to represent and manage, to a greater or lesser extent, the existent pluralism of their societies in cultural and ideological terms.[67] Notably, the Southeast Asian region appears to express a common pattern of constitutionalism that is sensitive to diversity and, for several reasons, differs from the liberal-democratic one. The structural commonalities of constitutionalism in this region – despite the significant internal diversity – make it worthy of analysis as a possible alternative or complementary tradition, adding to the global discourse on both constitutionalism and diversity accommodation.[68]

66 It must be noted that, as observed by Castellino, Joshua and Domínguez Redondo, Elvira, *Minority Rights in Asia: A Comparative Legal Analysis* (Oxford University Press, Oxford, 2006), 52–57, this region is the least willing to participate in the UN mechanisms, with several countries not bound by either the ICCPR or the ICESCR, i.e., Brunei, Cambodia, Malaysia, Myanmar, and Singapore.

67 See, Neo, Jacklyn L. and Bui, Ngoc Son (eds.), *Pluralist Constitutions in Southeast Asia* (Hart Publishing, Oxford-Portland, 2019), and esp. the introductory chapter, *Id.*, "Pluralist Constitutions and the Southeast Asian Context", 1–23.

68 This is a feature that seems to differentiate this region from others of the Global South, like the African continent, where (ethno-cultural) diversity is a very relevant political issue but a common regional pattern does not seem to be recognizable; furthermore, besides the experiences of Ethiopia and, especially, South Africa, and despite their very prominent internal diversity, most African states have followed the nation-state model – implying the need for a coincidence between the nation as a culturally and linguistically homogeneous entity and the state – in their nation-building projects; on this, see Dersso, Solomon, "Constitutional Accommodation of Ethnocultural Diversity in the Post-Colonial African State", 24(3) *South African Journal on Human Rights* (2008), 565–592.

A pluralist constitution has been defined as a constitution that "recognises and accommodates (and not eliminate) internal pluralities within a given society" and "clearly rejects . . . any attempt to ignore or *coercively* eliminate individual and group identity that is not in line with the predominant identity".[69]

Pluralist constitutionalism implies constitutions that are particularly "porous" to the diversity of the societal contexts they regulate. This also means that constitutional documents are not taken as permanent, even in terms of their foundational elements.[70] Rather, they are sites conducive to continuous interpretation and contestation from legal authorities and societal actors. This engenders dynamism and openness to change in a continuous search for a balance between the need for unity and respect for diversity. Consequently, even public and constitutional law are plural. These constitutions are not supposed to found a monist state legal system and, whether directly or indirectly, openly acknowledge the contribution of several authorities in the definition of the constitutional rules, models, and meanings. In addition, they are inherently structured so as not to eliminate plurality when creating a national identity. In other words, pluralist constitutions seem to give rise to a plurality of legal-political autonomous spaces expressing diversity beyond the usual and well-known territorial arrangements.[71]

The result is a variety of constitutional models, all sharing the described specific structural traits. In this category of constitutions, it is possible to include countries that explicitly envisage diversity and the accommodation thereof as a core element of their constitutional structure, for instance, Singapore, as well as states that, at least formally, do not display specific constitutional instruments for its management, such as Brunei Darussalam. Furthermore, pluralist constitutionalism is thought to be a wide category that encompasses various kinds of constitutions underpinned by different ideologies. This means that democratic as well as non-democratic or authoritarian constitutions may fit into the category of pluralist constitutions. The common feature of this broad category is that every constitution is, to some extent, infused or at least conditioned by the pluralism of the society it rules. Indeed, the Southeast Asian constitutional settings are, in various ways, formally and informally, informed by the multiple pluralities of the Southeast societies, which thus influence the constitutional system at the institutional, societal, and political levels. Diversity is a concept present in several constitutional texts, an object of judicial activity, and a core claim for political action directed at constitutional change.

Interestingly, pluralist constitutions have also been framed as minimalist in the sense that they "abjure attempts to eradicate pluralities" even if they "may at times provide incentives for individuals and groups to abandon pluralities"

69 Neo and Ngoc Son, Pluralist Constitutions . . . , 12.

70 Ibid.

71 On this, see Neo, Jacklyn L., "Space Still Matters: Towards More Pluralism in Public Law: Afterword to the Foreword by Ran Hirschl and Ayelet Shachar", 18(1) *International Journal of Constitutional Law (I Con)* (2020), 22–28, at 27.

and are mainly "minimalist in terms of the degree of inclusion and equality".[72] This opens the possibility of flexible and changeable solutions over time for the management of diversity, as well as a general openness as regards the active role of non-state actors, especially in the management of cultural and religious affairs.

In the end, a pluralist constitution is one that concretely and/or potentially embeds and does not explicitly deny or contrast pluralities through a minimalist structure open to diverse implementations over time. Several (but not all) countries marked by this type of constitution may be framed as soft constitutional states, where the regulation of diversity results from the interaction of sources of law stemming from various state and non-state authorities (with different balances in every country).[73] It is not by chance that most of the systems analyzed here, as explained below, employ and officially recognize legal pluralism through personal status law.

The solutions put forward by Southeast Asian states are varied and range from formal to substantive equality, protections similar to minority rights, legal exemptions, territorial autonomy, and legal pluralism. What seems to differentiate most Southeast Asian countries from the Global North tradition is that the rights discourse does not generally hold a central position in constitutional architecture, especially when it comes to diversity accommodation. In contrast, the concept of interests, together with the idea of societal harmony – which are related to what has been referred to as "Asian Values"[74] – are attributed major importance. In addition, as hinted, quite common is reliance on and official recognition of non-state legal orders that concur with the state in the management of the interests of ethnic-cultural and religious communities.[75]

The former element – namely, the construction of a model for the accommodation of diversity not centered on the language of rights and the presence and acknowledgment of legal pluralism – is especially observable in the

72 Neo and Ngoc Son, Pluralist Constitutions . . . , 12.

73 On the concept of soft state, as one of the manifestations of the Global South constitutional tradition, see Menski, Werner, "Beyond Europe", in Örücü, Esin and Nelken, David (eds.), *Comparative Law: A Handbook* (Hart Publishing, Oxford-Portland, 2007), 189–216, at 194.

74 "Asian Values" is an expression which emerged at the end of the Cold War, whose most active proponents were the governments of Malaysia and Singapore, and which denoted the refusal of a universal system of human rights protection in favor of a relativization of the human rights discourse. On the concept and content of this see Cauquelin, Josiane, Lim, Paul and Mayer-König, Birgit (eds.), *Asian Values: An Encounter with Diversity* (Curzon Press, Richmond, 2000); also, see Castellino and Domínguez Redondo, Minority Rights in Asia . . . , 11–22, who have offered interesting considerations (and several bibliographical references) on the problematic issues such a concept raises, specifically in regard to its possible instrumental use by authoritarian regimes.

75 Naturally, this phenomenon is not limited to this area of the world; however, this region shows a fairly widespread, common approach to this issue, which does not seem to be the case in other areas.

country that has arguably the most peculiar, sophisticated, and complex model of diversity accommodation amongst the ASEAN states, namely Singapore.[76]

SINGAPORE: UNIQUE NON-EXPORTABLE MODEL OR INTERESTING CASE FOR COMPARATIVE ANALYSIS?

The city-state of Singapore features a remarkably diverse society in terms of race, religion, and language. The main groups composing the Singaporean society, and around which the state system is structured, are the Chinese, Malay, Indian, and "Other" communities, with the latter composed of persons not included in the other categories. Besides "race", religion adds another significant dimension of diversity and complexity. According to a 2014 survey conducted by the Pew Research Center, slightly over a third of Singapore's population is Buddhist (34%), 18% are Christian, 16% are religiously unaffiliated, 14% are Muslim, 5% are Hindu, and less than 1% are Jewish. The rest of the population belongs to folk or traditional religions (2%) or other religions considered as a group (10%).[77]

Notably, the Singaporean legal system and its model for the management of diversity are not unknown to comparative constitutional scholarship, but they have certainly not gained the status of a model worth global consideration in mainstream comparative analysis. In other words, Singapore has been considered to be a special system with its own rules that operate in conditions that are not analogous to those present in other countries.

These considerations have been developed by Kymlicka and He. The authors, offering some consideration on the existence of alternatives to the models for the accommodation of diversity stemming from the Global North tradition, eventually affirmed that there is no other option for Southeast Asian countries that aspire to accommodate diversity than to look at the consolidated Global North standards and possibly participate in their definition at the international level.[78] Kymlicka further observed that the Singaporean solution cannot be considered a source of inspiration for addressing the issue of diversity in either the Western world or other Southeast Asian countries.[79] The reason lies in its societal context – made up of three major communities with immigrant backgrounds. This, according to the Canadian author, is not comparable to any other country, where

76 Naturally, several other countries in Southeast Asia display very interesting models and instruments. Among them, Malaysia certainly stands out; on this, see Harding, Andrew (ed.), *The Constitution of Malaysia: A Contextual Analysis* (Bloomsbury, London, 2012).

77 The data are available at the following link: https://www.pewresearch.org/religion/2014/04/04/global-religious-diversity/.

78 See Kymlicka, Will and He, Baobang, "Introduction", in Kymlicka, Will and He, Baobang (eds.), *Multiculturalism in Asia* (Oxford University Press, Oxford, 2005), 1–21, at 6.

79 Kymlicka, Will, "Liberal Multiculturalism: Western Models, Global Trends, and Asian Debates", in Kymlicka and He (eds.), Multiculturalism . . . , 22–55, at 43.

the issues related to the accommodation of diversity are traditionally linked instead to the existence of ethno-cultural groups whose claims can be framed in terms of minority (or indigenous) nationalism, similarly to those characterizing non-dominant groups in the Global North. Consequently, as Singapore has not faced classic minority and indigenous issues, it cannot be said to represent an exportable or inspirational model for countries that have experienced such a reality.[80]

However, it has been pointed out that this depiction of the Singaporean context as not having had to face the main questions shaping other models of multiculturalism – i.e., the typical minority or indigenous claims to historic ownership and thus exclusive government of the country or autonomous power in parts thereof – appears to be, firstly, debatable. It can be said to be based upon a historical reconstruction that underplays the pre-colonial past of the country.[81] Secondly, it seems Kymlicka considered non-dominant groups' claims as a non-dependent variable that is not conditioned by the existing societal and legal structures in the sense that the claim shapes the state's response to diversity issues. This seems to overlook the very role that cultural and especially legal structures have in determining the content of non-dominant demands. Indeed, it seems more accurate to consider that legal structures inevitably shape the form and type of claims made by non-dominant groups in that they create a set of legal possibilities through which non-dominant groups frame their assertions. In other words, the legal context of a country is not only conditioned by the type of existing minority claims, but it affects them itself as it envisages a set of legitimate options for their protection or empowerment. It is not by chance that non-dominant, unrecognized groups in Global North countries that are seeking protection or empowerment articulate their demands in terms of their available options, i.e., minority or indigenous rights.

Based on that, and following the theoretical and methodological approach endorsed in the present work, the Singaporean experience can be said to contribute to the global discourse on constitutionalism and diversity accommodation. For various reasons, it represents an alternative to the liberal-democratic approach to diversity issues that, due to the disregard it has experienced in the comparative literature, may be thought of as emergent. In other words, such a model is emergent, provided that it is given equal standing in comparative studies and not relegated to the realm of non-liberal or non-democratic and thus non-comparable systems, and is considered useful material for comparison in the interest of reciprocal learning. Bearing in mind the differences between

80 See Kymlicka, Liberal Multiculturalism . . . , 43.

81 Choo, John, "A Mimetic Theoretical Approach to Multiculturalism: Normalizing the Singaporean Exception", 26 *Contagion: Journal of Violence, Mimesis, and Culture* (2019), 209–235, at 211–212.

Global South[82] and Global North countries, fostering their communication on an equal footing seems particularly fruitful. This may facilitate a bilateral, rather than unidirectional, cross-fertilization among these areas of the world.

What seems particularly interesting about Singapore is that it offers perspectives that enrich the global debate over the management of diversity and solutions that may, if not inspire other constitutional systems and help them tackle the possible setbacks they are experiencing, at least relativize the centrality of Western-driven and rights-based discourse in this area of law.[83] In particular, the Singaporean experience tells the observer of a system where the accommodation of diversity is central but addressed without resorting to the rights discourse and where major importance is given to the balance of the collective interests of the communities making up the city-state society.

Singapore displays a model of diversity management with unique features that stem from the pluralist structure of its constitutional system.[84]

The constitutional framework – composed of the constitution and other founding documents that have been referred to as having acquired a quasi-constitutional status as material interpretations of the fundamental law[85] – provides for a structure that enables and guides an often robust regulation of diversity by the Singaporean government.

The written constitution addresses the issue of diversity in several parts. It does so by setting fundamental norms and principles as well as regulating some specific diversity-related institutions. For now, the focus will be on the main constitutional principles, while the institutions will be described in the following section.

82 Furthermore, the very position of Singapore as a Global South country is probably debatable, at least in economic terms; in fact, it is among the richest countries in the world and part of the "rich North", according to the Brandt line; for this reason, it may probably be more accurate to refer to Singapore as expressing a non-Western constitutional tradition.

83 Notably, recent publications on Singapore have moved in this direction: for instance, besides Neo, Jacklyn L. and Bui, Ngoc Son (eds.), Pluralist Constitutions . . . , see Chan, Heng Chee, Siddique, Sharon, Masron, Irna Nurlina and Cooray, Dominic, *Singapore's Multiculturalism: Evolving Diversity* (Routledge, London-New York, 2019), e-book version, 24, who have held that "Singapore is generally regarded as a success and may also hold lessons for Western developed nation-states that are increasingly aware of the weaknesses of their own multicultural models".

84 On the Singaporean model as a manifestation of pluralist constitutionalism, see Tan, Eugene B., "The Imperative of Integrative Pluralist Constitutionalism: Going Beyond Formal Equality, Eschewing Rights, and Accommodation of Differences in Singapore", in Neo and Ngoc Son (eds.), Pluralist Constitutions . . . , 51–81.

85 On the concept of material constitution, see Mortati, Costantino, *La Costituzione in senso materiale* (Giuffrè, Milan, 1940); on the importance of the White Paper on Shared Values and its status of quasi or soft constitutional law, in a country where governmental interpretations of constitutional provisions acquire further strength as they can be easily given effect due to the political dominance of the PAP government, see Thio, Li-Ann, *A Treatise on Singapore Constitutional Law* (Academy Publishing, Singapore, 2012), 76–82 and 104–106.

Article 12 of the constitution posits the fundamental principle of non-discrimination, which has a particularly wide scope of application. Article 12(2) indeed prohibits discrimination

> on the ground only of religion, race, descent or place of birth *in any law or in the appointment to any office or employment under a public authority or in the administration of any law relating to the acquisition, holding or disposition of property or the establishing or carrying on of any trade, business, profession, vocation or employment.* (italics added)

Furthermore, some other fundamental indications are found in Articles 152, 15, and 153, and 153A of the constitution. The first requires the state "constantly to care for the interests of racial and religious minorities in Singapore", and in the second paragraph, accords a special position to the Malays, recognized as indigenous people of the country. The latter is not considered justiciable[86] and has had more of a symbolic than a practical function, even if some measures, especially in the realm of the management of Islam (the vast majority of Malays are Muslims), have been adopted.

The second couple of provisions affirm the freedom of religion (Article 15)[87] and call on the Legislature to regulate "Muslim affairs" and constitute a "Council to advise the President in matters relating to the Muslim religion" (Article 153). Finally, Article 153A sets the official and national languages of the country: Malay, Mandarin, Tamil, and English fall within the first category, while only Malay is also attributed the status of national language. Such a provision is of utmost importance as it constitutes the backbone of the Singaporean multiracial system and bilingual school system.

Among the other foundational documents that have shaped Singapore's management of diversity, the Government White Paper on Shared Values[88] – released in 1991 at a moment of increasing ethnic awareness that could have led to societal fragmentation[89] – is of crucial importance. The "shared values" are the materialization of the core ideological values underlying the state, as well as the main guidance for state accommodation of diversity. The government defined five values to be shared by all the communities: a. Nation before community and society above self; b. family as the basic unit of society; c. regard and community support for the individual; d. consensus

86 Tan, The Imperative . . . , 64.

87 Article 15, constitution of Singapore.

88 *White Paper on Maintenance of Religious harmony* (Cmd 21 of 1989).

89 For a historical reconstruction of the Singaporean nation-building project and the ruling party's (People's Action Party, PAP) evolving approach towards the accommodation of diversity, starting from the end of the British colonial occupation, see Chan, Siddique, Masron, Irna and Cooray, Singapore's Multiculturalism . . . , 24–72.

rather than confrontation; e. racial and religious harmony.[90] The adoption of this set of values marked a shift in Singapore's approach towards diversity as it supported more incisive governmental action in this area.[91]

Based on this constitutional and ideological platform, the state of Singapore has created a complex system of diversity accommodation through legislation and other kinds of regulations and policies. Such a system is explicitly committed to the equality of the racial communities that make up its society in a bid to maintain societal harmony and avoid competition and jealousy among them. As for religious pluralism, it is addressed by the creation of a particular form of secular state that promotes individual religious freedom while at the same time allowing for potentially deep intervention by the state to protect the value of religious harmony.

The core concepts around which the entire system for the accommodation of ethno-cultural diversity is organized are multiracialism and meritocracy. Multiracialism, the Singaporean version of multiculturalism,[92] implies the recognition of the distinctiveness of every community and their equal treatment, along with the promotion of their interaction.[93] Notably, no special rights are provided for the members of the groups, but a strong emphasis is put on granting them the same opportunities for life development, which may also imply the enactment of positive measures to tackle social disparities, especially towards the Malays community (which is also entitled to a special position in the constitution). This goal connects multiracialism with meritocracy, which can be read as a market-driven version of the principle of equality. Indeed, the principle requires a "society that governs and rewards according to merit rather than other criteria of birth, wealth, ethnicity or religion",[94] whereby every race is supposed to enjoy equal social and economic opportunities.[95]

To reach such a comprehensive goal, the so-called CMIO multiracial model has been designed, which is based upon the division of the resident population

90 On the guiding role of the shared values and their connection with the discourse on Asian values, and for a thorough analysis of their content, see Thio, A Treatise . . . , 100–125.

91 Castellino and Domínguez Redondo, Minority Rights in Asia . . . , 201.

92 On this, see Chan, Siddique, Masron, Irna and Cooray, Singapore's Multiculturalism . . . , 73–158, and esp. 73–77; Tan, The Imperative . . . , 66, defined multiracialism as a "de facto constitutionally entrenched obligation, manifested through pluralist constitutionalism that employs both formal and substantive equality".

93 Thio, A Treatise . . . , 217.

94 On this, see Chan, Siddique, Masron, Irna and Cooray, Singapore's Multiculturalism . . . , 76.

95 On the concept of meritocracy in Singapore, see Quinn Moore, Robert, "Multiracialism and Meritocracy: Singapore's Approach to Race and Inequality", 58(3) *Review of Social Economy* (2000), 339–360; Cheang, Bryan and Choy, Donovan, *Liberalism Unveiled: Forging a New Third Way in Singapore* (World Scientific, Singapore, 2021).

in Singapore – i.e., citizens and permanent residents[96] – into four main ethnic or racial groups: Chinese, Malays, Indians, and Others.[97] According to this system, every Singaporean is attributed an ascriptive racial identity at birth – which is indicated on the identity card – with this marker being used for several purposes in the multiracial system. Notably, over time, the classification has witnessed an evolution that has provided some flexibility in the sense that it is now possible to indicate more than one race on the identity card.[98]

Around this categorization, numerous policies, institutions, and mechanisms have been put in place to foster equal treatment and pacific coexistence among every race. The measures envisaged may be classified according to their aims: coexistence in diversity, group empowerment and autonomy, and representation/participation.

In the first category, one can find the policy of public housing, which ensures proportionate distribution of the ethnic communities in housing blocks of the House Development Board estates.[99] Taking into account that 80% of the population of Singapore lives in HDB estates,[100] this measure appears to have a considerable integrative effect on the society of the city-state. Notably, the policy has been progressively adapted to the evolution of society in Singapore; for instance, proportions have been adjusted, and new types of quotas have been introduced (such as for non-Malays permanent residents).[101]

Also fitting into the first category is language regulation. The constitution of Singapore establishes multilingualism and, thereby, the equal standing of every community in terms of language. In the educational domain, a bilingual school system has been created. This uses English as the medium of instruction and teaches the mother tongue of the student community.[102] Such a model applies to all government schools in Singapore. The official mother tongue language of a student corresponds to that of the ethnic group indicated on the IC; those that fall into the category of Others are expected to choose a second language in addition to English.[103] The measures in this area

96 It is important to notice that, as observed by Chan, Siddique, Masron, Irna and Cooray, Singapore's Multiculturalism . . . , 146: "The non-resident members of the Singapore population are considered temporary inhabitants and therefore the race-based integration model of CMIO is not applicable to them".

97 A policy that was already practiced under British rule: for a historical background of this system, see Clammer, John, *Race and State in Independent Singapore 1965–1990: The Cultural Politics of Pluralism in a Multiethnic Society* (Routledge, London-New York, 1998), e-book version, 36–58.

98 Chan, Siddique, Masron, Irna and Cooray, Singapore's Multiculturalism . . . , 84.

99 This was introduced in 1989 as part of the Ethnic Integration Policy (EIP).

100 "Public Housing – A Singapore Icon", *Housing & Development Board*, www.hdb.gov.sg/cs/infoweb/about-us/our-role/public-housing-a-singapore-icon.

101 Chan, Siddique, Masron, Irna and Cooray, Singapore's Multiculturalism . . . , 92–95.

102 See "Mother Tongue Language Policy", *Ministry of Education*, www.moe.gov.sg/admissions/returning-singaporeans/singaporeans-returning-home/mother-tongue-policy.

103 Chan, Siddique, Masron, Irna and Cooray, Singapore's Multiculturalism . . . , 96–99.

appear to reflect a double aim: on the one hand, fostering the use of English as a *lingua franca* and an instrument to compete in a knowledge-based economy, while, on the other, "the teaching of the mother tongue is primarily for the purpose of cultural transmission and preservation of the languages of the different communities that make up Singapore".[104] It may be noticed that this area has also witnessed progressive adjustment in a bid to add a degree of flexibility to the system and reflect the cultural diversity of the members of the different groups.[105]

The third measure aimed at fostering inter-group cohesion and the limitation of inter-group tension is the establishment of Inter-racial and religious confidence circles (IRCCs), imagined as forums to enhance dialogue and reciprocal understanding among communities and religions.[106]

In addition, Singapore has developed tools that foster some types of group empowerment and autonomy. This is the case with the creation and funding of ethnic self-help groups. These organizations – funded by both the state and members of the race they have been set up for[107] – play a critical role in uplifting the socially and economically disadvantaged members of ethnic communities.[108] They essentially represent a layer of decentralization in the provision of some services that can arguably be framed in terms of group autonomy or functional non-territorial autonomy.[109] In other words,

104 In the words of the then Minister of State for Education, Dr. Aline Wong; the entire speech is available at the following link: www.moe.gov.sg/media/speeches/2000/sp24112000.htm; there are criticisms to these policies, as they have favoured the essentialization of communities and their languages and discouraged the internal linguistic plurality of every community; on this, see Jain, Ritu, "Multilingual Singapore: Language Policies, Challenges, and Responses", in Jain, Ritu (ed.), *Multilingual Singapore: Language Policies and Linguistic Realities* (Routledge, London-New York, 2021), 1–11.

105 For instance, as described by Chan, Siddique, Masron, Irna and Cooray, Singapore's Multiculturalism . . . , 155: "Since the early 1990s, a non-Tamil Indian may choose to do a non-Tamil Indian Language (Bengali, Gujarati, Hindi, Punjabi, or Urdu), which is in line with the cultural identity argument as non-Tamil Indian students can pursue their respective mother tongues since not all Indians are Tamils. A further flexibility is extended to students who have been living overseas for some years and have not been studying their MTL – they can apply for exemption from studying their official MTL, or consider a non-official language such as French, German, or Japanese, all on a case-by-case basis".

106 On this, see *Singapore: 2nd and 3rd Periodic Report to the UN Committee on the Rights of the Child* (CRC/C/SGP/2–3), paras. 2.9–2.14.

107 As described by Quinn Moore, Multiracialism and Meritocracy . . . , 345, they "receive funding from private donations, automatic payroll deductions, and from government matching funds up to a threshold amount".

108 The four ethnic SHGs are: Mendaki (set up in 1982); the Singapore Indian Development Association (SINDA) (set up in 1991); Chinese Development Assistance Council (CDAC) (set up in 1992); and the Eurasian Association (EA) which was first established in 1919 and accorded SHG status in 1994; interestingly, as indicated by Chan, Siddique, Masron, Irna and Cooray, Singapore's Multiculturalism . . . , 103, in 2017 the creation of a self-help group center run by all four communities was announced, which is now in function.

109 On this, see the next sections.

ethnic groups themselves are empowered by funding them so that they can assist their most disadvantaged members. This mechanism creates an ethnic eco-system of welfare – especially for education purposes – that resonates with the concept of institutional completeness, a term mainly employed to describe self-governance systems in Canada.[110] Additionally, religious associations cooperate with the state in the provision of social services.[111]

As far as the representation of groups or their interests is concerned, one finds several institutions and mechanisms specifically designed for this goal.

The first is the Presidential Council for Minority Rights (PCMR), which is regulated by Articles 68–92 of the constitution and was introduced in 1969. The PCMR is a consultative body that "consider and report on such matters affecting persons of any racial or religious community in Singapore as may be referred to the Council by Parliament or the Government"[112] and, specifically, "draw attention to any Bill or to any subsidiary legislation if that Bill or subsidiary legislation is, in the opinion of the Council, a differentiating measure".[113] By differentiating measures, the constitution means

> any measure which is, or is likely in its practical application to be, disadvantageous to persons of any racial or religious community and not equally disadvantageous to persons of other such communities, either directly by prejudicing persons of that community or indirectly by giving advantage to persons of another community.[114]

Interestingly, the body is meant to protect the interests of the racial groups but is not necessarily composed of members of those groups. Every individual citizen is eligible to be a member, but no racial quotas are in place.[115] The institution is generally considered to be weak and lacking coercive power since many

110 On the concept of institutional completeness, implying that minority groups best ensure their vitality through their own institutions, see Chapter 4; on the pragmatic use of this instrument by the government in order to outsource welfare and prevent the emergence of dependency tendencies toward a state-supported welfare system, see Quinn Moore, Multiracialism and Meritocracy . . . , 345–349; it must also be noted, as indicated by Teo, Terri-Anne, *Civic Multiculturalism in Singapore: Revisiting Citizenship, Rights and Recognition* (Palgrave Macmillan, Cham, 2019), 129, that such a system may risk leading to inequalities among races in that, as it is based on proportional redistribution of resources, the largest race group (Chinese) receives more funding and may therefore get more benefits from this system.

111 As illustrated by Thio, Li-Ann, "The cooperation of Religion and State in Singapore: A Compassionate Partnership in Service of Welfare", 7(3) *The Review of Faith & International Affairs* (2009), 33–45, at 38, this model, based on cooperation among ethnic and religious associations and the state, creates a composite welfare system referred to as "Many Helping Hands".

112 Article 76, constitution of Singapore.

113 Article 77, constitution of Singapore.

114 Article 68, constitution of Singapore.

115 See Articles 72 and 73, constitution of Singapore.

hurdles and limitations frustrate its functions.[116] A similar body, as explained below, has been established in the interest of the Muslim community.

The second mechanism is the so-called Group Representation Constituency (GRC) scheme for elections,[117] which coexists with single-member constituencies and grants race representation in the Legislature. The GRC scheme implies the creation of an enlarged constituency, where parties compete by presenting teams of between three and six candidates, of which at least one member must be a person belonging to the Malay community or, alternatively, the Indian or Other community. Today, although it has attracted several criticisms – especially related to its use as an instrument for PAP's self-renewal and reinforcement[118] – the GRC system determines the majority of the Parliament's seats and has favored wide racial representation. Of most interest is the fact that the GRC mechanism, albeit specifically aimed at promoting ethnic representation, has not led to an increased politicization of ethnicity. On the contrary, it has been pointed out that the system has contributed to depoliticizing ethnic affiliation, as it incentivizes politicians to moderate their discourse on potentially divisive issues and broaden their political perspectives.[119] Several reasons account for this. Among them, critical is the fact that candidates in the GRC constituencies compete and win in multi-ethnic teams. As such, a minority representative needs to appeal to a wider audience to get the chance to be elected. Moreover, the GRC makes ethnic parties unviable, as, due to the housing policy, there is no constituency where a party can win by only appealing to an ethnic minority.[120] Hence, the result is that the electoral system – specifically designed to take into consideration and promote the representation of ethnic groups – does not trigger a rise in ethnic conflict nor lead to the rigidification and major entrenchment of ethnic affiliations. Instead, it appears to encourage the exact opposite: easing of ethnic conflict, depoliticization of ethnic diversity, dialogue, and cooperation among representatives of ethnic groups.

116 On this, see Thio, Li-Ann, A Treatise . . . , 361–367.

117 See Article 39A(1), constitution of Singapore, introduced through the Constitution of the Republic of Singapore (Amendment) Act 1988 (Act No. 9 of 1988), and the Parliamentary Elections (Amendment) Act 1988 (Act No. 10 of 1988).

118 On this, see Thio, A Treatise . . . , 352–355; also, Neo, Jacklyn L., "Navigating Minority Inclusion and Permanent Division: Minorities and the Depoliticization of Difference", 17 *Jus Politicum* (2017), 607–627, at 614, who stated that: "Despite its seemingly noble aim, the GRC scheme is one of the most heavily criticized innovation to Singapore's electoral system, with many critics arguing for its abolition. Opposition politicians have, for instance, criticized the GRC system on the basis that it allows the ruling party to stifle opposition as it essentially increases barriers of entry for opposition parties"; it must indeed be noted that since the introduction of the GRC scheme (1988), the opposition to the PAP party succeeded in winning a constituency only once in 2011.

119 Neo, Navigating Minority Inclusion . . . , 620.

120 On this, see Neo, Navigating Minority Inclusion . . . , 620–626, who illustrated all the factors that determine the depoliticization of ethnicity through the GRC scheme.

The third tool fostering racial communities' political representation is the recent regulation as regards the elected Presidency (the direct election has been in force since 1991).[121] In 2016, an amendment to the Singaporean constitution introduced Article 19B, which reads as follows: "An election for the office of President is reserved for a community if no person belonging to that community has held the office of President for any of the 5 most recent terms of office of the President". In other words, this mechanism serves as an inter-generational safeguard of access to this office, which protects all racial communities.[122]

As regards religion, this identity marker almost totally overlaps with race in the case of the Malay community, though this is not always the case for other groups.[123] State response to religious diversity follows from a peculiar form of secularism. Singapore can arguably be described as a secular state insofar as it allows the practice of any cult and does not officially recognize a state religion. The principle of secularism is not entrenched in the constitutional text but was affirmed by the 1966 constitutional commission – a body appointed by the government to study racial and religious accommodation in Singapore following the declaration of independence – and subsequently put into practice by the state.[124]

At the same time, secularism in Singapore has specific traits if compared to a Western approach to this concept, especially as it provides for the possibility of robust governmental action to counter religious conflict and promote religious harmony. In addition, secularism is mitigated by the special position attributed to Islam and the (limited) official recognition of religious legal pluralism.

As for Islam, Singapore acknowledges and officially endorses legal pluralism in the form of the application of Sharia law for the Muslim community. This is stated by the Administration of Muslim Law Act of 1966, which also created the Islamic Religious Council of Singapore (as prescribed by the constitution), a Presidential consultative body also entitled to establish a Sharia court. Consequently, Muslims in Singapore are governed by Islamic law in matters of marriage, divorce, and succession.

Another notable element of the state management of religious pluralism is the creation of a legal framework that empowers the government to proactively intervene for the protection of the value of religious harmony. In order to avoid the emergence of religious conflict – which was violent at the end of

121 On the evolution of this institution, see Thio, A Treatise . . . , 385–428.

122 Tan, The Imperative . . . , 74; in this case, the racial groups are split into three categories: Chinese, Malay and Indian and other communities.

123 Interestingly, Castellino and Domínguez Redondo, Minority Rights in Asia . . . , 220, have underlined that "there appears to be a strong belief, reinforced by the 1980 census figures, that religion and religious affiliations coincide with ethnicity in Singapore".

124 Chan, Siddique, Masron, Irna and Cooray, Singapore's Multiculturalism . . . , 276.

the colonial period[125] – the Maintenance of Religious Harmony Act (MRHA) was passed in 1990. The statute allows the Minister of Home Affairs to issue restraining orders against religious leaders or members of religious institutions "who threaten Singapore's religious harmony by their words or actions, and those who conduct political activities under the guise of religion".[126] In a nutshell, actions that may be subject to control and limitation fall under the categories of proselytization, expression of intolerance towards other religions, and the employment of religion for political causes. Several criticisms have been leveled at a system that allows potentially very intrusive state action into religious affairs. Naturally, this could be instrumentalized to protect authoritarian state interests and delegitimize any form of opposition to the detriment of individual freedom. Nonetheless, other authors have stressed the fact that such regulation – never invoked, although threatened on some occasions[127] – has yielded significant results in fostering the peaceful coexistence of religions derived more from its expressive and persuasive power than its punishing provisions.[128]

The Singaporean model surely shows a distinctive approach to diversity accommodation and, more generally, constitutionalism. Its features evidently distance it from a traditional liberal perspective,[129] although it must be

125 In particular, two episodes of religious riots are generally referred to as "teaching points" in Singapore's history and political discourse: the 1950 Maria Hertogh riots and the 1964 racial riots; on these episodes, respectively, see Aljunied, Syed and Khairudin, Muhd, *Colonialism, Violence and Muslims in Southeast Asia: The Maria Hertogh Controversy and Its Aftermath* (Routledge, London-New York, 2009); Lau, Albert, *A Moment of Anguish: Singapore in Malaysia and the Politics of Disengagement* (Times Academic Press, Singapore, 2000).

126 *White Paper on Maintenance of Religious harmony*, 9–10.

127 However, it must be noticed that, as indicated by Neo, Jacklyn L., "Regulating Pluralism: Laws on Religious Harmony and Possibilities for Robust Pluralism in Singapore", 18(3) *The Review of Faith & International Affairs* (2020), 1–15, at 7–8, the MRHA "sits within a framework of other laws, which have been more often employed. The first is the Sedition Act, which criminalizes, among others, the causing of ill-will and hostility among different races and classes. The reference to race has been assumed to include religion. In addition, there is a chapter in the Penal Code, a British era law, containing offences against race and religion. While these laws have been employed in the past against speech and conduct deemed to be against religious harmony, they have been relatively rare, though no less impactful".

128 For instance, see Neo, Regulating Pluralism . . . , 1–12, esp. 4, where the author underlined that the liberal idea of the negative impact of deep regulation of the religious realm may be oversimplistic, as the relationships between regulation and freedom appear to be much more complex in practice.

129 As illustrated by Neo, Navigating Minority Inclusion . . . , 610, Singapore's constitutional system has been referred to as competitively authoritarian, authoritarian constitutionalist, or soft authoritarian; on these concepts, see Levitsky, Steven and Way, Lucan A., *Competitive Authoritarianism: Problems of International Politics* (Cambridge University Press, Cambridge, 2010); Tushnet, Mark, "Authoritarian Constitutionalism", 100(2) *Cornell Law Review* (2015), 391–461; Tan, Eugene B., *The Constitution of Singapore: A Contextual Analysis* (Hart Publishing, Oxford-Portland, 2015).

recognized that the constitutional system does have liberal underpinnings to a certain degree.[130]

From a liberal standpoint, there are several potentially problematic aspects. Prominent among them is the fact that the Singaporean model is designed according to the attribution of ascriptive racial identities from birth and a rather essentialized notion of race and ethnicity. Such points evidently clash with the foundational elements of the liberal-democratic tradition in this area, which considers free self-identification as a fundamental cornerstone of minority and indigenous peoples' rights law.

Furthermore, questionable from a liberal perspective is what has been defined as the "communitarian" leaning of the constitutional system of Singapore. As a matter of fact, the constitutional system – defined by both its constitution and quasi-constitutional documents – is ideologically committed to achieving harmony among races and religions and consequently allows for robust government intervention in these areas. In this regard, it has been pointed out that state regulation of racial and religious diversity goes so far as to resemble authoritarian social engineering, as the system potentially allows the government – ruled by the same party since Singapore's independence – to instrumentalize policies to silence opposing voices.[131]

More generally, the primacy accorded to community and state interests through the promotion of a specific ethos in the citizenry[132] is at odds with the centrality of the individual rights approach in Global North liberal-democratic settings.

However, a contextual reading of the Singaporean experience[133] seems to offer an opportunity to reflect and put into perspective the Global North tradition of diversity accommodation. Accordingly, it is possible to appreciate the existence of competing models featuring instruments that could, to some extent, be of global interest. This is particularly true when the challenges that arise from the increase in diversity that several societies are experiencing nowadays are taken into account.

Notably, the criticisms related to the Singaporean authoritarian government have been contested recently by advancing a contextual reading of the constitution of Singapore which situates the constitutional model in its cultural and social ecosystem. This means taking such an ecosystem seriously as well as evaluating the legal framework and its implementations in light of it.

A contextualized approach makes the observer aware that the risk of the essentialization of identities is not considered to be a threat in Singapore, as the system is internalized, and ethnicity is not a source of social or political

130 Thio, Li-Ann, "Singapore Relational Constitutionalism: The 'Living Institution' and the Project of Religious Harmony", *Singapore Journal of Legal Studies* (2019), 204–234, at 217.

131 On this, and for further references, see Neo, Regulating Pluralism . . . , 3–5.

132 Thio, Singapore Relational Constitutionalism . . . , 6.

133 Such a reading is proposed by Neo and Ngoc Son, Pluralist Constitutions . . . , 1–24.

divide.[134] The system, structured upon the four racial categories, does not create a climate of tension or exacerbate conflicts among them, as all the communities are given communal space to express their identities but also shared spaces of dialogue.[135] At the same time, while certainly prioritizing some identifications, it seems that the state does not seek to eliminate the internal diversity of the different communities and sometimes strives to adjust its legal regulations to fit the social reality. Examples include the addition of permanent residents into the CMIO system, the introduction of double racial identifications on the identity card, the adjustment of the housing policy to take into account the evolving societal composition, and the teaching of languages of specific communities beyond the most spoken ones. Also, the very category of "Others" reflects a clearly inclusive stance in the Singaporean system.

Furthermore, Neo has demonstrated how state intervention to achieve racial and religious harmony is more proactive than punishing, which means that the need for the state to intervene to punish misconduct is limited when compared to its persuasive power.[136] In addition, it must be said that the idea of a state promoting a particular ethos in the country is not unfamiliar to the liberal tradition,[137] which, despite professing the neutrality of the state, evidently endorses specific moral values that inform the constitutional system. The Singaporean constitutional model is different in that it makes this non-neutral perspective explicit from the very beginning through the foundational constitutional and quasi-constitutional documents.

Finally, what must be taken into account are the results of the Singaporean system. Regardless of the criticisms related to the possible authoritarian leaning of the state, no one has denied that the multiracial system has yielded notable results in managing its variegate society and fostering security as well as peaceful coexistence among citizens.[138]

Having clarified this, what appears to be of particular interest is the general approach taken by the country, as well as the use and regulation of some specific instruments. Of course, drawing attention to this case does not imply an endorsement of it. But from this, for instance, one could appreciate the variety of means – direct, indirect, soft/persuasive, or hard/direct – that the state can use to manage diversity and the role the state can take. Additionally, although no model can be thought to be exportable as a whole to other contexts, its instruments and approach may be of interest in other settings that are becoming increasingly diverse.

134 Neo, Regulating Pluralism . . . , 8.

135 Thio, A Treatise . . . , 217.

136 Neo, Regulating Pluralism . . . , 1–15 and *Id.*, "Dimensions of Religious Harmony as Constitutional Practice: Beyond State Control", 20 *German Law Journal* (2019), 966–985; see also, Thio, Singapore Relational Constitutionalism . . . , 206.

137 As explained by Macedo, Stephen, *Liberal Virtues: Citizenship, Virtue and Community in Liberal Constitutionalism* (Clarendon Press, Oxford, 1990), 163–183.

138 Also acknowledged by Kymlicka, Liberal Multiculturalism . . . , 43.

The general Singaporean approach is fascinating in that it is pragmatic, soft, and flexible, i.e., open to continuous adjustment.

Such a model suggests a relatively steady connection between diversity accommodation and the need for adjustment and flexibility so as to guarantee a continuous interaction between law and the society it rules and keep a balance – or harmony, or, in liberal terms, proportionality – in the protection of the various societal interests.

In addition, the limited role of minority rights (while fundamental rights are explicitly stated) diminishes the confrontational dimension of diversity accommodation. At the same time, the focus on communitarian and state interests increases the responsibility of the members of every racial and religious community in what can be seen as a multilevel governance system driven by the state. From this, it seems that the rights discourse loses its centrality when a societal approach to diversity accommodation is taken. However, this does not necessarily imply a decreased level of protection and empowerment offered to the components of the diverse society. In other words, it appears that diversity is managed through a (quite state-directed) governance system, where every actor has a – formal or informal – role in fostering the peaceful coexistence of diverse communities, and conditions are created for the communities to interact and exchange on a daily basis.

From a more theoretical standpoint, the Singaporean experience thus adds to the vocabulary and practice of constitutionalism, drawing on duty, trust, solidarity, and a conciliatory rehabilitative ethos in service of sustainable relationships[139] more than the attribution and possible extension of rights, which may result in power struggles and conflicts.

As regards this case, the concept of relational constitutionalism has been employed, which understands constitutionalism as aiming to "promote the relational well-being of individuals and groups and to preserve sustainable relationships in a polity where disparate religious groups and their members are able to co-exist, maintain their distinct identities while being unified by a national identity and a shared commitment to the public good".[140] A relational constitution is made up of hard and soft constitutional documents, the latter serving a fundamental role of exhortation, persuasion, and guidance, which enhances the interiorization of the values outlined in the constitution. They can be seen as part of the material constitution of Singapore, and their very influential role has been widely acknowledged. They prescribe desired standards of conduct that are regularly invoked and reiterated after disputes erupt, allowing the relevant actors to reaffirm their commitment to shared norms jointly.[141]

139 Thio, Singapore Relational Constitutionalism . . . , 205.

140 Thio, Li-Ann, "Relational Constitutionalism and the Management of Inter-Religious Disputes: The Singapore 'Secularism with a Soul' Model", 1(2) *Oxford Journal of Law and Religion* (2012), 446–469, at 448; *Id.*, Singapore Relational Constitutionalism . . . , 204–234.

141 Thio, Singapore Relational Constitutionalism . . . , 209.

Regardless of the content of the values put forward, what seems particularly interesting is the centrality of soft law regulations when it comes to diversity accommodation and the encouragement of peaceful coexistence. These complement hard state regulation to the point that they foster the recognition of its legitimacy and, at the same time, limit the application of its punitive provisions. Together with the flexible approach, this can arguably be considered a fundamental element of the Singaporean constitutional system.

Flexibility is also related to the instruments and domains through which the state intervenes in the accommodation of diversity. While the constitution and the statutes provide for a general legal framework, some tools to regulate diversity and foster peaceful coexistence are set forth through policies embedded in several types of other legal means and in areas that are generally ignored in other parts of the world. Take the example of the housing policy: this is a tool, not regulated by statutes but by bylaws or administrative means, which is mostly ignored by states in the Global North when it comes to diversity accommodation. This may actually represent a fruitful solution to avoid the phenomenon of the ghettoization of migrants or other marginalized minorities that often occur in large cities nowadays. In addition, the housing policy has a very significant impact on the functioning of the GRC scheme since the distribution of the population to avoid ethnic enclaves is one of the main explanations for the depoliticization effect of the electoral system.

Cooperation with and support from ethnic and religious associations, which leads to the creation of a multi-layered system of diversity governance, is another notable instrument that follows the logic of flexibility and softness in this complex system of governance. Such a model, which engenders the creation of spaces of autonomy in the provision of services for several communities (and is, notably, also consistent with the state meritocratic system aimed at avoiding citizens' dependency on the state)[142] is officially recognized and supported, unlike other experiences in the Global North. The idea of state-endorsed cooperation with communities, which creates the condition for the latter to create an ecosystem of welfare in a unitarian framework, is another interesting lesson one can draw from the Singaporean case.

Likewise, official recognition and state endorsement characterize legal pluralism in Singapore, which only concerns the Muslim community. The Singaporean approach to legal pluralism is in line with the widespread practice of officially recognizing (religious) legal pluralism in Southeast Asian countries, which consistently differs from the mostly non-official status accorded to it in Global North countries (naturally with exceptions, especially related to indigenous peoples). Although it has been argued that official recognition may lead to "weak" forms of legal pluralism – thereby running the risk of it being authoritatively controlled or directed by the state and its ideology of legal centralism[143] – state endorse-

142 See Thio, The Cooperation of Religion and State . . . , 37–38.

143 On this, see Griffiths, John, "What Is Legal Pluralism?", 24 *The Journal of Legal Pluralism and Unofficial Law* (1986), 1–55, at 8.

ment may also be interpreted as creating an enabling framework for legal pluralism to blossom and interact in a pluralized legal system. Official recognition entails a pluralization of law in terms of sources and contents and may foster clarity and legal certainty as, this way, clear boundaries or procedures may be designed to address possible conflicts of jurisdiction.

Finally, central is the government's commitment to creating conditions that favor encounters and dialogue between races and religions, both on a societal and a political level. The housing and the electoral policies, together with the creation of intercultural and inter-religious fora (the IRCCs) and wide state support for the communities' cultural expressions,[144] foster continuous interaction among groups, ease the risk of ethnic conflicts and contribute to depoliticizing ethno-cultural issues.

To sum up, the Singaporean model shows the significance of a pragmatic approach to diversity accommodation, which implies flexibility and constant adjustment. Moreover, it urges the observer to reflect on the importance of creating conditions for continuous societal and political interaction among different groups and for allowing the autonomous expression of diversity in different areas, including the provision of social services and religious justice. In addition, it must once more be highlighted that Singapore ensures pluralism through a – state-directed – governance system that does not rely on rights discourse, where the communities themselves are supposed to cooperate with the state, thereby playing an important role as subjects in diversity accommodation. Lastly, the analyzed case shows how (ethno-cultural) diversity can inform every aspect of state organization and activity without causing the pillarization of society or the polarization of political discourse along ethno-cultural lines.

Naturally, the conditions for such a system to work are peculiar to the case under study.[145] Nonetheless, its elements clearly integrate the language and practice of constitutionalism and provide an interesting approach compared to the more traditional ones in this area.[146]

The European macro-perspective

European international soft law, through its documents and the activity of its various monitoring bodies, seems to have grasped the ongoing challenges of

144 On this, see Chan, Siddique, Masron, Irna and Cooray, Singapore's Multiculturalism . . . , 100–104.

145 On the conditions that contribute to the peculiar functioning of the Singaporean system, see Clammer, Race and State . . . , 36–58.

146 Hence, it is not suggested that Singapore should be plainly transplanted into other settings, nor is it naïvely considered as a better model for the accommodation of diversity compared to the limits of Western systems, which are "risks" foreseen by Gaudreault-DesBiens, Jean-F., "Religious Courts, Personal Federalism, and Legal Transplants", in Ahdar, Rex and Aroney, Nicolas (eds.), *Shari'a in the West* (Oxford University Press, Oxford, 2010), 159–180, at 168–177. Rather, the case study is merely intended to relativize the discourse over constitutionalism and diversity accommodation and foster the interaction and communication among models within a tradition – constitutionalism – that is composite and multifaceted.

diversity accommodation, thus giving us a general picture of its concrete and potential developments. This is why it can be seen as a theoretical matrix that guides the understanding of the evolution of the legal instruments aimed at accommodating diversity in the Global North.

Not dissimilarly from the previous sections, the focus of this part of the work will be on the European region as expressing a common constitutional tradition that provides a comprehensive, innovative approach to the issue of the accommodation of diversity. In the same vein, the most advanced perspectives stemming from international soft law will be analyzed, and examples of state practices in line with them will be provided.

While some interesting insights can be gained from the UN bodies' activities, and among them, especially the Special Rapporteur on Minority Issues' reports,[147] the most innovative and comprehensive perspective on the evolution of the Law of Diversity comes from the activity of the HCNM and the ACFC, the monitoring body of the FCNM. Generally speaking, these documents embed a global or societal[148] perspective on diversity accommodation in two respects.

Firstly, diversity is taken as a general element of societies and not something only related to some minority groups. Following this approach, all the tools for the accommodation of diversity are designed to serve the interests of the entire diverse society and not only those of some specific communities. Consequently, the management of diversity acquires a much larger scope and includes legal instruments for both majorities and non-majority groups (and the internal minorities thereof), as well as for their reciprocal understanding and coexistence.[149] Notably, the "societal" and "global" framing of diversity results in distancing from the majority-minority discourse and focuses on the

147 For instance, the *Report of the Special Rapporteur on minority issues of 2019*, available at the following link: https://ap.ohchr.org/documents/E/GA/report/A_74_160.pdf, 18, offers a broad working definition of ethnic, religious, or linguistic minority in line with the UN bodies' jurisprudence: "An ethnic, religious or linguistic minority is any group of persons which constitutes less than half of the population in the entire territory of a State whose members share common characteristics of culture, religion or language, or a combination of any of these. A person can freely belong to an ethnic, religious or linguistic minority without any requirement of citizenship, residence, official recognition or any other status".

148 On this, see Palermo, Francesco, "Quanto è morbido il soft law? La tutela non giurisdizionale dei diritti delle minoranze nelle aree geogiuridiche europee", 1 *Rivista di Diritti Comparati* (2022), 74–94, available at the following link: https://www.diritticomparati.it/rivista/quanto-e-morbido-il-soft-law-la-tutela-non-giurisdizionale-dei-diritti-delle-minoranze-nelle-aree-geogiuridiche-europee/.

149 This is particularly interesting in that it implies taking into consideration diversity accommodation as a phenomenon that concerns both minorities and majorities; the effect of diversity accommodation mechanisms on majorities is often overlooked in theory and practice, with few exceptions: on this, see Basta, Karlo, *The Symbolic State: Minority Recognition, Majority Backlash, and Secession in Multinational Countries* (McGill-Queen's University Press, Montréal-Kingston-London-Chicago, 2021); this innovative perspective allows taking into account the societal effects of diversity accommodation and the needs of all the communities that compose the diverse society.

creation of a society where differences are integrated while at the same time respected through various means. In addition, such a perspective – which shies away from the conflation of diversity and some selected groups – opens up the possibility of extending the scope of positive diversity accommodation beyond "traditional" addressees and instruments.

Secondly, a dynamic reading of identity – and, specifically, minority identity – is purported. Based on that, the documents analyzed in this section encourage a flexible approach to the definition of minorities and groups entitled to protection and the equally flexible employment of instruments devoted to safeguarding and empowering diversity. Concretely, they thus emphasize the principle of free self-identification in (minority or majority) communities, which means that no legal ascription to one specific social grouping is tolerated without the consent of the involved person. As a consequence, they endorse a more blurred concept of minority and the possibility of extending minority rights provisions and instruments to non-citizens and members of groups that are not legally defined as national minorities on an article-by-article basis – especially those related to participation in public, economic, and social life. They also encourage the development of tools intended to foster mutual understanding among different components of society.

Importantly, the trends exposed here are to be considered as the developments that add up to the existing corpus of minority and indigenous peoples' rights law and do not envisage its demise. On the contrary, they are thought to be specifically related to a mature phase of diversity accommodation, where pressing issues like the survival and peaceful coexistence of groups are no longer contested, and basic safeguards for the promotion of diversity are put in place.[150]

The ACFC commentary of 2012

Early indications of the described approach can be found in the ACFC Thematic Commentary No. 3 of 2012 on the language rights of persons belonging to national minorities under the Framework Convention.[151]

Despite being a document devoted to language rights, it has been pointed out that it expresses a renovated attitude towards minority rights by considering them in the wider context of our contemporary diverse societies.[152]

150 On this, see Palermo, Francesco, "'The Borders of My Language Mean the Borders of My World': Language Rights and Their Evolving Significance for Minority Rights and Integration of Societies", in Ulasiuk, Iryna, Hadîrcă, Laurenţiu and Romans, William (eds.), *Language Policy and Conflict Prevention* (Brill-Nijhoff, Leiden-Boston, 2018), 135–154.

151 ACFC, Thematic Commentary no. 3, *The Language Rights of Persons Belonging to National Minorities under the Framework Convention*, 24 May 2012, ACFC/44DOC(2012)001 rev, hereinafter also referred to as Commentary or Commentary of 2012.

152 Palermo, The Borders . . . , 143.

In fact, along with more traditional language rights provisions,[153] the Commentary acknowledges that complexity characterizes diverse societies. It, therefore, takes on the challenge of addressing several issues related to its management through the abovementioned global approach. This means that the recommendations presented in the Commentary deal with the complex interactions that stem from a society where diversity is a multifaceted phenomenon that ought not to be conflated with just some minority groups.

The described attitude is visible in several parts of the document.

First, the Commentary tackles the role of language in identity formation and distances itself from a static conception thereof. In this respect, para. 7 reads as follows: "Increasing mobility and migration are current social phenomena that have also diversified means of communication. As a result, sociolinguistic approaches to the notion of language, which was long considered intimately linked to static concepts such as territory and belonging to a group, are changing as well. The Framework Convention is based on an individual rights approach. It is thus not focused on language itself, nor on a language community, but on the speakers. Their communicative repertoire, which may encompass a range of linguistic resources (standard and non-standard forms of languages, dialects, etc.) often develops throughout life as a result of interaction and mobility". Furthermore, para. 13, in Part II – which deals with the importance of language for the preservation of one person's identity – affirms that "language, like identity, is not static but evolves throughout a person's life. The full and effective guarantee of the right to use one's (minority) language(s) implies that authorities allow free identification of persons through language and abstain from constraining personal identities into rigid language categories. The choice of each person belonging to a national minority to choose freely to be treated or not to be treated as such must be respected in line with Article 3.1 of the Framework Convention". Para. 18 adds another important point concerning the issue of multiple linguistic affiliations. It encourages states to provide the conditions for multiple affiliations, thereby implying that a person may legitimately claim linguistic rights regarding several minority languages.

In addition, some considerations on the role of language and its regulation are offered. In this sense, for instance, para. 12 states that promoting language diversity has varying roles, which come down to being, on the one hand, "a crucial and identifying minority attribute" and, on the other, "an important tool for promoting full and effective equality and integration of multicultural and linguistically diverse societies".

Moreover, the Advisory Committee takes a clear position on the issue of the beneficiaries of language provisions by encouraging, at para. 15, states authorities "to pursue an open and inclusive approach and to consider extending the protection of the Framework Convention to groups that are not covered", and

153 Palermo, The Borders . . . , 147.

adding that “The personal scope of application should, where appropriate, also extend to non-citizens, particularly where exclusion on the grounds of citizenship may lead to unjustified and arbitrary distinctions, such as when such exclusion concerns stateless persons belonging to national minorities who permanently reside on a given territory” which is seen as “consistent with broader efforts at European level to develop a more nuanced approach to the application of the citizenship criterion in the protection of national minorities”.

Importantly, at para. 25, the Commentary unveils that targeting diversity rather than minorities implies a general reconsideration of all the legal instruments stemming from minority rights law as essential tools for the integration of society and not as purely defensive tools. In this sense, the purported concept of integration is key to understanding the approach underlying the Commentary. It is described as “a two-way process” that “requires recognition and respect on both sides [majority and minority cultures] and may often lead to changes within both the majority and minority cultures”. Therefore, while expectably distinguishing integration from the idea of assimilation, the Commentary also underlines the fact that the former has a dynamic character and is not supposed to be taken as a definitive and static result. This seems to suggest a dynamic view of the instruments for the accommodation of diversity themselves, which are supposed to adapt to changing societal conditions and varying power balances among groups, at least in those societies where basic rights and safeguards are no longer in danger. In other words, it is questioned whether the rigid legal safeguards for minorities – though still fundamental in some situations – are the only means to protect and empower diversity and fluid (or non-static) representation of society and groups is endorsed.

The Ljubljana Guidelines on Integration of Diverse Societies

The Ljubljana Guidelines on Integration of Diverse Societies of 2012[154] represent the second document bringing about a renewed perspective on diversity accommodation. The document is composed of an introduction and a set of recommendations organized in four parts: Structural principles, Principles for integration, Elements of an integration policy, and Key policy areas.

This document is primarily innovative through its general approach to the management of diversity. Not unlike the Commentary of 2012, the Guidelines shift the focus from posing the rights of some non-majority groups to indicating how to regulate diverse societies as a whole.

In keeping with this perspective, a societal, global, and, consequently, non-exclusivist and non-isolationist model of accommodation is proposed.

154 OSCE HCNM, *The Ljubljana Guidelines on Integration of Diverse Societies* (OSCE HCNM, The Hague, 2012), hereinafter referred to as Guidelines.

Such a model is, in turn, grounded in a specific reading of what diversity is and how it informs several societies nowadays. This resonates with the other documents analyzed in this section and implies the need for a fresh perspective on this issue.

Turning to the introduction, the Guidelines immediately show their original content as regards the framing of diversity. They describe contemporary societies as inherently and increasingly diverse and affirm the need to complement the traditional policies and legal approaches in this field accordingly. To do so, they suggest that specific regard be paid to instruments that are intended not only to recognize and accommodate minority culture, identity, and political interests but also to those that favor the "integration of multi-ethnic societies".[155]

> Subsequently, in their "principles for integration", the Guidelines describe diversity as a "feature of all contemporary societies and of the groups that comprise them".[156] Accordingly, Individual identities can be and in fact increasingly are ***multiple*** (a sense of having horizontal identities; for instance, belonging to more than one ethnicity), ***multilayered*** (various identities coexist and overlap in the same person, such as ethnic, religious, linguistic, gender, professional and the like), ***contextual*** (the context might determine which identity is more prominent at a given moment) and ***dynamic*** (the content of each identity and the attachment of individuals to it is changing over time).[157]

Of course, legal recognition of the more or less numerous factors of diversity characterizing every person is not unknown by law. However, from a legal standpoint, this issue has mostly been addressed by anti-discrimination law. The Guidelines affirm that such complexity should also be taken into consideration when it comes to instruments that are meant to manage diversity beyond non-discrimination.

Based on the described framing of diversity as a general societal phenomenon, the document goes on to lay down a set of principles and practical recommendations for the development of instruments and policies that are coherent with it.

As regards the models that the Guidelines encourage, the main change of perspective compared to the "traditional" approaches in this area specifically revolves around a renewed concept of integration. The latter is described – echoing the ACFC Commentary of 2012 – as implying both the inclusion of diversity in state organizations through various means as well as measures for

155 Guidelines, 4.
156 See Guideline no. 5, 14.
157 See Guideline no. 5, 14.

intercultural dialogue within a given society.[158] In other words, diversity is conceived of as an element that characterizes our reality, and its accommodation is not only in the interest of one or more minority groups but society as a whole.

As a consequence, the Guidelines support a flexible approach to diversity accommodation that distances itself from an exclusivist framing of identity and diversity issues. In this sense, one can clearly notice that such a framing – which has informed the evolution of minority and indigenous peoples' rights law – is considered to be limiting when it comes to the integration of increasingly diverse societies in two main respects. It may be so in that, firstly, it can sometimes reinforce the existing cleavages among majority and non-majority groups insofar as it is framed in exclusivist terms.[159] Secondly, a model of accommodation solely based on a minority-majority framing and rights discourse is regarded as practically limited as a means of managing diverse societies, which appear to require a different, more complex, and flexible strategy. The "traditional" model – which understands minority rights as special positive measures for specific disadvantaged groups with particular "objective" (and subjective) cultural features – has become so central theoretically and practically that it has generally been considered the only way to cope with diversity issues. Accordingly, the extension of minority rights and mechanisms in exclusivist terms to further groups through their legal recognition has been thought to be the main statecraft solution for managing emergent phenomena of diversity, like the so-called new minorities. Conversely, the Guidelines, not unlike the Commentary of 2012, uphold an inclusive reading of minority rights, as well as their integration through measures that foster societal cohesion using participatory means in diverse societies.

The Guidelines consider the essential role of law as providing an appropriate framework for this renewed perspective and offer numerous practical solutions. Particularly interesting is that this perspective emerges in every part of the document: the recommendations that are put forward do not specifically address minority groups but the larger phenomenon of diversity that

158 See, in particular, Guidelines, 3–4, which affirm that the process of integration "can lead to changes in majority and minority cultures. This is why the HCNM prefers to speak about the integration of multi-ethnic societies rather than integration of a minority group into a particular society"; this is an innovative use of the notion of integration, especially compared to the scholarly approach towards this area of study, which, as illustrated by McGarry, John, O'Leary, Brendan and Simeon, Richard, "Integration or Accommodation? The Enduring Debate in Conflict Regulation", in Choudry, Sujit (ed.), *Constitutional Design for Divided Societies: Integration or Accommodation?* (Oxford University Press, Oxford, 2008), 41–88, at 41, mostly employs integration in contrast to accommodation, where the former "promotes a single public identity coterminous with the state's territory", "commends a common and functional single public house . . ." and "primarily seek[s] the equality of individual citizens before the law and within the public institutions"; in contrast, the latter implies "equality with institutional respect for differences".

159 This is stated in the introduction of the Guidelines, 3.

characterizes society. Accordingly, the measures that are proposed are thus aimed at fostering the inclusion of diversity both in state structures and legislative frameworks rather than expressly requiring the extension of rights to other types of minorities through their legal recognition.[160]

The non-exclusivist approach underlying the Guidelines is apparent in some parts of the document. For instance, the definition of states (and minorities) in (mono-)ethnic and static terms as the property of one or several fixed ethnicities is discouraged as a strategy. It is considered that this should give way to acknowledging that members of minorities' and majorities' identities evolve owing to their reciprocal contact.[161] Moreover, connected to that, it is affirmed that free self-identification and contextual affiliations to different non-majority groups – as well as their voluntary change over time – should be authorized.[162] In other words, a rejection of rigid legal categorizations when it comes to diversity accommodation is endorsed, leading to diversity being considered as a global and multi-dimensional phenomenon that informs the entire society and requires various (and variable) means to manage it. This is further confirmed by a rejection of detailed definitions when it comes to diversity issues. An open conception of the term minority is visible in the Introduction, which reads as follows:

> The term "national minority", as used in the Guidelines, refers to a wide range of minority groups, including ethnic, religious, linguistic and cultural communities, regardless of whether these groups are recognized as such by the States where they reside and irrespective of the designation applied to or claimed by them.[163]

Notably, this standpoint does not engender the demise of minority rights. Quite to the contrary, it confirms their critical role. However, at the same time, it puts them in the context of our contemporary, diverse societies and conceives of them as just one of the tools that contribute to their peaceful integration. This is eloquently expressed by Guideline no. 7, part of the principles for integration, which recommends that a non-isolationist approach to minority issues be taken. On the one hand, this means that measures to ensure inter-community dialogue and participation in shared institutions should be adopted to complement minority rights and favor a process of integration that is respectful of diversity. On the other, it also implies that the reach of diversity accommodation should not be limited to the regulation of forms

160 See Guideline no. 18, 28: "Legislative frameworks, including constitutional law, should be inclusive and should explicitly recognize the diversity within plural societies and guarantee its protection and promotion".

161 See Guideline no. 5, 15.

162 Guideline no. 6, 15–16.

163 Guidelines, 4.

of diversity that have been traditionally addressed by the *corpus* of minority rights, nor to its underlying logic and structure. The open approach to the beneficiaries of minority rights is further confirmed by the inclusive conception of minorities that the introduction provides.[164]

Several guidelines and their commentaries provide interesting recommendations for setting up this model.

The second part introduces many "principles for integration", in line with the general rationale of the document, which is further detailed in parts III and IV. Guideline no. 7 states that a non-isolationist approach to minority rights may be encouraged through measures that complement them and favor inter-community dialogue. They may regard, for instance, the school system and imply the establishment of integrated curricula or housing policies, which should be more sensitive to the risk of residential segregation. Other indications come from Guideline no. 11, which affirms that further measures can be taken in the area of education[165] and in the context of media policies, such as encouraging the use of multilingual broadcasting. Guideline no. 12 specifies that the latter measures should target both the majorities and minorities of a given country and favor their mutual recognition and understanding. Again, the most promising areas where such a goal could be reached are identified within education and media.[166]

Furthermore, the Guidelines in Part III and IV bring about other concrete suggestions for the integration of diverse societies, which relate to the pluralism of the party system,[167] as well as inclusive and multiple citizenships.[168]

164 Guidelines, 4–5: "The term "national minority", as used in the Guidelines, refers to a wide range of minority groups, including ethnic, religious, linguistic and cultural communities, regardless of whether these groups are recognized as such by the States where they reside and irrespective of the designation applied to or claimed by them. In addition, "minority" is often used as a shorthand term for "persons belonging to national minorities". This does not imply that all principles, minority rights, and policy options presented in the document apply to every situation in the same way. It is clear that, while basic human rights standards apply to all, good integration policies will need to be tailored to some extent to meet the challenges and needs of different minority groups and different circumstances. The content of integration policies may depend on such factors as the numbers involved, the length of settlement and geographic concentration, and the particular social, economic and cultural needs, among other considerations. In addition, the fact that many individuals have multiple identities that may be asserted in different ways, times and contexts must also be recognized when developing integration policies".

165 Such as exchanges between schools providing education to minority and majority pupils to promote interaction and mutual understanding; see Guideline no. 11, 21, and also Guidelines nos. 44 and 45, 54–56.

166 See Guideline no. 12, 22–23.

167 See Guideline no. 27, 35, on the need for a legislative framework that allows party system to be inclusive across ethnic lines.

168 Guideline no. 32, 40 recommends that citizenship should be designed as inclusive and affirms that the vast majority of rights should be applied to everyone regardless of their status (apart from some political rights); see also Guideline no. 37, 44–45 on multiple citizenship.

Moreover, they detail the practical instruments that states can put forward in the areas of education and media,[169] as well as language regulation.

Regarding the latter, Guideline no. 42 indicates that states should find a balance between the protection of non-majority languages and the promotion of the state's official language(s) in the interest of all the components of the diverse society.[170] Such a balance is never reached once and for all and depends on the conditions of every country and its internal diversity. At the same time, some basic standards should be observed to guarantee that both official state and minority languages can thrive and serve their functions. For instance, it is affirmed that states can designate a national language, but they have to provide everyone with adequate opportunities to learn it and equally participate in cultural, social, and economic life as well as the public affairs of their wider society. Moreover, it is asserted that states should not restrict the use of minority languages in the private sphere. Additionally, any state-language requirements in the public sphere should be based on legitimate aims and be necessary and proportional. Very interesting is also the recommendation that states that

> Where a linguistically diverse State perceives and maintains a single official language as a tool of integration, allowing the use of other languages to some degree in public administration and services, education and the media can help accommodate the needs and promote the inclusion of minorities. The levels and nature of any language services and the incorporation of non-official languages into the public administration should be determined according to the specific circumstances of the communities concerned. Essential public services, such as healthcare, should have the capacity, to the extent possible, to also provide those services in minority languages when needed.

It thus seems clear that the document's approach to a typical minority area is rather flexible and not solely focused on the guarantee of rights to minorities. Rather, it adopts a broad societal perspective based on a non-exclusivist and non-isolationist rationale. Consequently, proposed instruments for the accommodation of diversity are always marked by an inclusive structure and seek to achieve peaceful integration of the entire society. Indeed, when legal tools for minorities are proposed, they are generally advanced as inclusive instruments and complemented by measures that foster dialogue with other groups. When posing instruments related to the interests of the majority of

169 In particular, see Guidelines nos. 44 and 45, 54–56, on education policies and intercultural and multilingual education; as for media and their role for mutual understanding, see Guideline no. 48, 60–61; on the need for a balance between state language(s) and minority language(s) in media, see Guideline no. 49, 61–63.

170 Guideline no. 42, 52–53.

a state (like the promotion of a national language), the Guidelines encourage their application to the entire diverse society, and especially to the non-majority groups.

Furthermore, the Guidelines appear to take a clear stance in favor of participatory instruments as means particularly conducive to the effective integration of diverse societies (read in the sense indicated above). This is expressed in the explanatory note of Guideline no. 8, which affirms that the state "needs to provide policies, legislation and mechanisms that enable and support the expression and negotiation of diversity within a shared institutional and legislative framework", and that "in the context of integration of diverse societies, individuals and/or groups can reach solutions acceptable to all to the issues they face through negotiation and mutual accommodation".[171] In addition, Guideline no. 9 proclaims the centrality of effective participation in social, economic, and cultural life to achieving an integrated, diverse society.[172]

Similarly notable is the critical role the Guidelines attribute to participation in all the other sections. In Part III ("Elements of an integration policy"), they underline that integration policies should be elaborated, implemented, and monitored, taking into account the competencies and roles of private actors and stakeholders, including members of minorities.[173] In this sense, members of non-majority groups are no longer considered as mere objects of minority protection but as subjects in the process of defining instruments for the accommodation of diversity.

Effective participation is indicated as one of the most important policy areas[174] for diversity accommodation and a fundamental right to which everyone, including members of minorities, is entitled. According to the Guidelines, members of non-majority groups should not only enjoy the right to participate but also be encouraged to do so in a more proactive manner.[175] Hence, states are asked to design instruments and policies proportionate to the degree and significance of diversity in their societies, as well as the needs of their different communities.

Participation involves several dimensions of life, including social and economic life, as well as cultural and religious affairs and democratic decision-making. Every aspect of participation is, once more, addressed following the non-isolationist and non-exclusivist approach featured in the Guidelines. This means that measures directed towards some groups are

171 Guideline no. 8, 18.
172 Guideline no. 9, 19–20.
173 Guidelines no. 13, 24; no. 14, 25; no. 18, 28; no. 23, 32; no. 24, 33; no. 28, 36–37; and no. 29, 37.
174 This is the area to which most attention is drawn in the Guidelines, also in terms of practical recommendations.
175 See Guidelines, 3.

always meant to benefit the entire society, their application is never restricted to one or more legally selected communities, and the instruments for the accommodation of diversity are not considered the exclusive property of some non-majority groups.

As regards social and economic life, states are mainly asked to remove the existing obstacles that hinder, in particular, the participation of persons belonging to non-majority groups.[176] Such obstacles may be various and relate to a large number of areas, including housing, healthcare, social protection, social welfare services, education, and employment (including inclusion in the labor market with both public and private employers and access to business and other self-employment opportunities).[177] Interestingly, as specified by the commentary of Guideline no. 40, participation also implies the active involvement of members of non-majority groups residing in depressed areas and the design and implementation of policies aimed at fostering their economic regeneration.

As for participation in cultural and religious life, the Guidelines affirm that preserving and promoting different cultural and religious traditions is as critical as encouraging interaction and intercultural exchange in a pluralist framework.[178] The promotion of non-majority cultures requires that members of minorities be effectively included in the decision-making processes concerning relevant policies and legislation and have a say on matters that pertain to them. Decentralization – which can also take the shape of non-territorial arrangements – is also advanced as a tool that can play a significant role in this area insofar as it is employed in a context where the principles of pluralism, participation, and democratization are respected.[179]

The final dimension of participation concerns democratic decision-making processes. Guideline no. 39 lays down a list of possible instruments that states can design to foster non-majority representation and participation. Apart from the arrangements aimed at encouraging or guaranteeing minority representation in elected assemblies and other public bodies, other tools appear to be of particular interest. On the one hand, territorial and non-territorial autonomous arrangements are framed as tools that facilitate minority representation so long as they keep an inclusive and open structure. This is particularly true of territorial autonomy, concerning which Guideline no. 39 maintains that it must be based on democratic principles

176 Guideline no. 40, 47–49.

177 Guideline no. 40, 47–49.

178 See Guideline no. 41, 49–50.

179 See Guideline no. 41, 49–50: "cultural policy should observe the principles of pluralism, participation, democratization and decentralization. Processes of decentralization, including non-territorial self-governance (cultural-autonomy) arrangements, can play an important role in creating the conditions necessary for persons belonging to minorities to participate effectively in cultural life".

and processes to ensure that it reflects the views of all the communities of the concerned territory and not solely of the regional majority. In other words, the Guidelines encourage an "integration-oriented" approach to autonomy that is distanced from the "pure" model of territorial autonomy for minority protection.[180]

On the other, the Guideline acknowledges that minority participation can be achieved by consultative or "dialogic" bodies and mechanisms marked by different degrees of institutionalization (in that they may be variously institutionalized channels of communication) as well as by "processes" designed to ensure and promote effective participation. In other words, the Guidelines expressly recognize the fact that more or less institutionalized participatory instruments that go beyond those that are traditional in this area may play a considerable role in creating the conditions for the accommodation of diverse societies. In a way, such recognition means that participatory democracy, including bottom-up and less institutionalized practices, is included in the instruments for the accommodation of diversity and considered worthy of specific attention. Such tools are of particular interest as they have evident inclusive potential and do not necessarily require that specific legal recognition of non-majority groups be accorded given their flexibility and possible lesser institutionalization.

Ultimately, one may conclude from the above that diversity accommodation is framed by the Guidelines as a complex, inclusive, and multi-layered governance system whereby public and private (minority) actors have an active role in the design and implementation of measures as well as their very application. They consequently recommend a system where minority rights are still fundamental but employed as non-exclusive tools – owing to their broader societal target – and are complemented by dialogic measures and instruments that distance themselves from the typical minority rights structure. As regards this latter category, a wide set of participatory democracy mechanisms – which include more and less institutionalized instruments and processes – are seen as the key to a successful accommodation of diversity and integration of diverse societies.

The ACFC commentary of 2016

The ACFC Thematic Commentary No. 4 of 2016[181] is the third soft law document that advances a societal and global approach to the accommodation of

180 Palermo, Francesco, "Owned or Shared? Territorial Autonomy in the Minority Discourse", in Malloy, Tove H. and Palermo, Francesco (eds.), *Minority Accommodation through Territorial and Non-Territorial Autonomy* (Oxford University Press, Oxford, 2015), 13–32.

181 ACFC, Thematic Commentary no. 4, *The Framework Convention: A Key Tool to Managing Diversity Through Minority Rights*, ACFC/56DOC(2016)001, hereinafter also referred to as Commentary or Commentary of 2016.

diversity, which is synthesized in its title, “The Framework Convention: a key tool to managing diversity through minority rights”.[182]

The Commentary’s main innovative contents delve into a reframing of minority rights as instruments, which are not exclusively targeted at minorities but have a wide societal reach and affect the (diverse) society globally. This is established at the very beginning of the document, where the Commentary underlines that “the Framework Convention addresses society as a whole and not just individuals or specific groups. Rather than asking ‘who’ should be protected, it asks ‘what’ is required to manage diversity most effectively through the protection of minority rights”.[183] In other words, this document also endorses a non-isolationist use of minority rights.

Notably, not dissimilarly from the Ljubljana Guidelines, this reconsideration of the instruments for the accommodation of diversity follows from a flexible and non-exclusivist framing of (minority) identity issues and an inclusive conception of the notion of integration.

Concerning identity and diversity issues, the Commentary is in line with the considerations indicated in the other documents. It emphasizes the fact that diversity is a general and dynamic phenomenon marking (several) societies and cannot be conceived of as a static and immutable feature of some specific (minority or majority) group. Rather, differences are present in and between the different components of diverse societies, and this should be taken into consideration when designing and implementing instruments for the accommodation of diversity.[184]

As for integration, this is here defined as

> a process of give-and-take and affects society as a whole. . . . This is particularly relevant in distinguishing successful integration from forced assimilation, which is explicitly prohibited in Article 5(2) of the Framework Convention. While assimilation forces persons belonging to a minority to relinquish their specific characteristics to blend into a society that is dominated by the majority, integration requires both the majority and the minorities to mutually adapt and change through an ongoing negotiation and accommodation process.[185]

Once more, integration is thus seen as a process that involves society as a whole and leads to societal cohesion without excluding or eliminating diversity. As a result, not only do the instruments for the accommodation of diversity serve

182 The document is structured in eight parts: an introduction (Part I); Part II dedicated to the right to free self-identification; Part III dealing with different state approaches to the application of the FCNM; Part IV, V, VI, and VI on the inclusive model of accommodation proposed by the ACFC; Part VIII containing the conclusions.

183 Commentary of 2016, 3.

184 Commentary of 2016, 5.

185 Commentary of 2016, para. 44, 18.

the interests of some selected and legally recognized groups, but they are also supposed to have a broader scope, as they are also beneficial for non-legally recognized groups and society as a whole.

It is consequently no surprise that the core concept around which the entire Commentary seems to revolve is flexibility.

Flexibility is firstly recommended when it comes to the definition of a national minority. The ACFC, in line with its long-established soft jurisprudence, affirms that

> The purpose of this commentary is to make it clear that the absence of a definition in the Framework Convention is indeed not only intentional but also necessary to ensure that the specific societal, including economic and demographic, circumstances of states parties are duly taken into account when establishing the applicability of minority rights. The Framework Convention was deliberately conceived as a living instrument whose interpretation must evolve and be adjusted regularly to new societal challenges.[186]

Put differently, no limitations on potential addressees have ever been established by the FCNM nor by its monitoring body. The latter approach has been frustrated by states, which, by contrast, have recurrently relied upon various kinds of legal recognition (and definitions) of minorities and/or other criteria to narrow down (or exclude) the application of positive measures that go beyond non-discrimination in their territories. The ACFC has criticized this practice numerous times, including in the Commentary of 2016.[187] In this case, the Commentary endorses a completely reversed perspective, whereby the factual evidence of a condition of diversity becomes the main criterion for the adoption of protective or empowering measures.[188]

From that, a flexible and broad employment of the instruments provided for by FCNM, in terms of its addressees, is put forward. In fact, in Part III, the document thoroughly describes the approaches taken by states to the application of the FCNM, typically intended to circumscribe its application, and contests them while at the same time proposing what is defined as a "context-specific article-by-article" approach. In practice, the model suggested by the ACFC requires that the application of the FCNM not be limited to legally recognized national minorities but variously and proportionally extended to persons that belong to groups that live in a similar situation.

186 Commentary of 2016, para. 5, 5.

187 Furthermore, the ACFC has underlined that while states have a margin of discretion in this area, this is not without its limitations, which are based on the international law principles of good faith and *pacta sunt servanda*; see Commentary of 2016, para. 5, 5.

188 Which is in line with the international approach to this issue and the indications coming from the PCIJ's advisory opinion of 31 July 1930, *Greco-Bulgarian Communities*, Ser. B, Fasc. No. 17, 3–36.

Interestingly, the document offers some concrete examples of possible further beneficiaries, such as members of the majority of a state living in a minority language-dominated area, groups enjoying special measures but not recognized as minorities, members of constituent people who live in a minority situation, and immigrants.[189]

Flexibility is, secondly, suggested when it comes to the implementation of legal instruments for the accommodation of diversity. The model recommended by the Commentary is marked by a non-exclusivist framing of diversity issues, which is strictly connected to the fundamental principle of free self-identification. The Commentary underlines that several contemporary societies are affected by constant transformation – due to not only mobility and migration but also mixed marriages and cases of state succession – with this impacting the development of individuals' identity perceptions.[190] As a result, identity formation may be conceived of as a lifelong dynamic process during which one may simultaneously affiliate with multiple groups that have a minority or majority status.[191] Following this view, free self-identification acquires critical significance for diversity accommodation, as it allows people to express which identity is relevant for them and avoid externally imposed ascription (which is frequently based upon specific identity markers, like religion, language, culture, ethnic background, or other visible features) and legal treatment.[192] Furthermore, a non-exclusivist approach to diversity accommodation acknowledges that groups are composed of people with diverse claims and desires – some members of minorities may prioritize integration, others the maintenance of their differential status – and that people may at the same time be and feel part of different groups and concurrently have different needs depending on the situation they find themselves in.[193]

In other words, the document aims to encourage a reconsideration of the models for managing diversity with a view to adapting them to the complex societal reality they rule. It endorses flexibility as, at least on some occasions, a traditional framing of diversity accommodation tools – based on static and exclusivist categorizations, rigid top-down instruments, and a minority-majority framing – appears to be distant from the reality they address

189 Commentary of 2016, para. 47, 19; specifically, on the application of the "contextual article-by-article approach" endorsed by the ACFC to immigrants, see Palermo, Francesco, "Deconstructing Myths: What's in the Debate on Extending the Scope of Minority Rights and Policies to Immigrants?", in Medda-Windischer, Roberta, Boulter, Caitlin and Malloy, Tove H. (eds.), *Extending Protection to Migrant Populations in Europe: Old and New Minorities* (Routledge, London-New York, 2020), 16–36.

190 See Commentary of 2016, 3.

191 On this, see Commentary of 2016, 3–5, and Part II, on the right to free self-identification.

192 Commentary of 2016, para. 37, 15.

193 On this, see Commentary of 2016, para. 11, 7: "free self-identification implies the right to choose on a situational basis when to self-identify as a person belonging to a national minority and when not to do so".

and may, therefore, be counterproductive to the successful integration of diverse societies.[194]

Such an approach has notable consequences for how the instruments for the accommodation of diversity are implemented.

For instance, fromthe recognition of multiple affiliations derives the right to selectively exercise the rights related to a particular group in different situations.[195] Put differently, people who identify with more than one group are not required to choose membership of one exclusively. Therefore, "This implies that practices by which an individual affiliates with a particular minority should not be seen as exclusive, as he or she may simultaneously identify with other minorities or with the majority".[196]

The non-exclusive membership of different groups constitutes a significant shift in how diversity issues are framed and may consequently be regulated. It implies softening the majority-minority framing that underpins traditional approaches to these issues, which in some cases may reinforce rather than weaken their logic of contraposition and exclusivity. In turn, this inspires models that rely on this contraposition and are consequently rigid, strongly institutionalized, and exceptional. Their rollout, therefore, generally demands adequate financial resources and cannot be indefinitely extended. In such a context, hierarchies among various minorities may be created,[197] and people belonging to groups that do not benefit from any kind of recognition or support are naturally inclined to claim instruments and protections that follow this model.

Notably, what the Commentary illustrates is that alternative and more inclusive approaches are possible without necessarily leading to the demise of the corpus of minority rights and the guarantees they provide.

Inclusivity and respect for diversity inform this model and appear to be particularly conducive to integration in societies where diversity is no longer

194 On this, Commentary of 2016, para. 38, 16: "The categorisation of the minority as a static and homogeneous group may reinforce stereotypes and does not pay adequate attention to the broad diversity and intersectionality that exists within minorities, as within all groups . . . . In some states parties, legislation makes reference to other externally imposed criteria, such as "ethnic minority threatened by social exclusion" or "citizens in a vulnerable socio-economic situation", while in others, an affiliation with a particular national minority may be presumed based on names. The Advisory Committee considers such practices of association of persons with a specific group based, without consent, on presumptions such as names, language, or visible features, as incompatible with Article 3(1) and the right to free self-identification".

195 An example is indicated in the Commentary of 2012, which, in paras. 16–18, 6–7, describes the situation of persons belonging to national minorities that may choose to have their name officially recognised in a minority language but, at the same time, decide not to use their minority language in contact with local administrative authorities.

196 Commentary of 2016, para. 13, 8.

197 Commentary of 2016, para. 43, 18.

taken as an exception or solely identified as some specific type of differential status when it comes to protection or empowerment.

The Commentary indicates that for this to happen, every element of a model for the accommodation of diversity should be structured following the same rationale. Importantly, for instance, it is necessary that the data upon which policies and instruments may be based[198] be collected in accordance with the principle of free self-identification and the renovated conception of diversity. Thus, the Commentary underlines that data collection must be voluntary, and

> no automatic inference from a particular indication (for example language use) to another indication (for instance, religion, ethnicity) and no assumption of certain linguistic, religious or ethnic affiliations is to be made based on a person's name or other characteristics.[199]

In addition, the list of possible responses to identity-related questions should be open, and the possibility of expressing multiple affiliations should be provided explicitly. Moreover, the ACFC cautions states against exclusively relying on official statistics and figures, which may not be a realistic representation of reality, as some people belonging to disadvantaged groups may be unwilling to participate in censuses due to fear of discrimination or persecution. In other words, flexibility is once more critical and much encouraged.

In addition, priority is given to the factual condition of diversity rather than legal recognition. Based on this rationale, the ACFC states that several measures provided for by the FCNM may be implemented without the need to recognize non-majority groups as national minorities formally. Indeed, the Commentary thoroughly describes the broad scope of the different rights laid down in the FCNM.[200] Some states have partially followed this approach; for instance, Cyprus and Finland. The former has included Roma under the protection of the FCNM, although they are not a legally recognized minority; the

198 For instance, when the enjoyment of particular rights is linked to numerical thresholds.

199 Commentary of 2016, para. 15, 8–9.

200 After analyzing different state practices concerning the definition of national minorities, Part IV of the Commentary goes on to propose a classification of the articles of the FCNM based on their general or specific scope; accordingly, a first set of guarantees applies to everyone, such as the protection against discrimination, the promotion of intercultural dialogue, the protection from hostility and hate crime, and the promotion of education and media as tools for integration; a second group of articles are considered as having a broad scope of application: these are those referring to equality, culture, association and religion, media, language, education, and participation; the last category includes, minority rights that have a specific scope of application and those where their exercise could be limited to certain areas of a country where the members of the minority reside traditionally and/or in substantial numbers; these are the right to use a minority language in relations with local administrative authorities, the right to have topographical indications and signposts displayed in the minority language, and the right to learn minority languages or receive instruction in minority languages.

latter has extended the protection afforded to "old Russians" to newer Russian speakers.[201]

Another critical issue that emerges from the perspective endorsed by the Commentary is that dialogic means, including participatory mechanisms, are to be considered as part of the instruments for the accommodation of diversity and play an important role as tools that are specifically targeted to the protection of minorities.[202] This is particularly true when non-recognized minorities are taken into consideration since it seems that participatory means constitute a first step, or even a precondition, in a process of gradual integration of non-majority groups that may eventually lead to further and more structured protection or empowerment.[203] Moreover, such instruments are thought to facilitate the design of "open and flexible solutions to issues that prevent access to rights, and may thereby promote societal cohesion and stability"[204] together with respect for diversity. Interestingly, the Commentary highlights that various virtuous state practices are observable, as in the cases of the Czech Republic and Finland. In both countries, immigrant groups like Somalis and Vietnamese are included in cultural consultation mechanisms and benefit from state support for their activities. In Finland, the Somali League is an active member of the Advisory Board on Ethnic Relations, which is a consultative body that advises the Ministry of Interior on matters related to minorities and integration. In the Czech Republic, an open definition of minorities is provided for by the Act on the Rights of Members of National Minorities (law no. 273/2001), which, among other things, established the Government Council for National Minorities – a permanent advisory and initiative body which is composed of representatives of the national minorities and of ministries and other public bodies responsible for minority policies. The inclusion

201 On this, see the Second State Report submitted by Cyprus and the ACFC Third Opinion on Finland; also, it seems that the Czech Republic is following the same approach, allowing the enjoyment of rights to non-citizens who share the ethnic identity of a national minority of the state, despite the fact that Article 2(1) of Act 273 of 2001 on the Rights of Members of National Minorities and other minority provisions refer to citizenship as a criterion to either define a minority or exercise some specific rights.

202 Commentary of 2016, para. 53, 21: "The Advisory Committee has consistently held . . . that an exclusive view that separates the issue of traditional minority protection from broader questions surrounding the integration of society does not do justice to the aim and purpose of the Framework Convention but rather hinders the enjoyment of the rights of persons belonging to national minorities; in several other parts of the document the importance of this dimension of diversity accommodation is highlighted, and not only in the section specifically dedicated to this issue (29–30); for instance, in the area of media, the Commentary indicates that it is important "to ensure that minority representative effectively participate in relevant decision-making processes as in media supervisory bodies".

203 As indicated by the Commentary of 2016, para. 75, 29, the ACFC has many times "underlined the importance of an inclusive approach to the application of Article 15, as effective participation is often a precondition to gaining access to the rights contained in the Framework Convention".

204 Commentary of 2016, para. 76, 29.

of the Vietnamese minority in that body has been a fundamental step for this community toward accessing structured forms of protection and empowerment and contributing to the design of minority accommodation measures.[205]

More generally, the Commentary affirms that broader questions about the integration of diverse society are not to be separated from the implementation of minority rights. This implies that measures that favor intercultural comprehension and exchange can also arguably be seen as part of an inclusive and open model of diversity accommodation. As already observable in the Ljubljana Guidelines, the media and the school system are the areas where the best results in terms of integration are thought to happen.[206]

Convergences and divergences between the Global North and Global South

From the described macro-constitutional perspectives, it is possible to sketch some brief considerations.

To begin with, the comparative overview has contributed to the relativization of a specific idea of constitutionalism and aimed to illustrate its various concrete materializations. As a political and legal concept, constitutionalism seems to be flexible enough to include many forms of organization and worldviews without losing its meaning and function. In other words, juxtaposing the Global South and Global North approaches contributes to pluralizing the contents of constitutionalism. Furthermore, both experiences seem to illustrate that the constitutional framework may embed pluralism to a significant extent without losing its guiding role.

Indeed, one can notice that in the analyzed Global South countries, constitutionalism and the state are not fused. This means that the constitutional structure – especially when it comes to diversity accommodation and the management of pluralism – decenters the state and its institutions, consistently favoring non-state or alternative public actors and putting a major accent on governance models.

Though this version of constitutionalism is not unknown in the Global North tradition – take, for instance, the English experience, where constitutionalism is a theory of law and not a theory of the state[207] – liberal theory has nonetheless significantly tied constitutionalism to the centrality of the state. From the perspective of the narrower area of interest in this work, the fusion between constitutionalism and state has implied the centrality of the latter

205 On this, see Kascian, Kiryl and Vasilevich, Hanna, "Czech Republic Acknowledgement of Belarusian and Vietnamese as New Minorities", 12 *European Yearbook of Minority Issues* (2013), 353–371.

206 Commentary of 2016, paras. 59–63, 23–24.

207 On this, see Torre, Alessandro, "Il Regno Unito", in Carrozza, Paolo, Di Giovine, Alfonso and Ferrari, Giuseppe F. (eds.), *Diritto costituzionale comparato* (Laterza, Rome-Bari, 2019), 5–54.

when it comes to the accommodation of diversity. In turn, this has led to a public, state-directed, top-down, paternalistic approach to this area based on the notion of recognition as a gateway to the enjoyment of special rights.

However, the latest developments, at least in international soft law, appear to adopt a different model, which, to a certain degree, resonates with some concepts of the Global South traditions. The soft law documents put forward the idea that diversity is a foundational feature of (several) contemporary societies and pluralism – a principle that should inform constitutional systems and states' approaches to managing diversity. Accordingly, European soft law upholds the importance of conceiving diversity accommodation as a complex and flexible governance model that needs the contribution of all relevant actors, be they public or not. Subsidiarity, cooperation, and a non-exclusivist approach to managing diversity are central elements of this model. Hence, it seems that a partial convergence is observable in this area, with a common theoretical and practical ground that consists of the concepts of governance and pluralism.

Nevertheless, it seems that the European perspective diverges from that of the analyzed Global South regions in terms of the theoretical framing of diversity. Indeed, the former puts a strong emphasis on the concept of diversity as a general phenomenon in societies. It, therefore, tries to distance itself from the traditional approach, which characterizes minority and indigenous peoples' rights law by relying on the conflation between diversity and some specific groups. By contrast, the Global South approach, albeit quite inclusive when it comes to diversity management, tends to identify diversity by reference to some specific groups. At the same time, a certain degree of flexibility and inclusiveness characterize this region, too.

Lastly, shifting the focus on the means that have introduced innovations in diversity accommodation in the studied areas, the described macro-constitutional perspectives show that constitutional design, especially in the Global South, has played a significant role in shaping models for the accommodation of diversity. This especially seems to be the case in those regions whose countries aspire to use the constitutional text as a privileged, transformative instrument conducive to wide societal and political changes through legal processes. In those areas of the world, the transformative use of constitutions has mainly sought to symbolically and practically break from past colonial, authoritarian, and racist state structures or to end violent conflicts and recompose diverse and divided societies.[208] However, in line with the comparative method endorsed in this work, one should not refrain from drawing attention to the possible lessons that the Global South may hold for general global discourse on diversity accommodation.

By contrast, it appears that the transformative use of constitutions has only been considered as an option for the Global North to a limited extent. Global

208 On this, see Klare, Legal Culture . . . , 146–188.

North countries – and especially the European region – have witnessed a pluralization of their constitutional systems without considerable constitutional reforms but through a strengthened (and more or less successful) dialogue between international (hard and soft) law developments and national constitutional frameworks. Among them, beyond the European continent, Canada stands out as an important case: the rigid constitutional federal design of that country has not been limiting but rather acted as an enabling structure for the emergence of manifold forms of "nested" governance.

Hence, constitutional reform is probably not a panacea when seeking solutions to the challenges diversity accommodation poses nowadays. Rather, this comparative overview has demonstrated that constitutional revision in some regions has been a significant instrument through which revolutionary concepts of state and law – based on strong pluralism and forms of governance that parallel traditional state structures – as well as other principles, like plurinationality and interculturalism, have been entrenched.

Bibliography

Aboultaif, Eduardo W., *Power-Sharing in Lebanon: Consociationalism since 1820* (Routledge, London-New York, 2019)

Acosta, Alberto, *El Buen Vivir: Sumak Kawsay, una oportunidad para imaginar otros mundos* (Abya-Yala, Quito, 2012)

Aguilar, Gonzalo, Lafosse, Sandra, Rojas, Hugo, and Steward, Rébecca, "The Constitutional Recognition of Indigenous Peoples in Latin America", 2(2) *Pace International Law Review Online Companion* (2010), 44–96

Akgönül, Samim, "Le statut personnel des musulmans de Grèce: vestiges ottomans et réalités contemporaines", in Aoun, Marc (ed.), *Les statuts personnels en droit comparé: Evolutions récentes et implications pratiques* (Peeters, Leuven, 2009), 279–291

Aljunied, Syed and Khairudin, Muhd, *Colonialism, Violence and Muslims in Southeast Asia: The Maria Hertogh Controversy and Its Aftermath* (Routledge, London-New York, 2009)

Ávila Santamaría, Ramiro, "Ecuador Estado constitucional de derechos y justicia", in Ávila Santamaría, Ramiro (ed.), *La Constitución del 2008 en el contexto andino: análisis desde la doctrina y el derecho comparado* (Ministerio de Justicia y Derechos Humano, Quito, 2008), 19–38

Àvila Santamaría, Ramiro, *El neoconstitucionalismoa andino* (Universidad Andina Simón Bolivar, Sede Ecuador and Huaponi Ediciones, Quito, 2016)

Bagni, Silvia, *Il ruolo delle Corti costituzionali tra pluralismo giuridico, plurinazionalità e interculturalità*, at: https://www.robertotoniatti.eu/contributi/il-ruolo-delle-corti-costituzionali-tra-pluralismo-giuridico-plurinazionalita-e-interculturalita

Barié, Cletus Gregor, "Representation of Indigenous Peoples in Times of Progressive Governments: Lessons Learned from Bolivia", 17(2) *Latin American and Caribbean Ethnic Studies* (2022), 167–192

Barrantes-Reynolds, Maria-Paula, *Legal Pluralism in the Constitution of Bolivia of 2009: Between Multiculturalism and Plurinationalism* (PhD dissertation, University of Leicester, Leicester, 2016)

Barrera, Anna, "Turning Legal Pluralism into State-Sanctioned Law: Assessing the Implications of the New Constitutions and Laws in Bolivia and Ecuador", in Nolte, Detlef and Schilling-Vacaflor, Almut (eds.), *New Constitutionalism in Latin*

America: Promises and Practices (Routledge, London-New York, 2016), 575–604 (e-book version)

Barrios, Franz, "The Bolivian Invention: Plurinationality and Indigenous People within an Unusual Composite State Structure", in Requejo, Ferran and Caminal, Miquel (eds.), *Federalism, Plurinationality and Democratic Constitutionalism: Theory and Cases* (Routledge, London-New York, 2012), e-book version, 436–482

Basta, Karlo, *The Symbolic State: Minority Recognition, Majority Backlash, and Secession in Multinational Countries* (McGill-Queen's University Press, Montréal-Kingston-London-Chicago, 2021)

Bhamra, Meena K., *The Challenges of Justice in Diverse Societies: Constitutionalism and Pluralism* (Ashgate, Farnham-Burlington, 2011)

Boaventura de Sousa Santos, "Cuando los excluidos tienen derecho: justicia indígena, plurinacionalidad e interculturalidad", in Boaventura, de Sousa Santos and Grijalva Jiménez, Agustín (eds.), *Justicia indígena, plurinacionalidad e interculturalidad en Ecuador* (Abya Yala-Fundación Rosa Luxembourg, Quito, 2012), 13–50

Boaventura de Sousa, Santos and Exeni Rodríguez, José Luis (eds.), *Justicia indígena, plurinacionalidad e interculturalidad en Bolivia* (Abya Yala-Fundación Rosa Luxembourg, Quito, 2012)

Boaventura de Sousa, Santos and Grijalva Jiménez, Agustín (eds.), *Justicia indígena, plurinacionalidad e interculturalidad en Ecuador* (Abya Yala-Fundación Rosa Luxembourg, Quito, 2012)

Bonilla Maldonado, Daniel (ed.), *Constitutionalism of the Global South: The Activist Tribunals of India, South Africa and Colombia* (Cambridge University Press, Cambridge, 2013)

Bonilla Maldonado, Daniel, "Multicultural Constitutions", in Mendes, Conrado H., Gargarella, Roberto and Guidi, Sebastián (eds.), *The Oxford Handbook of Constitutional Law in Latin America* (Oxford University Press, Oxford, 2022), 832–845

Castellino, Joshua and Domínguez Redondo, Elvira, *Minority Rights in Asia: A Comparative Legal Analysis* (Oxford University Press, Oxford, 2006)

Cauquelin, Josiane, Lim, Paul and Mayer-König, Birgit (eds.), *Asian Values: An Encounter with Diversity* (Curzon Press, Richmond, 2000)

Chan, Heng Chee, Siddique, Sharon, Masron, Irna Nurlina and Cooray, Dominic, *Singapore's Multiculturalism: Evolving Diversity* (Routledge, London-New York, 2019), e-book version

Chassagne, Natasha, *Buen Vivir as an Alternative to Sustainable Development: Lessons from Ecuador* (Routledge, London-New York, 2021)

Cheang, Bryan and Choy, Donovan, *Liberalism Unveiled: Forging a New Third Way in Singapore* (World Scientific, Singapore, 2021)

Choo, John, "A Mimetic Theoretical Approach to Multiculturalism: Normalizing the Singaporean Exception", 26 *Contagion: Journal of Violence, Mimesis, and Culture* (2019), 209–235

Clammer, John, *Race and State in Independent Singapore 1965–1990: The Cultural Politics of Pluralism in a Multiethnic Society* (Routledge, London-New York, 1998), e-book version

Coertzen, Pieter, "Religion and the Constitutional Experience of South Africa", in Bottoni, Rossella, Cristofori, Rinaldo and Ferrari, Silvio (eds.), *Religious Rules, State Law, and Normative Pluralism: A Comparative Overview* (Springer, Cham, 2016), 343–355

Colque Fernández, Gonzalo, *Autonomías indígenas en las tierras altas* (Instituto Internacional para la Democracia y la Asistencia Electoral (IDEA), La Paz, 2009)

De Domingo Soler, Carlos, "Brief Introduction of Andean Neoconstitutionalism for Europeans: Possibilities and Impossibilities", 9(1) *Ius Humani, Revista de Derecho* (2020), 9–44

Dersso, Solomon, "Constitutional Accommodation of Ethnocultural Diversity in the Post-Colonial African State", 24(3) *South African Journal on Human Rights* (2008), 565–592

Englert, Franziska and Schaub-Englert, Jonathan, "A Fruitless Attempt Towards Plurinationality and Decolonization? Perplexities in the Creation of Indigenous Territorial Autonomies in Bolivia", 52(1) *VRÜ Verfassung und Recht in Übersee* (2019), 67–89

Ferrarese, Maria Rosaria, *La governance tra politica e diritto* (Il Mulino, Bologna, 2010)

Ferrari, Silvio, "Religiously Based Personal Laws and Management of Diversity in Europe", 25 *Law and Business* (2022), 1–15

Gargarella, Roberto, "Equality", in Dixon, Rosalind and Ginsburg, Tom (eds.), *Comparative Constitutional Law in Latin America* (Edward Elgar, Cheltenham-Northampton, 2017), 176–197

Gaudreault-DesBiens, Jean-F., "Religious Courts, Personal Federalism, and Legal Transplants", in Ahdar, Rex and Aroney, Nicolas (eds.), *Shari'a in the West* (Oxford University Press, Oxford, 2010), 159–180

Ghosh, Partha S., *The Politics of Personal Law in South Asia: Identity, Nationalism and the Uniform Civil Code* (Routledge, London-New York, 2018)

Griffiths, John, "What Is Legal Pluralism?", 24 *The Journal of Legal Pluralism and Unofficial Law* (1986), 1–55

Grijalva Jiménez, Agustín, "Del presente se inventa el futuro: justicias indígenas y estado en Ecuador", in Boaventura de Sousa, Santos and Grijalva Jiménez, Agustín (eds.), *Justicia indígena, plurinacionalidad e interculturalidad en Ecuador* (Abya Yala-Fundación Rosa Luxembourg, Quito, 2012), 51–76

Harding, Andrew (ed.), *The Constitution of Malaysia: A Contextual Analysis* (Bloomsbury, London, 2012)

Huneeus, Alexandra, "The Limits of Inter-American Constitutionalism", in Dixon, Rosalind and Ginsburg, Tom (eds.), *Comparative Constitutional Law in Latin America* (Edward Elgar, Cheltenham-Northampton, 2017), 300–324

Jain, Ritu, "Multilingual Singapore: Language Policies, Challenges, and Responses", in Jain, Ritu (ed.), *Multilingual Singapore: Language Policies and Linguistic Realities* (Routledge, London-New York, 2021), 1–11

Kascian, Kiryl and Vasilevich, Hanna, "Czech Republic Acknowledgement of Belarusian and Vietnamese as New Minorities", 12 *European Yearbook of Minority Issues* (2013), 353–371

Klare, Karl E., "Legal Culture and Transformative Constitutionalism", 14(1) *South African Journal on Human Rights* (1998), 146–188

Kymlicka, Will, "Liberal Multiculturalism: Western Models, Global Trends, and Asian Debates", in Kymlicka, Will and He, Baobang (eds.), *Multiculturalism in Asia* (Oxford University Press, Oxford, 2005), 22–55

Kymlicka, Will and He, Baobang, "Introduction", in Kymlicka, Will and He, Baobang (eds.), *Multiculturalism in Asia* (Oxford University Press, Oxford, 2005), 1–21

Langa, Pius, "Transformative Constitutionalism", 17(3) *Stellenbosch Law Review* (2006), 351–360

Lau, Albert, *A Moment of Anguish: Singapore in Malaysia and the Politics of Disengagement* (Times Academic Press, Singapore, 2000)

Levitsky, Steven and Way, Lucan A., *Competitive Authoritarianism: Problems of International Politics* (Cambridge University Press, Cambridge, 2010)

Llasag Fernández, Raúl, "Plurinacionalidad: una propuesta constitucional emancipadora", in Ávila Santamaria, Ramiro (ed.), *Neoconstitucionalismo y sociedad* (Ministerio de la Justicia y Derechos Humanos, Quito, 2008), 311–355

Macedo, Stephen, *Liberal Virtues: Citizenship, Virtue and Community in Liberal Constitutionalism* (Clarendon Press, Oxford, 1990)

Malik, Maleiha, *Minority Legal Orders in the UK: Minorities, Pluralism and the Law* (The British Academy, London, 2012)

Maoz, Asher, "The Application of Religious Law in a Multi-Religion Nation State: The Israeli Model", in Bottoni, Rossella, Cristofori, Rinaldo and Ferrari, Silvio (eds.), *Religious Rules, State Law, and Normative Pluralism: A Comparative Overview* (Springer, Cham, 2016), 209–227

Martínez Novo, Carmen, "Managing Diversity in Postneoliberal Ecuador", 19(1) *The Journal of Latin American and Caribbean Anthropology* (2014), 103–125

McGarry, John, O'Leary, Brendan and Simeon, Richard, "Integration or Accommodation? The Enduring Debate in Conflict Regulation", in Choudry, Sujit (ed.), *Constitutional Design for Divided Societies: Integration or Accommodation?* (Oxford University Press, Oxford, 2008), 41–88

Menski, Werner, "Beyond Europe", in Örücü, Esin and Nelken, David (eds.), *Comparative Law: A Handbook* (Hart Publishing, Oxford-Portland, 2007), 189–216

Menski, Werner, "Law, State and Culture: How Countries Accommodate Religious, Cultural and Ethnic Diversity, the British and Indian Experiences", in Foblets, Marie-Claire, Gaudreault-DesBiens, Jean-F. and Dundes Renteln, Alison (eds.), *Cultural Diversity and the Law: State Responses from Around the World* (Bruylant-Yvonne Blais, Bruxelles-Montréal, 2010), 403–446

Merino, Roger, "Reimagining the Nation-State: Indigenous Peoples and the Making of Plurinationalism in Latin America", 31(4) *Leiden Journal of International Law* (2018), 773–792

Mortati, Costantino, *La Costituzione in Senso Materiale* (Giuffrè, Milan, 1940)

Neo, Jacklyn L., "Dimensions of Religious Harmony as Constitutional Practice: Beyond State Control", 20 *German Law Journal* (2019), 966–985

Neo, Jacklyn L., "Navigating Minority Inclusion and Permanent Division: Minorities and the Depoliticization of Difference", 17 *Jus Politicum* (2017), 607–627

Neo, Jacklyn L., "Regulating Pluralism: Laws on Religious Harmony and Possibilities for Robust Pluralism in Singapore", 18(3) *The Review of Faith & International Affairs* (2020), 1–15

Neo, Jacklyn L., "Space Still Matters: Towards More Pluralism in Public Law: Afterword to the Foreword by Ran Hirschl and Ayelet Shachar", 18(1) *International Journal of Constitutional Law (I Con)* (2020), 22–28

Neo, Jacklyn L., "State Legal Pluralism and Religious Courts: 'Semi-Autonomy and Jurisdictional Allocations in Pluri-Legal Arrangements'", in Berman, Paul S. (ed.), *The Oxford Handbook of Global Legal Pluralism* (Oxford University Press, Oxford, 2020), e-book version, 1628–1668

Neo, Jacklyn L. and Bui, Ngoc Son (eds.), *Pluralist Constitutions in Southeast Asia* (Hart Publishing, Oxford-Portland, 2019)

Ortino, Sergio, *La struttura delle rivoluzioni economiche* (Cacucci, Bari, 2010)

Ortiz Tirado, Pablo, "El laberinto de la autonomía indígena en el Ecuador: las circunscripciones territoriales indígenas en la amazonía central, 2010–2012", 10(1) *Latin American and Caribbean Ethnic Studies* (2015), 60–86

Ost, François and Van de Kerchove, Michel, *De la pyramide au réseau? Pour une théorie dialectique du droit* (Université Saint-Louis, Bruxelles, 2002)

Pacari, Nina, "Naturaleza y territorio desde la mirada de los pueblos indigenas", in Acosta, Alberto and Martinez, Esperanza (eds.), *Derechos de la naturaleza: el futuro es ahora* (Abya-Yala, Quito, 2009), 129–132

Palermo, Francesco, "Deconstructing Myths: What's in the Debate on Extending the Scope of Minority Rights and Policies to Immigrants?", in Medda-Windischer, Roberta, Boulter, Caitlin and Malloy, Tove H. (eds.), *Extending Protection to Migrant Populations in Europe: Old and New Minorities* (Routledge, London-New York, 2020), 16–36

Palermo, Francesco, "Owned or Shared? Territorial Autonomy in the Minority Discourse", in Malloy, Tove H. and Palermo, Francesco (eds.), *Minority Accommodation through Territorial and Non-Territorial Autonomy* (Oxford University Press, Oxford, 2015), 13–32

Palermo, Francesco, "'The Borders of My Language Mean the Borders of My World': Language Rights and Their Evolving Significance for Minority Rights and Integration of Societies", in Ulasiuk, Iryna, Hadîrcă, Laurenţiu and Romans, William (eds.), *Language Policy and Conflict Prevention* (Brill-Nijhoff, Leiden-Boston, 2018), 135–154

Palermo, Francesco, "Quanto è morbido il soft law? La tutela non giurisdizionale dei diritti delle minoranze nelle aree geogiuridiche europee", 1 *Rivista di Diritti Comparati* (2022), 74–94

Pegoraro, Lucio, "Comparare l'America Latina (e in America Latina): introduzione critica", in Bagni, Silvia e Baldin, Serena (eds.), *Latinoamérica: viaggio nel costituzionalismo comparato dalla Patagonia al Río Grande* (Giappichelli, Turin, 2022), 3–15

Pogrebinschi, Thamy, "Turning Participation into Representation Innovative Policy Making for Minority Groups in Brazil", in Girouard, Jennifer (ed.), *Varieties of Civic Innovation: Deliberative, Collaborative, Network, and Narrative Approaches* (Vanderbilt University Press, Nashville, 2014), e-book version, 321–365

Pogrebinschi, Thamy and Ros, Melisa, "Democratic Innovations in Latin America", in Elstub, Stephen and Escobar, Oliver (eds.), *Handbook of Democratic Innovation and Governance* (Edward Elgar, Cheltenham-Northampton, 2019), 389–403

Pozzolo, Susanna, "Neoconstitucionalismo=Neoconstitutionalism", 11 *Eunomía: Revista en Cultura de la Legalidad* (2016), 142–151

Quinn Moore, Robert, "Multiracialism and Meritocracy: Singapore's Approach to Race and Inequality", 58(3) *Review of Social Economy* (2000), 339–360

Ramírez, Silvina and Maisley, Nahuel, "The Protection of the Rights of Indigenous Peoples", in Gonzalez-Bartomeu, Juan F. and Gargarella, Roberto (eds.), *The Latin American Casebook: Courts, Constitutions, and Rights* (Routledge, London-New York, 2016), 189–208

Ruggiu, Ilenia, *Culture and the Judiciary: The Anthropologist Judge* (Routledge, London-New York, 2019)

Rynkowski, Michael, *Religious Courts in the Jurisprudence of the European Court of Human Rights* (Brill, Leiden-Boston, 2019)

Saffon, Maria Paula, "Property and Land", in Mendes, Conrado H., Gargarella, Roberto and Guidi, Sebastián (eds.), *The Oxford Handbook of Constitutional Law in Latin America* (Oxford University Press, Oxford, 2022), 578–597

Salazar, Daniela, "Ecuador", in Mendes, Conrado H., Gargarella, Roberto and Guidi, Sebastián (eds.), *The Oxford Handbook of Constitutional Law in Latin America* (Oxford University Press, Oxford, 2022), 174–202

Schavelzon, Salvador, *El nacimiento del Estado plurinacional de Bolivia: etnografía de una asamblea constituyente* (Plural editores, La Paz, 2012)

Schavelzon, Salvador, *Plurinacionalidad y Vivir Bien/Buen Vivir: dos conceptos leídos desde Bolivia y Ecuador post-constituyentes* (Abya Yala, Quito, 2019)

Schilling-Vacaflor, Almut and Kuppe, René, "Plurinational Constitutionalism: A New Era of Indigenous-State Relations?", in Nolte, Detlef and Schilling-Vacaflor, Almut (eds.), *New Constitutionalism in Latin America: Promises and Practices* (Routledge, London-New York, 2016), e-book version, 538–574

Tan, Eugene B., *The Constitution of Singapore: A Contextual Analysis* (Hart Publishing, Oxford-Portland, 2015)

Tan, Eugene B., "The Imperative of Integrative Pluralist Constitutionalism: Going Beyond Formal Equality, Eschewing Rights, and Accommodation of Differences in Singapore", in Neo, Jacklyn L. and Bui, Ngoc Son (eds.), *Pluralist Constitutions in Southeast Asia* (Hart Publishing, Oxford-Portland, 2019), 51–81

Teo, Terri-Anne, *Civic Multiculturalism in Singapore: Revisiting Citizenship, Rights and Recognition* (Palgrave Macmillan, Cham, 2019)

Thandabantu, Nhlapo and Chuma, Himonga (eds.), *African Customary Law in South Africa: Post-Apartheid and Living Law Perspectives* (Oxford University Press, Southern Africa, Cape Town, 2014)

Thio, Li-Ann, "The Cooperation of Religion and State in Singapore: A Compassionate Partnership in Service of Welfare", 7(3) *The Review of Faith & International Affairs* (2009), 33–45

Thio, Li-Ann, "Relational Constitutionalism and the Management of Inter-Religious Disputes: The Singapore 'Secularism with a Soul' Model", 1(2) *Oxford Journal of Law and Religion* (2012), 446–469

Thio, Li-Ann, *A Treatise on Singapore Constitutional Law* (Academy Publishing, Singapore, 2012)

Thio, Li-Ann, "Singapore Relational Constitutionalism: The 'Living Institution' and the Project of Religious Harmony", *Singapore Journal of Legal Studies* (2019), 204–234

Tockman, Jason and Cameron, John, "Indigenous Autonomy and the Contradictions of Plurinationalism in Bolivia", 56(3) *Latin American Politics and Society* (2014), 46–69

Tomaselli, Alexandra, *Indigenous Peoples and Their Right to Political Participation* (Nomos, Baden-Baden, 2016)

Toniatti, Roberto, "Il paradigma costituzionale dell'inclusione della diversità culturale in Europa e in America Latina: premesse per una ricerca comparata sui rispettivi modelli", 6 *The Pluralist Papers* (2015), at http://www.jupls.eu/images/JPs_WP6_RT__paradigma_costituzionale_dellinclusione_culturale.pdf

Torre, Alessandro, "Il Regno Unito", in Carrozza, Paolo, Di Giovine, Alfonso and Ferrari, Giuseppe F. (eds.), *Diritto costituzionale comparato* (Laterza, Rome-Bari, 2019), 5–54

Tushnet, Mark, "Authoritarian Constitutionalism", 100(2) *Cornell Law Review* (2015), 391–461

Tushnet, Mark, "The New 'Bolivarian' Constitutions: A Textual Analysis", in Dixon, Rosalind and Ginsburg, Tom (eds.), *Comparative Constitutional Law in Latin America* (Edward Elgar, Cheltenham-Northampton, 2017), 126–152

Vela-Almeida, Diana and Torres, Nataly, "Consultation in Ecuador: Institutional Fragility and Participation in National Extractive Policy", 48(3) *Latin American Perspectives* (2021), 172–191

Vintimilla Saldaña, Jaime, *Ley orgánica de cooperación y coordinación entre la justicia indígena y la jurisdicción ordinaria ecuatoriana: ¿Un mandato constitucional necesario o una norma que limita a los sistemas de justicia indígena?* (Cevallos, Quito, 2012)

Von Bogdandy, Armin, Ferrer Mac-Gregor, Eduardo, Antoniazzi Morales, Mariela, Piovesan Flávia and Soley, Ximena (eds.), *Transformative Constitutionalism in Latin America: The Emergence of a New Ius Commune* (Oxford University Press, Oxford, 2017)

Walsh, Catherine, "The Plurinational and Intercultural State: Decolonization and State Re-founding in Ecuador", 1 *RUDN Journal of Philosophy* (2012), 103–115

Wright, Claire and Tomaselli, Alexandra (eds.), *The Prior Consultation of Indigenous Peoples in Latin America: Inside the Implementation Gap* (Routledge, London-New York, 2020)

4 Innovative instruments for the accommodation of diversity

From theory to practice: emergent instruments for the accommodation of diversity in the Global North

Along with the macro-constitutional perspectives and their concrete implementations analyzed previously, several interesting instruments for the accommodation of diversity have emerged recently. The following overview will show how variegate and evolving this area of law is and how all the instruments, albeit in different ways and to varying extents, diverge from the structure of the traditional tools for diversity accommodation. Consequently, they can be framed as a varied category of emerging tools whose distinctive feature is their divergence from the consolidated instruments that stem from the liberal-democratic tradition.

Whereas macro-developments have received quite a structured theoretical framing from a (constitutional) legal (and political) perspective – even if often country-specific and with limited consideration of the Global South –, the latest micro-innovations of the Global North in this field appear to lack comprehensive recognition or conceptual framing. They will, therefore, be the focus of the remainder of this work, in a bid to include them in a comprehensive and enabling theoretical framework that recognizes them as part of the corpus of diversity accommodation.[1]

This section aims to propose a classification of the emergent models divided into three main categories – non-territorial autonomy, legal pluralism, and participatory democracy – providing several examples that are touched upon but not delved into as comprehensive case studies. This is in line with the method employed in the previous parts of the work that have dealt with the instruments for the accommodation of diversity in the liberal-democratic tradition of constitutionalism.

The instruments analyzed in this section are considered to differ from the "traditional" ones for several reasons, which are sketched here and will be illustrated in depth in the next chapter.

1 However, when useful, examples from Global South legal systems that follow liberal-democratic models will be presented.

DOI: 10.4324/9781003493518-5

First, some of them are characterized by being less institutionalized or governance-focused, in the sense that they do not have the shape of a full-fledged, top-down, or "hard" arrangement foreseen by the state but emerge as bottom-up forms of self-governance that take numerous forms. However, constitutional and legal frameworks seem to play a critical role in enabling their emergence.

Secondly, other tools are part of generally emergent innovative phenomena but acquire a special meaning when designed for the empowerment of diversity. This is the case with participatory mechanisms that foster the participation or consultation of the components of a diverse society. Participatory democracy is an emerging democratic practice that has considerable potential when it comes to ensuring the inclusion of the multiple views embedded in a society. This potential has been (partially) explored regarding the representation of the views of non-dominant groups and communities.

Thirdly, it seems that classic instruments are also evolving and distancing themselves from their traditional features. One can observe, for example, cases of subnational territorial and non-territorial autonomy that are marked by non-isolationist and non-exclusivist features in a bid to foster integration through the tools that were once utilized to accommodate the interest of one specific group (constituting a majority in a subnational entity).

Emerging governance forms of autonomy

A shift toward governance

A first trend that can be observed in this area is the emergence of what here is referred to as governance forms of autonomy. This term is meant to encapsulate various types of self-government or self-governance, which are differentiated from the classic structure of territorial and non-territorial autonomy. The latter, as instruments for the accommodation of diversity, are marked by the following characteristics: a. they are forms of autonomy based on the top-down institution of public bodies that are attributed or delegated wide or general competences; b. those bodies are vested with administrative and legislative functions (at least in theory, this is also the case for non-territorial cultural autonomy); c. they are entrenched in the legal system of a country through constitutional provisions or statutes, and as such, form a part of the state system of government;[2] d. they are designed to protect the interests of a specific minority: in territorial arrangements, the minority is turned into a majority in a given territory, while in non-territorial ones, the minority "owns" the

2 Cornell, Steve E., "Autonomy as a Source of Conflict: Caucasian Conflicts in Theoretical Perspective", 54(2) *World Politics* (2002), 245–276, at 249; Steiner, Henry J., "Ideals and Counter-Ideals in the Struggle Over Autonomy Regimes for Minorities", 66(5) *Notre Dame Law Review* (1991), 1539–1560, at 1542.

institution; e. they have been created for security and/or protection reasons;[3] f. ultimately, their functioning resonates with nation-state logic as they are institutionalized public forms of political self-government that reproduce the state in small-scale.[4]

All the types of autonomy analyzed here deviate from this structure to different extents and complement the traditional approaches to the issue of autonomy in diversity accommodation. For this reason, the expression "non-orthodox", "non-governmental", or "governance" forms of autonomy may be employed to describe them.

Functional non-territorial autonomy

This category of autonomy is an emerging form of self-governance that shies away from the well-known classic models. Its formation seems to be related to a general trend occurring in several contexts, namely the change from purely state-managed institutions to new types of governance in societal management. It has indeed been observed that, in this epoch, several kinds of governance bodies along the public-private divide complement the state in the provision of services and functions that were once exclusively managed by public structures.[5] In other words, there is empirical evidence that the production of public policy is increasingly the result of interactions between a plurality of public, semi-public, and private actors that self-organize horizontally around interests, thus creating a complex system of governance.[6]

Notably, some authors have observed that the same phenomenon is taking place in the area of diversity accommodation, as flexible and less

3 Malloy, Tove H., "Functional Non-Territorial Autonomy in Denmark and Germany", in Malloy, Tove H., Osipov, Alexander and Vizi, Balázs (eds.), *Managing Diversity through Non-Territorial Autonomy: Assessing Advantages, Deficiencies and Risks* (Oxford University Press, Oxford, 2015), 183–204, at 184; on this, see also Weller, Marc and Wolff, Stefan, *Autonomy, Self-Governance and Conflict Resolution: Innovative Approaches to Institutional Design in Divided Societies* (Routledge, London-New York, 2005).

4 See Poirier, Johanne, "Autonomie politique et minorités francophones du Canada: réflexions sur un angle mort de la typologie classique de Will Kymlicka", 1 *Minorités linguistiques et société/Linguistic Minorities and Society* (2012), 66–89.

5 On this, see Sørensen, Eva and Torfing, Jacob (eds.), *Theories of Democratic Network Governance* (Palgrave Macmillan, Basingstoke-New York, 2007).

6 More precisely, Sørensen, Eva and Torfing, Jacob, "Introduction: Governance Network Research: Towards a Second Generation", in Sørensen and Torfing (eds.), Theories . . . , 1–21, at 9, have employed the notion of network governance "to refer to a particular type of networks and a particular form of governance", and defined a governance network as "1. a relatively stable horizontal articulation of interdependent, but operationally autonomous actors; 2. who interact through negotiations; 3. which take place within a regulative, normative, cognitive and imaginary framework; 4. that is self-regulating within limits set by external agencies; and 5. which contributes to the production of public purpose".

institutionalized forms of autonomy are emerging. These have been referred to as functional non-territorial autonomy arrangements.[7]

Functional autonomy is the outcome of bottom-up processes whereby private organizations are created to cooperate with the state in the provision of services in favor of a non-dominant group. This way, non-majority groups, rather than being the object of top-down provisions or being attributed or delegated powers by the state for protective or security purposes, become subjects of diversity accommodation in a bid to empower themselves and promote their own rights and interests.[8] In other words, functional autonomous arrangements stem from active action from a community that aims to self-regulate or self-manage areas of concern without resorting to claiming rights[9] to obtain state protection. Focusing on this form of non-territorial autonomy and theoretically framing it as such determines a better understanding of how broad the universe of tools for the accommodation of diversity is beyond the most consolidated and top-down, hard, defensive, and paternalistic models.[10] Moreover, interestingly, functional non-territorial autonomy has been considered to foster societal integration and the par-

7 The most comprehensive study on these phenomena, which explicitly connected emerging forms of functional autonomy to the concepts of network governance and legal pluralism, is Malloy, Tove H. and Salat, Levente (eds.), *Non-Territorial Autonomy and Decentralization: Ethno-Cultural Diversity Governance* (Routledge, London New York, 2021), and esp. the introductory and final chapters. These, however, do not specifically use the expression "functional non-territorial autonomy"; this section follows the conceptualization offered by Malloy, Tove H., "Non-Territorial Autonomy: Traditional and Alternative Practices", in Romans, William, Ulasiuk, Iryna and Petrenko Thomsen, Anton (eds.), *Effective Participation of National Minorities and Conflict Prevention* (Brill-Nijhoff, Leiden-Boston, 2020), 105–122, who aimed to theoretically consolidate and give some sort of conceptual clarity to the concept, as it has been attributed different (albeit related) meanings; for instance, see Suksi, Markku, "Non-Territorial Autonomy: The Meaning of '(Non-)Territoriality'", in Malloy, Tove H. and Palermo, Francesco (eds.), *Minority Accommodation through Territorial and Non-Territorial Autonomy* (Oxford University Press, Oxford, 2015), 83–115, who emphasized the fact that functional autonomy has always had some sort of public dimension, be it in the form of the delegation of powers from the state to bodies that, for this reason, are made part of the public administration, or through the creation of specific branches of administration in the interest of the minority group; the concept of functional autonomy has also been used to describe (or propose innovative) forms of territorial autonomy: on this, see Frey, Bruno S., "Functional, Overlapping, Competing Jurisdictions: Redrawing the Geographic Borders of Administration", 25(3–4) *European Journal of Law Reform* (2003), 544–555; Keating, Michael, "Rethinking Territorial Autonomy", in Gagnon, Alain-G. and Keating, Michael (eds.), *Political Autonomy and Divided Societies: Imagining Democratic Alternatives in Complex Settings* (Palgrave Macmillan, London, 2012), 13–31, also referred to functional autonomy as an innovative form of territorial autonomy.

8 On the concept of empowerment, see Wolf, Sonja, "Minority Empowerment", in Malloy, Tove H. and Boulter, Caitlin (eds.), *Minority Issues in Europe: New Ideas and Approaches* (Franck&Timme, Berlin, 2019), 97–112, and the final section of this chapter.

9 Although the recognition of the value of pluralism – and for some authors, of minority rights – seems to be a precondition for this phenomenon to take place.

10 Malloy, Functional Non-Territorial Autonomy . . . , 187.

ticipation of non-majority groups, i.e., their engagement and participation in the management of public affairs within a cohesive societal context that values diversity.[11]

In effect, empowered non-dominant groups contribute to the development of policies and provision of services that are in their interests. They do so in conjunction with the state through private organizations, with this model of autonomy having neither a strong legal basis nor an institutionalized public form. Indeed, these autonomous arrangements are not usually codified in a united framework of law: they may sometimes (and partly) be regulated by *ad hoc* provisions of public law, but they are mostly sanctioned through private law registration while, at the same time, often being variously supported by states.[12] In the end, it appears that functional autonomy does not imply the demise of the role of the state (rather, the demise of the state as a community of destiny and home of a nation), but it places it in a broad framework of cooperation between powers and components of society, without denying the role of public and constitutional law as enabling frameworks for these innovations.

In practice, functional non-territorial autonomy may assume several forms and take place through "informal mechanisms, such as dialogue mechanisms, specific management agreements, a*d hoc* and footnote budgeting, specific programming, or public-private partnerships".[13]

Interesting cases of functional non-territorial autonomy can be found in South Africa – related to Afrikaners' self-governance[14] – and, to a certain extent, the UK,[15] Ireland, and Northern Ireland, with the latter concerning patterns of functional self-rule of the Irish-speaking population.[16]

However, one of the most interesting – and by far the most structured – examples is located at the border between the German Land of Schleswig-Holstein and the regions of Southern Denmark, which serves the interests of, respectively, the Danish and German minorities. Those groups are not recognized

11 Ibid.

12 Malloy, Non-Territorial Autonomy . . . , 115.

13 Malloy, Functional Non-territorial Autonomy . . . , 188.

14 On this, see Geldenhuys, Deon, "Autonomy Initiatives of the Afrikaner Community in South Africa", in Malloy and Salat (eds.), Non-Territorial Autonomy . . . , 91–114; De Villiers, Bertus, "Community Government for Cultural Minorities: Thinking beyond 'Territory' as a Prerequisite for Self-government", 25(4) *International Journal on Minority and Group Rights* (2018), 561–590, at 576, where he described the case of the Helpmekaar Kollege MSV (RF) operating in Johannesburg and providing education in Afrikaans: this private institution has been set up by the Afrikaans community, and is entirely self-funded as it does not receive any government grant.

15 As for the UK, Topidi, Kyriaki, "Faith Education in Britain", Malloy and Salat (eds.), Non-Territorial Autonomy . . . , 215–239, described the expansion of faith schools as a form of functional non-territorial autonomy for different religious communities, including Sikh, Jewish, and Muslim groups.

16 On this, see Coleman, Steve and Ó Ciosáin, Éamon, "The Irish Gaeltacht as a Trans-Local Phenomenon", in Malloy and Salat (eds.), Non-Territorial Autonomy . . . , 153–164.

as national minorities by the constitutions of Germany and Denmark, but both countries have signed and ratified the most important European and international documents related to minority protection. Moreover, they recognized the two minorities as national minorities at the moment of signing the FCNM. In addition, the condition of the minorities is specifically taken into account by the so-called Bonn-Copenhagen Declarations and the constitution of Schleswig-Holstein.

Besides the international and constitutional framework, Germany and, especially, the Land of Schleswig-Holstein have approved some legislative acts that concern the Danish minority, while Denmark has been more reluctant to do so.[17]

Notably, non-territorial autonomy in the border region between Denmark and Germany has been found in numerous areas. In every sector, numerous Danish and German minority associations have been established, which are coordinated by umbrella bodies that function as the decision-making institutions and manage the minorities' relationships with the states.[18]

In the political realm, alongside political minority parties, a range of other representative and consultative bodies have been constituted.[19] They have been considered proper consultative platforms for minorities and have played a significant role in influencing decision-making processes in the region.

Moreover, several minority bodies operate in the cultural sector and self-manage a vast array of cultural organizations, including theatres, museums, libraries, and newspapers. All these institutions are entirely managed by minorities themselves and are sometimes funded by the two states.

In addition, minority organizations are very active when it comes to the provision of services for their respective communities. For instance, both minorities have created social centers that offer services to elderly and needy members, counseling, medical care, maternity advice, economic support, and cooperation.[20] Such a private minority system of social welfare is

17 On this, see Malloy, Functional Non-Territorial Autonomy . . . , 192–193.

18 Malloy, Non-Territorial Autonomy . . . , 116.

19 Malloy, Functional Non-Territorial Autonomy . . . , 195, listed the following associations: The Liaison Committee for the German Minority to the Danish State (1964); the Advisory Committee for Danish Minority Issues (1965); the Committee for Issues Concerning the German Minority in North Schleswig (1975); the Representation Office of the Germany Minority in Copenhagen (1983); the European Bureau for Lesser-Used Languages (EBLUL) in Germany (1986); the Commissioner of the Minister-President for Minority Affairs and Culture, Schleswig-Holstein (1988); the Representation Office of the Danish Minority to the Danish Parliament (1992); the Commissioner for German Minority Issues and German Embassy Contacts in the Border Region (2000); the German Federal Government Commissioner for Emigrant Issues and National Minorities (2002); the Trans-Factional Initiative for Regional and Minority Languages (2003); DialogForumNorden (2004) and the Secretariat for Minorities to the Bundestag (2005).

20 For instance, minority organizations in the economic sector are farmers' associations and credit unions and banks.

managed by two main institutions, the Dansk *Sundhedstjeneste for Sydslesvig* in Schleswig-Holstein and *Sozialdienst Nordschleswig* in Denmark, which operate in parallel to state and regional structures. In the economic sector, several other associations serve minority interests.

Specific attention should be drawn to education, as in both parts of the border region, minorities have created and self-administered their schools.[21] These educational institutions are private and run by minorities but receive funding and recognition from both states. Therefore, without the adoption of specific legal frameworks that establish special arrangements for minorities,[22] the two groups have taken up a public service through private minority institutions, thus acting directly to take care of their interests through the provision of services rather than claiming top-down protection or the formal endowment of specific entitlement.

Based on the foregoing, functional non-territorial autonomy seems to emerge as a very flexible tool for the accommodation of diversity. Less institutionalization does not imply legal irrelevance. Quite the contrary, taking into account such forms of autonomy urges legal scholars to enlarge their observations and conceptions of law, its role, and its forms. In this case, the law is much less direct and "hard", but not less significant in the functioning of this model. Similarly, autonomy is much less institutionalized but not less functioning. Moreover, such autonomous arrangements appear to be potentially very inclusive in the sense that state legal recognition does not appear to be a precondition for the exercise of self-governance instruments. Hence, the groups potentially using them are not limited to traditional or classic minorities. The integration function that less institutionalized models for the accommodation of diversity can serve, therefore, should not be overlooked. They are tools that coexist and operate alongside the institutions of the majority society in a common societal system where societal interactions are possible and usual. Notably, the peculiar private form of the functional non-territorial autonomous arrangements allows them to operate regardless of existing political boundaries, including international ones.[23]

21 The Danish minority operates 50 kindergartens, 46 schools, and two high schools, and the German minority operates 21 kindergartens, 14 schools, and one high school (sources: https://www.skoleforeningen.org/institutioner and http://www.dssv.dk).

22 The Education Act of 1990 of Schleswig-Holstein provides for general regulation of the education system, acknowledging its private-public structure; however, no specific provision addresses the issue of minority schools; similarly, the German schools in Denmark operate under the Act on Free Schools, which provides for an exemption from the requirement of proficiency in Danish for their teachers and attributes some powers to the *Deutscher Schul- und Sprachverein für Nordschleswig* (the German Association of School and Language for Northern Schleswig) when it comes to the allocation of financial resources.

23 Another very interesting example is offered by De Villiers, Bertus, Community Government…, 576, who illustrated the case of the Transcarpathian Hungarian Institute in Ukraine, funded by private actors and the government of Hungary, which provides higher education in Hungarian in the interest of the Hungarian community in Ukraine.

The rights of the minorities enjoying this form of autonomy are much more proactively practiced than affirmed in symbolic documents (especially at the national level), and their exercise flows from active involvement in legal systems where horizontal subsidiarity is encouraged or at least admitted. Interestingly, state support for minority activities and institutions is not lacking. This creates a form of horizontal cooperation – resonating with the concept of subsidiarity – which is in the interest of both parties. In any case, the public legal frameworks serve a significant function as they enable various forms of non-territorial autonomous arrangements to blossom rather than directly regulating them. This is so in the sense that they provide for the legal principles and conditions that allow and, to some extent, encourage the creation of this form of diversity accommodation based on activist-type citizenship and cooperation between private entities and public powers. Such legal systems enable autonomous action and institutions for diversity accommodation by attributing a "power to" take autonomous action, unlike the traditional minority rights law approach to autonomy that gives minorities "freedom from" state institutions and control.[24] In other words, functional non-territorial autonomy may be understood as something that persons belonging to minorities or other groups make use of because they are entitled to it as civic freedom and not as anything granted by the state under the public law of a country.[25]

Lastly, it is of interest to note that, in 2014, the constitution of Schleswig-Holstein was amended to explicitly recognize the existence of private Danish schools and secure their state financing. From this, one could notice that functional non-territorial autonomy, a less institutionalized and more flexible form of self-government based on the provision of services rather than on the language of rights, can also constitute a first step towards further institutionalization by the state. Put differently, it seems that the concrete creation of a minority-friendly ecosystem through a network of associations taking up services in cooperation with public structures not only allows for the protection of the rights of the relevant minorities (through their active exercise) but also acts as a "claim" of recognition and support that may possibly foster increasing legal recognition and protection in the long term.[26]

24 Malloy, Functional Non-Territorial Autonomy . . . , 199.

25 Suksi, Markku, "Personal Autonomy as Institutional Form: Focus on Europe Against the Background of Article 27 of the ICCPR", 15(2–3) *International Journal on Minority and Group Rights* (2008), 157–178, at 163.

26 For an overview of other experiences of functional non-territorial autonomy and their dynamics, see Smith, David J., Dodovski, Ivan and Ghencea, Flavia (eds.), *Realising Linguistic, Cultural and Educational Rights Through Non-Territorial Autonomy* (Palgrave Macmillan, Cham, 2023).

Institutional completeness and administrative autonomy in Canada and beyond

Institutional completeness is a concept that has been recently used to describe forms of self-governance in Canada. The expression is of particular interest to this work in that it emphasizes the relationship between the endurance of a community and the existence of a manifold set of non-governmental institutions that operate in its interest in various sectors.

The expression was coined by the sociologist Raymond Breton in a study that delved into the forms of integration of ethnic communities.[27] The analysis revealed that the integration of immigrant communities is directly influenced and shaped by their institutional completeness, i.e., the extent to which those communities have created their own institutions, i.e., formal and informal organizations operating in numerous areas, such as religion, welfare, information, and culture. This is so in the sense that the more ethnic institutions are present in a society, the more likely that an immigrant of the same group will be attracted to this "societal ecosystem".[28] More importantly, Breton demonstrated how the degree of institutional completeness – i.e., the extent to which ethnic institutions exist and are stable – has a direct impact on a given community's survival and endurance.[29] The notion was subsequently used by the sociologist as regards the francophone minority communities (FMCs) in Canada (outside Québec) and the dynamics of their integration.[30]

From a legal perspective, research has been conducted on the phenomenon of institutional completeness with regard to the FMCs in Canada and, to a lesser extent, the English community in Québec.

27 Breton, Raymond, "Institutional Completeness of Ethnic Communities and the Personal Relations of Immigrants", 70(2) *American Journal of Sociology* (1964), 193–205; see also *Id.*, "The Structure of Relationships Between Ethnic Collectivities", in Driedger, Leo (ed.), *The Canadian Ethnic Mosaic* (McClelland and Stewart, Toronto, 1978), 55–73; *Id.*, "La communauté ethnique, communauté politique", 15(2) *Sociologie et Sociétés* (1983), 23–37.

28 Breton, Institutional Completeness . . . , esp. 196.

29 Ibid., 196–200; this thesis was also affirmed by Raymond Breton and Roger Bernard in the known *Lalonde* case (*Lalonde v Ontario* (Health Services Restructuring Commission) of 1999, 131 O.A.C. 201 (DC) and *Lalonde v Ontario* (Health Services Restructuring Commission) of 2001, 56 O.R. (3D) 577 (C.A.)), which accorded the francophone community of Ontario the right to have a francophone hospital; on this, and the role of courts in the development of the concept of institutional completeness, see Chouinard, Stéphanie, "The Rise of Non-territorial Autonomy in Canada: Towards a Doctrine of Institutional Completeness in the Domain of Minority Language Rights", 13(2) *Ethnopolitics* (2014), 141–158, at 146–154.

30 Breton, Raymond, "L'intégration des francophones hors Québec dans des communautés de langue française", 55(2) *Revue de l'Université d'Ottawa* (1985), 77–90; *Id.*, "Les institutions et les réseaux d'organisations des communautés ethnoculturelles", in VV.AA., *État de la recherche sur les commu- nautés francophones hors Québec: Actes du premier colloque national des chercheurs* (Fédération des francophones hors Québec, Ottawa, 1985), 4–19.

Chouinard has demonstrated that this concept has been increasingly employed by courts in Canada to recognize forms of autonomy in the provision of services that favor FMCs in several areas and, in particular, in the realm of education and health services.[31] Her studies illustrate that the courts – and, gradually, the Legislatures – have increasingly recognized the importance of self-managed organizations delivering services in French to ensure the preservation of this community. In addition, Foucher and Bourgeois have provided an overview of the vast array of autonomous arrangements for the FMCs that have emerged in Canada, referred to by the authors as forms of sectorial (or administrative) autonomy.[32]

Regardless of the different categorizations employed, all the accounts have essentially drawn attention to the same phenomenon, namely, the creation of public or private-public autonomous arrangements that do not correspond to traditional – and more frequently discussed – state-like autonomies (be they territorial or non-territorial). These instruments for the accommodation of diversity provide the targeted non-majority group with different degrees of self-governance over the institutions that deliver specific services – including but not limited to schools – in its favor. In other words, all the tools analyzed here are related to the participation in or direct government of institutions and organizations that serve minority interests in specific areas. The model analyzed here adds to the general theorization of the legal instruments for the accommodation of diversity as it enlarges and pluralizes the concept of autonomy, which may take numerous forms and does not always involve the creation of state-like institutions vested with general powers and political-governmental autonomy.

Institutional completeness and sectorial autonomy may take two general forms: the first consists of self-managed private institutions that cooperate with public structures, while the second – much more developed – involves the creation of public independent organisms governed by the non-majority group in

31 See Chouinard, The Rise of Non-territorial Autonomy . . .; *Id.*, "Quand le droit linguistique parle de sciences sociales: l'intégration de la notion de completude institutionnelle dans la jurisprudence canadienne", 3 *Revue de Droit Linguistique* (2016), 60–93; the rulings are *Lalonde v Ontario* (Commission de restructuration des services de santé); *Gigliotti v Conseil d'administration du Collège des Grands Lacs; Fédération franco-ténoise v Attorney General of Canada; Galganov c. Russell (township); Yukon Francophone School Board, Education Area #23 v Yukon (Attorney General); Northwest Territories (Attorney General) v Commission Scolaire Francophone, Territoires du Nord-Ouest; Association des Parents ayants droit de Yellowknife et al. v Attorney General of the Northwest Territories et al.*; the author interestingly connected the concept of institutional completeness to functional non-territorial autonomy, which, in her opinion, provides a better theoretical framing of the Canadian developments; such a perspective is criticized by Léger, Rémi, "Non-territorial Autonomy in Canada: Reply to Chouinard", 13(4) *Ethnopolitics* (2014), 418–427.

32 See Foucher, Pierre, "Autonomie des communautés francophones minoritaires du Canada: le point de vue du droit", 1 *Minorités linguistiques et société/Linguistic Minorities and Society* (2012), 90–114; Bourgeois, Daniel, "Administrative Nationalism", 39(5) *Administration & Society* (2007), 631–655; *Id.*, "Territory, Institutions and National Identity: The Case of Acadians in Greater Moncton, Canada", 42(7) *Urban Studies* (2005), 1123–1138.

certain administrative sectors. The main areas where institutional completeness and sectorial autonomy have been envisaged are education and healthcare.

In the former area, one can find the most developed minority autonomy arrangements in Canada. This is also due to the constitutional protection of the right to minority education in that country. In fact, it must be noticed that the right to receive minority – English or French – education in Canada enjoys strong constitutional entrenchment. As of 1982, Article 23 of the Canadian Charter of Rights and Freedoms has explicitly recognized minority educational rights and affirmed the English and French minority members' rights to receive primary and secondary school instruction in their language – when numbers warrant. Such provision does not explicitly include a right to self-management of schools, but this has been very clearly derived by courts[33] by referring to other constitutional provisions and pieces of provincial legislation that have further implemented Article 23 of the Canadian Charter of Rights and Freedoms. In particular, the two major French-speaking communities outside Québec – settled in Ontario and New Brunswick – enjoy further forms of legal protection. The Acadians of New Brunswick are directly addressed by the Canadian constitution, which states that the English and French communities in that Province enjoy an "equal status and equal rights and privileges, including the right to distinct educational institutions and such distinct cultural institutions as are necessary for the preservation and promotion of those communities".[34] This principle is refrained by the Law on the equality of New Brunswick's linguistic communities. In Ontario, the Law on services in French constitutes the legal basis for the creation of autonomous arrangements in several sectors, including education.[35]

The main form of minority self-management employed in Canada in the realm of education is the school board of public (minority) schools. It is a public institution created by municipalities and is vested with vast and varied competencies, ranging from hiring teachers to defining school curricula.[36] In

33 The most important decision of the Supreme Court of Canada on this matter is *Mahé v Alberta*, [1990] 1 S.C.R. 342: in this case, the Supreme Court of Canada affirmed that minority school boards should be managed by representatives of the minorities, on the basis of the "sliding scale" principle, i.e., the higher the number of parents, the more powers they could manage exclusively; on this, see Bourgeois, Daniel, "Minority Educational Self-Management in Canada", in Malloy, Osipov and Vizi (eds.), Managing Diversity . . . , 141–162.

34 Article 16, Canadian Charter of Rights and Freedoms.

35 As indicated by Foucher, Autonomie des communautés . . . , 104, this law has also constituted the legal basis for the *Lalonde case*.

36 On this, see Bourgeois, Minority Educational Self-Management . . . , 141–143; according to the author, one school board autonomously manages the school curriculum, and another, in the Southeast region of New Brunswick has declared itself "an order of government"; such an expression and has been employed by the same author to describe the powers of Canadian school boards in Bourgeois, Daniel, "Bilan de la pleine gestion scolaire assurée par l'application de l'article 23 de la Charte canadienne des droits et libertés [Assessment of the School Management Guaranteed by Section 23 of the Canadian Charter of Rights and Freedoms]", in Henry, Yves and Mougeot, Catherine (eds.), *Recherche en éducation en milieu minoritaire francophone* (Ottawa University Press, Ottawa, 2007), 212–217.

general, "All twenty-nine Francophone school boards go beyond their pedagogical mandate to play a key cultural and community role that majority schools do not".[37] Given their particularly conducive legal frameworks, the most advanced cases of self-managed educational systems are to be found in Ontario and New Brunswick.

As far as the healthcare sector is concerned, the courts have played a major role in acknowledging the importance of institutional completeness,[38] which is more developed in the two Provinces of Ontario and New Brunswick. In these two subnational entities, the French minorities enjoy forms of autonomy in the governance of the healthcare system, generally in the form of participation in public health boards.[39]

Interestingly, this type of autonomy is not unknown in other countries, such as, for instance, Finland, Sweden, and Italy (in South Tyrol). However, in the latter cases, such arrangements appear to be included and operate in wider legal frameworks that foresee further forms of autonomy.[40] By contrast, in Canada, the arrangements seem to be the main tool employed to accommodate FMCs' interests and needs.

It must also be noted that forms of private-public partnerships have emerged in several parts of Canada through agreements for the provision of some services between various levels of government and minority associations. Research in this area is very limited and focuses more on the evolution of the role of representative associations than on their actual powers and duties.[41] However, this seems to be another promising area of diversity accommodation that resonates with the other instruments already analyzed.

The models of institutional completeness and sectorial autonomy are of great interest and seem to add to the general theory of diversity accommodation. In this case, it must be noted that the legal framework – at a constitutional (federal and provincial) and statutory level, together with fundamental courts' rulings – has played a significant active role in fostering the emergence of these autonomous arrangements, especially when it comes to the two major French-speaking communities outside Québec. Moreover, a notable element favoring the establishment of sectorial autonomies is the fact that French is the official language of the country (and of New Brunswick, too). Therefore, the French-speaking communities (partially) enjoy a legally recognized differential position in the constitutional system (often referred to as official language minorities). In other words, "hard" legal frameworks concerning these

37 Bourgeois, Minority Educational Self-Management . . . , 142.

38 The most significant decision on this matter is *Lalonde v Ontario*, which has led to the maintenance of the Montfort hospital, the only entirely francophone healthcare facility in Ontario; on this, see Chouinard, The Rise . . . , 146–154; *Id.*, Quand le Droit Linguistique . . . , 69–91.

39 Foucher, Autonomie des communautés . . . , 106.

40 On this, see Suksi, Non-Territorial Autonomy . . . , 90.

41 Foucher, Autonomie des communautés . . . , 108.

communities are present, even if they are not considered national or traditional minorities.[42]

While the analyzed tools, unlike those studied in the previous section, are more institutionalized and potentially less inclusive, they nonetheless seem to offer interesting and innovative perspectives as regards the evolution of instruments for the accommodation of diversity. This is so in the sense that they imply a form of autonomy that shies away from the idea of a full-fledged system of government and instead applies the concept to a limited area of governance that contributes to the minority's survival. Particularly interesting is the very relativization of the concept of autonomy, which takes multiple forms according to the different conditions and situations being managed. In turn, this relativizes the centrality of a rather univocal discourse over this topic in literature dealing with diversity accommodation. Finally, it has been demonstrated that this model has proved successful, at least for the FMCs residing in Ontario and New Brunswick, as it has played out as a win-win scenario that has eased minority claims to further political options and, consequently, societal tensions.[43]

Nested federalism(s)

Nested federalism(s) is an expression that refers to complex governance structures where public and private bodies exert several duties for the sake of (generally indigenous) communities within the existent constitutional (generally) federal structure without modifying its fundamental features.[44] Put differently, there is evidence of the emergence of further layers of decentralization in federal states. These differentiate from the traditional model of self-government, as they are forms of self-management that do not fully fit into the classical model of political subnational autonomy.

At the same time, such autonomous systems, which are to different degrees related to the notion of functional non-territorial autonomy, rely upon the basic logic of federalism. This is visible in the fact that they are based on modern treaties or agreements between state and (indigenous) groups.

Cases of nested federalism(s) have been found in Canada and Australia, and all concern innovative forms of indigenous self-governance.

42 On the rather difficult systematization of the FMCs within the consolidated theoretical categories of minority rights law, see Poirier, Autonomie politique . . . , 73–84.

43 On this, see Bourgeois, Administrative Nationalism . . . , 642–652; Bourgeois, Daniel and Bourgeois, Yves, "Minority Sub-State Institutional Completeness", 22(2) *International Review of Sociology* (2012), 293–304.

44 The concept of nested federalism has been derived from Wilson, Gary N., Alcantara, Christopher and Rodon, Thierry, *Nested Federalism and Inuit Governance in the Canadian Arctic* (University of British Columbia Press, Vancouver, 2020), who, in turn, were inspired by Hooghe, Liesbet and Marks, Gary, *Community, Scale, and Regional Governance: A Post-Functionalist Theory of Governance* (Oxford University Press, Oxford, 2016).

Though different autonomy instruments for the accommodation of First Nations' interests and rights have been adopted in Canada,[45] the establishment of nested federal layers of governance – based on some of the so-called modern treaties,[46] also referred to as comprehensive land claims agreements[47] – is certainly the most interesting approach for this work. Recently, three specific cases have drawn scholarly attention, namely, the Inuit self-governance models of Inuvialuit, Nunavik, and Nunatsiavut, all located in the Canadian Arctic.[48] While all present peculiar features – not least as they are all nested in and

45 In Canada, self-government for indigenous peoples follows different paths: the general form of autonomy is provided for by the Indian Act of 1867, which regulates the so-called band governments in the reserves and, despite having being amended on several occasions, is still marked by an assimilatory approach and the establishment of a single model of government for all the indigenous groups; in addition, several forms of self-government that take various shapes are defined by old and new treaties, under the protection of Article 35 of the Constitution Act, 1982, which allows indigenous peoples to "escape" the general system foreseen by the Indian Act; for a general overview of the possible forms of self-government stemming from the modern treaties, see Abele, Frances and Prince, Michael J., "Four Pathways to Aboriginal Self-Government in Canada", 36(4) *American Review of Canadian Studies* (2006), 568–595; on the significance and the interpretation of Article 35 of the Canadian constitution, Kuokkanen, Rauna, *Restructuring Relations: Indigenous Self-Determination, Governance, and Gender* (Oxford University Press, Oxford, 2019), 74 (footnote 68), indicated that: "Notwithstanding the federal government's interpretation of section 35 recognizing self-government as part of existing Aboriginal rights, Canadian courts have not yet explicitly confirmed the constitutional protection of the right to self-government. The Supreme Court of Canada has left the question open while some lower courts maintain the right does not exist. . . . There are exceptions such as Campbell v British Columbia (2000) that provides that Aboriginal self-government rights are constitutionally protected and have not been extinguished . . . . Canadian courts have also recognized the pre-existing sovereignty of Indigenous peoples" (Supreme Court of Canada decision of Haida Nation, 2004).

46 On the different types of treaties employed to accommodate indigenous peoples' interests, the difference between numbered treaties – those signed between 1871 and 1921 marked by the Dominion of Canada's land acquisition purposes – and modern treaties and the evolution of the relationships between the Canadian government and First Nations, see, among others, Miller, James R., *Compact, Contract, Covenant: Aboriginal Treaty-Making in Canada* (University of Toronto Press, Toronto, 2009).

47 According to Wilson, Alcantara, and Rodon, Nested Federalism . . . , 51, "modern treaties, . . . , are similar to historical treaties in that the communities have exchanged their rights to large portions of traditional territories for ownership over a much smaller portion of those lands. However, the lands they have received and the rights they have gained are much more expansive than those that indigenous communities revived through historical treaties prior to 1921"; on the modern treaty-making process, and, specifically, on the difference and similarities between land claim negotiations and self-government negotiations, see Wilson, Alcantara and Rodon, Nested Federalism . . . , 36–37.

48 On this, Wilson, Alcantara and Rodon, Nested Federalism . . . , esp. 43–158; other forms of nested federalism, similarly stemming from modern treaties, have been established for the Nisga'a indigenous peoples in British Columbia and 11 First Nations in Yukon (Wilson, Alcantara and Rodon, Nested Federalism . . . , 9).

parallel to an unchallenged constitutional federal structure – the Inuvialuit is arguably the most fascinating case.[49]

The latter model is of specific interest in that it is not structured following a public autonomy model, but rather, it is completely centered on private corporations that serve the needs of the relevant community. Indeed, the Inuvialuit Final Agreement (IFA) provides for a unique private governance structure nested within the Northwest Territories.

After the signing of the IFA, a variety of land claims organizations were created to implement the treaty. At the regional level, the Inuvialuit Regional Corporation (IRC) and the Inuvialuit Game Council (IGC) are tasked with administering "all the rights, jurisdictions, monies, and lands contained in the Inuvialuit Final Agreement".[50] In particular, the IRC manages the financial resources foreseen by the treaty in the interest of the Inuvialuit. Over time, the corporation has undertaken a wide range of activities to foster the development of the indigenous community, including the creation of subsidiaries specialized in different sectors.[51] Among these, of much importance are the programs and services adopted to ameliorate the conditions of the beneficiaries. For

49 On the Nunatsiavut and Nunavik self-governance arrangements, see Wilson, Alcantara and Rodon, Nested Federalism . . . , 91–96 and 133–140; Wilson, Gary N. and Alcantara, Christopher, "Mixing Politics and Business in the Canadian Arctic: Inuit Corporate Governance in Nunavik and the Inuvialuit Settlement Region", 45(4) *Canadian Journal of Political Science/Revue canadienne de science politique* (2012), 781–804. It must nonetheless be noticed that the Inuit self-governance system is not the only emerging model of self-management occurring in Canada, as several other forms of complex governance have also arisen over the last decades; among them, Métis self-governance has also been described as innovative; on this, see Dubois, Janique and Saunders, Kelly, "'Just Do It!': Carving Out a Space for the Métis in Canadian Federalism", 46(1) *Canadian Journal of Political Science/Revue canadienne de science politique* (2013), 187–214: the model has several similarities to the cases of functional non-territorial autonomy previously addressed, whereby a community carves out spaces of self-governance through the establishment of a network of private organizations that provide services to and representation of the relevant group; on the evolution of indigenous forms of self-governance and the changing position of these communities in the constitutional federal framework, see Papillon, Martin, "Canadian Federalism and the Emerging Mosaic of Aboriginal Multilevel Governance", in Bakvis, Herman and Skogstad, Grace (eds.), *Canadian Federalism: Performance, Effectiveness, and Legitimacy* (Oxford University Press, Oxford, 2012), 284–301; Macklem, Patrick, "The Constitutional Identity of Indigenous Peoples in Canada: Status Groups or Federal Actors?", in Arato, Andrew, Cohen, Jean and von Busekist, Astrid (eds.), *Forms of Pluralism and Democratic Constitutionalism* (Columbia University Press, New York-Chichester, 2018), 117–148; another community that has been developing non-orthodox models of self-management is the francophone Franzaskois group, located in Saskatchewan: on this, see Dubois, Janique, "The Fransaskois' Journey from Survival to Empowerment through Governance", 11(1) *Canadian Political Science Review* (2017), 37–60.

50 Wilson, Alcantara and Rodon, Nested Federalism . . . , 110.

51 They are the Inuvialuit Development Corporation (IDC), the Inuvialuit Investment Corporation (IIC), the Inuvialuit Land Corporation (ILC), the Inuvialuit Land Administration (ILA) and the Inuvialuit Petroleum Corporation (IPC).

instance, the IRC and its subsidiaries have provided job training, employment, employment support, education assistance, prenatal nutrition and child development programs, and day care services.[52]

The IGC's goal is to represent Inuvialuit interests in all matters concerning the management of wildlife and wildlife habitat in the Inuvialuit settlement area; consequently, it has critical functions as regards policies related to harvesting rights, renewable resource management, and conservation.[53] The corporate body has been attributed regulatory functions in these areas; additionally, it appoints Inuvialuit representatives to the co-management boards of the region that have been established by the IFA.[54]

At the local level, six corporations have been established for each of the Inuvialuit communities (Aklavik, Inuvik, Palatuk, Sachs Harbour, Tuktoyaktuk, and Ulukhaktok). The latter are discharged with several duties, among which: setting the criteria for membership according to the provisions of the Inuvialuit Final Agreement; participating as a member of (and together with the other Community Corporations) the IRC; exercising control over any development activity on Inuvialuit land approved by Inuvialuit Land Administration or IRC; receiving and distributing funding from all sources for community purposes.[55]

It has been pointed out that the corporate governance structure of the Inuvialuit region – defined as Corporate Inuit Governance – has had a function that goes far beyond the management of financial assets, as, firstly, it has provided internal and external representation to the community. In fact, the beneficiaries of the treaty elect their representatives and hold them accountable, and the corporations have given voice to the community in its relations with regional political institutions on several issues. Furthermore, the corporation system has offered social services and programs, income redistribution, and contributed to adopting important regulations in areas of particular interest to the community.[56]

52 Wilson and Alcantara, Mixing Politics and Business . . . , 796.

53 Ibid., 794.

54 These boards are responsible for advising the Minister of Indian Affairs regarding proposed developments, environmental reviews, and fisheries or wildlife management in the ISR; see Wilson and Alcantara, Mixing Politics and Business . . . , 797; participation through co-management seems to be another innovative aspect of Inuit governance as well as an interesting emerging model of non-majority groups participation and will be addressed in the next sections.

55 Other functions are identifying Inuvialuit who qualify to be active members of the corporation; identifying Inuvialuit who qualify to be honorary members of the corporation; regulating matters of local concern to the members of the corporation; establishing the Inuvialuit Community Corporation Hunters and Trappers Committees (HTCs); determining the qualifications for membership (source: https://irc.inuvialuit.com/about-irc/communities/community-corporations).

56 Wilson and Alcantara, Mixing Politics and Business . . . , 789–797.

Hence, it is no coincidence that some authors have argued for a better appreciation of the model.[57] Through its representative function, together with the range of policies put in place and their sizeable benefits for the relevant community, it can arguably be considered as an innovative *de facto* self-governance structure for the accommodation of diversity, based on an architecture of private corporations, designed by a treaty under constitutional protection.

As far as the role of law is concerned, it seems that this case confirms the important role of the legal framework as an enabler for First Nations empowerment. Although it recognizes the condition of the First Nations and their entitlement to rights, it does not rule their rights in depth. Rather, it provides for a model that requires them to engage in negotiations with the state (and the Provinces) to co-decide better conditions for their empowerment through a form of self-governance. It thus seems that major emphasis is put on the community's active role as a subject rather than understanding them as an object of legal provision and diversity accommodation.

The case of the Noongar indigenous people in Australia has several similarities with the Canadian experience of nested federalism. Although Australia has followed a different path to other settler nations like Canada, the US, and New Zealand – where different forms of arrangements have been established by means of old and new treaties between the state and indigenous peoples – a legal framework for the emergence of indigenous autonomous arrangements has been provided for since the early 1990s. The legal framework results from the so-called Mabo decision of 1992,[58] the federal Native Title Act of 1993, and the federal Corporations (Aboriginal and Torres Strait Islander) Act (CATSI Act) of 2006. The Mabo decision of 1992 acknowledged indigenous claims of land rights, and since then, the native title has been recognized and determined in several parts of the country. In addition, the two statutes constitute the basis for native title to be claimed and regulate several aspects related to it. Notably, this regulatory framework does not go so far as to recognize legal protection for indigenous public self-government,[59]

57 Ibid., 797.

58 On this fundamental ruling, see, among others, Stephenson, Margaret A. and Ratnapala, Suri (eds.), *Mabo: A Judicial Revolution* (Queensland University Press, St. Lucia, 1993); Hyndman, David, "Mabo and the Demise of Terra Nullius: Regaining Ancestral Domain in Australia", 2(3) *Fourth World Bulletin* (1993), 4–5.

59 According to De Villiers, Bertus, "Privatised Autonomy for the Noongar People of Australia: A New Model for Indigenous Self-Government", in Klain-Gabbay, Liat (ed.), *Indigenous, Aboriginal, Fugitive and Ethnic Groups Around the Globe* (Intech Open, London, 2019), 127–157, at 134: "Native title is seen as a "bundle of rights" which relate principally to the proprietary interests an Aboriginal community has in land, for example, caring of country, but not to self-government or autonomy as understood in a public law sense"; an exception is represented by the state of Western Australia, where the Aboriginal Communities Act of 1979 has provided for a form of local/municipal public self-government for indigenous peoples in that area of the country.

but it nonetheless offers interesting avenues for the self-management of indigenous affairs. The two statutes stipulate that Aboriginal people who have successfully filed a land claim must register a not-for-profit corporation to manage their affairs. Through the corporation, the Aboriginal community manages its interests concerning land; receives benefits; negotiates; undertakes activities; protects its heritage; and does other actions that a legal entity is capable of doing in regard to the native title.[60]

This opportunity has been seized by the Noongar indigenous people, settled in the state of Western Australia, whose self-governance has been described as an innovative form of "privatized autonomy".[61] Interestingly, not only does their self-management derive from the federal legal framework, but, most importantly, it also stems from a settlement between the Aboriginal community and the state of Western Australia,[62] which resulted in the Indigenous Land Use Agreement and two further pieces of state legislation that have sealed the settlement.[63] Put differently, despite having gone through a litigation process pursuant to the Native Claim Act of 1993,[64] the self-governance of the Noongar community eventually came about as a result of a negotiation and agreement between the community itself and the state, thus reproducing the covenantal logic of federalism.

The outcome of the negotiation is a peculiar form of non-territorial self-governance featuring the following fundamental elements.

First, the agreement covers the entire region where the Noongar are settled rather than only the small parcels of territory where the native title has been recognized.[65]

Second, several corporations have been established to manage the community's interests, which operate in parallel to the other public territorial jurisdictions, i.e., on a non-territorial basis for the Noongar residing in the region. More precisely, the region has been divided into six sub-regions, each managed by a corporation. The six bodies work in a federal-type structure, with a central corporation (Central Service Corporation) discharged with the duty to coordinate the activities of the others. Interestingly, the Central Service Corporation is tasked with representing the community in negotiations with public governments and advocating on behalf of the Noongar people.

60 De Villiers, Privatised Autonomy . . . , 133.

61 Ibid., 127–157.

62 The settlement came about after a land claim had been lodged by the Noongar community in 2005.

63 The Noongar Recognition Act and the Noongar Land Administration Act of 2016.

64 In fact, a special section of the Federal Court has been created to this end.

65 De Villiers, Privatised Autonomy . . . , 143; the settlement has the same structure as the treaties agreed upon in Canada, USA, and New Zealand, whereby the indigenous community accepts to exchange their rights to large portions of their territories for ownership over a smaller part and the entitlement to a set of rights including financial support, joint management of land, transfer of land and houses, cultural programs, and heritage protection.

Third, the corporations provide a vast range of (more or less developed) services and may also take up activities on behalf of the public government, thereby resulting in a "hybrid of civil and public law bodies".[66] In particular, such a system implies that the community's corporations manage land, are consulted in decision-making processes concerning the Noongar people and its lands, are financially supported by the federal government, manage housing and heritage protection policies, and provide social, health, welfare, economic and educational services and programs.

All the functions are managed through a network of private entities, which they exercise functions akin to those generally held by public governments. According to De Villiers, this private form of autonomy may be better suited to delivering and managing services for the indigenous community than ordinary government departments. Its private (or hybrid) structure is relevant to this.[67] As a result, the Noongar agreement and the related legislation have established a unique, one-of-a-kind fourth level of government in Australia.

As in the Canadian case, the peculiar nature of the bodies entitled to serve the community's interests challenges the monolithic theoretical concept of autonomy that revolves around public forms and urges the observer to appreciate the variety of shapes an autonomous arrangement can take. The private or quasi-private status of the autonomous models seems to allow a high degree of flexibility and appears to be a pragmatic tool whereby priority is given to practical solutions based on mutual consent rather than focusing on traditional public law issues like the question of sovereignty, the type of public powers exercised, and the allocation of competencies. At the same time, though the legal framework is not absent, it mainly offers a platform for negotiation and sealing agreements. In fact, besides the private-law nature of the corporations discharged with the management of community interests, another notable element of this model is, in both cases, the centrality of negotiation. This implies an active role of the relevant communities as subjects in the definition of the rules governing diversity.

In addition, this model has been defined as holistic[68] in the sense that it implies a (peculiar) form of non-territorial self-governance that is designed to accommodate diversity by serving all the needs of the community and not only cultural ones. In other words, the corporation system seems to provide a model underpinned by a comprehensive view of the relevant community's interests and suggests a strict interlinkage between cultural and socio-economic needs.

Lastly, it must be noted that both forms of autonomy imply a different relationship between the territory and the communities exercising powers over it, as well as a different conception of autonomous jurisdiction. Both are peculiar forms of non-territorial autonomy where a softer connection with the territory

66 De Villiers, Privatised Autonomy . . . , 143.
67 Ibid., 152.
68 Ibid., 145.

is observable, as both provide services and activities that add to and do not exclude the action of governmental bodies. Therefore, it seems that rather than being a precondition for the achievement of autonomy, territory (and land rights) act as an avenue[69] or extension for the exercise of autonomous powers.

Besides, the authority exercised by these bodies is different from traditional state-like jurisdiction, which is linked to traditional liberal theorizations of territorial and non-territorial autonomy that either refer to the concept of sovereignty or echo it. The focus here is on delivering services and redistributing wealth, with this implying a fundamentally practical approach to the issue of diversity accommodation that shies away from reproducing traditional liberal public forms of government and instead aims to employ flexible private instruments to achieve community survival and empowerment in every aspect of life.

The particular role of territory is a central element of the last case analyzed in this section, namely, the so-called urban reserves for indigenous peoples in Canada.

The establishment of urban reserves is an emerging phenomenon occurring in Canada, whereby First Nations acquire ownership of lands outside their traditional reserves through special treaties called Treaty Land Entitlement Framework Agreements (TLEFA). The most implemented examples of urban reserves are located in the Province of Saskatchewan, where a TLEFA was adopted in 1992.[70] There, unlike several other cases, this type of autonomous arrangement has not resulted from urban expansion nor municipal annexation of lands but is a consequence of a precise strategizing by indigenous peoples.[71]

The establishment of an urban reserve means attributing reserve status to portions of urban areas, with this implying the application of the same special regime in force in the indigenous homelands. This means, for instance, that those areas can be governed by bands under the Indian Act and subject to the same tax exemptions.[72] At the same time, the management of an urban reserve is nested within the complex institutional framework of the cities and Provinces where it has been established and coexists with them.

69 Ibid., 132, indeed stated that land rights constitute an avenue to privatized autonomy for the Noongar people.

70 Already in 1988, the city of Saskatoon created the urban reserve of Muskeg Lake Cree Nation, which was the first case in Canada.

71 On this, see Garcea, Joseph, "First Nations Satellite Reserves: Capacity-Building and Self-Government in Saskatchewan", in Belanger, Yale D. (eds.), *Aboriginal Self-Government in Canada: Current Trends and Issues* (Purich Publishing, Saskatoon, 2008), 240–259.

72 On this, see Peters, Evelyn, "Urban Reserves", Research paper for the National Centre for first Nations Governance, August 2007, available at the following link: https://fngovernance.org/wp-content/uploads/2020/09/e_peters.pdf, 1–27, at 3.

The most interesting feature of this case concerns the relationship between territory and self-governance. Indeed, urban reserves constitute an interesting example of self- and shared governance, whereby the indigenous communities residing in cities are allowed to create and develop their own institutions, businesses, and services for their socio-economic and cultural survival and empowerment. The acquisition of land ownership (which in any case grants some additional advantages for the indigenous communities) allows them to exercise a rather flexible form of self-governance that consists of managing their institutions – from businesses to service-delivering bodies – in an urban setting and not on isolated reserves.

What appears interesting is that, as in the previous cases, self-governance is exercised through non-orthodox and complex structures aimed at creating a non-isolationist ecosystem conducive to economic and cultural survival and self-sufficiency. Consequently, territory is not a fundamental precondition but an enabling element.[73] Additionally, as in the previous cases, the control over territory does not entail exclusive sovereign jurisdiction but a more pragmatic and relational form of autonomy.[74]

Revitalized inclusive forms of territorial and non-territorial subnational autonomy for diversity accommodation

A final category of autonomous arrangement that appears to diverge from the traditional employment of autonomy for diversity accommodation purposes – based on the idea that a national minority becomes a regional majority – is what can be referred to as "revitalized forms of subnational autonomy". These arrangements exhibit an inclusive structure in that they are not premised on the reproduction of the nation-state logic on a smaller scale. On the contrary, they are designed to embed and foster the expression of the many diversities that characterize their societies. This idea of self-government represents yet another manifestation of the integration turn that the European soft law has endorsed as regards the accommodation of diversity, which focusses on the need to overcome rather simplistic views that can hinder the achievement of peaceful coexistence between diverse groups in contemporary societies.

Such a model, which implies an inclusive revision of autonomy for diversity accommodation, has been encouraged by European international soft law and has increasingly drawn scholarly interest. In this sense, it has been

73 Dubois, Janique, "Beyond Territory: Revisiting the Normative Justification of Self-Government in Theory and Practice", 2(2) *The International Indigenous Policy Journal* (2011), 1–10, at 5–10.

74 On the concept of relational autonomy, which entails the need for complex, shared or co-operative forms of governance to manage diverse societies, especially in urban areas, see Murphy, Michael, "Indigenous Peoples and the Struggle for Self- Determination: A Relational Strategy", 8(1) *Canadian Journal of Human Rights* (2019), 67–102.

pointed out that the model of subnational ethnic government based on "minority ownership" is becoming outdated. It is limited in its ability to manage the growing complexity that characterizes several contemporary societies.[75] This is the case with what has been referred to as "pure minority autonomous arrangements",[76] but also for complex regional multinational power-sharing systems. These forms of autonomy, which already go beyond models designed exclusively for the benefit of a single regional majority, are also confronted with the challenge of increasing diversity that originates from migration flows and, in general, the rise of "others" that challenge the rigid structure of arrangements based on an ethnic distribution of power and ethnic representation in administration.[77]

It seems that this model is attracting growing attention in the Global North, and, in some cases, the need to update self-government systems in this direction has been on the agenda for several years or practiced to a limited extent. For instance, the Province of South Tyrol in Italy has slowly been moving towards more flexibility in its organization and activity. Though still based on a complex system of power-sharing between the German, Italian, and Ladin communities, one can see that

> the role of the Autonomy Statute is being transformed from a mechanism for the imposition of peaceful co-existence by law into (also) a governmental instrument. The focus is increasingly on . . . enlarging the scope of self-government and less on the measures for group protection, although both elements will always be the two pillars upon which the whole autonomy is grounded.[78]

A fascinating – though still evolving – case is represented by the experiment of democratic confederalism in the Autonomous Administration of North and East Syria (Rojava), which has elements of both territorial and non-territorial

75 Palermo, Francesco, "Owned or Shared? Territorial Autonomy in the Minority Discourse", in Malloy, Tove H. and Palermo, Francesco (eds.), *Minority Accommodation Through Territorial and Non-Territorial Autonomy* (Oxford University Press, Oxford, 2015), 13–32, at 19–21.

76 Palermo, Owned or Shared . . . , 21–24.

77 On this, see Piacentini, Arianna, "'Others' and Consociational Democracy: Citizens, Civil Society, and Politics in South Tyrol and Bosnia Herzegovina", *Project Report* (Eurac Research-Provincia Autonoma di Bolzano, Bolzano-Bozen, 2021) on others in autonomous arrangements; see also Agarin, Timofey and McCulloch, Allison, "How Power-Sharing Includes and Excludes Non-Dominant Communities: Introduction to the Special Issue", 41(1) *International Political Science Review* (2020), 3–14, and the other articles in this issue.

78 Palermo, Francesco, "Implementation and Amendment of the Autonomy Statute", in Woelk, Jens, Marko, Joseph and Palermo, Francesco (eds.), *Tolerance Through Law: Self Governance and Group Rights in South Tyrol* (Martinus Nijhoff, Leiden-Boston, 2008), 143–159, at 158; the possible revision of the power-sharing system has been on the agenda in South Tyrol for several years and is still a politically contentious matter.

autonomy.[79] However, at this stage, it is more of an ideal-typical theoretical model rather than a fully implemented arrangement.

Legal pluralism as a form of autonomous self-governance

This section deals with legal pluralism as an emergent model for accommodating diversity. It uses examples from countries of the Global North, where it is generally not legally recognized or endorsed by state law, unlike several other regions and states of the world (especially in the Global South). Hence, the instrument could be framed as emergent in that it seems to be gaining relevance in Western legal systems, but it has also been theoretically overlooked or undertheorized as a general tool for the accommodation of diversity in this area of the world, especially on the European continent.[80]

The expression legal pluralism[81] refers to the coexistence of legal orders in the same geographical and temporal space[82] and challenges the liberal assumption that law must equate to state law.

79 As indicated in the introduction, the inclusion of Global South models in this part of the work is based on their usefulness in the general development of models for the accommodation of diversity; moreover, the Syrian case appears to rely on a democratic form of subnational government that seems in line with the theoretical underpinnings of the liberal-democratic constitutional tradition; on this experience, and for further references, see Burç, Rosa, "Non-Territorial Autonomy and Gender Equality: The Case of the Autonomous Administration of North and East Syria – Rojava", 31(3) *Philosophy and Society* (2020), 321–340.

80 This is highlighted by Morondo Taramundi, Dolores, "Legal Pluralism and Reasonable Accommodation of Religious Diversity", 24(4) *International Journal on Minority and Group Rights* (2017), 467–483; naturally, as observed by Morondo Taramundi, Legal Pluralism . . . , 468–469, there are exceptions, especially pertaining to the accommodation of religious diversity and with regard to some countries, such as Canada; on this, see also Ferrari, Silvio, "Religiously Based Personal Laws and Management of Diversity in Europe", 25 *Law and Business* (2022), 1–15.

81 The present section employs the expression legal pluralism, although, in legal studies, legal and normative pluralism are generally used interchangeably; a possible distinction between legal and normative pluralism is offered by Quane, Helen, "Legal Pluralism, Autonomy and Ethno-Cultural Diversity Management", in Malloy and Salat (eds.), Non-Territorial Autonomy . . . , 67–87, at 69: "Legal pluralism has generated considerable academic debate, but for present purposes, it refers to the co-existence of more than one legal or 'law like' normative system within the same geographical and temporal space. Of course, this presupposes that the relevant normative systems can be classified as 'law' or 'law like'. If not, it may be more correct to refer to normative rather than legal pluralism".

82 Twining, William, "Normative and Legal Pluralism: A Global Perspective", 20 *Duke Journal of Comparative and International Law* (2010), 473–518, at 488–489; Turner, Bryan S., "Legal Pluralism: Freedom of Religion, Exemptions and the Equality of Citizens", in Bottoni, Rossella, Cristofori, Rinaldo and Ferrari, Silvio (eds.), *Religious Rules, State Law, and Normative Pluralism: A Comparative Overview* (Springer, Cham, 2016), 61–73, at 62.

Theories of legal pluralism arose in the 1970s[83] and are now a central theme of legal research. Although several definitional conundrums characterize this area of legal study – especially when it comes to the definition of what law is[84] – legal pluralism's core idea is that the legal phenomenon is not limited to official sources of law produced by the state[85] but comprises a variety of legal arrangements stemming from numerous state and non-state authorities and processes. Theories of legal pluralism have significant theoretical and policy implications. Firstly, presenting examples and varieties of legal pluralism aims to

> persuade jurists, theorists, and law and development practitioners to set aside the vision of the monist law state and be open to new ways of conceiving of law that recognizes the pervasiveness of legal pluralism and the variety of ways law exists within, across, and outside of state systems.[86]

In turn, this allows for the shedding of light on the dynamics of cohesion, competition, and conflict occurring among legal institutions to understand them better[87] and possibly contribute to their better coexistence. Secondly, from a policy standpoint, legal pluralist theory warns the jurist against applying uniform (generally Global North and state-centered) categories to different experiences to better grasp their functioning and develop policy recommendations.[88]

Among the phenomena taken into account by legal pluralist theory,[89] prominent are experiences of legal pluralism that derive from the coexistence

83 Tamanaha, Brian Z., *Legal Pluralism Explained: History, Theory, Consequences* (Oxford University Press, Oxford, 2021), 1, illustrated that, after the 1970s, there was an explosion of literature dealing with legal pluralism; for a comprehensive historical and literature overview of legal pluralism and its relationship with emerging nation state structures, and then, in the context of colonial and post-colonial societies, see Tamanaha, Legal Pluralism . . . , 19–96.

84 On this, see, for instance, the pioneering work of Ehrlich, Erlin, *Fundamental Principles of the Sociology of Law* (Harvard University Press, Cambridge, 1913); Griffiths, John, "What Is Legal Pluralism", 24 *The Journal of Legal Pluralism & Unofficial Law* (1986), 1–55; Moore, Sally Falk, "Law and Social Change: The Semi-autonomous Social Field as an Appropriate Subject of Study", 7(4) *Law & Society Review* (1973), 719–746; *Id., Law as Process: An Anthropological Approach* (Routledge and Kegan Paul, London, 1978); Boaventura de Sousa, Santos, "Law: A Map of Misreading: Toward a Postmodern Conception of Law", 14(3) *Journal of Law and Society* (1987), 279–302; *Id., Toward a New Common Sense: Law, Science and Politics in the Paradigmatic Transition* (Routledge, London, 1995); Teubner, Gunter, "Two Faces of Janus: Rethinking Legal Pluralism", 13 *Cardozo Law Review* (1992), 1443–1462; Tamanaha, Brian Z., "Understanding Legal Pluralism: Past to Present, Local to Global", 30 *Sidney Law Review* (2008), 375–411.

85 Rinella, Angelo, "La controversa categoria del pluralismo giuridico e le sue intersezioni con il pluralismo religioso", available at https://www.robertotoniatti.eu, 1–7, at 2.

86 Tamanaha, Legal Pluralism . . . , 9.

87 Ibid.

88 Ibid., 9–10.

89 Davies, Margaret, "Legal Pluralism", in Rosenfeld, Michel and Sajó, András (eds.), *The Oxford Handbook of Comparative Constitutional Law* (Oxford University Press, Oxford, 2012), 805–827, at 811, has identified three major strands of legal pluralist theory: the first related to colonialism, the second as a result of ordinary normative pluralism in any complex society and a third that has globalization and the consequent loss of power by states to supra- and international organizations and the diminishment of its traditional legal functions as its central focal point.

of state law and non-state legal orders originating from ethnic (generally indigenous) or religious communities. This strand of literature has analyzed cases of legal pluralism in Global North and Global South countries and their varying relationship with state law, with specific regard to the issues of state recognition and management of them.

In this part of the work, attention is drawn to emergent phenomena of legal pluralism that, similarly to the other instruments here analyzed, add to classic theorizations as they have blossomed from the self-empowered actions of non-majority groups favored by conducive (or at least not constraining) legal systems. Once more, this observation is also meant to analyze how the state legal system interacts with these models of diversity accommodation. For instance, these forms of legal pluralism can benefit from public regulations, although these are not specifically or exclusively aimed to address them.[90] In other words, not dissimilarly from the other instruments studied, it seems that emergent models of legal pluralism may arise thanks to general legal provisions and legal frameworks that create room for autonomous self-regulation and self-management.

Concretely, the emergent models of legal pluralism here analyzed take the shape of private courts or arbitration systems that apply religious (or customary) law to settle controversies of several types – including but not limited to family law – within a given community.

Specifically, the focus is either on non-institutionalized forms or types that are established following legal models provided by non-minority-specific legislation. This implies a shift away from the strict focus on top-down legal measures that can be adopted to regulate or acknowledge diversity to appreciate the effect legal systems can have on the development of empowered forms of diversity accommodation. In other words, such a perspective requires scholars to widen their observations about the legal phenomenon of diversity management to take into account the role of general legal frameworks as platforms for non-majority empowerment through their principles and sectorial regulations. Following this approach, the law is considered to provide several access points for non-majority groups to manage their own affairs beyond the enjoyment of individual minority rights, some of which do not originate from minority-specific instruments and public law institutions. It is here that it is argued that the role of general legal frameworks and their strategic employment by non-majority groups to achieve functional forms of self-management has been overlooked so far.[91]

Thus, this section aims to recognize and validate these phenomena in order to shed light on and better understand them, as well as give them theoretical standing as part of the broad universe of diversity accommodation. And, just like the other cases studied in this chapter, the objective is

90 On this, with regard to this phenomenon in the realm of religious diversity, see Ferrari, Silvio, "Religious Rules and Legal Pluralism: An Introduction", in Bottoni, Cristofori and Ferrari (eds.), Religious Rules . . . , 1–25, at 16–17.

91 Partial exceptions are the cases described in Malloy and Salat (eds.), Non-Territorial Autonomy . . . , and the literature quoted in this section.

not only descriptive but also analytical, as it aims to evaluate the structural elements of the emerging instruments for the accommodation of diversity and how they diverge from their classical counterparts. Similarly to the other tools, legal pluralist arrangements that stem from general rules and not from "hard" minority rights laws and instruments imply a significant integrationist and a possible inclusive potential as forms of non-territorial governance of non-majority groups that do not isolate the group from the wider society, shy away from rigid public law structures and do not require specific state recognition to operate.

To be clear, it is not argued here that the instruments for the accommodation of diversity presented constitute the best-performing models or are the best suited to this end. Indeed, this work does not aim to provide normative solutions to the issue of managing diversity. More modestly, it attempts to provide a comprehensive look into the variety of (variously institutionalized) legal arrangements in this area. This is to enable and encourage research interest in these less theorized – but evidently equally important – issues. The aim is thus the inclusion of less theorized tools within the general legal discourse over diversity accommodation and their thorough understanding to appreciate the evolution of models in this area of law.

Addressing such tools for the accommodation of diversity implies taking an approach that differs from classic accounts of minority rights and autonomy as instruments for diversity accommodation, which mainly rely on macro-level studies of top-down public law regulations that involve governments devolving powers to minority institutions for strategic reasons, either based on security threats or paternalistic protection.[92] Yet, this does not mean that such phenomena cannot be studied from a public legal perspective for the following reasons. First, nowadays, no one could argue that legal pluralism is not part of legal theory and that law is a plural phenomenon stemming from various state and non-state forms of authority. Second, forms of legal pluralism and, in general, of self-management aimed at providing services and utilities for a given group and originating from communities' active engagement may be seen as the expression of public and constitutional principles applied in several legal systems such as in particular, the principle of horizontal subsidiarity.

From a theoretical standpoint, it seems that these forms of legal pluralism can be related to the concept of institutional completeness in the sense that the courts or arbitration tribunals addressed in this part of the work constitute institutions that are conducive to the survival and endurance of a community. This is so in the sense that, broadly speaking, they are representative institutions whose activities impact the social and political arenas. Furthermore, they contribute to the survival of a group as they apply norms that have been created by the community itself. At the same time, legal

92 See Malloy, Non-Territorial Autonomy . . . , 108.

pluralism appears to express a form of functional autonomy, as quasi-judicial organizations are essentially the outcome of the empowered action of a community and provide services in the interest of the relevant non-majority group.

Hence, it appears that legal pluralism may be framed as a form of autonomous arrangement, with this possibly providing interesting avenues for its further theorization and development.[93] In the same vein, it has been pointed out that

> there is limited discussion in the literature of the relationship between autonomy arrangements and legal pluralism or the broader implications of this relationship for managing ethno-cultural diversity within a State. All too often, proposals for autonomy arrangements fail to make explicit their potential to generate legal pluralism or map out the implications to which this pluralism can give rise.[94]

Accordingly, legal theory may benefit from broadening the conceptual framework through which legal pluralism is traditionally viewed and linking it with the concept of autonomy, with this contributing to a more calibrated assessment of their functioning and implications.[95] To this end, the expression legal pluralist autonomous arrangements may be used to describe them.[96]

Two cases appear to be of particular interest as examples of pluralist autonomous arrangements.

The first is the case of religious alternative dispute resolution (ADR) occurring in the UK and the United States. As described by Broyde,[97] interesting examples of non-majority community arbitration have arisen in these two countries. In the US, the operation of judicial religious bodies is not a new phenomenon, but it has recently become increasingly significant.[98] Nowadays, several religious arbitration bodies operate under the aegis of the Federal Arbitration Act (FAA), which is underlain by a contractual approach to dispute

93 On this, see Malloy, Tove H., "A New Research Agenda for Theorizing Non-Territorial Autonomy?", in Malloy and Salat (eds.), Non-Territorial-Autonomy . . . , 3–22; Quane, Legal Pluralism . . . , 67–87.

94 Quane, Legal Pluralism . . . , 67.

95 An exception to this approach is Capotorti, Francesco, *Study on the Rights of Persons Belonging to Ethnic, Religious and Linguistic Minorities* (United Nations, New York, 1977) (UN Doc. E/CN.4/sub.2/384/Rev.1, UN sales Nr. E.78.XIV.1)/Geneva UN Center for Human Rights, UN Doc E/CN.4/sub.2/384/Add.1-7, 1–114, at 66–68, who emphasized the link between autonomy and legal pluralism.

96 The expression is borrowed from Quane, Legal Pluralism . . . , 68.

97 Broyde, Michael J., *Sharia Tribunals, Rabbinical Courts, and Christian Panels Religious Arbitration in America and the West* (Oxford University Press, Oxford, 2017).

98 On the evolution and increasing significance of religious arbitration in the US and the UK, see Broyde, Sharia Tribunals . . . , 3–28, 71–111, 177–185.

resolution.[99] Accordingly, decisions of arbitration bodies to which parties have voluntarily resorted are binding and enforceable by state courts, provided that their selection of the forum and decisional norms is voluntary and the arbitration procedures are clear and reasonably fair.[100] ADR bodies are entitled to rule over a vast range of matters, such as family law, property, employment, and commercial transactions.[101]

Notably, several communities have created ADR bodies pursuant to the FAA, and they include non-majority as well as majority religious groups, such as respectively, Muslims, Jews,[102] and Catholic Christians on the one side and Protestant Christians on the other.[103]

As for the UK, Muslim quasi-judicial bodies, in particular, have gained an important role in the management of justice along with state courts. Not unlike the US, in this country, a general regulation over alternative dispute resolution – the Arbitration Act of 1996 – offers a platform for these phenomena to emerge.[104] According to the Act, courts must respect parties' contracts and enforce decisions issued by an arbitral tribunal following a valid arbitration agreement.[105]

While several private Shari'a councils exist in the UK and operate in an informal way,[106] Muslim arbitration under the Arbitration Act is managed by the Muslim Arbitration Tribunal (MAT), which is entitled to decide over matters of civil and personal law and specializes in commercial issues.[107] Interestingly, it has been reported that the MAT has been resorted to by an increasing number of non-Muslims.[108]

These experiences offer valuable insights for the purpose of this work. Both arbitration models function according to a general regulation of

99 This means that, as explained by Holm, Søren and García Oliva, Javier, "Religion and Law in Twenty-First Century England: Tradition and Diversity", in Bottoni, Cristofori and Ferrari (eds.), Religious Rules . . . , 375–393, at 381: "decisions of religious arbitrations are enforced by the secular courts, not because they are decisions of religious courts, but because the parties have agreed to be bound by the decisions in question".

100 Broyde, Sharia Tribunals . . . , 22.

101 Ibid.

102 According to Broyde, Sharia Tribunals . . . , 14–15 and 76–82, the Jewish arbitration system is the most developed in the US.

103 The concrete organization and functioning of ADR bodies differ among the different communities; on this, see Broyde Sharia Tribunals . . . , 10–20 and 137–201.

104 It must also be noticed that religion has been addressed by UK law: The Divorce (religious Marriages) Bill of 2001 has recognized that rulings of the *Beth Din* (the Jewish Rabbinical Court) are binding on people that voluntarily consent to be guided by those rulings.

105 Broyde, Sharia Tribunals . . . , 178.

106 On less institutionalized cases of legal pluralism, see the following part of this section.

107 On this, also see Prief, Yvonne, "Muslim Legal Practice in the United Kingdom: The Muslim Arbitration Tribunal", in Oberauer, Norbert, Prief, Yvonne and Qubaja, Ulrike (eds.), *Legal Pluralism in Muslim Contexts* (Brill, Leiden-Boston, 2019), 12–42.

108 See Hirsch, Afua, "Fears over Non-Muslim's Use of Islamic Law to Resolve Disputes", *The Guardian* (March 14, 2010), http://www.guardian.co.uk/uk/2010/mar/14/non-muslims-sharia-law-uk.

arbitration provided for by the state (or subnational entities). As such, the communities that employ them do not enjoy special forms of protection or recognition. In other words, the non-majority groups that use arbitration entities to regulate a vast range of issues – that is not limited to the family realm but also matters, such as commercial relations – are not addressees of specific arrangements that recognize them as minorities but make use of general legal frameworks that enable them to apply their own community or religious rules. Such a legal framework acts as a platform for communities of different kinds to self-manage wide sectors of their life relying on private-contractual forms of justice without special public regulations. Thus, one could argue that the establishment of comprehensive arbitration regulation has provided an access point for private and community-based forms of justice to communities that seek to maintain their own way of living and, accordingly, employ their own systems of law.

Based on the foregoing, two main points of interest may be highlighted, which confirm the considerations proposed previously. First, the creation of a legal platform enabling private voluntary forms of conciliation and arbitration has considerable inclusive potential as a tool for the accommodation of diversity if compared to instruments that have been provided for in the interest of a (some) given community(ies) only. It allows the establishment of legal pluralism without confining it to some selected groups through the valorization of agreements among private parties to be judged according to religious norms. Accordingly, it is through private, voluntary,[109] and contractual forms – through which parties agree to solve their conflicts in an arbitration tribunal – that legal pluralism has gained a central and accepted position in those legal systems.[110]

Secondly, the forms of judicial arbitration that are established according to this model are not necessarily close and exclusive and may result in fostering exchange and coexistence in diverse societies, be it at a judicial – as religious and secular courts are compelled to interact – or a societal and political level.[111] Of much interest in this regard is the fact that, in 2010, a significant rise in the use of MAT as a method to solve controversies among non-Muslims in the UK was reported. Additionally, this arbitration body has become an important

109 However, the fact that members of a given community may be socially or religiously compelled to resort to this form of justice must not be underestimated.

110 This does not come without criticisms, especially as regards the Muslim arbitration courts, on the grounds that religious courts may produce substantive injustice, be coercive and used to entrench unjust power relations in religious communities, encourage illiberal practices, or foster separation and isolation of religious communities; on this, see Broyde, Sharia Tribunals . . . , 205–232; counterarguments to these opinions are proposed by Broyde, Sharia Tribunals . . . , 237–268.

111 It has been pointed out that, in turn, the continuous interaction in the judicial and societal arenas and the consequent need to find ways to coexist is supposed to decrease the risk of societal tensions and foster practices of mutual understanding; on this, see Broyde, Sharia Tribunals . . . , 254–260, and in part. 264.

representative actor of the Muslim community in the societal and political arenas.[112]

The second case dealt with in this section is the experience of Gypsy law and, in particular, the functioning of Gypsy tribunals – called *Kris* – in several European and North American countries.

The existence and functioning of Romani legal orders have been addressed from different angles in the literature. Besides anthropological and ethnographic studies, scholars of legal pluralism have addressed Gypsy law as a self-standing comprehensive legal system operating in parallel to state law in several jurisdictions.[113] One of the central institutions of this system is the *Kris*, which has been defined as "the core element of arbitration, adjudication and lawmaking in Roma communities".[114] These judicial bodies apply Romani Law – which is orally transmitted and defined – to the settlement of disputes about economic interests, family issues, moral and ethical questions, and problems of the whole community or some parts of it.[115]

Interestingly, the operation of the *Kris* is neither legally endorsed nor recognized by the states, but it has been pointed out that some forms of *de facto* recognition, deference, or informal agreements are in place.[116] Thus, the role of law is significantly softer than in the previous examples, as the *Kris* is a substantially non-institutionalized instrument that contributes to the regulation of several aspects of the relevant community's members.

However, this case being a clear example of diversity accommodation, there is still reason to consider it from a public legal perspective. This is so not only in the sense of considering Gypsy law as actual law – as endorsed by a legal pluralist conception of law – but also in that this allows the scholar to reflect on the

112 See Broyde, Sharia Tribunals . . . , 184–185; Choksi, Bilal M., "Religious Arbitration in Ontario: Making the Case Based on the British Example of the Muslim Arbitration Tribunal", 33(3) *University of Pennsylvania Journal of International Law* (2012), 791–840, at 828.

113 Starting from the work of Weyrauch, Walter Otto and Bell, Maureen A., "Autonomous Lawmaking: The Case of the Gypsies", in Weyrauch, Walter Otto (ed.), *Gypsy Law: Romani Legal Traditions and Culture* (University of California Press, Berkeley, 1997), 11–87; on this, and for further references, see Nafstad, Ida, "Gypsy Law: The Non-State Normative Orders of Roma: Scholarly Debates and the Scandinavian Knowledge Chasm", 48(1) *The Journal of Legal Pluralism and Unofficial Law* (2016), 92–109.

114 Salat, Levente and Miscoiu, Sergiu, "Roma Autonomous Lawmaking: The Romanian Case", in Malloy and Salat (eds.), Non-Territorial Autonomy . . . , 167–194, at 168: the authors have provided a thorough account on the functioning of the Romani legal order in Romania.

115 Among the various classifications, the one selected here was offered by Marushiakova, Elena and Popov, Vesselin, "The Gypsy Court in Eastern Europe", 17(1) *Romani Studies* (2007), 67–101; on other possible classifications, see Salat and Miscoiu, Roma Autonomous Lawmaking . . . , 177–178.

116 On this, warning of the possible risks of a *de facto* recognition of Romani legal orders in cases where they allow practices contrary to human rights (especially when it comes to women's rights), see Cahn, Claude, "Lawmaking in Traditional Romani Communities and International Human Rights Law and Norms: Case Study of the Real and Potential Role of the Romani Kris", 7(1) *European Yearbook of Minority Issues* (2007), 93–134.

traditional theoretical approach applied to diversity accommodation. Indeed, the focus on macro-level and top-down regulation attributing rights to selected communities hinders and limits observations regarding the wider legal phenomenon of diversity accommodation. In this sense, scholars have mainly drawn attention to state action or regulation and their outcomes in terms of recognition, special regulations and/or creation of special public law bodies.

By contrast, the *Kris* case (but also the others presented previously) illustrates that official recognition and authorization by the state may not be necessary conditions for a (non-territorial) autonomous arrangement to prove effective.[117]

Hence, what seems to be missing is a legal conceptual approach that is capable of understanding and explaining the variety of legal arrangements for the management of diversity beyond the traditional macro-public law perspective. Accordingly, it seems that what one can refer to as the "silent effects" of the legal frameworks – consequences of constitutional principles and general regulations – have been overlooked. A legal system can, in fact, be an enabler for empowered action by non-majority groups as subjects and not objects of regulation. It must be noted that this is not supposed to demonstrate that legal systems that do not have special measures necessarily allow for the efficient promotion of diversity. These considerations are aimed at showing that keeping the traditional focus on the issue of the accommodation of diversity can lead to overlooking the complexity of this legal phenomenon. For instance, some liberal scholarship has insisted that special arrangements have a detrimental effect on state unity and, as a consequence, are unnecessary – or even incompatible with liberal principles, as a common legal framework that allows the equal enjoyment of rights is considered to be sufficient to protect minorities and other groups.[118] Such a perspective relies on a public law approach and does not offer a complete account of this matter as it does not take into consideration the "empowering" function a non-minority-specific regulation may serve within a constitutional framework that allows pluralism, thus overlooking the variety of forms the accommodation of diversity can take.

The studied case presents an opportunity not only to recognize and validate such a model theoretically but also to give it an analytical framing that permits its

117 Salat and Miscoiu, Roma Autonomous Lawmaking . . . , 186.

118 On this, see the positions illustrated in Räikkä, Juha (ed.), *Do We Need Minority Rights?* (Martinus Nijhoff, The Hague-Boston-London, 1996); on this debate, see for instance, Habermas, Jürgen, "Struggles for Recognition in the Democratic Constitutional State", in Gutmann, Amy and Taylor, Charles (eds.), *Multiculturalism: Examining the Politics of Recognition* (Princeton University Press, Princeton, 1995), 203–236; Barry, Brian, *Culture and Equality: An Egalitarian Critique of Multiculturalism* (Blackwell Publishers, Oxford, 2001); an exception may be Henrard, Kristin and Dunbar, Robert (eds.), *Synergies in Minority Protection: European and International Law Perspectives* (Cambridge University Press, Cambridge-New York, 2008), who has focused on the "minority effects" of non-minority-specific legal frameworks.

inclusion in the wider discourse over diversity accommodation. A means of filling this theoretical gap as regards less-institutionalized manifestations of diversity accommodation might be to add a new conceptual category to the classic classification of state approaches to this issue. In this sense, it seems that the concept of "toleration" – sometimes employed when analyzing the Gypsy's autonomous arrangements[119] – may serve a useful function. This is so in the sense that it allows one to recognize state models and constitutional frameworks that do not necessarily encourage bottom-up forms of diversity accommodation but, at the same time, do not attempt to eliminate them – and indeed sometimes (formally or informally) defer to them – and more or less willingly provide for general (or non-minority-specific) instruments or principles for their emergence. The concept of toleration helps with the analysis of all the cases studied in this section.

In conclusion, the present section has offered a snapshot of emerging forms of legal pluralism as a means to accommodate diversity, attempted to classify them, and analyzed their structure. Not unlike the cases of non-orthodox autonomy, such legal phenomena appear to illustrate the existence and potential of autonomous arrangements that, to different degrees, diverge from the traditional structure of minority rights and instruments based on public law recognition, hard regulations, and exclusive entitlements. Although these models are not free from criticism[120] and significantly rely on constitutional and legal systems that are conducive to their emergence, they nonetheless contribute to expanding the legal and constitutional discourse over diversity accommodation.

Participatory democracy and democratic innovations: consultative bodies and inclusive, participatory practices between reality and potential

The goal of the following section is to present the third category of instruments that emerges as an innovative strand in the area of the accommodation

119 Toleration is used by Salat and Miscoiu, Roma Autonomous Lawmaking . . . , 168, with regard to the Romanian state approach to the Romani legal order operating within its borders.

120 On this, see the considerations of Ferrari, Religious Rules . . . , 21: "Is legal pluralism the best strategy to give citizens the opportunity to live according to their convictions without endangering social cohesion and fostering segregation? At first glance one could think that the more religious rules that are recognized and implemented in a State legal system, the more citizens have the possibility to run their lives according to the rules of their choice. . . . Sometimes legal pluralism has encouraged religious conservatism . . . , in other cases the legal application of the principle of religious pluralism turned out to strengthen dominant cultural and religious identities . . . . It is therefore wise to accept Michele Graziadei's remark that "legal pluralism as a theory, or as a set of theories, does not necessarily address how diversity can be turned into a resource for individuals and for society as a whole, rather than becoming a cause of fragmentation and anomie" (see Graziadei, Michele, "State Norms, Religious Norms, and Claims of Plural Normativity under Democratic Constitutions", in Bottoni, Cristofori and Ferrari (eds.), Religious Rules . . . , 29–43, at 38).

of diversity. The latter has to do with the development of various channels of participation by non-majority groups in decision-making. In a way, these innovations may be included in the general theoretical category of participatory democracy or democratic innovations.

Participatory democracy and democratic innovations[121] are catch-all expressions that refer to institutions and mechanisms that foster the interaction between citizens and public bodies in decision-making processes aimed at enriching democratic procedures and complementing – not substituting – representative democracy.[122] In general, experiences of democratic innovations started to emerge during the 1970s and 1980s in various parts of the world. They have attracted the attention of scholars from a range of disciplines, most notably political science.[123]

Shifting the focus to the subject of the work, the employment of participatory democratic means for the accommodation of diversity is arguably quite developed and consolidated, at least from a theoretical and international law perspective.[124] Instruments that bolster the participation of minorities beyond the traditional parliamentary channels have been theorized and recognized as necessary to guarantee effective participation in public life.[125] The adoption of key international documents – such as the Lund Recommendations on the Effective Participation of National Minorities in Public Life of 1999 and the ACFC Commentary on Effective Participation of Minorities of

121 It must be said that part of the literature on this theme prefers the expression "democratic innovations"; on this, amongst others, see Smith, Graham, *Democratic Innovations: Designing Institutions for Citizen Participation* (Cambridge University Press, Cambridge, 2009).

122 Trettel, Martina, *La democrazia partecipativa negli ordinamenti composti: studio di diritto comparato sull'incidenza della tradizione giuridica nelle democratic innovations* (ESI, Naples, 2020), 23–52; Smith, Democratic Innovations . . . , 8–29.

123 For an overview of the different strands of research concerning this area, see Trettel, La democrazia partecipativa . . . , 8–22.

124 On the international level and the activity of international bodies regarding this issue, see Weller, Marc, "Effective Participation of Minorities in Public Life", in Weller, Marc (ed.), *Universal Minority Rights: A Commentary on the Jurisprudence of International Courts and Treaty Bodies* (Oxford University Press, Oxford, 2007), 477–516; De Varennes, Fernand and Kuborska-Pucha, Elżbieta, "Effective Participation of National Minorities in Public Life: The UN's Perspective", in Romans, Ulasiuk and Petrenko Thomsen (eds.), Effective Participation . . . , 17–42; specifically, concerning national minorities, see, among others, Weller, Marc, "Article 15", in Weller, Marc (ed.), *The Rights of Minorities in Europe: A Commentary on the European Framework Convention for the Protection of National Minorities* (Oxford University Press, Oxford, 2005), 429–462; on indigenous peoples, see Tomaselli, Alexandra, *Indigenous Peoples and Their Right to Political Participation* (Nomos, Baden-Baden, 2016); Wright, Claire and Tomaselli, Alexandra, *The Prior Consultation of Indigenous Peoples in Latin America: Inside the Implementation Gap* (Routledge, London-New York, 2020).

125 On this, see Djordjević, Ljubica, "Consultative Bodies as Channels for Minority Participation in Public Affairs", in Malloy and Boulter (eds.), Minority Issues in Europe . . . , 197–227.

2008[126] – proves the importance of this area. Furthermore, international indigenous peoples' rights law – especially the ILO convention no. 169 and the UNDRIP – has traditionally attributed a significant role to participatory practices and promoted the (variously implemented) right to free, prior, and informed consent of indigenous peoples on matters that concern them.

Additionally, several state practices confirm the increased attention given to such mechanisms, both for minorities and indigenous peoples.

However, it has been noticed that participatory democracy is still largely overshadowed in theory and practice by the interest in traditional channels of participation through representation in elected assemblies.[127] Accordingly, while participatory instruments are implemented to different degrees or at least widely accepted, they seem to suffer from being overlooked theoretically and experience troublesome practical applications.

It must be noted that attributing practical priority and theoretical superiority to representation and participation in elected political bodies – and, accordingly, underestimating other means of representing non-majority groups' views – is a limiting and not completely realistic perspective of the effective possibilities of this kind of participation. The conception of participation as necessarily tied to representation in legislative bodies may be the consequence of the continuous application of traditional categories and classical ideas of representation and decision-making. This may not lead to useful theoretical and practical results. Moreover, it has been argued that the focus on this channel of participation is also explained by the fact that this is the easiest and, at the same time, least effective form of participation.[128] For instance, while reserved seats in assemblies may give the relevant groups real opportunities to influence decision-making processes that concern them – especially when adopted by local or subnational legislatures or when veto rights (whose establishment is not without several problematic aspects) are attributed to the groups – the risk of purely symbolic representation is not negligible, as several cases can demonstrate.[129]

Hence, it could be said that the turn towards participatory instruments and processes to complement representative tools has not been completely consolidated from an academic or practical standpoint.

126 See, OSCE HCNM, *The Lund Recommendations on the Effective Participation of National Minorities in Public Life* (OSCE HCNM, The Hague, 1999); ACFC, Thematic Commentary no. 2, *The Effective Participation of Persons Belonging to National Minorities in Cultural, Social and Economic Life and in Public Affairs*, 27 February 2008, ACFC/31DOC(2008)001 (hereinafter ACFC Commentary of 2008).

127 Palermo, Francesco and Roter, Petra, "The Lund Recommendations from the Perspective of the Framework Convention", in Romans, Ulasiuk and Petrenko, Thomsen (eds.), Effective Participation . . . , 81–104.

128 Palermo and Roter, The Lund Recommendations . . . , 86.

129 As described by Palermo and Roter, The Lund Recommendations . . . , 91 and Kymlicka, Will, *Multicultural Citizenship: A Liberal Theory of Minority Rights* (Clarendon, Oxford, 1995), 150.

For this reason, participatory means beyond classic forms of representation – especially in the form of consultative bodies and co-management mechanisms[130] – are presented here as at least partially innovative avenues of this area of law.[131] After a brief categorization of the general models, one may find in international law and state practice, some of the most innovative examples will be presented. These are conceived of as original means in the sense that, similar to the previously-mentioned examples, they present a potentially ample degree of inclusivity; sometimes seem to imply a conception of diversity management that does not coincide with the protection of one specific group (or a closed list of them); shy away from the classic well-trodden idea of representation (in legislatures or other political or judicial bodies); and imply participation and co-management in boards and other governance bodies rather than in government institutions.

Theoretically, it has been observed that participatory democracy may be seen as a method of governance that aims to bolster a pluralization of voices in the democratic process. It has also been pointed out that every voice that is included in the democratic arena through participatory means is essentially the expression of an autonomous point of view in processes leading to public decisions. Put differently, democratic innovations have essentially engendered a multiplication of coexisting decision-making centers that are representative of various parts of society.[132] Interestingly, as will be further elaborated in the following chapters, other authors have noticed a strong connection between federalism and participatory democracy in the sense of conceiving decision-making as a complex federal process that coordinates numerous coexisting autonomous voices.[133] Such a conceptual depiction of democratic innovations seems to suggest that this instrument can also be analyzed through the lens of autonomy, i.e., as an autonomous arrangement primarily guaranteeing

130 It must be noted that the variety of representative mechanisms is not limited to representation in legislatures, but also includes representation in executives and judiciary, which are not less important and arguably far more effective than the former, as illustrated by Palermo and Roter, The Lund Recommendations . . . , 92–94. However, major attention is directed here to the two selected types of consultation mechanisms, as they seem the most promising tools, especially when it comes to their innovative potential.

131 This does not mean that consultative bodies can substitute electoral representation or other forms of participation, such as representation in public administration or judicial bodies; in other words, whilst potentially very important and inclusive, as stated by the ACFC Commentary of 2008, 28 (para. 106): "Consultation alone does not, however, constitute a sufficient mechanism for ensuring effective participation of persons belonging to national minorities".

132 These considerations have been brought forward by Trettel, La democrazia partecipativa . . . , 231–235.

133 See Gerken, Heather K., "Federalism All the Way Down", in 124(1) *Harvard Law Review* (2010), 4–74; Palermo, Francesco, "Regulating Pluralism: Federalism as Decision-Making and New Challenges for Federal Studies", in Palermo, Francesco and Alber, Elisabeth (eds.), *Federalism as Decision-Making: Changes in Structures, Procedures and Policies* (Brill-Nijhoff, Leiden-Boston, 2015), 499–513; on this, see Chapter 6.

the expression of autonomous voices to influence general decisions.[134] As will become apparent, the suggested conceptual framing appears to be conducive to a better appreciation of this instrument and, possibly, further development based on solid theoretical grounds.

Several instruments have been developed to promote the participation of non-majority groups in public life. Among them, it is possible to find *ad hoc* bodies and processes as well as stable institutions that are encouraged by international law. According to a classification provided by Weller based on their study of state activity in the area of minority rights law,[135] consultative mechanisms may take the shape of co-decision, consultation, coordination, and minority self-governance mechanisms.

The first category generally takes place through consultative institutions attached to national or subnational parliaments and occurs either where minority consultative councils must be heard before certain decisions are made or minority consultative councils have genuine decision-making powers.

Consultation mechanisms include three main models: minority consultative bodies that are principally composed of and organized by minority organizations; minority consultative bodies attached to a high-ranking governmental office or a governmental contact office; consultative institutions led by governmental representatives, who may sometimes constitute the majority of the membership.

The third category, coordination mechanisms, encompasses generally expert bodies, coordination points, or round tables established to take minority issues in governmental activities into consideration. They are not considered genuine consultative bodies due to their limited role.

The last group of consultative institutions concerns non-territorial self-governance bodies that are also discharged with significant advisory functions. Among the instruments indicated here, these are emerging as one of the most implemented mechanisms for participation through consultation, especially in Eastern Europe. Indeed, although their autonomous functions are oftentimes described as limited, unclear, or limitedly implemented, their activity as consultative bodies has been widely considered more effective (and pledged by international monitoring bodies). Cases of non-territorial

134 Also, Nimni, Ephraim, "Cultural Minority Self-Governance", in Weller, Marc and Nobbs, Katherine (eds.), *Political Participation of Minorities: A Commentary on International Standards and Practice* (Oxford University Press, Oxford, 2010), 634–660, who, while analyzing Article 14 of the Explanatory Note of the Lund Recommendations of 1999, defined self-governance as "a measure of control by a cultural a community over matters affecting it", with this general definition thus including forms of (classic) autonomy and participation.

135 Weller, Marc, "Minority Consultative Mechanisms: Towards Best Practices", 7(1) *European Yearbook of Minority Issues* (2007), 425–448; similarly (also based on Weller's studies), see Council of Europe's Committee of Experts on Issues Relating to the Protection of National Minorities (DH-MIN), *DH-MIN Handbook on Minority Consultative Mechanisms* (Council of Europe, Strasbourg, 2006).

self-governance bodies with comprehensive consultative functions are to be found, for instance, in Hungary, Croatia, Serbia, Estonia, Finland, Norway, and Sweden (for the Sami indigenous people).[136]

Among the consultative bodies presented here, of particular interest for the purpose of this work, are the advisory and co-decision structures, as they are "transversal bodies". The latter are not aimed at representing the voice of just one minority but rather are designed to gather all the minority groups, thus creating a consultative body that does not serve the interest of a single group. This structure appears to be consistent with the approach of the European international soft law documents indicated previously, which consider diversity accommodation as a complex system of governance that must take into account the composite societal reality and not only focus on a specific group's needs and demands. Put differently, they seem to imply a conception of diversity that does not exclusively identify a single minority that "owns" the body but represents all groups bearing diversity. An example is Germany: The Minority Council, established in 2005, advises the federal government and federal parliament about matters that affect the Frisians, Sinti and Roma, Sorbian, and Danish minorities, particularly as concerns the protection and promotion of their language and culture. What has been noticed is that the "German Council's functioning and initiatives are not aimed at support for the interests of a specific language community, but rather to promote a culture and atmosphere that is, in general, conducive to tolerance and language diversity in Germany".[137]

In this sense, even more in line with this perspective are what can be referred to as "transversal inclusivist bodies", which are characterized by having open membership criteria[138] and do not – at least formally – exclude any form of (ethno-cultural) group from being part of it. Accordingly, this model distances itself from the exclusivist idea of diversity accommodation and favors the con-

136 For in-depth analyses of these cases, and their actual functioning as autonomy arrangements and consultative mechanisms, see Malloy, Tove H., Osipov, Alexander and Vizi, Balázs (eds.), *Managing Diversity through Non-Territorial Autonomy: Assessing Advantages, Deficiencies and Risks* (Oxford University Press, Oxford, 2015) and Malloy, Tove H. and Palermo, Francesco (eds.), *Minority Accommodation through Territorial and Non-Territorial Autonomy* (Oxford University Press, Oxford, 2015); on the relationships between non-territorial autonomy and participation, see Vizi, Balázs, Dobos, Bálazs and Shikova, Natalia (eds.), *Non-Territorial Autonomy as an Instrument for Effective Participation of Minorities* (Centre for Social Sciences & University American College Skopje, Skopje, 2021).

137 On this, see De Villiers, Bertus, "Is an Advisory Body for Aboriginal People in Australia Progress to Rectify Past Injustices or Toy Telephone: Insights from European and other Experiences", 17(1) *Journal on Ethnopolitics and Minority Issues in Europe* (JEMIE) (2018), 24–49.

138 This generally goes along with open legal definitions of minority; it must nonetheless be noticed that the actual inclusive potential of the consultative bodies depends on the will of the authority that is discharged with the appointment of members; on this, Djordjević, Ljubica, Consultative Bodies . . .

ceiving of diversity as a general phenomenon that has to do with the existence of several communities that are not always recognized as minorities. In this sense, these bodies put together all the relevant groups and foster the creation of transversal diversity fora.

The Croatian Council for National Minorities, established by the Constitutional Law on the Rights of National Minorities of 2002, follows the described structure. Besides the creation of non-territorial autonomous arrangements (national minority councils), the legal framework for minority protection in Croatia has established a government-funded structure that serves the interests of all minorities and manages the distribution of public funding to minority self-governments and associations. Neither the constitution nor the institutive law contain a closed list of national minorities. Two other examples are the already mentioned cases of Finland and the Czech Republic.[139]

Notably, consultative bodies mainly composed of minority associations also offer such inclusive potential. These, too, may arguably be considered promising emerging instruments for the accommodation of diversity. This is so in that their private form (at least potentially) allows them to escape public recognition of their minority status as a pre-condition for participation in consultation processes.

Besides consultative bodies, a further noteworthy model of participation has been labeled as "co-management". This expression refers to the cooperative management between state or public institutions and non-majority (generally indigenous) groups in areas of interest to the latter. These bodies are attractive models for the accommodation of diversity as they focus on pragmatic governance issues and methods instead of traditional representation in elected bodies. While those instruments may seem less "appealing" than classic representative channels, they could serve very important, concrete functions and foster the protection of non-majority needs through their empowerment in policymaking. In a way, co-management as a form of participation shifts the focus from (possibly symbolic) representation in legislative procedures to concrete involvement in decision-making processes at various levels of government. In other words, these are governance instruments rather than government ones: much like the other models, the governance dimension majorly features emerging participatory instruments.

In general, although the idea of participation has been a core element of indigenous peoples' claims from the beginning, a trend towards co-management as a form of participation by indigenous peoples has recently become apparent in Canada. This form of participation – established through the so-called modern treaties – has mainly concerned wildlife management, land use planning, environmental regulation, cultural policies such as education and

139 On this, see Chapter 3.

social welfare, and healthcare.[140] A paradigmatic case is that of Inuit governance in Inuviatsluit. Indeed, the IFA has established several boards that are co-managed by members appointed by the Province and the IGC, one of the private corporations serving the Inuviatsluit's interests.[141] Other (more or less successful) experiences concern other Northern indigenous peoples in Nunavut, Yukon, and the Northwest Territories.[142]

However, co-management is not confined to experiences regarding indigenous peoples. For instance, FMCs' participation in school and health boards may be seen as fitting within this category, at least in cases where the latter do not control these bodies and cooperate with members of the majority.[143]

Apart from these concrete examples, democratic innovations appear to be a particularly promising area of development when it comes to instruments for the accommodation of diversity, as they are conducive to opening up spaces for dialogue, exchange, and enrichment of democratic decisions beyond the application of the majority principle. In other words, besides their concrete implementation, enriching democratic processes and complementing representative decision-making is in line with the underlying inclusive logic of the innovative trends of diversity accommodation. For this reason, it could be said that while participatory democracy may already be instrumental to wider societal inclusion in democratic processes, it still has a considerable potential to exploit and could significantly contribute to further innovations in the area of diversity accommodation.

Some preliminary conclusions and open questions on the structure of the emerging instruments

The present chapter aimed to provide an overview of the emerging dynamics concerning the accommodation of diversity in the Global North, where, as seen, a range of innovations are taking place and complementing the most consolidated models stemming from this tradition.

To set the stage for the next part of the work, which mainly deals with a theoretical appraisal of the latter developments, it is important to preliminarily underline that all the tools here analyzed share some common structural

140 On this, and for further references, see Wilson, Alcantara and Rodon, Nested Federalism . . .; White, Graham, *Indigenous Empowerment through Co-Management: Land-Claims Boards, Wildlife Management, and Environmental Regulation* (University of British Columbia Press, Vancouver, 2020).

141 Similarly, as seen previously, in several South American countries notable instruments of participation through bodies that could be included in the category of co-management have been set up; the participatory bodies in Ecuador and Bolivia serve significant agenda-setting functions and thus contribute to the definition of government political priorities and policies.

142 They are, respectively, the Nunavut Wildlife Management Board, the Yukon Fish and Wildlife Management Board, the Mackenzie Valley Environmental Impact Review Board and the Mackenzie Valley Land and Water Board.

143 Bourgeois, Minority Educational Self-Management . . . , 147–162.

characteristics that differentiate them from the classical configuration of minority and indigenous peoples' rights instruments and mechanisms.

As seen, the first common element is the flexible structure and (consequent) inclusive potential of those tools. Indeed, be they forms of non-orthodox autonomy, legal pluralist autonomous arrangement, or participatory democratic means, almost all of them feature a private or hybrid configuration and/or open criteria for membership. The result is a tendency towards a complex system of governance, where private or hybrid bodies coexist and cooperate with public institutions in the management of various forms of diversity. What must be emphasized is that the (often) inclusive structure of the tools is a critical element that differentiates them from the minority and indigenous rights law's mechanisms. This is arguably the most original element of the analyzed instruments because their structure allows for the accommodation of a potentially wide – and not completely explored – range of differential conditions beyond those traditionally addressed.

Moreover, the private form of the autonomous tools allows the rigidity of public regulations to be escaped, particularly their underlying logic, which suggests that only recognized groups have access to forms of self-management. In other words, private or hybrid entities potentially accommodate a greater variety of diversity in social and political arenas via less traditional channels. Furthermore, the peculiar legal shape of the arrangements allows them to operate regardless of existing political borders and provide services or grant voices to the relevant communities on a personal basis. This results in prioritizing the pragmatic interests of the community over theoretical and political considerations.

It must be said that in all these cases, constitutional and legal structures have maintained a significant role. Depending on the case, the constitutional and legal framework of the state has contributed to the emergence of innovative instruments through its constitutional provisions and principles (for instance, recognition of linguistic pluralism, some rights of the relevant communities or subsidiarity) as well as on some occasions, non-minority-specific regulations (as, for instance, in the case of religious arbitration). Accordingly, law plays a softer but no less important function, as it acts as a platform from which these innovations may blossom.

Lastly, it should be emphasized that all the emergent phenomena embed autonomous features in the sense that all have been framed as forms of self-management and active participation in public life. Additionally, several of the instruments shown in this chapter are the result of empowerment through the bottom-up actions of the relevant communities, backed by governments in various ways. The non-majority groups are consequently often subjects of diversity management and contribute to elaborating tools, mechanisms, and solutions to this end.

At this point, it is important to clarify the meaning of empowerment for the sake of this work. This notion has been employed to frame non-majority groups' actions in different disciplines, including philosophy, gender studies, and psychology.[144] In the research field of this work, some authors have started to employ the concept to grasp non-majority groups' struggles and activities to transform the societal and political structures in which they find themselves.[145] Empowerment theories provide a description and an explanation of the dynamics where a community makes use of the available opportunities a given (legal, political, and societal) system offers to manage and protect its interests. Accordingly, minority empowerment has been defined as:

> a process of transition in a minority community from a situation of relative powerlessness to a position of relative power and control over community affairs. This process includes developing the authority, ability, and self-perception to influence the environment in the choices that can be made by the community, institutionalization of this change and independence from oppressive helping systems.[146]

Notably, Dubois has connected empowerment with governance, illustrating the existence of a strict link between various and multifaceted forms of participation in governance and the struggle for survival and endurance of communities that are not the recipient of special regulations.[147] The use of "empowerment" in the present work is aimed at conveying this idea, i.e., at

144 On this, see Wolf, Minority Empowerment . . . , 99–106, who indicated that the first theorization of the concept stems from community psychology and that, subsequently, empowerment theory has been used to understand women's struggles to access power positions and break gender stereotypes, to analyze the dynamics of the black civil rights movements in the 1950s and 1960s and in the framework of studies concerning poor people's access to economic development.

145 Since the late 2000s increasing studies have been devoted to minorities' empowerment: for instance, see Benton Lee, MaryJo, *Ethnicity, Education and Empowerment: How Minority Students in Southwest Chine Construct Identities* (Ashgate, Aldershot, 2002); al Haj, Majid and Mielke, Rosemarie, *Cultural Diversity and the Empowerment of Minorities: Perspectives from Israel and Germany* (Berghahn, New York, 2007); a great deal of studies have addressed the Roma communities in Europe: among others, see Lajcakova, Jarmila, "Advancing Empowerment of the Roma in Slovakia through a Non-Territorial National Autonomy", 2 *Ethnopolitics* (2010), 171–196; Richardson, Joanna and Ryder, Andrew, *Gypsies and Travellers: Empowerment and Inclusion in British Society* (The Policy Press, Bristol, 2012); research on the concept of empowerment has also been conducted with regard to the French communities in Canada: on this, see, for instance (and for further references) Léger, Rémi, "De la reconnaissance à l'habilitation de la francophonie Canadienne", 37 *Francophonie canadienne et pouvoir* (2014), 17–38.

146 Wolf, Minority Empowerment . . . , 108.

147 On this, see Dubois, The Fransaskois' Journey . . . , 37–60; similarly, Malloy, Tove H., "National Minorities between Protection and Empowerment: Towards a Theory of Empowerment", 13(2) *Journal on Ethnopolitics and Minority Issues in Europe* (2014), 11–29, provided some interesting considerations aimed at laying the foundations for a theory of minority communities' empowerment.

underlining the existence of instruments for the accommodation of diversity that originate from the action of non-majority groups and are characterized by a strong governance dimension, generally being non-governmental forms of autonomy that often display private or hybrid legal features.[148] Accordingly, the concept is employed for descriptive purposes to make sense of the difference between top-down institutionalized traditional instruments and those analyzed in this chapter.

To sum up, the common structural elements underlying the studied instruments are flexibility, potential inclusivity, empowerment through participation (allowed or tolerated through principles like subsidiarity), and governance-like autonomy.

As already clear, and further illustrated in the next chapter, the structure of the analyzed tools for the accommodation of diversity diverges significantly from the consolidated models of minority and indigenous peoples' rights law, thus adding a layer of complexity to this area and determining the need for new theoretical frameworks to grasp this evolution.

To conclude, it should be noted that the described instruments for the accommodation of diversity, though interesting working models, may not correspond to the relevant communities' demands, which are often tied to the idea of achieving political autonomy in the form of full-fledged self-government. This perspective is also perpetuated by some theorists, who see the emerging models as intermediate steps in a gradual path toward political autonomy.[149]

This raises several important questions. Are the presented models viable but temporary solutions for the accommodation of diversity with a view to continued institutionalization or further entrenchment, or are they supposed to keep their particular and less orthodox structure since this is an essential element for their emergence and successful functioning? These questions also pertain to the importance given to institutionalization: are further legal institutionalization and the creation of full-fledged political autonomies always the desired and most fruitful outcomes of self-management demands and claims?

Arguably, there is no general answer to these questions, as each situation has peculiar features that need to be taken into account. Furthermore, such

148 Interestingly, some of the autonomous arrangements presented in this chapter have already been framed in light of empowerment, as is the case with functional non-territorial autonomy in the Danish-German border: on this, see Wolf, Minority Empowerment . . . , 104–105; Malloy, Non-Territorial Autonomy . . . , 122.

149 On this, as regards the FMCs communities, see Poirier, Johanne, "Au-delà des droits linguistiques et du fédéralisme classique: favoriser l'autonomie institutionnelle des francophonies minoritaires du Canada", in Cardinal, Linda, Gilbert, Anne and Thériault, Joseph-Y. (eds.), *L'espace francophone en milieu minoritaire au Canada: nouveau enjeux, nouvelles mobilisations* (Fides, Montréal, 2008), 513–563; see also Wilson and Alcantara, Mixing Politics and Business . . . , 799, who have described Inuit governance as both a transitory and permanent form of governance, since the Inuit communities are still negotiating forms of self-government with the Crown, but at the same time do not envisage their private self-governance bodies ceasing when this is agreed.

issues pertain to normative perspectives on diversity accommodation, which are not specifically the focus of this work. Accordingly, no normative justification is provided here in favor of one arrangement.

Nevertheless, the study conducted previously allows some general considerations on this matter to be sketched, especially as regards the fact that political or governmental autonomy is often thought to be the final and better functioning arrangement for non-majority communities seeking to protect their interests.

From the foregoing, what can firstly be affirmed is that the emerging instruments, while showing flexible features and less institutionalized or entrenched forms of self-governance, do have a permanent character once created. All the arrangements that have been analyzed appear to confirm that the persistence of a self-governance system may benefit from institutionalization, but the latter is not a condition for their creation nor for their successful functioning.

At the same time, on some occasions, establishing less institutionalized self-management arrangements may also lead to further recognition from the state (or the subnational governments), acting as a claim through action. This has been the case with the experience of functional non-territorial autonomy in Germany and Denmark, where communities provide public services in areas concerning them and have increasingly entered partnerships with public governments – therein receiving both their recognition and support. However, this has not led to the creation of public systems of self-government for the communities, which does not appear to be the communities' final aim.

Moreover, besides their permanent character, in some cases, such as the FMCs' forms of self-governance, establishing forms of self-management that do not correspond to political self-government has yielded interesting results in terms of decreasing tensions between majority and non-majority communities. This has also led to the de-prioritization of self-government demands within the relevant community.

Based on these considerations, one may argue that the studied cases contribute to relativizing the practical and theoretical prioritization of full-fledged self-government for diversity accommodation. Though this may doubtlessly be the final goal of some communities, the stability and results yielded by the non-completely institutionalized arrangements addressed in this chapter urge the observer to question the idea that political self-government necessarily represents the ultimate goal of non-majority groups wishing to endure through self-management.

Bibliography

Abele, Frances and Prince, Michael J., "Four Pathways to Aboriginal Self-Government in Canada", 36(4) *American Review of Canadian Studies* (2006), 568–595

Agarin, Timofey and McCulloch, Allison, "How Power-Sharing Includes and Excludes Non-Dominant Communities: Introduction to the Special Issue", 41(1) *International Political Science Review* (2020), 3–14

al Haj, Majid and Mielke, Rosemarie, *Cultural Diversity and the Empowerment of Minorities: Perspectives from Israel and Germany* (Berghahn, New York, 2007)

Barry, Brian, *Culture and Equality: An Egalitarian Critique of Multiculturalism* (Blackwell Publishers, Oxford, 2001)

Benton Lee, MaryJo, *Ethnicity, Education and Empowerment: How Minority Students in Southwest Chine Construct Identities* (Ashgate, Aldershot, 2002)

Boaventura de Sousa, Santos, "Law: A Map of Misreading: Toward a Postmodern Conception of Law", 14(3) *Journal of Law and Society* (1987), 279–302

Boaventura de Sousa, Santos, *Toward a New Common Sense: Law, Science and Politics in the Paradigmatic Transition* (Routledge, London, 1995)

Bourgeois, Daniel, "Administrative Nationalism", 39(5) *Administration & Society* (2007), 631–655

Bourgeois, Daniel, "Bilan de la pleine gestion scolaire assurée par l'application de l'article 23 de la Charte canadienne des droits et libertés [Assessment of the School Management Guaranteed by Section 23 of the Canadian Charter of Rights and Freedoms]", in Henry, Yves and Mougeot, Catherine (eds.), *Recherche en éducation en milieu minoritaire francophone* (Ottawa University Press, Ottawa, 2007), 212–217

Bourgeois, Daniel, "Minority Educational Self-Management in Canada", in Malloy, Tove H., Osipov, Alexander and Vizi, Balázs (eds.), *Managing Diversity Through Non-Territorial Autonomy: Assessing Advantages, Deficiencies and Risks* (Oxford University Press, Oxford, 2015), 141–162

Bourgeois, Daniel, "Territory, Institutions and National Identity: The Case of Acadians in Greater Moncton, Canada", 42(7) *Urban Studies* (2005), 1123–1138

Bourgeois, Daniel and Bourgeois, Yves, "Minority Sub-State Institutional Completeness", 22(2) *International Review of Sociology* (2012), 293–304

Breton, Raymond, "Institutional Completeness of Ethnic Communities and the Personal Relations of Immigrants", 70(2) *American Journal of Sociology* (1964), 193–205

Breton, Raymond, "La communauté ethnique, communauté politique", 15(2) *Sociologie et Sociétés* (1983), 23–37

Breton, Raymond, "Les institutions et les réseaux d'organisations des communautés ethnoculturelles", in VV.AA., *État de la recherche sur les commu- nautés francophones hors Québec: Actes du premier colloque national des chercheurs* (Fédération des francophones hors Québec, Ottawa, 1985), 4–19

Breton, Raymond, "L'intégration des francophones hors Québec dans des communautés de langue française", 55(2) *Revue de l'Université d'Ottawa* (1985), 77–90

Breton, Raymond, "The Structure of Relationships Between Ethnic Collectivities", in Driedger, Leo (ed.), *The Canadian Ethnic Mosaic* (McClelland and Stewart, Toronto, 1978), 55–73

Broyde, Michael J., *Sharia Tribunals, Rabbinical Courts, and Christian Panels Religious Arbitration in America and the West* (Oxford University Press, Oxford, 2017)

Burç, Rosa, "Non-Territorial Autonomy and Gender Equality: The Case of the Autonomous Administration of North and East Syria – Rojava", 31(3) *Philosophy and Society* (2020), 321–340

Cahn, Claude, "Lawmaking in Traditional Romani Communities and International Human Rights Law and Norms: Case Study of the Real and Potential Role of the Romani Kris", 7(1) *European Yearbook of Minority Issues* (2007), 93–134

Capotorti, Francesco, *Study on the Rights of Persons Belonging to Ethnic, Religious and Linguistic Minorities* (United Nations, New York, 1977) (UN Doc. E/CN.4/ sub.2/384/Rev.1, UN sales Nr. E.78.XIV.1) / Geneva UN Center for Human Rights, UN Doc E/CN.4/sub.2/384/Add.1–7, 1–114

Choksi, Bilal M., "Religious Arbitration in Ontario: Making the Case Based on the British Example of the Muslim Arbitration Tribunal", 33(3) *University of Pennsylvania Journal of International Law* (2012), 791–840

Chouinard, Stéphanie, "Quand le droit linguistique parle de sciences sociales: l'intégration de la notion de completude institutionnelle dans la jurisprudence canadienne", 3 *Revue de Droit Linguistique* (2016), 60–93

Chouinard, Stéphanie, "The Rise of Non-territorial Autonomy in Canada: Towards a Doctrine of Institutional Completeness in the Domain of Minority Language Rights", 13(2) *Ethnopolitics* (2014), 141–158

Coleman, Steve and Ó Ciosáin, Éamon, "The Irish Gaeltacht as a Trans-Local Phenomenon", in Malloy, Tove H. and Salat, Levente (eds.), *Non-Territorial Autonomy and Decentralization: Ethno-Cultural Diversity Governance* (Routledge, London-New York, 2021), 153–164

Cornell, Steve E., "Autonomy as a Source of Conflict: Caucasian Conflicts in Theoretical Perspective", 54(2) *World Politics* (2002), 245–276, at 249

Davies, Margaret, "Legal Pluralism", in Rosenfeld, Michel and Sajó, András (eds.), *The Oxford Handbook of Comparative Constitutional Law* (Oxford University Press, Oxford, 2012), 805–827

De Varennes, Fernand and Kuborska-Pucha, Elżbieta, "Effective Participation of National Minorities in Public Life: The UN's Perspective", in Romans, William, Ulasiuk, Iryna and Petrenko Thomsen, Anton (eds.), *Effective Participation of National Minorities and Conflict Prevention* (Brill-Nijhoff, Leiden-Boston, 2020), 17–42

De Villiers, Bertus, "Community Government for Cultural Minorities: Thinking Beyond 'Territory' as a Prerequisite for Self-Government", 25(4) *International Journal on Minority and Group Rights* (2018), 561–590

De Villiers, Bertus, "Is an Advisory Body for Aboriginal People in Australia Progress to Rectify Past Injustices or Toy Telephone: Insights from European and other Experiences", 17(1) *Journal on Ethnopolitics and Minority Issues in Europe* (JEMIE) (2018), 24–49

De Villiers, Bertus, "Privatised Autonomy for the Noongar People of Australia: A New Model for Indigenous Self-Government", in Klain-Gabbay, Liat (ed.), *Indigenous, Aboriginal, Fugitive and Ethnic Groups Around the Globe* (Intech Open, London, 2019), 127–157

Djordjević, Ljubica, "Consultative Bodies as Channels for Minority Participation in Public Affairs", in Malloy, Tove H. and Boulter, Caitlin (eds.), *Minority Issues in Europe: New Ideas and Approaches* (Franck&Timme, Berlin, 2019), 197–227

Dubois, Janique, "Beyond Territory: Revisiting the Normative Justification of Self-Government in Theory and Practice", 2(2) *The International Indigenous Policy Journal* (2011), 1–10

Dubois, Janique, "The Fransaskois' Journey from Survival to Empowerment through Governance", 11(1) *Canadian Political Science Review* (2017), 37–60

Dubois, Janique and Saunders, Kelly, " 'Just Do It!': Carving Out a Space for the Métis in Canadian Federalism", 46(1) *Canadian Journal of Political Science / Revue canadienne de science politique* (2013), 187–214

Ehrlich, Erlin, *Fundamental Principles of the Sociology of Law* (Harvard University Press, Cambridge, MA, 1913)

Ferrari, Silvio, "Religiously Based Personal Laws and Management of Diversity in Europe", 25 *Law and Business* (2022), 1–15

Ferrari, Silvio, "Religious Rules and Legal Pluralism: An Introduction", in Bottoni, Rossella, Cristofori, Rinaldo and Ferrari, Silvio (eds.), *Religious Rules, State Law, and Normative Pluralism: A Comparative Overview* (Springer, Cham, 2016), 1–25

Foucher, Pierre, "Autonomie des communautés francophones minoritaires du Canada: le point de vue du droit", (1) *Minorités linguistiques et société / Linguistic Minorities and Society* (2012), 90–114

Frey, Bruno S., "Functional, Overlapping, Competing Jurisdictions: Redrawing the Geographic Borders of Administration", 25(3–4) *European Journal of Law Reform* (2003), 544–555

Garcea, Joseph, "First Nations Satellite Reserves: Capacity-Building and Self-Government in Saskatchewan", in Belanger, Yale D. (ed.), *Aboriginal Self-Government in Canada: Current Trends and Issues* (Purich Publishing, Saskatoon, 2008), 240–259

Geldenhuys, Deon, "Autonomy Initiatives of the Afrikaner Community in South Africa", in Malloy, Tove H. and Salat, Levente (eds.), *Non-Territorial Autonomy and Decentralization: Ethno-Cultural Diversity Governance* (Routledge, London-New York, 2021), 91–114

Gerken, Heather K., "Federalism All the Way Down", in 124(1) *Harvard Law Review* (2010), 4–74

Graziadei, Michele, "State Norms, Religious Norms, and Claims of Plural Normativity under Democratic Constitutions", in Bottoni, Rossella, Cristofori, Rinaldo and Ferrari, Silvio (eds.), *Religious Rules, State Law, and Normative Pluralism: A Comparative Overview* (Springer, Cham, 2016), 29–43

Griffiths, John, "What Is Legal Pluralism", 24 *The Journal of Legal Pluralism & Unofficial Law* (1986), 1–55

Habermas, Jürgen, "Struggles for Recognition in the Democratic Constitutional State", in Gutmann, Amy and Taylor, Charles (eds.), *Multiculturalism: Examining the Politics of Recognition* (Princeton University Press, Princeton, 1995), 203–236

Henrard, Kristin and Dunbar, Robert (eds.), *Synergies in Minority Protection: European and International Law Perspectives* (Cambridge University Press, Cambridge-New York, 2008)

Holm, Søren and García Oliva, Javier, "Religion and Law in Twenty-First Century England: Tradition and Diversity", in Bottoni, Rossella, Cristofori, Rinaldo and Ferrari, Silvio (eds.), *Religious Rules, State Law, and Normative Pluralism: A Comparative Overview* (Springer, Cham, 2016), 375–393

Hooghe, Liesbet and Marks, Gary, *Community, Scale, and Regional Governance: A Post-Functionalist Theory of Governance* (Oxford University Press, Oxford, 2016)

Hyndman, David, "Mabo and the Demise of Terra Nullius: Regaining Ancestral Domain in Australia", 2(3) *Fourth World Bulletin* (1993), 4–5

Keating, Michael, "Rethinking Territorial Autonomy", in Gagnon, Alain-G. and Keating, Michael (eds.), *Political Autonomy and Divided Societies: Imagining Democratic Alternatives in Complex Settings* (Palgrave Macmillan, London, 2012), 13–31

Kuokkanen, Rauna, *Restructuring Relations: Indigenous Self-Determination, Governance, and Gender* (Oxford University Press, Oxford, 2019)

Kymlicka, Will, *Multicultural Citizenship: A Liberal Theory of Minority Rights* (Clarendon, Oxford, 1995)

Lajcakova, Jarmila, "Advancing Empowerment of the Roma in Slovakia through a Non-Territorial National Autonomy", 2 *Ethnopolitics* (2010), 171–196

Léger, Rémi, "De la reconnaissance à l'habilitation de la francophonie Canadienne", 37 *Francophonie canadienne et pouvoir* (2014), 17–38

Léger, Rémi, "Non-territorial Autonomy in Canada: Reply to Chouinard", 13(4) *Ethnopolitics* (2014), 418–427

Macklem, Patrick, "The Constitutional Identity of Indigenous Peoples in Canada: Status Groups or Federal Actors?", in Arato, Andrew, Cohen, Jean and von Busekist, Astrid (eds.), *Forms of Pluralism and Democratic Constitutionalism* (Columbia University Press, New York-Chichester, 2018), 117–148

Malloy, Tove H., "A New Research Agenda for Theorizing Non-Territorial Autonomy?", in Malloy, Tove H. and Salat, Levente (eds.), *Non-Territorial Autonomy and Decentralization: Ethno-Cultural Diversity Governance* (Routledge, London-New York, 2021), 3–22

Malloy, Tove H., "Functional Non-Territorial Autonomy in Denmark and Germany", in Malloy, Tove H., Osipov, Alexander and Vizi, Balázs (eds.), *Managing Diversity Through Non-Territorial Autonomy: Assessing Advantages, Deficiencies and Risks* (Oxford University Press, Oxford, 2015), 183–204

Malloy, Tove H., "National Minorities between Protection and Empowerment: Towards a Theory of Empowerment", 13(2) *Journal on Ethnopolitics and Minority Issues in Europe* (2014), 11–29

Malloy, Tove H., "Non-Territorial Autonomy: Traditional and Alternative Practices", in Romans, William, Ulasiuk, Iryna and Petrenko Thomsen, Anton (eds.), *Effective Participation of National Minorities and Conflict Prevention* (Brill-Nijhoff, Leiden-Boston, 2020), 105–122

Malloy, Tove H., Osipov, Alexander and Vizi, Balázs (eds.), *Managing Diversity Through Non-Territorial Autonomy: Assessing Advantages, Deficiencies and Risks* (Oxford University Press, Oxford, 2015)

Malloy, Tove H. and Palermo, Francesco (eds.), *Minority Accommodation through Territorial and Non-Territorial Autonomy* (Oxford University Press, Oxford, 2015)

Malloy, Tove H. and Salat, Levente (eds.), *Non-Territorial Autonomy and Decentralization: Ethno-Cultural Diversity Governance* (Routledge, London-New York, 2021)

Marushiakova, Elena and Popov, Vesselin, "The Gypsy Court in Eastern Europe", 17(1) *Romani Studies* (2007), 67–101

Miller, James R., *Compact, Contract, Covenant: Aboriginal Treaty-Making in Canada* (University of Toronto Press, Toronto, 2009)

Moore, Sally Falk, "Law and Social Change: The Semi-autonomous Social Field as an Appropriate Subject of Study", 7(4) *Law & Society Review* (1973), 719–746

Moore, Sally Falk, *Law as Process: An Anthropological Approach* (Routledge and Kegan Paul, London, 1978)

Morondo Taramundi, Dolores, "Legal Pluralism and Reasonable Accommodation of Religious Diversity", 24(4) *International Journal on Minority and Group Rights* (2017), 467–483

Murphy, Michael, "Indigenous Peoples and the Struggle for Self- Determination: A Relational Strategy", 8(1) *Canadian Journal of Human Rights* (2019), 67–102

Nafstad, Ida, "Gypsy Law: The Non-State Normative Orders of Roma: Scholarly Debates and the Scandinavian Knowledge Chasm", 48(1) *The Journal of Legal Pluralism and Unofficial Law* (2016), 92–109

Nimni, Ephraim, "Cultural Minority Self-Governance", in Weller, Marc and Nobbs, Katherine (eds.), *Political Participation of Minorities: A Commentary on International Standards and Practice* (Oxford University Press, Oxford, 2010)

Palermo, Francesco, "Implementation and Amendment of the Autonomy Statute", in Woelk, Jens, Marko, Joseph and Palermo, Francesco (eds.), *Tolerance Through Law: Self Governance and Group Rights in South Tyrol* (Martinus Nijhoff, Leiden-Boston, 2008), 143–159

Palermo, Francesco, "Owned or Shared? Territorial Autonomy in the Minority Discourse", in Malloy, Tove H. and Palermo, Francesco (eds.), *Minority Accommodation Through Territorial and Non-Territorial Autonomy* (Oxford University Press, Oxford, 2015), 13–32

Palermo, Francesco, "Regulating Pluralism: Federalism as Decision-Making and New Challenges for Federal Studies", in Palermo, Francesco and Alber, Elisabeth (eds.), *Federalism as Decision-Making: Changes in Structures, Procedures and Policies* (Brill-Nijhoff, Leiden-Boston, 2015), 499–513

Palermo, Francesco and Roter, Petra, "The Lund Recommendations from the Perspective of the Framework Convention", in Romans, William, Ulasiuk, Iryna and Petrenko Thomsen, Anton (eds.), *Effective Participation of National Minorities and Conflict Prevention* (Brill-Nijhoff, Leiden-Boston, 2020), 81–104

Papillon, Martin, "Canadian Federalism and the Emerging Mosaic of Aboriginal Multilevel Governance", in Bakvis, Herman and Skogstad, Grace (eds.), *Canadian Federalism: Performance, Effectiveness, and Legitimacy* (Oxford University Press, Oxford, 2012), 284–301

Peters, Evelyn, "Urban Reserves", *Research Paper for the National Centre for first Nations Governance*, August 2007, 1–27, at https://fngovernance.org/wp-content/uploads/2020/09/e_peters.pdf

Piacentini, Arianna, " 'Others' and Consociational Democracy: Citizens, Civil Society, and Politics in South Tyrol and Bosnia Herzegovina", *Project Report* (Eurac Research-Provincia Autonoma di Bolzano, Bolzano-Bozen, 2021)

Poirier, Johanne "Au-delà des droits linguistiques et du fédéralisme classique: favoriser l'autonomie institutionnelle des francophonies minoritaires du Canada", in Cardinal, Linda, Gilbert, Anne and Thériault, Joseph-Y. (eds.), *L'espace francophone en milieu minoritaire au Canada: nouveau enjeux, nouvelles mobilisations* (Fides, Montréal, 2008), 513–563

Poirier, Johanne, "Autonomie politique et minorités francophones du Canada: réflexions sur un angle mort de la typologie classique de Will Kymlicka", 1 *Minorités linguistiques et société / Linguistic Minorities and Society* (2012), 66–89

Prief, Yvonne, "Muslim Legal Practice in the United Kingdom: The Muslim Arbitration Tribunal", in Oberauer, Norbert, Prief, Yvonne and Qubaja, Ulrike (eds.), *Legal Pluralism in Muslim Contexts* (Brill, Leiden-Boston, 2019), 12–42

Quane, Helen, "Legal Pluralism, Autonomy and Ethno-Cultural Diversity Management", in Malloy, Tove H. and Salat, Levente (eds.), *Non-Territorial Autonomy and Decentralization: Ethno-Cultural Diversity Governance* (Routledge, London-New York, 2021), 67–87

Räikkä, Juha (ed.), *Do we need Minority Rights?* (Martinus Nijhoff, The Hague-Boston-London, 1996)

Richardson, Joanna and Ryder, Andrew, *Gypsies and Travellers: Empowerment and Inclusion in British Society* (The Policy Press, Bristol, 2012)

Rinella, Angelo, *La controversa categoria del pluralismo giuridico e le sue intersezioni con il pluralismo religioso*, 1–7, at https://www.robertotoniatti.eu

Salat, Levente and Miscoiu, Sergiu, "Roma Autonomous Lawmaking: The Romanian Case", in Malloy, Tove H. and Salat, Levente (eds.), *Non-Territorial Autonomy and Decentralization: Ethno-Cultural Diversity Governance* (Routledge, London-New York, 2021), 167–194

Smith, David J., Dodovski, Ivan and Ghencea, Flavia (eds.), *Realising Linguistic, Cultural and Educational Rights Through Non-Territorial Autonomy* (Palgrave Macmillan, Cham, 2023)

Smith, Graham, *Democratic Innovations: Designing Institutions for Citizen Participation* (Cambridge University Press, Cambridge, 2009)

Sørensen, Eva and Torfing, Jacob, "Introduction: Governance Network Research: Towards a Second Generation", in Sørensen, Eva and Torfing, Jacob (eds.), *Theories of Democratic Network Governance* (Palgrave Macmillan, Basingstoke-New York, 2007), 1–21

Sørensen, Eva and Torfing, Jacob (eds.), *Theories of Democratic Network Governance* (Palgrave Macmillan, Basingstoke-New York, 2007)

Steiner, Henry J., "Ideals and Counter-Ideals in the Struggle Over Autonomy Regimes for Minorities", 66(5) *Notre Dame Law Review* (1991), 1539–1560

Stephenson, Margaret A. and Ratnapala, Suri (eds.), *Mabo: A Judicial Revolution* (Queensland University Press, St. Lucia, 1993)

Suksi, Markku, "Non-Territorial Autonomy: The Meaning of '(Non-)Territoriality'", in Malloy, Tove H. and Palermo, Francesco (eds.), *Minority Accommodation Through Territorial and Non-Territorial Autonomy* (Oxford University Press, Oxford, 2015), 83–115

Suksi, Markku, "Personal Autonomy as Institutional Form: Focus on Europe Against the Background of Article 27 of the ICCPR", 15(2–3) *International Journal on Minority and Group Rights* (2008), 157–178

Tamanaha, Brian Z., *Legal Pluralism Explained: History, Theory, Consequences* (Oxford University Press, Oxford, 2021)

Tamanaha, Brian Z., "Understanding Legal Pluralism: Past to Present, Local to Global", 30 *Sidney Law Review* (2008), 375–411

Teubner, Gunter, "Two Faces of Janus: Rethinking Legal Pluralism", 13 *Cardozo Law Review* (1992), 1443–1462

Tomaselli, Alexandra, *Indigenous Peoples and Their Right to Political Participation* (Nomos, Baden-Baden, 2016)

Topidi, Kyriaki, "Faith Education in Britain", in Malloy, Tove H. and Salat, Levente (eds.), *Non-Territorial Autonomy and Decentralization: Ethno-Cultural Diversity Governance* (Routledge, London-New York, 2021), 215–239

Trettel, Martina, *La democrazia partecipativa negli ordinamenti composti: studio di diritto comparato sull'incidenza della tradizione giuridica nelle Democratic Innovations* (ESI, Naples, 2020)

Turner, Bryan S., "Legal Pluralism: Freedom of Religion, Exemptions and the Equality of Citizens", in Bottoni, Rossella, Cristofori, Rinaldo and Ferrari, Silvio (eds.), *Religious Rules, State Law, and Normative Pluralism: A Comparative Overview* (Springer, Cham, 2016), 61–73

Twining, William, "Normative and Legal Pluralism: A Global Perspective", 20 *Duke Journal of Comparative and International Law* (2010), 473–518, at 488–489

Vizi, Balázs, Dobos, Bálazs and Shikova, Natalia (eds.), *Non-Territorial Autonomy as an Instrument for Effective Participation of Minorities* (Centre for Social Sciences & University American College Skopje, Skopje, 2021)

Weller, Marc, "Article 15", in Weller, Marc (ed.), *The Rights of Minorities in Europe: A Commentary on the European Framework Convention for the Protection of National Minorities* (Oxford University Press, Oxford, 2005), 429–462

Weller, Marc, "Effective Participation of Minorities in Public Life", in Weller, Marc (ed.), *Universal Minority Rights: A Commentary on the Jurisprudence of International Courts and Treaty Bodies* (Oxford University Press, Oxford, 2007), 477–516

Weller, Marc, "Minority Consultative Mechanisms: Towards Best Practices", 7(1) *European Yearbook of Minority Issues* (2007), 425–448

Weller, Marc and Wolff, Stefan, *Autonomy, Self-Governance and Conflict Resolution: Innovative Approaches to Institutional Design in Divided Societies* (Routledge, London-New York, 2005)

Weyrauch, Walter Otto, and Bell, Maureen A., "Autonomous Lawmaking: The Case of the Gypsies", in Weyrauch, Walter Otto (ed.), *Gypsy Law: Romani Legal Traditions and Culture* (University of California Press, Berkeley, 1997), 11–87

White, Graham, *Indigenous Empowerment through Co-Management: Land-Claims Boards, Wildlife Management, and Environmental Regulation* (University of British Columbia Press, Vancouver, 2020)

Wilson, Gary N. and Alcantara, Christopher, "Mixing Politics and Business in the Canadian Arctic: Inuit Corporate Governance in Nunavik and the Inuvialuit Settlement Region", 45(4) *Canadian Journal of Political Science / Revue canadienne de science politique* (2012), 781–804

Wilson, Gary N., Alcantara, Christopher and Rodon, Thierry, *Nested Federalism and Inuit Governance in the Canadian Arctic* (University of British Columbia Press, Vancouver, 2020)

Wolf, Sonja, "Minority Empowerment", in Malloy, Tove H. and Boulter, Caitlin (eds.), *Minority Issues in Europe: New Ideas and Approaches* (Franck&Timme, Berlin, 2019), 97–112

Wright, Claire and Tomaselli, Alexandra, *The Prior Consultation of Indigenous Peoples in Latin America: Inside the Implementation Gap* (Routledge, London-New York, 2020)

5 Building the "Law of Diversity"

The evolution of the treatment of diversity in the constitutional tradition and the comparative overview of the most innovative models appear to suggest the need for a renewed conceptual framework capable of encapsulating the described dynamics. This is the aim of the present chapter, which will propose the employment of the expression "Law of Diversity" as a new theoretical semantic supposed to enable a better understanding of the phenomena of interest and create a solid ground from which they might develop. To this end, some considerations about the position of diversity and the paradigms underpinning its treatment will be proposed in order to set the stage for the final sections. These will then clarify the conceptual proposal and its theoretical usefulness.

The evolving position of diversity

The next sections constitute the first step in the gradual path that leads to the construction of the conceptual framework based on the expression "Law of Diversity". They will analyze the position of diversity within the constitutional tradition. Accordingly, it will become apparent that the provision of rules to manage differentiated conditions has become increasingly significant within this tradition.

Diversity and liberal constitutionalism: diversity as a derogation from the constitutional order

Liberal constitutionalism's approach to equality and diversity can be described as follows.

First of all, equality was undeniably the primary concern of the liberal state. It originally took the form of equality before the law – which applied to a very limited number of people, i.e., white, rich, and healthy men – and was a condition protected by the constitutional framework, enforced by legislation, and implemented by administration and courts. The recognized condition of equality implied the free enjoyment of rights without infringement by the state or other public bodies. Notably, "the fact that general laws applied to

DOI: 10.4324/9781003493518-6

everybody and were the product of parliaments elected by the empowered body politic was generally considered an adequate protection of equality".[1] Accordingly, equality was not a principle capable of conditioning the lawmaker's activity.[2] Quite the contrary, generally, the parliament was the institution entrusted to materialize rights through legislation, its activity being the incontestable expression of the general will. In other words, equality was tantamount to legality, whatever its source was.[3] Nevertheless, although "the constitutional equality principle guaranteed equality before the law", it did not ensure "equal protection of the law".[4]

Against this backdrop, measures dedicated towards specific groupings were thus not necessary since all (male) citizens were supposed to enjoy the same status and opportunities through this new enabling structure of the state.

As for diversity, it was either ignored or, when taken into account as a ground for the introduction of specific rules for its protection or promotion,[5] conceived of as a derogation determined by *extra ordinem* sources of law. This was also true in the sense that the latter were international obligations (or the like) imposed on systems that were by nature theoretically sovereign, closed, and complete.[6] These mechanisms of diversity protection shared a common core element: they were (albeit differently) negotiated (not always even with the groups themselves) derogations from the ordinary constitutional systems

1 Brydc, Brun-O. and Stein, Michael A., "General Provisions Dealing with Equality", in Tushnet, Mark, Fleiner, Thomas and Saunders, Cheryl (eds.), *Routledge Handbook of Constitutional Law* (Routledge, London-New York, 2013), 287–300, at 288.

2 Ibid.

3 In the UK system, legality can be described as the complex outcome of different lawmakers' activities. This is different from the continental European experience where parliaments gained the monopoly over the production of law; on this see, Torre, Alessandro, "Il Regno Unito", in Carrozza, Paolo, Di Giovine, Alfonso and Ferrari, Giuseppe F., *Diritto costituzionale comparato* (Laterza, Rome-Bari, 2019), 5–54; on the connection between equality and legality, Fioravanti, Maurizio, "Il principio di eguaglianza nella storia del costituzionalismo moderno", 2(4) *Contemporanea* (1999), 609–630. As regards the US constitutional system, if it is true that the judicial review of legislation was (officially) in place following the leading ruling *Marshall v Madison*, at the same time, its use to limit the government's activity and enforce rights and equality provisions was gradual: thus, it seems reasonable to affirm that the US system followed the described trend as regards equality and its enforcement at that time.

4 Bryde and Stein, General Provisions . . . , 288.

5 By contrast, specific rules allowing discrimination were in place in several legal orders; for instance, in the US, as early as 1865, thus immediately after the end of the Civil War and the abolition of slavery, several states enacted the so-called "black codes" – laws intended to limit the rights and freedoms of African Americans and grant their availability as cheap labor force.

6 And, thus, they had not formally developed legal tools to give effect to international law on the relationships between domestic and international law and their evolution, leading to the adoption of rules for the incorporation of the latter into the former in most countries during the twentieth century, see De Wet, Erika, "The Constitutionalization of Public International Law", in Rosenfeld, Michel and Sajó, András (eds.), *The Oxford Handbook of Comparative Constitutional Law* (Oxford University Press, Oxford, 2012), 1209–1230.

in place in a given territory. Hence, the recognition of diversity – in the sense of a condition that justifies differential treatments and/or underlies the establishment of autonomous legal orders – is laid outside the perimeter of the formally uniform legal systems of the liberal epoch and their constitutions. It was therefore considered exceptional and thus needed exceptional reasons to be justified and exceptional means to be implemented.[7]

It must be recognized that the description of the relationships between equality and diversity within the tradition of liberal constitutionalism is not universal, and exceptions exist, for instance, in the case of federal countries. In these cases, diversity became, to a greater or lesser extent, part of the constitutional organization. In other words, it was included within the constitutional perimeter through a model based on covenantal logic, which resonates with the rationale of minority rights treaties.

That being said, it should also be highlighted that, with the partial exception of Switzerland,[8] the management of diversity within those federal structures emanated from the liberal philosophical and political tradition and was, therefore, tied to its fundamental categories. This is evident if one draws attention to the management of indigenous peoples in federal states; the liberal assumptions underlying the organization of those states[9] led to the exclusion of these populations from the constitutional order and their relegation to a different and inferior legal status compared to that characterizing the citizens of those countries.

Diversity and democratic constitutionalism: diversity as a legitimate exception to the ordinary rule

The democratic turn of constitutionalism has been accompanied by a growing awareness of the significance of diversity in contemporary societies, which is increasingly accepted in international and national jurisdictions and addressed from an organizational and – most often – rights-based standpoint.

Consequently, diversity has acquired a stronger and less precarious position. Indeed, it has begun to be considered as a structural element of liberal democratic constitutional systems that inherently seek the realization of pluralism. As such, state regulation of diversity beyond non-discrimination – previously an option that certain states for some reasons chose – turned into an increasingly

7 See Belser, Eva Maria, "Concluding Remarks", in Belser, Eva Maria, Bächler, Thea, Egli, Sandra and Zünd, Lawrence (eds.), *The Principle of Equality in Diverse States: Reconciling Autonomy with Equal Rights and Opportunities* (Brill-Nijhoff, Leiden-Boston, 2021), 415–428, at 415.

8 On the reasons why Switzerland can be considered as a partial exception, see Chapter 2, "Models for the accommodation of diversity in the liberal epoch and their targets".

9 On the monist assumptions that have underpinned constitutional theory and practice, especially in their origins, see Tierney, Stephen, *The Federal Contract: A Constitutional Theory of Federalism* (Oxford University Press, Oxford, 2022), 83–100.

consolidated international (regional) standard, albeit to varying extents.[10] Hence, the position of diversity has been reinforced and has acquired a legitimate place in several constitutional traditions, i.e., it has become a differential condition that can legitimately justify differential treatments (be they in the form of temporary affirmative measures or more stable provisions aimed at maintaining diversity).

Hence, diversity entails a condition that is protected by norms that not only include non-discrimination and its by-products but also permanent positive rights and enabling instruments like autonomy – albeit the balances struck depend on the targeted group.[11] International law – in the shape of minority rights law (mainly in the European regional area) and indigenous rights law – thus equipped itself with legal instruments that complemented the established individual approach of human rights law, recognizing specific rights for non-majority groups which share, to some extent, a collective dimension. When it comes to the mentioned legal measures intended to protect or promote diversity beyond non-discrimination, they are, once more, directed to specific groups of citizens that have, to a certain extent, recognizable cultural, linguistic, religious, or ethnic characteristics, though no binding definition of them – be they minorities or indigenous people – is retrievable in the international legal system. This implies that a large margin of appreciation is left to states when selecting the subjects entitled to these forms of protection or promotion.

Based on the foregoing, diversity seems to have been gradually embedded within the perimeter of constitutionalism and is no longer seen as a derogation. At the same time, it also appears to be true that, even in cases where diversity goes so far as to become the basis of the state structure, it nonetheless maintains an exceptional dimension in constitutional legal systems. Put

10 This is especially the case in Europe; on this, see Palermo, Francesco, "Current and Future Challenges for International Minority Protection", 10 *European Yearbook of Minority Issues* (2011), 21–36.

11 Chapter 2 has illustrated that national minorities and indigenous peoples have generally been the targets of differential measures beyond non-discrimination, while "new minorities" and other non-dominant groups have been theoretically distinguished from the former and practically excluded from these forms of protection; the established categorization of non-majority groups mainly relies on the work of Kymlicka, Will, *Multicultural Citizenship: A Liberal Theory of Minority Rights* (Clarendon, Oxford, 1995), which has significantly marked the literature (and international developments) in this area; for instance, see, among others, and besides the literature indicated in Chapters 1 and 2, Eide, Asbjørn, "The Rights of 'Old' versus 'New' Minorities", in Malloy, Tove H. and Marko, Joseph (eds.), *Minority Governance in and Beyond Europe: Celebrating 10 Years of the European Yearbook of Minority Issues* (Brill-Nijhoff, Leiden, 2014), 23–38; for a critique of this perspective, and the introduction of alternative theorizations, see Poirier, Johanne, "Autonomie politique et minorités francophones du Canada: réflexions sur un angle mort de la typologie classique de Will Kymlicka", 1 *Minorités linguistiques et société/Linguistic Minorities and Society* (2012), 66–89; Medda-Windischer, Roberta, *Old and New Minorities: Reconciling Diversity and Cohesion* (Nomos, Baden-Baden, 2009).

differently, the recognition of diversity by law leads to legitimate special treatments in favor of specific groups that diverge from the general rule, which is still conceived of as the ordinary rule.

Such a dimension is distinguishable in agnostic liberal and promotional systems, where the lesser or greater recognition of diversity – in many forms – is the result of the majority's (top-down) decisions and represents an exception to the general rules of the legal system.[12] In other words, regulating, protecting, and promoting diversity is legitimate to different degrees but is a special treatment compared to the general rules.

The same goes for multi-national legal systems since the promotion of diversity, albeit integrated into the constitutional order as a foundational rule, is tantamount to the exclusive entitlement of two or more "constituting communities" to equal group rights and prerogatives. Accordingly, although the treatment of those communities is based on group equality, diversity represents a core element of the whole constitutional system and is equated to the dominant groups that compose the state. The principle of majority and its by-products do not apply, for they are substituted by the principle of consensus, which *per se* creates a special system where only the interests of some groups can be balanced. In a way, the limitation of the special rule's scope makes it exceptional. In other words, while the protection of diversity is the basis of these systems – underpinning a constitutional structure that recognizes the plural composition of the society – it nonetheless remains an exception, as the scope of the differential measures is limited to some groups and most often implies the exclusion of others.[13]

Moving to the international dimension, the described exceptional framing seems further confirmed, given that international instruments endorse an understanding of diversity as the source of special rules for the special needs of selected groups, thereby showing a cautious approach to its regulation beyond non-discrimination.

Diversity and plural constitutionalism: diversity as the general rule

The emergent dynamics related to the accommodation of diversity illustrated in Chapters 3 and 4 reveal a renovated approach to diversity. They attribute to it a more central and founding role and depart from framing it exclusively in terms of majority-minority relations. Accordingly, the expression plural constitutionalism may be used to describe the models underpinned by this logic.

12 Palermo, Francesco and Woelk, Jens, *Diritto costituzionale comparato dei gruppi e delle minoranze* (CEDAM, Padua, 2021), 53–58 and 311–344.

13 On this issue, and for further references, Agarin, Timofey and McCulloch, Allison, "How Power-Sharing Includes and Excludes Non-Dominant Communities: Introduction to the Special Issue", 41(1) *International Political Science Review* (2020), 3–14 and the other articles of this issue, and in part. Stojanović, Nenad, "Democracy, Ethnoicracy and Consociational Demoicracy", 41(1) *International Political Science Review* (2020), 30–43.

The adjective plural is here intended to describe, on the one hand, the variety of macro-perspectives and legal tools that, in different ways, imply a reconsideration of the traditional position and framing attributed to diversity; on the other, the fact that the studied models and instruments are marked by a pluralization of the very idea of diversity, which is no longer (or at least potentially not anymore) equated to some specific (ethno-cultural) archetypes.

This is the case, firstly, with the emerging traditions of constitutionalism in the Global South that have been illustrated in Chapter 3. The South American and Southeast Asian macro-perspectives and related instruments have brought about several novelties that complement and enlarge the traditional discourse over constitutionalism writ large and the accommodation of diversity (the latter being traditionally based on the exclusive concepts of national minorities and indigenous peoples).[14] The former, and, in particular, the cases of Bolivia and Ecuador, testify to the creation of a state structure that is pluralized from its foundations due to the introduction and implementation of the principles of plurinationality and interculturalism. The latter is embedded in a large variety of constitutional systems – with Singapore being the most complex and refined case – where diversity informs so much of state organization and policies that the expression "pluralist constitutions" has been employed to describe them. In both cases, diversity is a foundational element of the constitutional legal system and entails a pluralization of law in terms of both sources and contents, which are internally differentiated based on their different recipients. Furthermore, both traditions value and bolster the idea that the accommodation of diversity requires a complex system of – more or less state-driven – governance, where the components of the diverse society work alongside public institutions to achieve peaceful coexistence and respect for diversity. Additionally, governance emerges both theoretically and practically as a fundamental means of guaranteeing the empowerment of the relevant communities and finally protecting their interests and rights. Lastly, both experiences depart from framing and consequently deal with diversity as something attributed by majorities to minorities but attempt to incorporate diversity into mainstream state structures through both integrative and autonomous flexible measures.

Secondly, the recent developments in European international soft law and the innovative instruments that have been developed in Global North countries provide a new lease of life to the issue of diversity accommodation from within the liberal tradition.[15]

The European macro-perspective implies a double global approach to diversity accommodation. On the one hand, diversity is considered to be a global phenomenon in our societies. On the other hand, and consequently, the means to manage it are considered to have a global reach that goes beyond the exclusive protection of one or more given groups, as they contribute to

14 For bibliographical references, see Chapter 3.

15 On this, see Chapter 4 and the bibliographical references in that chapter.

the integration of societies respectful of their internal differences. In other words, diversity is supposed to permeate society as a whole, and, as a consequence, legal systems are encouraged to consider diversity to be an ordinary situation. Therefore, differential conditions are the source of differentiated measures, which are no longer conceived of as derogations or exceptions but as ordinary rules. Based on that, one could affirm that European soft law bolsters a normalization of diversity – framed as a generalized element of several societies – which engenders a normalization of the instruments designed to manage it.

A similar conception of diversity infuses the emerging instruments analyzed in Chapter 4. These all exhibit significant inclusive potential that implies a possible wide scope of application beyond the traditional groups that have been targeted by minority and indigenous rights laws and mechanisms. Consequently, they are instruments that can potentially accommodate numerous non-majority groups' interests beyond the traditional targets of minority and indigenous peoples' rights law. Several of these instruments are characterized by a flexible structure that makes them potentially very inclusive tools for diversity accommodation. This potential inclusiveness is one of the most notable elements of the innovative tools for diversity accommodation, and it distances them from the models informed by what will be referred to as the mono- and multi-national paradigms in the next sections. The reason predominantly lies in their less institutionalized legal status, which means they are not exclusive "property" of a (recognized) minority and are accessible to several types of non-majority groups – potentially without the need for preliminary public action to recognize their rights. If the implementation of these instruments has mainly concerned non-majority groups that enjoy some sort of legal recognition, their inclusive potential must not be overlooked as a fundamental structural feature. Possible further applications should be explored. Therefore, diversity acquires a more ordinary position in legal systems that have experienced this evolution, as its manifold accommodation is becoming increasingly common and practiced.

The concurrent paradigms underlying the treatment of diversity

The notion of paradigm as a guide

The description of the role and management of diversity in constitutionalism provided previously highlights the variety of variously institutionalized legal instruments that already exist or are emerging. This overview was intended to set the stage for a reconsideration of a specific theoretical standpoint that seems to have monopolized and restrained scientific endeavors in this field of study. It seems that the (minority) rights discourse has theoretically overshadowed interest in other forms of accommodation of diversity, such that the latter have been analyzed but not included in comparative studies nor, most importantly, considered as part of the same phenomenon.

The next section will be a further step toward the final theoretical aim of the chapter, which is the proposal of a renewed and enabling theoretical framework regarding this area of law. It looks at the evolution of instruments for the accommodation of diversity in light of their essential structure and elements to eventually underscore the innovations that emergent models are introducing in this field of law. Based on this, it will be possible to move the scientific standpoint from consolidated models to emergent ones and finally develop a wider perspective on and a better understanding of the instruments for the accommodation of diversity. Once equipped with the wider picture, the need for a more open and inclusive theoretical framework that is able to include both traditional and contemporary models to manage diversity will be evident.

To do so, the notion of paradigm[16] provides a useful analytical lens to understand the basic elements – and political-sociological views, in turn, affected by global economic and legal dynamics – underlying the legal definition and treatment of diversity. The notion of paradigm may be read as the basic and founding principle, which, like genetic makeup, profoundly and transversally characterizes the development of the instruments for the accommodation of diversity. By using this analytical tool, it will be possible to depict the historically changing position of diversity in constitutionalism, its varying meaning, and the basic structure of the legal instruments that aim to manage it.

Finally, the application of the described scientific standpoint is supposed to provide a clear picture of the contemporary trends in the area of diversity accommodation.

The mono-national and the multi-national paradigms: rigidity and homogeneity

As pointed out by several authors, even if through the use of different terms, the accommodation of diversity beyond non-discrimination within liberal and democratic constitutionalism has long been characterized by the existence of what is here referred to as a national paradigm.[17] While both strands of constitutionalism seem to share some core elements of the national paradigm,

16 The term paradigm is borrowed from two main authors who have dedicated imponent works on this idea and how it affects the (revolutionary) evolution of scientific thought, as well as economic, political and legal systems: Ortino, Sergio, *La struttura delle rivoluzioni economiche* (Cacucci, Bari, 2010) who, in turn, took inspiration from Kuhn, Thomas S., *The Structure of Scientific Revolutions* (University of Chicago Press, Chicago, 4th ed., 2012).

17 Other authors refer to the monocultural paradigm or the racial paradigm; on this, see, respectively, Dundes Rendeln, Alison, "The Cultural Defense: Challenging the Monocultural Paradigm", in Foblets, Marie-Claire, Gaudreault-DesBiens, Jean-F. and Dundes Relteln, Alison (eds.), *Cultural Diversity and the Law: State Responses Around the World* (Bruylant-Yvon-Blais, Bruxelles-Montréal, 2010), 791–818; Heinze, Eric, "The Construction and Contingency of the Minority Concept", in Fottrell, Deirdre and Bowring, Bill (eds.), *Minority and Group Rights in the New Millennium* (Martinus Nijhoff, Leiden-Boston, 1999), 25–74.

they differ when it comes to the position of diversity within the constitutional framework. For this reason, it appears possible to affirm that liberal constitutionalism was underpinned by a mono-national paradigm and democratic constitutionalism by a multi-national one.

The mono-national paradigm

In a nutshell, the mono-national paradigm essentially consisted of and legally reproduced the natural correspondence between a homogeneous national community and a state, thus leading to the exclusion or neglect of other diversities.[18]

Such a perspective affected the limited way the management of diversity beyond non-discrimination – which had, at that time, a very circumscribed reach – was put in place. Besides the fact that diversity accommodation represented an extraordinary derogation of the constitutional order,[19] it must be noted that the recipients of the treaty provisions intended to protect diversity were groups that were recognizable in terms of national characteristics. In essence, they were a small-scale reproduction of the national (ideal) communities.[20]

Another significant feature of the mono-national paradigm is the connection between diversity accommodation and security concerns. Minorities

18 The absolute centrality of homogeneity may be further understood if put in the context of a global analysis of this epoch, based on Ortino's account; the author identified the modern state as the legal and political manifestation of a specific human era based on what he called the paradigm of homogeneity, emergence of which was driven by the technological innovations related to the industrial revolution; for what concerns the interest of this section, Ortino's investigation is particularly helpful in the sense that it explains the deep interiorization of the logic of uniformity from a global point of view. As explained by Tully, James, *Strange Multiplicity: Constitutionalism in an Age of Diversity* (Cambridge University Press, Cambridge, 1995), 71, such a theorization also aimed to justify European settlers' domination and the creation of modern states in North America. Hence, the political-constitutional manifestation of Ortino's uniformity paradigm is to be found in the homogeneous nation-state and its by-products.

19 With the exception of federal systems in the liberal epoch, which, as seen, imply some inclusion of diversity in the constitutional structure; in the US, this mainly meant the recognition of territorial diversity, while, in Switzerland, a wider degree of cultural diversity was part of the original federal covenant, in a system where cantons were entitled to wide competencies on cultural matters and at the federal level no specific cultural cleavage was of major political salience as the different existing cleavages cross-cut each other.

20 To a certain extent, that applied to Switzerland too, as the cantonal communities were mainly homogeneous and internally treated diversity following liberal assumptions; furthermore, the groups that successively received constitutional recognition would have been linguistic communities, on the connection between the nation-state model and minority rights, so that the former conditioned the features of the latter, which, in turn, was the tolerated by-product of nation-state building processes, see Arato, Andrew and Cohen, Jean L., "Introduction: Forms of Pluralism and Democratic Constitutionalism", in Arato, Andrew, Cohen, Jean L. and von Busekist, Astrid (eds.), *Forms of Pluralism and Democratic Constitutionalism* (Columbia University Press, New York-Chichester, 2018), 1–30.

were seen as causes of instability in the emergent nation-state model as well as major contributors to tensions at the international level.[21] As a consequence, if not forced into assimilation, transfers, or, worse, made victims of genocides, they were provided with forms of protection to avoid domestic and especially international conflicts. The security dimension of the emerging minority provisions – at the time, predominant – is still a significant component, albeit to different extents, of minorities' and groups' safeguards.[22]

Finally, from the security perspective stems a last element of the mono-national paradigm, which would have informed, to different degrees, the evolution of diversity accommodation – namely, what has been called a paternalistic approach to diversity issues.[23] This originally materialized in two ways. First, safeguards for minorities and groups were imposed on weaker states in peace treaties based on geopolitical concerns and nationalistic aims. Second, the accommodation took the form of top-down protection, which beneficiary communities often did not have a say in. Hence, the latter were considered objects of protection rather than subjects.[24]

21 On the security approach towards minority issues, see Malloy, Tove H., "Introduction", in Malloy, Tove H., Osipov, Alexander and Vizi, Balázs (eds.), *Managing Diversity through Non-Territorial Autonomy: Assessing Advantages, Deficiencies, and Risks* (Oxford University Press, Oxford, 2015), 1–15, at 12–13; see also Marko, Joseph, Marko-Stöckl, Edith, Harzl, Benedikt and Unger, Hedwig, "The Historical-Sociological Foundations: State Formation and Nation Building in Europe and the Construction of the Identitarian Nation-cum-State Paradigm", in Marko, Joseph and Constantin, Sergiu (eds.), *Human and Minority Rights Protection by Multiple Diversity Governance: History, Law, Ideology and Politics in European Perspective* (Routledge, London-New York, 2019), 33–95, at 36: the authors have described the traditional framing of minorities in legal and political discourses as "framed by the identitarian nation-cum-state paradigm, so that groupings of people which are, in particular in terms of religion and language, seen as culturally different from the rest of the population and living on the territory of a given national state allegedly pose a threat to security, political unity, governability and the social cohesion of a given state an society".

22 On the continuing significance of the security dimension, see Nimni, Ephraim, "Minorities and the Limits of Liberal Democracy: Demoicracy and Non-Territorial Autonomy", in Malloy, Tove H. and Palermo, Francesco (eds.), *Minority Accommodation through Territorial and Non-Territorial Autonomy* (Oxford University Press, Oxford, 2015), 57–82, at 62–66, and esp. at 64: "Securitization is not a contemporary innovation as many international relations users of securitization argue, but a by-product of the historical conflation of nations, popular sovereignty, and territorial states. In whatever way one defines national-popular sovereignty, it is a concept dependent upon the definition of cultural-territorial boundaries, which inexorably creates outsiders and cultural insiders".

23 See Malloy, Introduction . . .; *Id.*, "National Minorities between Protection and Empowerment: Towards a Theory of Empowerment", 13(2) *Journal on Ethnopolitics and Minority Issues in Europe* (2014), 11–29, at 11–13.

24 Of course, this is a generalization, and, to a certain extent, exceptions to this model existed; for instance, as seen, the Polish community was given (at least formally) the right to have its own political institutions, as well, the autonomy of the Åland Islands, which implied a strong form of self-government and thus major involvement of the Ålandic community as a subject of minority protection. This dates back to 1919.

This framing is not put forward to criticize the protection of minorities and groups that followed this model, which was predominant in the nineteenth and twentieth centuries. It simply makes clear that the features of diversity accommodation characterizing liberal constitutionalism still play a considerable role in affecting the design, theorization, and study of several current models.

Hence, to sum up, it seems that homogeneity – in the ideal legal reality created by constitutionalism, exceptionalism, security concerns, top-down protection, and paternalism as regards the accommodation of diversity, are to be seen as the basic contents of the mono-national paradigm.

The multi-national paradigm

The democratic turn of constitutionalism has brought about several significant developments as regards the legal treatment of diversity. Nevertheless, it can be said that the evolution of the instruments for the accommodation of diversity shows several points of continuity with the basic liberal structure of diversity accommodation described previously.[25]

This is why one may describe the paradigm underlying diversity accommodation stemming from the democratic evolution of constitutionalism as multi-national.[26]

Though the inclusion of the largest number of people and their diversities in the political community of a state is implicit in the democratic turn of constitutionalism,[27] the way diversity is managed resonates with many of the

25 On the (mono- and multi-) national paradigm underpinning the evolution of the accommodation of diversity in liberal and liberal-democratic constitutionalism, see Marko, Marko-Stöckl, Harzl and Unger, The Historical-Sociological Foundations . . . , 33–95; Marko, Joseph, "Law and Ideology: The Ideological Conundrums of the Liberal-Democratic State", in Marko and Constantin (eds.), Human and Minority Rights . . . , 96–137.

26 On this, see Marko, Marko-Stöckl, Harzl and Unger, The Historical-Sociological Foundations . . . , 33; the authors have used the expression "monist-identitarian nation-cum-state paradigm" to describe the hegemonic approach that has marked the developments of social sciences, normative principles and institutional models since the XVI century in Europe; in addition, Marko, Law and Ideology . . . , 96, demonstrated that this paradigm has framed "our understanding of social and political relations between and within national states to this day".

27 On this, see Spiliopoulou Åkermark, Sia, "Multiculturalism in Crisis?", in Ruiz Vieytez, Eduardo J. and Dunbar, Robert (eds.), *Human Rights and Diversity: New Challenges for Plural Societies* (University of Deusto, Bilbao, 2007), 35–49, at 45: the author suggested that, besides conflict prevention, preservation of cultural diversity and protection of human dignity, "another justificatory ground has gained in prominence. That is the principle of democracy and democratic participation. This argument emphasises two reasons why minorities should be included in democratic decision-making. First of all, there is a right to participation in public affairs and in matters affecting minorities . . . . Secondly, . . . the views of minorities must be heard and be taken seriously. This improves the quality and legitimacy of the decisions".

features of the mono-national paradigm and rests on a similar conceptualization of diversity.[28]

The multi-national paradigm seems to embed several models that share a defensive (or protective), national, "hard", and exclusive (or proprietary) approach to minority and diversity issues.

The defensive or protective attitude in diversity accommodation is linked to the undeniable centrality of the state regarding these issues,[29] which has re-emerged in recent decades.[30] Although a refined legal framework has developed at the international level in certain regions, this is largely composed of soft law disciplines, which are reinforced by monitoring mechanisms whose functioning is very much affected by geopolitical developments.[31] This implies that – even though the development of an international regulatory framework has led to significant successes in the prohibition of gross violations and the enforcement of the principle of non-discrimination in the enjoyment of fun-

28 According to Marko, Law and Ideology . . . , 105, the structural characteristics of the nation-cum-state paradigm, which deeply inform the legal categories in this area of law, are: the naturalization of cultural diversity, which is redefined "into ethnic difference when belonging to a group or the possession of a territory is made a precondition for the social and political recognition of collective identity, legal equality, and effective participation"; identity formation is "one-dimensional, all-encompassing not allowing for multiple identities and requiring absolute loyalty towards state and nation"; exclusivism of identity framings.

29 On this, see Ortino, Sergio, "La tutela delle minoranze nel diritto internazionale: evoluzione o mutamento di prospettiva?", 76(2) *Studi trentini di scienze storiche. Sezione prima* (1997), 203–212; Bíró, Anna-Mária and Lennox, Corinne, "International Order, Diversity Regimes and Minority Rights: A Longue Durée Perspective", Bíró, Anna-Mária and Newman, Dwight (eds.), *Minority Rights and Liberal Democratic Insecurities: The Challenge of Unstable Orders* (Routledge, London-New York, 2022), 7–38, at 33; and, as indicated by Malloy, Tove H., "A New Research Agenda for Theorizing Non-Territorial Autonomy?", in Malloy, Tove H. and Salat, Levente (eds.), *Non-Territorial Autonomy and Decentralization: Ethno-Cultural Diversity Governance* (Routledge, London-New York, 2021), 3–22, at 3, such a centrality has not generally been challenged by legal and political theory, although, as seen in the previous chapters, alternative models are emerging.

30 Palermo, Francesco, "'The Borders of My Language Mean the Borders of My World': Language Rights and Their Evolving Significance for Minority Rights and Integration of Societies", in Ulasiuk, Iryna, Hadîrcă, Laurenţiu and Romans, William (eds.), *Language Policy and Conflict Prevention* (Brill-Nijhoff, Leiden-Boston, 2018), 135–154, at 141.

31 In fact, the pressing need to stop the violence and wars that erupted in the Balkans reinforced the international community and led to international soft law's significant influence on state legal systems from the 1990s until the 2000s and to the correlated dynamic of internationalization of constitutional law and constitutionalization of international minority rights law; the change of the geopolitical conditions, and, particularly, the re-emergence of the role of states in the international arena, account for the weakening of international law in this area; on this, see the Introduction and Palermo, Francesco, "The Protection of Minorities in International Law: Recent Developments and Trends", in VV.AA., *Les minorités: un défi pour les États: Actes du colloque international (22 et 23 mai 2011)* (Académie Royale de Belgique, Bruxelles, 2012), 165–185.

damental human rights[32] – it does not go as far as to condition the sovereignty of the states and impose the implementation of positive measures (be they structural or merely financial support) in favor of groups and minorities within their territory.[33] The latter are put in place following specific domestic options (besides legal conditionalities and pressure of the international community in certain situations[34]) based on the overall internal approach to diversity. The decision to take positive measures directed toward groups and communities beyond non-discrimination is, therefore, still much reserved to the discretion of states, although they are, especially in Europe, to some extent guided by international documents and mechanisms. From this, generally, a defensive, paternalistic, and top-down approach in diversity accommodation follows, whereby institutional protection and safeguards are provided for members of certain groups, the recognition of which is attributed exclusively to the state.[35] In other words, the multi-national paradigm is characterized by a similar protective approach as the mono-national, which conceives national minority groups as vulnerable or dangerous for state unity and, therefore, more often objects of protection than subjects of empowerment.[36]

Furthermore, the multi-national paradigm also entails a reproduction of the nation-state model in framing and regulating diversity issues. Some authors have observed that the national framing (variously labeled) is a cryptotype

32 Of course, these are notable results and, as seen, have been achieved also thanks to the jurisprudence of the ECHR and the CJEU.

33 Besides the cases where positive measures derive from the protection of fundamental human rights; on this, see Bíró and Lennox, International Order . . . , 10.

34 For instance, the Copenhagen criteria serve a significant function in this sense.

35 On this, see Malloy, National Minorities . . . , 11–12, where the author underlined that "the protection paradigm holds a hegemonic position in policy-making. Legal Instruments and social programmes are written in the mode of protection. Thus, agents of the protection of minorities are governments acting on behalf of the majority, and because governments have the agency to hold control of state power, protection becomes a top-down process"; interestingly, the author, at 13, also affirmed that "this paternalistic approach on behalf of dominant groups is mirrored in the academic literature where the view remains largely unchallenged. The protection paradigm is ever present not only in the normative literature but also in the systematic empirical analysis of government behaviour and state/supra-level institutions".

36 Malloy, Tove H., "Towards a New Paradigm of Minority Law-Making: A Rejoinder to Palermo and Woelk's Law of Diversity", 4 *European Yearbook of Minority Issues* (2004–2005), 5–28, at 5–9; *Id.*, *National Minority Rights in Europe* (Oxford University Press, Oxford, 2005); *Id.*, National Minorities . . . , 13: "One might argue that the notion of protection portrays minorities as victims, or recipients of a type of entitlement, the entitlement of protection. It brackets minorities as objects rather than subjects of their own lives"; also, on the concept of non-majority groups as objects or subjects of diversity accommodation, see, Bisaz, Corsin, "Minority Protection and the Neglected Importance of Authority: A Fundamental Challenge from Groups Rights", in Thürer, Daniel (ed.), *International Protection of Minorities: Challenges in Practice and Doctrine* (Schulthess, Zurich, 2014), 237–258; on the notion of empowerment, see Chapter 4 and the next section.

that directs and shapes the development of the legal categories in this field.[37] Accordingly, groups with characteristics corresponding to those of a national group are deemed worthy of protection (beyond non-discrimination): homogeneity, (often) long-standing tie with territory and citizenship in the state where they reside, and "cultural" identification criteria.

Based on that ideal-typical model, different kinds of groups are consequently not deemed worthy of protection as they do not correspond to the legally endorsed idea of the beneficiaries of minority protection. This is the case with groups with a migratory background. Indeed, a neat distinction between "old" and "new" minorities has been widely consolidated in legal and political literature and has been put into practice by legal regulation.[38] According to this view, national minorities are generally considered – also from a scholarly point of view – as legitimately entitled to wide positive rights and instruments compared to more recent non-majority groups.[39] As pointed out by Heinze, the same reasoning has been applied to several other societal groups that have traditionally been addressees of non-discrimination measures but excluded from the enjoyment of further positive rights and measures on the basis that they are not ethno-cultural groups.[40] In keeping with his view, the national framing of diversity issues exclusively through the notion of a national minority, which is mostly taken for granted and not questioned in literature either, is a contingent selective process that has (also) been affected by the predominance of a specific system of thought and approach to these issues.[41]

37 On this, see Heinze, The construction . . . , 42–56; Palermo, Current and Future Challenges . . . , 31–32; Marko, Marko-Stöckl, Harzl and Unger, The Historical-Sociological Foundations . . . , 33–95; Marko, Law and Ideology . . . , 96–137.

38 For an in-depth analysis of the topic, the challenges it poses, and the possible theoretical solutions to overcome the distinction between old and new minorities with a view to extending protection and empowerment to the latter, see Medda-Windischer, Old and New Minorities . . .

39 This is the well-known and rather uncontested theorization that originates from Kymlicka, Multicultural Citizenship . . . ; see "The notion of paradigm as a guide" section in this Chapter.

40 Heinze, The construction . . . , 72, made the example of sexual minorities: "Sexual minorities are no more, but also no less 'collectivised' than many ethnic, religious or linguistic groups whose claims are predominantly individual, but also who also may, in exceptional and modest cases, collectivise their interests in order to bolster their claims and enhance respect for them".

41 Naturally, other reasons account for the predominance of an ethno-cultural framing of diversity issues, among them historical and geo-political factors; the minority question was indeed a national question that arose in parallel to the birth of the modern state and was evidently one of the most compelling questions related to diversity management at that time; however, what these pages aim to underline is that after that epoch, the notion of minority has continued to be approached and studied exclusively through a national lens; consequently, national minorities were the only natural beneficiaries of positive measures, with this idea generally not having being challenged and taken for granted; on this, see Bíró and Lennox, International Order . . . , 33: "we accept that minority rights norms have become more universal since the League of Nations period, but the use of recognised categories also denotes that the "authorised forms of cultural difference" are strictly controlled and limited".

As regards the ways the multi-national paradigm affects the management of diversity, national minorities are attributed rights and instruments that resonate with the concept of state sovereignty, especially when it comes to forms of autonomy for minorities that turn them into a subnational majority.[42]

A corollary of the previous considerations is that generally, the rules governing diversity under the multi-national paradigm are hard or rigid as they are structured around a specific idea of targeted groups – i.e., a static and monolithic conception of minorities and groups as homogeneous entities[43] – and strongly institutionalized instruments, provided for from above by the state.[44]

Finally, the influence of the nation-state's legal and political categories may also be found in the use of an exclusive (or proprietary) model in the design of instruments for accommodating diversity in two respects. First, rights and instruments like autonomy are framed in terms of exclusive ownership by a specific community (or its members);[45] second, the communities themselves are conceived of as owned by a given ethnic or cultural (majority) group.[46]

The described paradigm which underpins the reproduction of the nation-state model in this field (which, of course, has achieved considerable success and varied applications, some of which are remarkably sensitive to diversity), on the one hand, has inspired the design of instruments whose exclusivity is reminiscent of the concept of sovereignty and which are based on a presumption of homogeneity (of the national community or protected groups) similar to that underpinning the concept of nation. On the other, it implies that the state is the only legitimate source of diversity accommodation beyond the guarantee of fundamental human rights and the principle of formal equality (non-discrimination), which is provided for by top-down institutionalized rights and instruments in favor of specific minority groups.

The plural paradigm

From the description of the recent developments in this area of law, it seems possible to affirm that a renewed approach is emerging. Several experiences and legal sources, as well as innovative theoretical accounts, indicate that the national paradigm – in its mono-national and multi-national versions – is

42 On this, see Palermo, Francesco, "Owned or Shared? Territorial Autonomy in the Minority Discourse", in Malloy and Palermo (eds.), Minority Accommodation . . . , 13–32.

43 See Palermo, Current and Future Challenges . . . , 31–33.

44 On the concept of rigidity and its role in the management of diversity, see Burri, Thomas, "The Rigidity of Structures to Protect Minorities: Hidden Facets of the Strasbourg Court's Judgement in *Sejdić* and the Banjul Commission's Decision in *Endorois*", in Thürer (ed.), International Protection . . . , 201–233; on the concept of institutionalization of the instruments for the accommodation of diversity and the general oversight that less institutionalized forms have suffered, Malloy, A New Research Agenda,. . . , 3–22.

45 On this, see Palermo, Owned or Shared . . . , 21–32.

46 See Palermo, Current and Future Challenges . . . , 32–33.

being complemented to various degrees while naturally not set aside. What this section aims to put forward is the idea that what one may refer to as a plural paradigm is (slowly) juxtaposing with the national one. This underpins several models for the accommodation of diversity that, to different extents, diverge from the classic features and structure of the traditional instruments.[47]

The Global South strands of constitutionalism that have been studied in this work appear to be informed by a plural paradigm in that they – albeit in different ways – distance themselves from the nation-state model (underpinning the other paradigms) for the following reasons. They markedly refuse the identification of one state with one (or more identified) nation(s)[48] – which entails the idea that diversity holds the position of a derogation or an exception – and consider (ethnic and societal) pluralism as a constitutive part of their systems; they relativize the position of the state (and its public organization) as the exclusive actor as concerns diversity management and provider of top-down protective measures; consequently, they make use of the language of rights, but strongly endorse governance means of various types as one of the main vehicles to peaceful diversity accommodation; lastly, they imply, albeit to varying extents, a considerable degree of inclusiveness and flexibility when it comes to the concrete instruments put in place for the management of diversity.

European developments also exhibit a trend away from the most established models of diversity accommodation. European soft law (and its concrete implementations at the domestic level) emphasizes participation and dialogue among the different groupings of the diverse society; additionally, it supports the integration of diversity through self-government and self-governance means where non-majority groups are not only recipients of protective measures but active actors. Moreover, European international soft law encourages the softening of rigid legal categories when it comes to the definition of non-majority groups based on a more dynamic (and realistic) conception of individual and group identity.[49] In other words, pluralism, participation and

47 The plural paradigm may also be seen as a specific manifestation of Ortino's paradigm of connection, which entails a growing inclusion of complexity in human thought and organization: see Ortino, La struttura . . . , 395–415 and 558–593; this connection between the evolution of the "Law of Diversity" and the general dynamics concerning state organization and public affairs has also been described by Palermo, Francesco, "Legal Solutions to Complex Societies: The Law of Diversity", in Ruiz Vieytez, Eduardo J. and Dunbar, Robert (eds.), *Human Rights and Diversity: New Challenges for Plural Societies* (University of Deusto, Bilbao, 2007), 63–82, at 66, as the phenomenon of polycentric diffusion of power.

48 Both the concepts of plurinationality and pluralist constitution, respectively characterizing the South American and Southeast Asian macro-perspectives, suggest the overcoming of a monist conception of the state.

49 With regard to the process of erosion of state definitions of minorities by international bodies, see, for instance, the *First Opinion of the ACFC on Estonia* (2002), ACFC/INF/OP/I(2002)5, para. 17 and the *Second Opinion of the ACFC on Italy* (2005), ACFC/INF/OP/II(2005)003, para. 11.

governance, together with an inclusive conception of diversity – as a phenomenon informing every aspect of most contemporary European societies and not an exclusive marker of national minorities – are the founding elements of the renewed European macro-perspective.[50] Consequently, the instruments that are endorsed by the soft law documents are flexible and continuously adjusted according to the evolution of societies and their processes of diversity integration.[51] As a result, the distancing from rigid categorizations and instruments characterizing the mono- and multi-national paradigms is evident.

Likewise, a renovated approach appears to infuse the emerging instruments analyzed in Chapter 4. Several such instruments are characterized by a flexible structure that makes them potentially very inclusive mechanisms through which to accommodate diversity. Another notable element of the structure of these instruments is that they determine the relativization of the centrality of state law – with its top-down paternalistic approach – when it comes to the accommodation of diversity, which is increasingly complemented by empowered forms of self-management and voice.[52] All the instruments share a strong governance dimension and testify to a functional turn in the accommodation of diversity based on empowerment and participation that complements the established human rights-based model of protection and security.[53] Besides that, if all the studied tools structurally diverge from the exclusivist and hard

50 These are developments in the area of the accommodation of diversity that have been envisaged by Palermo, Legal Solutions . . . , 63–82.

51 Palermo, Francesco, "Quanto è morbido il soft law? La tutela non giurisdizionale dei diritti delle minoranze nelle aree geogiuridiche europee", 1 *Rivista di Diritti Comparati* (2022), 74–94, at 93.

52 As observed by Malloy, Tove H., "Non-Territorial Autonomy: Traditional and Alternative Practices", in Romans, William, Ulasiuk, Iryna and Petrenko Thomsen, Anton (eds.), *Effective Participation of National Minorities and Conflict Prevention* (Brill Nijhoff, Leiden-Boston, 2020), 105–122, at 109, where the author referred to the emergence of other paradigms in diversity accommodation (and especially in autonomy studies) that challenge the traditional model.

53 These expressions are borrowed from Cabrera Ormaza, Maria Victoria, "From Protection to Participation? Shifting Perceptions towards Indigenous Peoples under International Law", in Hauser-Schäublin, Brigitta (ed.), *Adat and Indigeneity in Indonesia: Culture and Entitlements between Heteronomy and Self-Ascription* (Göttingen University Press, Göttingen, 2013), 31–41; the author illustrated that the functional approach is gaining increasing importance when it comes to the accommodation of indigenous peoples' interests: as demonstrated in the previous chapters, a similar trend is occurring in general in the area of diversity accommodation, so that the remarks made about the indigenous peoples may arguably be generalized; see also Malloy, Tove H., "From Security Threat to Citizen Deeds: A Paradigm Shift in European Minority Governance?", in Gaitanides, Charlotte and Grözinger, Gerd (eds.), *Diversity in Europe* (Nomos, Baden-Baden, 2015), 13–28, at 13–14: "Minorities are no longer the quiet bystander to their own lives allowing stigmatization on the basis of their belonging, religion or ethnicity. They seek participation in politics and society, and they seek decision-rights over their own affairs. In other words, by actively showing their agency as proactive subjects rather than passive objects, they are reformulating the conflict stereotyping that has for so many years defined minority governance".

logic underlying the mono- and multi-national paradigms, non-orthodox autonomous arrangements, especially in the forms of functional autonomy and nested federalism, deserve a particular mention. Indeed, such forms of self-governance reduce the importance of territory and political boundaries, which do not act as a prerequisite (and a constraint) for the development of these tools.

Based on the foregoing, it thus seems possible to propose a definition of the plural paradigm. It must be pointed out that none of the concrete experiences analyzed is a full-fledged manifestation of the latter, but nonetheless, together, they contribute to defining its main elements in what can be imagined as a process of incremental construction. Thus, the plural paradigm is sketched as an ideal-typical model here.

The latter underpins and inspires models for the accommodation of diversity that is "comprehensive" or global, multilevel, and flexible.

The paradigm can be defined as global or comprehensive since it implies the conception of the instruments for the accommodation of diversity as a set of tools (starting with minority rights) that benefit the diverse society as a whole – understood as a (culturally) composite society in which diversity is not only relevant to traditional minorities. These instruments consist not only of defensive measures against legally recognized minorities but also of devices and processes broadly aimed at the integration of diversity of all components of a society.

The plural paradigm, emerging out of theoretical and practical developments established in sources of soft law and variously implemented in certain contexts at the domestic level, evidently puts the mono and multi-national paradigm underpinning minority and indigenous rights law under stress, informing innovative instruments and consolidated ones employed in an inclusive and plural manner. In other words, the plural paradigm is a principle underlying a range of potential models, all characterized by their divergence from traditional approaches. Notably, the plural paradigm does not negate models inspired by the mono- and multi-national paradigms but rather incorporates them while suggesting their reinterpretation. Therefore, the accommodation of diversity, from the perspective of the plural paradigm, encompasses the instruments and rights typical of minority and indigenous peoples' rights law but rejects its exclusively national, hard, and strongly institutionalized character.

Furthermore, the plural paradigm underlies innovative instruments, as it expresses the need for flexibility in diversity accommodation and recognizes the role played by various actors in this field. In addition, it invokes the concepts of network, governance, and non-centralization and requires exploring the potential of not fully institutionalized forms of diversity management.

Notably, such a paradigm does not deny the role of the state as an organization – rather, it questions the role of the state as a community of destiny and a nation – but it places it in a broad framework of cooperation between powers and components of society. Nor does it diminish the guiding role of public and constitutional law.

Concretely, the plural paradigm inspires models that include an appropriate mix of measures guaranteeing autonomy (not only of culturally distinct groups, communities, and territories) and those aimed at the integration of societies in diversity.[54] Accordingly, the accommodation of diversity is the result of a different balance between these poles, moving along an imaginary autonomy-integration axis. The plural paradigm embeds a vast range of solutions to manage diversity, from variously institutionalized forms of autonomy – territorial, cultural, functional, or non-orthodox autonomy – to mechanisms for integration in diversity – representative, participatory, deliberative, consultative (instruments that, as seen, may also be framed as forms of autonomy).

Not unlike the evolution of human organization from a global perspective, what will be referred to as the "Law of Diversity" is arguably going through a phase of paradigm transition, with all the overlaps and contradictions that characterize such periods. This implies that different paradigms dialogue and sometimes clash within the same legal experiences, with this highlighting their different ways of governing diversity and their greater or lesser preparedness for the upcoming challenges.

The "Law of Diversity" as a gate-opener: why a renovated conceptual framework

The "Law of Diversity" as an enabling theoretical standpoint

The description provided previously has hopefully offered a clear picture of the evolution of the accommodation of diversity within the realm of constitutionalism, complemented by an analysis based on the notion of paradigm. The latter was supposed to unveil the essential structure of the legal instruments that have been put forward to manage differential human conditions in the various epochs up to today.

Based on this, one can see that the emergent practices add an innovative dimension to this area of law and to different extents, move away from the models informed by the mono-national and multi-national paradigm. If the previous analysis has successfully served its function of uncovering the innovative dynamics of this area of law and its structural features, the stage is finally set for proposing a renovated theoretical framework aimed at grasping the ongoing evolution of the instruments for the accommodation of diversity.

54 Fundamental, in this sense, from the point of view of the content of the measures taken, is the principle of proportionality and, with regard to the interaction between the components of society and the institutions at different levels, the subsidiarity principle.

To this end, the introduction of a new comprehensive standpoint that relies on the expression "Law of Diversity" is suggested here. This expression is borrowed from Palermo and Woelk[55] but at the same time expanded as a theoretical framework for existing developments occurring in this area. Indeed, the authors have used this expression to build a normative argument for the development of instruments for the accommodation of diversity in an age of "maturity", essentially taking inspiration from the most recent developments in European soft law regulations.[56] The present work may thus be conceived of as a follow-up to their account, for it takes into consideration further concrete developments that indicate that the evolution in diversity management they anticipated would complement traditional approaches is, to a certain extent, already emerging. In other words, the theoretical proposal is here more descriptive and analytical than normative.[57]

Importantly, choosing this concept unveils some specific theoretical (and, in part, normative) aims.

It is, first, intended to demonstrate that the legal instruments for the accommodation of diversity are evolving out of institutional experimentation, and emerging approaches are complementing those that have traditionally been studied. Hence, not only is the aim descriptive, but the proposed theoretical framing also implies the academic validation of these emerging phenomena. The theoretical recognition of these legal phenomena gives them a solid ground from which to develop since it sheds light on them, lures research interest, and possibly inspires further concrete implementations.[58]

Second, the "Law of Diversity" is brought forward to encourage scholars and practitioners to open up their theoretical and applicative perspectives, free of the epistemological limits the non-discrimination/rights discourse seems to be posing. In other words, the proposed notion is thought to act as an enabling conceptual framework that allows scholars and practitioners to appreciate the existing variety of legal instruments for the accommodation of diversity, their broad applicative possibilities, and their current developments.

Hence, this concept reveals that today, the management of diversity embeds and goes beyond non-discrimination and minority rights law and offers a unitary framework for both "traditional" and emerging models. The use of the

55 Palermo, Francesco and Woelk, Jens, "From Minority Protection to a Law of Diversity? Reflections on the Evolution of Minority Rights", 3 *European Yearbook of Minority Issues* (2003–2004), 5–13.

56 See, on this, Malloy, Towards a New Paradigm . . . , 9–11.

57 However, a normative dimension is also present in this theoretical proposal, as the most recent innovations in this area are seen as the most developed and refined tools for the accommodation of diversity, conducive to further inclusion and integration of diverse societies; in addition, it is normative in the sense explained in the following parts of the section.

58 Similar considerations are made by Trettel, Martina, *La democrazia partecipativa negli ordinamenti composti: studio di diritto comparato sull'incidenza della tradizione giuridica nelle democratic innovations* (ESI, Naples, 2020), as concerns democratic innovations.

proposed expression recommends refraining from framing diversity management only through the lens of the dichotomy that has traditionally characterized this field of study.

A theoretical framing based on the distinction between non-discrimination and rights discourse – which, in turn, implies a framing of diversity issues in terms of minority-majority relations and marks the mono-national and multi-national paradigms – may not be the most appropriate method to analyze the developments in this area of law consistently. As far as positive measures for accommodating diversity are concerned, the minority (and indigenous peoples') rights discourse affects the theoretical (and, consequently, legal and political) approach in a way that may be limiting, especially when it comes to the analysis of emergent models, which, to different extents, diverge from the traditional ones. Such a view implies that one focuses on diversity accommodation in terms of contraposition between alleged majorities and specific types of minorities, where the latter are in a position of subalternity needing top-down and institutionalized protective measures.

While this is most certainly the case, such a perspective is not able to theoretically grasp the forms of diversity accommodation that are characterized by different rationales, such as those addressed in the previous sections. In these cases, often (but not always) observable in legal systems where the management of diversity has reached a certain degree of consolidation, forms of accommodation become more fluid, less institutionalized, inclusive, and function-oriented. The significance of both the minority concept – with all its definitional hurdles – and the rights discourse thus seem to fade and give way to a major focus on the regulation of diversity (and pluralism) as a general phenomenon, as well as on the proactive role of the various component of diverse societies, where law mainly serves as an enabling framework rather than a detailed and rigid set of protective provisions.

As a result, framing and studying such phenomena through a non-discrimination/minority rights lens may be misleading. In particular, the minority rights discourse is generally underlain by what Malloy called security and protection paradigms and state-centrism in the management of diversity. Conversely, the emergent models imply a major focus on a flexible governance dimension where groups and communities play an active role in the accommodation of diversity.[59] These tools may indeed not originate from the legal recognition of a specific group and a consequent top-down attribution of a set of rights, including the "right" to autonomy. Moreover, they are forms of less institutionalized self-management that emerge due to the existence of an empowering legal framework.

The limitations of this perspective can be shown by taking the example of new or not legally recognized minorities. What is generally observable in literature is that opinions diverge as to whether or not they may be entitled to

59 Thus, expressing forms of empowerment.

forms of institutional protection that are granted to national minorities and whether or not coherent legal protection is given to the different non-majority groups present in a country. Thus, the entire debate revolves around the possible extension of minority rights mechanisms to non-legally recognized minorities, which at the moment enjoy protection through the non-discrimination legal framework.[60] Owing to the institutionalized and rigid structure of minority rights mechanisms, which requires the state to put in place a significant organizational (and economic) effort, this logic cannot but lead to the conclusion that an extension of minority rights must be subject to limitations and to the prioritization of selected kinds of diversity over others. What this theoretical framing and its applicative consequences may engender is oversight of the fact that other alternatives can exist beyond using instruments for non-discrimination or applying minority rights and that, to various extents, they are effectively emerging. According to Gaudreault-DesBiens, the idea of conflating the rights of some selected groups with diversity accommodation comes as a consequence of the comprehensive rights revolution that occurred in Europe and partially worldwide in the second half of the twentieth century. Notably, this has implied a monopolization of the rights discourse in terms of political agendas and theoretical perspectives that have conditioned the framing, development, and understanding of the complexity of accommodating diversity, thus acting as an epistemological constraint in this area of research.[61]

The present work, conversely, aims to illustrate that the models presented as emergent are also part of the broad universe of diversity accommodation and, in a way, represent the most refined and complex set of tools developed so far. Furthermore, several have critical inclusive potential as tools for the accommodation of diversity given their less institutionalized and flexible structure, as well as openness in terms of possible groups that can benefit from them. The privileged standpoint provided by the notion of "Law of Diversity" thus offers a theoretical platform to appreciate the dynamicity and evolutionary aspect of this area of law, which can be useful to scholars and practitioners.

Accordingly, the "Law of Diversity" can be imagined both as a unitary conceptual framework and a practical toolbox containing all the instruments aimed at accommodating differential human aspects. It thus serves theoretical and practical functions. Indeed, first, a unitary framework that gathers all the instruments for the accommodation of diversity from a legal perspective makes it possible to recognize their fundamental commonalities, foster their

60 For a thorough analysis of the academic debate on this issue, see Medda-Windischer, Old and New Minorities . . .

61 See Gaudreault-DesBiens, Jean-F., "Introduction to Part II", in Foblets, Gaudreault-DesBiens and Dundes Relteln (eds.), Cultural Diversity . . . , 367–380, esp. at 379; as a consequence, the author affirmed that "tackling issues pertaining to legal and cultural diversity through the prism of rights encourages a reliance on Manichean approaches, strengthens primary oppositions and therefore increases fundamentalist thought, be it secular or religious, statist or anti-statist, or 'European' or 'subaltern'".

dialogue, and somewhat relativize their normative content, i.e., the idea that some tools are to be applied to specific groups while others are not. A set of legal instruments detached from their specific addressees highlights what is the principal outcome of the increasing legal significance of diversity, namely the elaboration of a set of tools to manage differential human conditions. Unifying all the instruments illustrates both the commonality of their function and, at the same time, what Heinze called the contingency of the selection of their addressees, determined by historical, political, and philosophical factors.[62]

Correlated to that, a unified standpoint on the models for the accommodation of diversity, freed from its normative content, can help practitioners look at the available options without biases connected to the fact that some diversities only deserve forms of protection or empowerment beyond non-discrimination and the latter only correspond to a specific model.

Furthermore, the proposed concept can be enabled in the sense that it may help move this area of study's focus from the Global North and equally consider the Global South constitutional systems and models. Such a standpoint widens constitutional scholars' observations and makes them more aware of the variety of legal instruments available to accommodate diversity in contemporary constitutional settings. As a result, this could, once more, raise the awareness that the (national minorities and indigenous peoples') rights discourse is but one side of diversity accommodation in contemporary societies.

Hence, the concept "Law of Diversity" is brought forward as a category of analysis that implies a renovated awareness of how diversity impacts societies and affects the evolution of legal systems, as well as, consequently, a different methodological standpoint of legal inquiry. This category of analysis is thought to provide a unitary conceptual framework capable of representing and taking into account both the story and the evolution towards new models of what is generally referred to as minority and indigenous peoples' rights law.

The "Law of Diversity" as a gate-opener: support for the theoretical proposal from Diversity Studies

Central to the proposed research standpoint is the notion of diversity. In general, the term diversity is used here as a concept encompassing the differential aspects that characterize every human being.

The concept of diversity is not straightforward: it is generally interpreted in several ways and means different things depending on the perspective endorsed. For this reason, diversity is widely viewed with suspicion, as it entails an excessively generic standpoint that eventually ends up being deemed meaningless to scientific inquiry. In general, diversity is often seen as too vague, such that it is impossible to effectively use and operationalize it, especially in legal and political analyses.

62 Heinze, The construction . . . , 43–74.

In legal and political literature, the term diversity is mostly addressed in federal and minority rights literature. The accounts referring to this term have generally made use of it either by assigning vague content to it (generally federal studies) or defining it in ethno-cultural terms. This has led to it being conflated with different specific kinds of diversity, whereby a special position is given to linguistic, religious, and ethnic diversity, both theoretically and practically.

Therefore, diversity does not seem generally to be employed as a scientific concept in itself but mostly as either a descriptive or an evocative term in this area of research.

Nevertheless, diversity as a social scientific concept is attracting growing interest in research.

This is especially the case in sociology, whose findings may give some interesting insights and inspiration for this work. Within this field of research, diversity as an autonomous concept is gaining consensus. The emerging field of Diversity Studies addresses this concept as a notion that, while naturally involving many dimensions that have been generally studied as watertight and discrete, has a unitary meaning worth deepening. Following this perspective, diversity is looked at as a general category that affects the development of the economic, social, political, and legal orders.[63]

Diversity Studies is an emerging area of sociological research that shows undoubted potential, as is confirmed by several authors in this field.[64] The reasons why they support this are worth considering, as they seem to reflect to the conceptual shift that is proposed here through the notion of the "Law of Diversity".

Importantly, diversity has been described as a term that "at present, 'comes without baggage'. That is, there is to date not much conceptualization, theory-building, or methodological reflection surrounding it. It is still to be shaped".[65] This is thought to be an advantage because, on the one hand, it

63 More specifically, quoting Vertovec, Steven, "Introduction: Formulating Diversity Studies", in Vertovec, Steven (ed.), *Routledge International Handbook of Diversity Studies* (Routledge, London-New York, 2015), 1–20, at 10–11, diversity studies are meant to focus on the "***modes of social differentiation***: how categories of difference are constructed, manifested, utilized, internalized, socially reproduced – and what kind of social, political and other implications and consequences they produce", and on "diversity as ***complex social environments***: this includes studies of how social relations evolve in a context that comprises multiple classifications across a single mode of difference (e.g. a neighbourhood that is home to numerous ethnicities) or research on how a multiplicity of difference interact to condition social relations in a single site (e.g. class and sexuality, race and gender)".

64 Vertovec, Introduction . . . , 4; the next quotations are taken from a selection of interviews with numerous scholars who have addressed diversity in their studies from various perspectives (many of them are also quoted in Vertovec's chapter), carried out by the Max Planck Institute for the Study of Religious and Ethnic Diversity, and available at the institute's website (www.mmg.mpg.de); the footnotes will indicate the name of the interviewed scholar, together with the link to the interview.

65 Vertovec, Introduction . . . , 4.

may be helpful to complement consolidated scientific standpoints as regards diversity issues, such as, for instance, the centrality of the concept of minority groups and their rights as opposed to a majority as a perspective of analysis; on the other, it proves to be a "transportable" and adaptable theoretical concept.[66] In other words, diversity is meant to bring about substantive and methodological innovations.

The substantive innovations are connected to the idea that diversity could help research move from traditional categories of thought and provide a fresh theoretical perspective when it comes to the contemporary developments of (several) societies and their regulation. Thomas Blom Hansen explained this in the following terms:

> diversity opens the possibility of thinking of any group of human beings as being fundamentally diverse . . . . diversity can be an advance, especially if used to dissolve or challenge some of the hidden presuppositions about the homogeneity of the native populations in Europe. We need to get beyond the notion that minorities "have" diversity whilst natives do not.[67]

This seems particularly interesting regarding the specific focus of this work since diversity seems to serve as a theoretical tool that opens up scientific observation and moves the focus from specific minorities to the issue of diversity as a general phenomenon. The latter shift of perspective appears particularly helpful for legal studies, too, as the emergent models for the accommodation of diversity appear to be marked by a plural paradigm whereby the legal notion of recognized minority partially loses its centrality. The "Law of Diversity" thus serves as an enabling theoretical framework insofar as it allows such innovation in legal practice to be grasped and highlights its potential even beyond its current implementation.

Andreas Wimmer shared a similar opinion, stating that the use of this term has "the advantage of avoiding essentialization, because diversity is a concept that describes a plurality of modes of differentiation that are internally complex, etc. So, it avoids all of the more problematic essentialized notions of gender or sexuality or ethnicity".[68] Among others, Rainer Bauböck came to the same conclusion: the notion of diversity forces the scholar to avoid the essentialization of identity and its association "with distinct groups identities or minorities that suffer various kind of disadvantages", which are depicted

66 In these terms, Hiebert, Daniel, available at https://www.mmg.mpg.de/53721/interview-with-daniel-hiebert.

67 Blom Hansen, Thomas, available at https://www.mmg.mpg.de/50833/interview-with-thomas-blom-hansen, quoted in Vertovec, Introduction . . . , 4.

68 Wimmer, Andreas, available at https://www.mmg.mpg.de/65148/interview-with-andreas-wimmer.

"as clearly distinct from each other and as sharing a strong form of collective identity that binds them together".[69]

Similarly, according to Kim Knott, diversity "appears to be a more neutral term that does not bring with it ideal or a particular kind of ideological baggage which certainly multiculturalism now does both in academic circles and in political circles".[70]

Furthermore, and linked to the previous considerations, Nina Glick-Schiller highlighted that diversity is a concept able to describe the multiple, dynamic, and, at the same time, coexistent dimensions of differentiation that characterize human life.[71] Put differently, diversity is thus both multiple and unitary, with this suggesting one considers that "there is diversity within any designated group and that boundaries are not absolute".[72]

As regards the specific focus of this book, these considerations should not be read as suggesting the uselessness of the legal concept of minority due to the discovery that diversity is inherent in every social phenomenon. The law needs categories and categorization to manage reality, and minority rights concepts maintain absolute theoretical and practical value. Furthermore, the law has not been insensitive to the issue of the internal diversity of groups nor to the innumerable identity markers that characterize human life, especially from a non-discrimination law perspective. What such references make clear for the sake of this work is the potential that the notion of diversity has to help relativize the monopoly of a specific theoretical approach as regards this area of law.

Therefore, diversity has been portrayed as a fresh theoretical category that implies going beyond categories of thought that have typically characterized social (and especially political and legal) scientific endeavors, especially when it comes to the analysis of the legal instruments for the accommodation of diversity that goes beyond non-discrimination.

As mentioned previously, along with this original substantive content, diversity is consequently supposed to bring an innovative methodological viewpoint.

In this sense, Appadurai insists that this category could lead to studying broad phenomena and trends with a transformed view.[73] This appears to

69 Bauböck, Rainer, available at https://www.mmg.mpg.de/460210/interview-with-rainer-bauboeck; on this, see also Brubaker, Rogers, available at https://www.mmg.mpg.de/50980/interview-with-rogers-brubaker.

70 Knott, Kim, available at https://www.mmg.mpg.de/63109/interview-with-kim-knott.

71 Glick-Schiller, Nina, available at https://www.mmg.mpg.de/53046/interview-with-nina-glick-schiller.

72 Hylland Eriksen, Thomas, available at https://www.mmg.mpg.de/53772/interview-with-thomas-hylland-eriksen.

73 Appadurai, Arjun, available at https://www.mmg.mpg.de/50202/interview-with-arjun-appadurai.

provide a wider angle of analysis, one that comprehends numerous phenomena, recognizing their fundamental commonalities.

Wimmer added that theoretically, putting diversity in operation is methodologically worthwhile as it "runs against the tendency to see these different modes of differentiation and categorization as separate domains that are unrelated to each other. It forces us to adopt a holistic perspective on social processes looking from different angles" by outlining a "comparative horizon" that brings in "all these other constellations and other forms of non-immigration-based diversity and differentiation".[74]

This is an idea supported by Micheal Keath, who argued that "because the term might mean very different things in different places", "we should be prepared to use the concept as much a propagation, as an analytical variable through which we taxonomize and analyze the world".[75]

The previous references appear to unveil the methodological innovation that the conceptual framework based on the notion of the "Law of Diversity" is intended to offer, i.e., a dynamic standpoint through which one can observe the instruments for the accommodation of diversity and their evolution in terms of addresses and structure. Such a perspective aims to show that over time, the models and their addressees have evolved depending on changing historical and geopolitical factors that have shaped the paradigms informing the accommodation of diversity. This leads to relativizing the centrality of the theoretical (and practical) standpoint relying on the mono- and multi-national paradigms to realize that forms of diversity accommodation that diverge from it are emerging. Finally, the observer may be more aware that legal categories and instruments are constructs that are subject to change over time and that neither the structure nor the addressees of diversity accommodation are immutable. Rather, they are actually evolving.

Moreover, as Bauböck put it,[76] diversity may be a conceptual instrument able to span different environments and traditions (and, one may add, legal systems) and foster their comparison. While diversity has received different recognition and treatment, it has nevertheless been a common element in the organization of societies. Taking this into consideration engenders an extension of the field of scientific observation that may lead to a deeper understanding of the phenomenon, especially as numerous countries currently experience the same condition of growing complexity mostly determined by migration flows. In other words, according to Robert Brubaker, such a perspective

74 Wimmer, Andreas, available at https://www.mmg.mpg.de/65148/interview-with-andreas-wimmer; yet afterwards, he highlighted that this, in his opinion, is the only function of the term, which thus can provide another approach to studying these phenomena, but additional analytical instruments are necessary to further explain them.

75 See Keith, Michael, available at https://www.mmg.mpg.de/62619/interview-with-michael-keith.

76 Bauböck, Rainer, available at https://www.mmg.mpg.de/460210/interview-with-rainer-bauboeck.

implies that one recognizes that "there is not a sharp distinction between immigration societies and societies with longstanding forms of ethnic and religious pluralism".[77] Consequently, one may find it inspiring to focus on "the connections between long-established patterns of diversity and newer forms of migration-generated diversity", as they unravel that "historically established ways of accommodating diversity", at least in certain domains, have affected and inspired the patterns of diversity management of new diversities, especially in the religious realm.[78] Employing diversity, therefore, results in a wide standpoint and enlarged comparison among various models devoted to its accommodation, which, once more, helps relativize the centrality of the minority discourse,[79] especially when it comes to the study of models for the accommodation of diversity that go beyond non-discrimination.

In a way, diversity can thus be described as a theoretical picklock, or a "gate-opener",[80] in that, in Jan Blommaert's words, "it basically changes the whole spectrum with which we work, and it makes a range of huge questions inevitable". Therefore, it causes us to move from consolidated categories and a "robust vocabulary" towards new, less defined, and more nuanced – albeit at times uncomfortable – semantics.[81]

As a result, according to Ash Amin, one may consider diversity as a tool that "signals a particular turning point in social scientific thinking away from the world of specialisms, linear thinking, linear dynamics, towards a sense that we need a new social science that is able to grasp the world in both its complexity and its everyday evolution. In this attempt to renew and rethink the social sciences . . . diversity can play a more interesting role as part of a new social science lexicon".[82]

77 Brubaker, Rogers, available at https://www.mmg.mpg.de/50980/interview-with-rogers-brubaker.

78 Brubaker, Rogers, available at https://www.mmg.mpg.de/50980/interview-with-rogers-brubaker.

79 Koenig, Matthias, available at https://www.mmg.mpg.de/63140/interview-with-matthias-koenig: "I think 'diversity' is a very good umbrella term for this agenda since it captures very different phenomena that were previously categorized in separate disciplinary fields of research, including migration studies, ethnic-conflict studies, political sociology of plural societies, and post-colonial studies. I think it is very important to have such an umbrella term, since it encourages us to draw comparisons between the many varieties in which different collectivities may coexist within a given social context".

80 On this, see Faist, Thomas, available at https://www.mmg.mpg.de/51636/interview-with-thomas-faist.

81 Blommaert, Jan, available at https://www.mmg.mpg.de/50898/interview-with-jan-blommaert; also, see Bruno Riccio, available at https://www.mmg.mpg.de/64060/interview-with-bruno-riccio: "I think diversity is not a precisely analytical concept, but in not being precise, I think it's got some precise aspect. It cuts across common-sense boundaries – splitting and separating the different units of analysis. I think it comes from the attempt to going beyond methodological nationalism, beyond the ethnic lens, beyond the culturally bounded concept, beyond a lot of things".

82 Amin, Ash, available at https://www.mmg.mpg.de/49734/interview-with-ash-amin.

What is interesting to retain from the latter considerations is that while diversity may be a less comfortable concept for legal studies, it anyhow can provide significant innovations in this area of research. It indeed forces one to distance oneself from a well-known set of categories, which, albeit well-structured and still of great use, may act as a limit to scientific inquiry in this area.

To sum up, whereas the aims of sociology and legal inquiry are different, it seems that Diversity Studies can provide inspiration and support for the introduction of the concept "Law of Diversity". This paragraph has tried to demonstrate that diversity as a scientific notion serves at least two functions from a sociological standpoint, from which one can draw lessons regarding legal studies. Firstly, the notion of diversity emphasizes both the innumerable dimensions of differentiation existing within several contemporary societies and the fact that they are all interrelated and part of a unitary phenomenon. As for legal studies, this perspective makes it possible to grasp and theoretically validate the emergent legal tools that are, to different extents, informed by a paradigm that implies a dynamic view of identity and diversity.

Secondly, and related to that, this conceptual framework acts as a methodological gate-opener or enabling notion that encourages the observer and practitioner to take into account all the available instruments for the accommodation of diversity – from the most consolidated to the most innovative – and see them as communicating sets of tools that evolve over time in terms of structure and addressees in accordance with societal, political and historical developments.

The "Law of Diversity" applied: a proposal to classify the instruments for the accommodation of diversity

Having defined the "Law of Diversity" as the new conceptual framework to grasp the ongoing evolution of this area of law, the last section of this chapter aims to propose a brief classification of the instruments for the accommodation of diversity based on the previous considerations about their underlying paradigms and essential purpose.

Accordingly, it is possible to conceive the "Law of Diversity" as composed of four main categories of instruments, classified on the basis of their rationale: a. survival; b. recognition and protection; c. higher promotion; d. unity in diversity.

The first refers to the legal guarantees against the elimination, discrimination, and forced assimilation of given non-majority groups. International law has developed important standards to protect minorities and other groups from genocide and other forms of ethnic cleansing.[83]

The second category contains a vast array of legal instruments that include non-discrimination (a first and primary form of recognition of a differential

83 On this, see Chapter 2.

status and *conditio sine qua non* for further protection), the guarantee of equality in the enjoyment of basic rights, and entitlement to specific rights that accord differential treatments to people belonging to recognized non-majority groups, such as national minorities and indigenous peoples. The FCNM may be considered a framework of reference for this category.

Higher promotion tools are essentially directed to guarantee minority governance and minority rule[84] through representative, participatory, and autonomous arrangements, which are supposed to strengthen their protection as these mechanisms allow the non-majority groups to have a say or a degree of self-management over the matters that concern them.

The instruments for unity in diversity constitute a manifold group of tools (beyond non-discrimination), in some cases expressions of innovative constitutional traditions, characterized by their divergence from the traditional paradigm and structure featuring minority and indigenous peoples' rights law models. Among them, one can find variously institutionalized arrangements in the shape of non-orthodox autonomy, legal pluralist autonomous arrangements, and self-governance participatory means, together with revitalized forms of traditional instruments, such as territorial and non-territorial autonomy.

This brief classification, which ties together the discourse of the previous chapters, does not only have a descriptive character. It also seems useful in that it provides a historical and logical *continuum* of measures that follows a trend of attributing increased centrality and importance to the issue of diversity. It also reflects the incremental growth in sophistication and complexity of the instruments for its accommodation. In other words, each category may be seen as a step on a path of growing refinement of the instruments, each representing different epochs and stages of diversity accommodation and their underlying paradigms.

At the same time, every category of the "Law of Diversity" seems connected to different societal settings and specific needs, with this shedding light on the reciprocal influence between society and law and the potential transformative function of the latter when it comes to diversity accommodation. It seems that the more diversity is a source of conflict or tension, the more the tools for managing it are informed by security and paternalistic logics, must be strongly institutionalized (and legally entrenched), and rely on a legal (and discursive) distinction or separation between majority and minority groups (or among constitutive peoples). Conversely, the more diversity is legally incorporated and socially accepted as a general phenomenon – as a consequence of the success of protective measures or particularly open and inclusive constitutional approaches – the less need there is for exclusive measures and minority-majority framings and the more openness to further forms of diversity beyond the ones

84 Expressions borrowed from Bourgeois, Daniel, "Administrative Nationalism", 39(5) *Administration & Society* (2007), 631–655, at 635.

traditionally addressed.[85] The latter scenario does not imply the demise of the existing tools for the accommodation of diversity but rather a revision of their logic and functioning, like in the case of the latest theoretical and practical developments concerning territorial autonomy.[86] Hence, it could be affirmed that every category of the "Law of Diversity" incorporates and, to a certain extent, revises the others.

Based on the foregoing, the "Law of Diversity" therefore contains all the legal developments related to the accommodation of diversity and provides a guide for both scholars and practitioners on the trends of this area of law and the related instruments available. This guiding function is particularly helpful in that it clarifies the structure and the rationale of the various instruments: it, therefore, emphasizes their different underlying goals and their relationships to the different epochs and stages of diversity accommodation. Furthermore, thanks to this renewed conceptual framework, it has been possible to theoretically validate and include in the analysis the instruments for unity in diversity. Their underlying logic or paradigm denotes a substantive qualitative change that concerns the accommodation of diversity as a consequence of legal and societal settings that have incorporated the idea of diversity as a value rather than a source of conflict.

Bibliography

Agarin, Timofey and McCulloch, Allison, "How Power-Sharing Includes and Excludes Non-Dominant Communities: Introduction to the Special Issue", 41(1) *International Political Science Review* (2020), 3–14

Arato, Andrew and Cohen, Jean L., "Introduction: Forms of Pluralism and Democratic Constitutionalism", in Arato, Andrew, Cohen, Jean L. and von Busekist, Astrid (eds.), *Forms of Pluralism and Democratic Constitutionalism* (Columbia University Press, New York-Chichester, 2018), 1–30

Belser, Eva Maria, "Concluding Remarks", in Belser, Eva Maria, Bächler, Thea, Egli, Sandra and Zünd, Lawrence (eds.), *The Principle of Equality in Diverse States: Reconciling Autonomy with Equal Rights and Opportunities* (Brill-Nijhoff, Leiden-Boston, 2021), 415–428

Bíró, Anna-Mária and Lennox, Corinne, "International Order, Diversity Regimes and Minority Rights: A Longue Durée Perspective", Bíró, Anna-Mária and Newman, Dwight (eds.), *Minority Rights and Liberal Democratic Insecurities: The Challenge of Unstable Orders* (Routledge, London-New York, 2022), 7–38

Bisaz, Corsin, "Minority Protection and the Neglected Importance of Authority: A Fundamental Challenge from Groups Rights", in Thürer, Daniel (ed.), *International Protection of Minorities: Challenges in Practice and Doctrine* (Schulthess, Zurich, 2014), 237–258

Bourgeois, Daniel, "Administrative Nationalism", 39(5) *Administration & Society* (2007), 631–655

85 Such a dynamic has been highlighted by Palermo and Woelk, From Minority Protection . . . , 10–13.

86 On this, see Chapter 4.

Bryde, Brun-O. and Stein, Michael A., "General Provisions Dealing with Equality", in Tushnet, Mark, Fleiner, Thomas and Saunders, Cheryl (eds.), *Routledge Handbook of Constitutional Law* (Routledge, London-New York, 2013), 287–300

Burri, Thomas, "The Rigidity of Structures to Protect Minorities: Hidden Facets of the Strasbourg Court's Judgement in *Sejdić* and the Banjul Commission's Decision in *Endorois*", in Thürer, Daniel (ed.), *International Protection of Minorities: Challenges in Practice and Doctrine* (Schulthess, Zurich, 2014), 201–233

Cabrera Ormaza, Maria Victoria, "From Protection to Participation? Shifting Perceptions towards Indigenous Peoples under International Law", in Hauser-Schäublin, Brigitta (ed.), *Adat and Indigeneity in Indonesia: Culture and Entitlements between Heteronomy and Self-Ascription* (Göttingen University Press, Göttingen, 2013), 31–41

De Wet, Erika, "The Constitutionalization of Public International Law", in Rosenfeld, Michel and Sajó, András (eds.), *The Oxford Handbook of Comparative Constitutional Law* (Oxford University Press, Oxford, 2012), 1209–1230

Dundes Rendeln, Alison, "The Cultural Defense: Challenging the Monocultural Paradigm", in Foblets, Marie-Claire, Gaudreault-DesBiens, Jean-F. and Dundes Relteln, Alison (eds.), *Cultural Diversity and the Law: State Responses Around the World* (Bruylant-Yvon-Blais, Bruxelles-Montréal, 2010), 791–818

Eide, Asbjørn, "The Rights of 'Old' versus 'New' Minorities", in Malloy, Tove H. and Marko, Joseph (eds.), *Minority Governance in and Beyond Europe: Celebrating 10 Years of the European Yearbook of Minority Issues* (Brill-Nijhoff, Leiden, 2014), 23–38

Fioravanti, Maurizio, "Il principio di eguaglianza nella storia del costituzionalismo moderno", 2(4) *Contemporanea* (1999), 609–630

Gaudreault-DesBiens, Jean-F., "Introduction to Part II", in Foblets, Marie-Claire, Gaudreault-DesBiens, Jean-F. and Dundes Relteln, Alison (eds.), *Cultural Diversity and the Law: State Responses Around the World* (Bruylant-Yvon-Blais, Bruxelles-Montréal, 2010), 367–380

Heinze, Eric, "The Construction and Contingency of the Minority Concept", in Fottrell, Deirdre and Bowring, Bill (eds.), *Minority and Group Rights in the New Millennium* (Martinus Nijhoff, Leiden-Boston, 1999), 25–74

Kuhn, Thomas S., *The Structure of Scientific Revolutions* (University of Chicago Press, Chicago, 4th ed., 2012)

Kymlicka, Will, *Multicultural Citizenship: A Liberal Theory of Minority Rights* (Clarendon, Oxford, 1995)

Malloy, Tove H., "From Security Threat to Citizen Deeds: A Paradigm Shift in European Minority Governance?", in Gaitanides, Charlotte and Grözinger, Gerd (eds.), *Diversity in Europe* (Nomos, Baden-Baden, 2015), 13–28

Malloy, Tove H., "Introduction", in Malloy, Tove H., Osipov, Alexander and Vizi, Balázs (eds.), *Managing Diversity through Non-Territorial Autonomy: Assessing Advantages, Deficiencies, and Risks* (Oxford University Press, Oxford, 2015), 1–15

Malloy, Tove H., "National Minorities between Protection and Empowerment: Towards a Theory of Empowerment", 13(2) *Journal on Ethnopolitics and Minority Issues in Europe* (2014), 11–29

Malloy, Tove H., "Non-Territorial Autonomy: Traditional and Alternative Practices", in Romans, William, Ulasiuk, Iryna and Petrenko Thomsen, Anton (eds.), *Effective Participation of National Minorities and Conflict Prevention* (Brill Nijhoff, Leiden-Boston, 2020), 105–122

Malloy, Tove H., "A New Research Agenda for Theorizing Non-Territorial Autonomy?", in Malloy, Tove H. and Salat, Levente (eds.), *Non-Territorial Autonomy and Decentralization: Ethno-Cultural Diversity Governance* (Routledge, London-New York, 2021), 3–22

Malloy, Tove H., "Towards a New Paradigm of Minority Law-Making: A Rejoinder to Palermo and Woelk's Law of Diversity", 4 *European Yearbook of Minority Issues* (2004–2005), 5–28

Marko, Joseph, "Law and Ideology: The Ideological Conundrums of the Liberal-Democratic State", in Marko, Joseph and Constantin, Sergiu (eds.), *Human and Minority Rights Protection by Multiple Diversity Governance: History, Law, Ideology and Politics in European Perspective* (Routledge, London-New York, 2019), 96–137

Marko, Joseph, Marko-Stöckl, Edith, Harzl, Benedikt and Unger, Hedwig, "The Historical-Sociological Foundations: State Formation and Nation Building in Europe and the Construction of the Identitarian Nation-cum-State Paradigm", in Marko, Joseph and Constantin, Sergiu (eds.), *Human and Minority Rights Protection by Multiple Diversity Governance: History, Law, Ideology and Politics in European Perspective* (Routledge, London-New York, 2019), 33–95

Medda-Windischer, Roberta, *Old and New Minorities: Reconciling Diversity and Cohesion* (Nomos, Baden-Baden, 2009)

Nimni, Ephraim, "Minorities and the Limits of Liberal Democracy: Demoicracy and Non-Territorial Autonomy", in Malloy, Tove H. and Palermo, Francesco (eds.), *Minority Accommodation through Territorial and Non-Territorial Autonomy* (Oxford University Press, Oxford, 2015), 57–82

Ortino, Sergio, *La struttura delle rivoluzioni economiche* (Cacucci, Bari, 2010)

Ortino, Sergio, "La tutela delle minoranze nel diritto internazionale: evoluzione o mutamento di prospettiva?", 76(2) *Studi trentini di scienze storiche. Sezione prima* (1997), 203–212

Palermo, Francesco, "Current and Future Challenges for International Minority Protection", 10 *European Yearbook of Minority Issues* (2011), 21–36

Palermo, Francesco, "Legal Solutions to Complex Societies: The Law of Diversity", in Ruiz Vieytez, Eduardo J. and Dunbar, Robert (eds.), *Human Rights and Diversity: New Challenges for Plural Societies* (University of Deusto, Bilbao, 2007), 63–82

Palermo, Francesco, "Owned or Shared? Territorial Autonomy in the Minority Discourse", in Malloy, Tove H. and Palermo, Francesco (eds.), *Minority Accommodation through Territorial and Non-Territorial Autonomy* (Oxford University Press, Oxford, 2015), 13–32

Palermo, Francesco, "The Protection of Minorities in International Law: Recent Developments and Trends", in VV.AA., *Les minorités: un défi pour les États: Actes du colloque international (22 et 23 mai 2011)* (Académie Royale de Belgique, Bruxelles, 2012), 165–185

Palermo, Francesco, "'The Borders of My Language Mean the Borders of My World': Language Rights and Their Evolving Significance for Minority Rights and Integration of Societies", in Ulasiuk, Iryna, Hadîrcă, Laurenţiu and Romans, William (eds.), *Language Policy and Conflict Prevention* (Brill-Nijhoff, Leiden-Boston, 2018), 135–154

Palermo, Francesco, "Quanto è morbido il soft law? La tutela non giurisdizionale dei diritti delle minoranze nelle aree geogiuridiche europee", 1 *Rivista di Diritti Comparati* (2022), 74–94

Palermo, Francesco and Woelk, Jens, "From Minority Protection to a Law of Diversity? Reflections on the Evolution of Minority Rights", 3 *European Yearbook of Minority Issues* (2003–2004), 5–13

Palermo, Francesco and Woelk, Jens, *Diritto costituzionale comparato dei gruppi e delle minoranze* (CEDAM, Padua, 2021)

Poirier, Johanne, "Autonomie politique et minorités francophones du Canada: réflexions sur un angle mort de la typologie classique de Will Kymlicka", 1 *Minorités linguistiques et société / Linguistic Minorities and Society* (2012), 66–89

Spiliopoulou Åkermark, Sia, "Multiculturalism in Crisis?", in Ruiz Vieytez, Eduardo J. and Dunbar, Robert (eds.), *Human Rights and Diversity: New Challenges for Plural Societies* (University of Deusto, Bilbao, 2007), 35–49
Stojanović, Nenad, "Democracy, Ethnoicracy and Consociational Demoicracy", 41(1) *International Political Science Review* (2020), 30–43
Tierney, Stephen, *The Federal Contract: A Constitutional Theory of Federalism* (Oxford University Press, Oxford, 2022)
Torre, Alessandro, "Il Regno Unito", in Carrozza, Paolo, Di Giovine, Alfonso and Ferrari, Giuseppe F. (eds.), *Diritto costituzionale comparato* (Laterza, Rome-Bari, 2019), 5–54
Trettel, Martina, *La democrazia partecipativa negli ordinamenti composti: studio di diritto comparato sull'incidenza della tradizione giuridica nelle* democratic innovations (ESI, Naples, 2020)
Tully, James, *Strange Multiplicity: Constitutionalism in an Age of Diversity* (Cambridge University Press, Cambridge, 1995)
Vertovec, Steven, "Introduction: Formulating Diversity Studies", in Vertovec, Steven (ed.), *Routledge International Handbook of Diversity Studies* (Routledge, London-New York, 2015), 1–20

6 Can federalism help frame the emergent models for the accommodation of diversity?

Main assumptions

The present chapter aims to offer further analytical tools that contribute to theoretically framing the emergent instruments for the accommodation of diversity, which, as seen, are the most in need of a solid theoretical ground. It will do so by resorting to the concept of federalism and to federal theory and practice.

In the following paragraphs a theoretical account of the concept of federalism and its use in this work will be provided.

The main assumptions are that federalism: a) is an abstract legal concept (besides being an organizing principle) embedding some core elements common to any of its manifestations; b) the essential logic expressed by this abstract legal concept appears to have been replicated and applied in a variety of ways, not limited to the classical theorization of federalism as ontologically linked to the territorial distribution of powers and the nation-state model: as a result, federalism can be imagined as an adaptable matrix; c) conceived like this, federalism finally appears to be a useful interpretive paradigm to frame and explain the theoretical and practical evolution of the "Law of Diversity", as well as to provide some concrete mechanisms that could inspire it, at least in some respects: in this sense, federalism is thought of not only as a matrix, but also as an analytical lens and a practical method.

This inevitably implies a departure from what can be referred to as the legal and political[1] "mainstream modern approach" in this field. This phrase is used

1 Legal and political federal studies are inextricably intertwined; many reasons account for this, not least the fact that the boundaries of the mentioned disciplines depend on the scholarly tradition underlying the single approach, thus always being somewhat flexible and malleable; the comparative legal approach chosen for this inquiry abstracts from a pure institutional perspective but does not go as far as providing a normative or prescriptive theory on federalism (and on the "Law of Diversity"; in other words, echoing King, Preston, *Federalism and Federation* (John Hopkins University Press-Croom Helm, Baltimore-London, 1982), 9–15, and his classification of political science, the empirical political theories are the object of attention more than the philosophical ones, which are, nonetheless, taken into consideration in a general way.

DOI: 10.4324/9781003493518-7

to indicate the predominant modern literature which has been almost exclusively built from the standpoint of the nation-state, its structures, and (the reproduction of) its model.[2]

Conversely, the present work adheres to those still minoritarian voices who have made a case for the "necessity of a rethinking of the federal phenomenon in a theoretical framework larger than that of an essentially institutional reflection upon the organization of states"[3] with a view to "pluralizing a theoretical model which, to date, has served as the principal framework for most legal inquiries in this area".[4] Concretely, this results in reinterpreting and extending the scope of the traditional fundamental concepts of modern federal theory, starting from a reconsideration of federalism itself, but also taking into consideration the less well-trodden paths of previous literature which have hinted at possibly fruitful suggestions.

All these contributions have in common the underlying idea of federalism as a concept theoretically independent from its manifestations, which deserves renewed definition and recognition to express a potential that goes much further than what has been explored so far, i.e., beyond its "nation-state" or statist expression.[5] Following this rationale, the main goal of the inquiry is to underscore a meta-theoretical connotation and function of federalism. This is largely for analytical and practical purposes, which, in a way, also require that a basic conceptualization (but not a definition) of federalism be offered. The final aim of the chapter is to provide the emergent models for the accommodation of diversity analyzed in Chapter 4 with a structured theoretical foundation for their understanding and further development.[6]

2 On this, see Gaudreault-DesBiens, Jean-F. and Gélinas, Fabien, "Opening New Perspectives on Federalism", in Gaudreault-DesBiens, Jean-F. and Gélinas, Fabien (eds.), *The States and Moods: Governance, Identity and Methodology* (Éditions Yvon Blais-Bruylant, Cowansville-Bruxelles, 2005), 51–96, at 51–52; furthermore, it should be noted that the "mainstream modern approach" to federalism has generally been based on the analysis of case studies rather than on comparison intended to define a general (constitutional) concept of federalism, as indicated by Tierney, Stephen, *The Federal Contract: A Constitutional Theory of Federalism* (Oxford University Press, Oxford, 2022), 1–55.

3 Gaudreault-DeBiens and Gélinas, Opening New Perspectives . . . , 52.

4 Ibid.

5 As suggested by Gaudreault-DesBiens and Gélinas, Opening New Perspectives . . . , 66.

6 Interestingly, Berman, Paul S., *Global Legal Pluralism: A Jurisprudence of Law Beyond Borders* (Cambridge University Press, New York, 2012), 10, stressed the need for procedural rules that foster and manage the interactions between the state and non-state legal systems: such considerations may be extended to all the emerging instruments for the accommodation of diversity, which, in different ways, contribute to the creation of complex systems of governance that imply strong pluralism and the continuous interplay between public, quasi-public and private bodies; see also Neo, Jacklyn L., "State Legal Pluralism and Religious Courts: Semi-Autonomy and Jurisdictional Allocations in Pluri-Legal Arrangements", in Berman, Paul S. (ed.), *The Oxford Handbook of Global Legal Pluralism* (Oxford University Press, Oxford, 2020), e-book version, 1628–1668, at 1646–1647; to this end, as will be demonstrated, federal theory appears to offer interesting practical solutions.

Of course, any theoretical proposal is somewhat stipulative and subjective[7]: what counts is its logical internal coherence or plausibility[8] and its practical usefulness for the development of the research in a given field,[9] which, in turn, requires that the concept maintains a clear and distinguishable character in order to be successfully operationalized. These objectives are thus given due consideration within this section and will constitute the yardstick against which it will be possible to justify the proposed approach.

Finally, methodological clarification is necessary. This section focusses on recent literature, which does not exclude the possibility of taking practices and classic works on federalism-related concepts that occurred in pre-modern and early-modern times into consideration. Nevertheless, the modern and contemporary literature – that which has grown along with the birth and development of the (nation) state – is privileged. This is firstly due to the comparative public law standpoint characterizing this study, strictly connected to the emancipation of public (political and legal) spheres and structures. Secondly, recent literature may be considered as the latest stage in the evolution of federal thought and, in a way, a synthesis of it. Therefore, these classics will be mainly addressed through secondary literature, paying attention to those authors who have explored pre- and early- modern views in the context of contemporary investigations of federalism, with a view to understanding how they have been affected by those ideas and the consequences of this.

Theoretical references: the emergence of a meta-theoretical approach to federalism and its applications

Four approaches to federalism in recent literature

Drawing upon a classification made by Lépine, four main approaches to the concept of federalism may be observed in recent literature.[10]

The first is the one that questions both the possibility and the concrete value of defining federalism as a political or legal category, affirming that federal

7 See King, Federalism . . . , 9–15 on the stipulative character of definitions especially in the field of federal studies.

8 On this, and in particular, on the characteristics of what the author called the analytical political thought, see King, Federalism . . . , 9–15.

9 On the importance of theorizing about federalism, see Popelier, Patricia, *Dynamic Federalism: A New Theory for Cohesion and Regional Autonomy* (Routledge, London-New York, 2021), 7–45, esp. at 12–14.

10 Lépine, Frédéric, "A Journey through the History of Federalism: Is Multilevel Governance a Form of Federalism?", 363(1) *L'Europe en formation* (2012), 21–62, at 27–31; his account is here employed as a guideline, but has been modified or implemented in some respects.

arrangements are nothing but political bargains.[11] Accordingly, federalism is "no more than a constitutional legal fiction" that could be given 'whatever content' seemed appropriate at the moment".[12] In other words, federalism as a political or legal notion on its own either does not exist or is useless: it is thus a contingent and politically shaped organizational means.

The second main strand of thought is based upon a more or less explicit conflation of federalism with a specific institutional manifestation. Indeed, while a theoretical distinction between federalism and federation is widely acknowledged,[13] concretely the former has, in one way or another, been fused to the latter, generally leading to terminological confusion. Specifically, federalism has been defined as a normative principle or an ideology which implies advocating for a multi-tiered government combining shared rule and self-rule,[14] but the concrete and common focus of these analyses has been the study of the institutional manifestations of the principle, and on which among them should be considered as an expression of "true" federalism.

Among the different positions, it is possible to identify those who have conflated federalism with federation, i.e., with a particular form of government essentially characterized by the existence of two layers of territorial government and a constitution defining the respective areas of jurisdiction.[15] Upon this common essential reading, different, more specifical institutional definitions of federation have been built.[16]

Others have equated federalism with an ideal-typical model[17] (generally based on the US example), namely, the so-called federal democracy, the authentic expression of the liberal democratic values which are supposed to

11 See Riker, William H., *Federalism: Origin, Operation, Significance* (Little, Brown & Company, Boston, 1964), 2 and 11; for more on Riker's thought, see Burgess, Michael, *Comparative Federalism: Theory and Practice* (Routledge, London-New York, 2006); differently from Lépine's classification, R. Davis is not included in this category, since his account on federalism seems favorable to further developments of the concept in line with the aims of the chapter.

12 Riker, William H., "Six Books in Search of a Subject or Does Federalism Exist and Does It Matter?", 2(1) *Comparative Politics* (1969), 135–146, at 146.

13 From King's account onwards.

14 Watts, Ronald L., *Comparing Federal Systems* (McGill-Queen's University Press, Montréal, 3rd ed., 2008), 8; also, Burgess, Comparative Federalism . . . , 2.

15 See Wheare, Kenneth C., *Federal Government* (Oxford University Press, London, 4th ed., 1963), 10; see also Watts, Comparing . . . , 29 who, after specifying the differences between federalism, federal political system and federation, focuses on a classification of the latter, implicitly prioritizing them in his work.

16 For instance, Watts, Comparing . . . , 9; Gamper, Anna, "A 'Global Theory of Federalism': The Nature and Challenges of a Federal State", 6(10) *The German Law Journal* (2005), 1297–1318; for further literature on this perspective: Popelier, Dynamic Federalism . . . , 15–32, who defined this approach as the "Hamiltonian approach" to federalism.

17 On this, see Gamper, A Global Theory of Federalism . . . , 1298.

underlie and constitute the core of federalism.[18] In other words, federalism is seen as a form of liberal-democratic constitutional government.[19] Therefore, on the one hand, it is attributed an ideological and normative value,[20] while on the other it cannot be separated from its specific ideal-typical manifestation; as a consequence, any supposedly federal political system is compared to that model to assess the degree of development of concrete institutional solutions and the embedment of its values.

The third view is grounded in the idea that no specific agreed definition of federalism can be reached, nor is it desirable.[21] Nevertheless, this does not give rise to the demise of the concept, but to a refined pragmatical use of it that has been referred to as the "institutional toolbox approach".[22] Hence, the topic is

18 A perspective that seems implicitly or explicitly endorsed by most American modern authors; as noted by Tierney, Stephen, "Federalism and Constitutional Theory", in Jacobsohn, Gary and Schor, Miguel (eds.), *Comparative Constitutional Theory* (Edward Elgar, Cheltenham-Northampton, 2018), 45–66, esp. at 53–54; see, among the authors that have explicitly elaborated on this connection, Burgess, Michael, *In Search of the Federal Spirit* (Oxford University Press, Oxford, 2012); similarly, Stepan, Alfred, "Federalism and Democracy: Beyond the U.S. Model", in Karmis, Dimitrios and Norman, Wayne (eds.), *Theories of Federalism: A Reader* (Palgrave Macmillan, New-York-Basingstoke, 2005), 255–268.

19 In this sense, Friedrich, Carl J., "Federal Constitutional Theory and Emergent Proposals", in Macmahon, Arthur (ed.), *Federalism. Mature and Emergent* (Russell&Russell, New York, 1962), 510–533.

20 Tierney, The Federal Contract . . . , 42–50, classified this body of literature in two main strands, the first according to which "Federalism is often presented as an instrumentally useful way of achieving broader moral goods" and "assesses federalism for the moral consequences of its effects. In doing so it adopts a number of benchmarks for evaluating the moral efficacy of federalism"; this line of reasoning has characterized the origins of American thought on federalism: see, for instance, Hamilton, Alexander, "Federalist No. 28", in Rossiter, Clinton (ed.), *The Federalist Papers* (The New American Library, New York, 1961), 178–182; see also the American Supreme Court ruling *Gregory v Ashcroft* 501 U.S. 452, 458 (1991), per Justice O'Connor; the second strand "posits the inherent moral worth of federalism as an ideal system of government", a perspective that "transcends ideological and empirically situated political theory, turning instead to the evaluative register of moral political philosophy" and that "contends that federalism is a model of government well suited to the nature of the human condition, in particular to the range of social interconnections that characterise the communal and social dimensions of human nature"; authors taking this approach refer to the work of Althusius, try to modernize it and apply it to post-modernity: on this, see Hueglin, Thomas O., *Early Modern Concepts for a Late Modern World: Althusius on Community and Federalism* (Wilfried Laurier University Press, Waterloo, 1999); *Id.*, "Johannes Althusius: Medieval Constitutionalist or Modern Federalist?", 9(4) *Publius* (1979), 9–41; Aroney, Nicolas, "The Federal Condition: Towards a Normative Theory", 61(1) *The American Journal of Jurisprudence* (2016), 13–31.

21 Palermo, Francesco and Kössler, Karl, *Comparative Federalism: Constitutional Arrangements and Case Law* (Hart Publishing, Oxford-Portland, 2019), 3.

22 Palermo and Kössler, Comparative Federalism. . . , 2–4; also, this expression was used by Gaudreault-DesBiens, Jean-F., "Towards a Deontic Axiomatic Theory of Federal Adjudication", in Lev, Amnon (ed.), *The Federal Idea* (Hart Publishing, Oxford-Portland, 2017), 75–103, at 76, to describe the perspective that, in his view, "envisages this constitutional regime as a mere tool that can be used to solve particular problems in certain institutional contexts".

addressed from a pragmatical perspective, focusing "on the toolbox of federalism, on how it works and why", and, as a consequence, on all the manifestations of a vertical division of territorial powers.[23] However, it must be noted that the described position preliminarily implies a – albeit implicit or only sketched – perception of what federalism denotes, namely, a broad concept embedding every combination of territorial division of powers, or self-rule and shared rule.[24] The basic idea that federalism is worth being operationalized rather than defined as (and confined to) a specific model constitutes one of the main sources of inspiration for the analysis conducted here, as integrated by the fourth standpoint that will be examined further on.

The fourth perspective characterizes the studies underscoring what has been defined as a "meta-theoretical" dimension of federalism, which have shown a holistic standpoint and have been inspired, to a greater or lesser extent, by the critical contributions of some modern federal scholars.[25]

Following their accounts, federalism is theorized as an autonomous legal (and/or political) concept[26] that is derived from the observation of the so-called "federal phenomenon". A legal concept is here regarded as the outcome of a process of abstraction of general legal categories typical of the comparative inquiry.[27] In this sense, federalism is meant to be a general, synthetical and analytical legal notion, not unlike a constitution, for instance. And, like "constitution", federalism may thus be seen as an interpretive legal model embodying some essential features replicated in innumerably varied ways.[28] It is, finally, the meta-theoretical common core, super-code or framework able to bring all of these concrete manifestations together.[29]

Federalism is intertwined and inseparable from its materializations, which form the so-called federal phenomenon. Therefore, as a legal concept, federalism relies on the idea that the federal phenomenon is resolutely multifaceted, with its concrete shape being affected by the cultural, political, economic, and philosophical contexts underlying the different epochs of human history and acting as contingencies of the federal theme.[30] Accordingly, the state-related dimension of federalism as a form of government is but one of the possible

23 Palermo and Kössler, Comparative Federalism. . . , 3 and 34–35.
24 Ibid., 3–4; similarly, Popelier, Dynamic Federalism . . . , 12.
25 Namely, Elazar, Friedrich and Davis; see the following sections.
26 Gaudreault-DesBiens and Gélinas, Opening New Perspectives . . . , 70.
27 As indicated by Hirschl, Ran, *Comparative Matters: The Renaissance of Comparative Constitutional Law* (Oxford University Press, Oxford, 2014), 238, one of the most sophisticated activities of comparative constitutional lawyers is to use comparison to "generate concepts and analytical frameworks for thinking critically about constitutional norms and practices".
28 Gaudreault-DesBiens and Gélinas, Opening New Perspectives . . . , 70–71.
29 For more on this, see section 6.3.
30 In this sense, Lépine, Frédéric, "Federalism: Essence, Values and Ideologies", in Gagnon, Alain-G., Keil, Soeren and Mueller, Sean (eds.), *Understanding Federalism and Federation* (Ashgate, Farnham-Burlington, 2015), 31–48, at 36–37.

replications of the legal concept – or, one of the manifestations of the federal phenomenon – possibly having a legal-constitutional significance.

To be clear, the employment of the adjective "meta-theoretical" to describe the perspective adopted in this work is meant to suggest that federalism is taken at a more abstract level than a (conceptual or) theoretical one. It is used as a lens or a framework of understanding through which one may grasp the structure and functioning of several phenomena – especially those analyzed in Chapter 4 – and consequently apply to them the federal wisdom that derives from federal theory and practice, as will be further explained in what follows. A theoretical perspective, which would arguably imply analyzing federalism as a constitutional concept, i.e., as a specific form of government provided by a constitution (as has been done recently),[31] would limit the scope of the observation to institutional or governmental features.[32] The approach taken here is aimed at demonstrating that federalism can be used as a frame to recognize a vast range of more or less institutionalized instruments for the accommodation of diversity that have public legal relevance, and to verify what are the theoretical benefits of such an operation for a better understanding of the latter instruments. Accordingly, it is not the aim of this chapter to dive into the very essence of federalism, but to provide arguments that sustain the idea of employing it as a general inter-temporal matrix for understanding complex systems of governance (as those stemming from the evolution of the "Law of Diversity"), which implies going beyond its traditional description as a model of government or a principle embedding a set of moral values.

The meta-theoretical view therefore represents the building block underpinning the use of the term federalism in this study, which complements the "institutional toolbox approach". While the latter approach implicitly delimits the research interest to the institutional and territorial expressions of the "toolbox of federalism", this viewpoint suggests that federalism embeds a logic that can be replicated and concretized without limits of any sort in forms that have a public law significance.[33]

At the same time, the pragmatic aim of the institutional toolbox approach is maintained. In a nutshell, the assumption is that not only is the meta-theoretical angle able to extend the scope of federalism as an analytical tool but, as a result, it also broadens its potential as an inspiring method for the regulation

31 On this, see Tierney, The Federal Contract . . . , esp. 151–182; another author that dove into the definition of federalism as a "constitutionally defined concept" implying a form government characterized by the existence of a multi-tiered structure is Popelier, Dynamic Federalism . . . , esp. 46–74.

32 This perspective is in line with Lépine's study on federalism; in particular, see Lépine, A Journey . . . , 60, who described federalism in the framework of his research as follows: "federalism must be seen in a meta-theoretical perspective, as a general approach of politics, or a paradigm considered in its more general sense. This is what can be called the 'federalist idea' or the 'federalist principle'".

33 And not only public for some authors: see Macdonald's account further on.

of pluralism which embeds a large and varied "baggage" (or "wisdom") made up of institutions and practices. Consequently, once an observed phenomenon is framed as part of the phenomenon of federalism, it will be possible to apply "federal wisdom" to understand it and eventually draw practical lessons (stemming from federal theory and trends) related to its possible developments.

Such a theoretical operation has added value in the context of Global North constitutional settings, which are the main interest of these last chapters. Indeed, in these contexts, the democratic element is firmly entrenched in constitutional theory and practice and forms common ground for the general development of federalism and diversity accommodation. Global North constitutional systems in particular are characterized by increasing openness to democratic pluralism, which often leads to increasing complexity in state organization and democratic practices, as well as integration of traditional decision-making processes, an evolution that can be subsumed within the concept of governance.[34] Such development of democracy and state organization seems to ask for a renewed reading of both federalism and diversity accommodation that shies away, respectively, from the unitarian[35] or (mono-/multi-) national theoretical paradigm[36] that has long marked their development and study. As regards the latter, a renovated reading appears necessary to grasp the evolution of the instruments for the accommodation of diversity and give them a theoretical framing. As for the former, the contemporary epoch constitutes an opportunity for federal theory to enlarge its theoretical, analytical and practical potential in a time of democratic pluralism and complexity.[37]

That being said, it must be noted that the accounts that underpin the approach here proposed do not represent a cohesive school of thought. Rather, they are an ensemble of past and contemporary indications coming from political and legal research. The next sections thus attempt to unify these suggestions to create the theoretical basis of this investigation into federalism and to make it clear that the literature drawn on has roots in some classical work as well. Moreover, they finally aim to explain how and why federalism may be fruitfully used as an analytical lens for the study of the emergent models for the accommodation of diversity.

It is also necessary to emphasize that the aim of the proposed conceptual framework is not to provide an additional definition of what "true" federalism is, and thus which account, among the numerous interpretations, is more authentic and connected to reality. No normative or prescriptive set of features

34 See Chapters 4 and 5.

35 On the fact that constitutional theory has long lacked a specific theorization of federalism and approached it through traditional categories created having the unitarian state as a model (as is the case, for instance, with sovereignty), see Tierney, The Federal Contract . . . , 57–282.

36 See Chapter 5.

37 On this, see Palermo, Francesco, "Regulating Pluralism: Federalism as Decision-Making and New Challenges for Federal Studies", in Palermo, Francesco and Alber, Elisabeth (eds.), *Federalism as Decision-Making: Changes in Structures, Procedures and Policies* (Brill-Nijhoff, Leiden-Boston, 2015), 499–513, at 504–508.

is sought, nor is an ideal-typical model conceived. Quite the contrary, the primary aim is to provide clarification of what the proposed standpoint signifies and explain its almost unexplored[38] analytical and practical potential; this is done through the analysis of the contributions that have underscored federalism as an interpretive legal framework encompassing manifold manifestations that share a common core or nature.

Feder(ation)alism v the meta-theoretical potential of federalism: general overview and first connections with the "Law of Diversity"

The latter perspective rests upon the idea that federalism has a far-reaching analytical scope. As a consequence, it claims that the traditional focus of legal and political federal thought – what one may call the form-of-government dimension of federalism or "feder(ation)alism", given that it essentially identifies it as a political system based upon two or more layers of territorial government – could hinder the potential of federalism.

The introduction of the term feder(ation)alism aims to highlight the elision between federalism and federation (as an overarching term for federal systems) as a form of government that most literature in this area appears to take as a given. The term thus seems useful as it emphasizes the implicit connection that political and constitutional theory establishes between the concept of federalism (taken in constitutional or philosophical terms) and its state-related manifestations.

More specifically, feder(ation)alism intrinsically ties federalism to two main themes. This choice has significant epistemological consequences as it evidently affects the scope of the analysis on federalism.

On the one hand, federalism has constantly been described as a *form of territorial governance*, having to do with the relations between territorial layers of authority. A great number of studies take the territorial dimension of federalism as a postulate, generally without thoroughly justifying that choice.[39]

On the other, and more generally, one may notice the widespread framing of federalism in terms of a *form of government*. This corresponds to a specific model of state organization – not necessarily the federal state in a strict sense – based on the institutionalization of two or more orders of full-fledged *polities*. These reproduce or resemble the state and are entitled to varying degrees of legislative and administrative powers.[40]

38 As will be seen, Lépine, A Journey . . . , esp. 51–62, used federalism as a tool to frame multilevel governance.

39 For instance, Popelier, Dynamic Federalism . . . , 50, justified her perspective with the following statement: "There is a common understanding that federalism is about the relationship between territorial levels of authority"; similarly, Tierney, The Federal Contract . . . , 161.

40 This is particularly apparent in Popelier, Dynamic federalism . . . , who built a theory of federalism as a value concept to be identified in a "proper balance" among layers of territorial government; however, the theoretical framework is somewhat conditioned by the basic initial tenet, stated at 50: "Federalism pre-supposes a subdivision of the political system in territorial entities with some political power", which is justified by the general statement indicated in the previous footnote.

This is not to say that federal research has not witnessed renovation. One can see an increase in studies that have revolved around the "post-modern epoch" and their consequences for the Westphalian model of state, mostly elaborating on the variety of new (and often asymmetric) federal arrangements to manage ethnic diversity[41] and the process of European integration.[42] However, the centrality of the two previously mentioned elements does not appear to have been called into question.

In particular, increasing attention to political behaviors and cultural components of federalism is observable. However, while it is true that today non-institutional factors affecting the dynamics of federal political systems are generally considered crucial to any analysis, this does not mean that the general focus has shifted to something different from the federal form of government. Rather, it is only that more attention has been devoted to the actors who live and perform within federal systems as well as to the social-cultural context.

Moreover, the analysis of the ongoing transition from the modern era to the so-called "post-modern epoch" has given rise to another parallel trend. Many authors have grasped the impact of post-modernity on the Westphalian model of the (federal) state. Generally, this has led to the acknowledgment of the increasing complexity characterizing the exercise of power, as a consequence of upward and downward drives stemming from global economic trends and the emergence of compelling ethno-cultural diversity issues in contemporary societies.[43] Nonetheless, this has by no means led to a considerable change in the heart of most inquiries, which have always directly or indirectly placed state-like full-fledged polities at the core of their analysis.

Conversely, the meta-theoretical position is intended to show that federalism, far from corresponding to a specific yardstick model, may be read

41 On the relationship between constitutional asymmetries and what are referred to as "multi-tiered multinational systems" – i.e., states composed of multiple tiers of government in which the central level is mixed with sub-national entities with lawmaking power that host territorially embedded groups with differences based on linguistic, religious, cultural, and ethnic markers, which claim important political autonomy around these differences – see Sahadžić, Maja, *Asymmetry, Multinationalism and Constitutional Law: Managing Legitimacy and Stability in Federalist States* (Routledge, London-New York, 2021); specific attention is also drawn to federal arrangements for conflict resolution; on this, see Keil, Soeren and Alber, Elisabeth (eds.), *Federalism as a Tool of Conflict Resolution* (Routledge, London-New York, 2021); Keil, Soeren and Kropp, Sabine (eds.), *Emerging Federal Structures in the Post-Cold War Era* (Palgrave Macmillan, Cham, 2022).

42 In addition, one can also consider within this category those authors who have investigated the replication of federal patterns in state organization only with regard to some parts of the state territory, that is to say, those who have addressed autonomy as a form of federal arrangement; for instance, see Palermo and Kössler, Comparative Federalism. . . , 58–61.

43 See Elazar, Daniel J., "From Statism to Federalism: A Paradigm Shift", 17(4) *International Political Science Review/Revue internationale de science politique* (1996), 417–429; *Id.*, "The State System + Globalization (Economic plus Human Rights) = Federalism (State Federations Plus Regional Confederations)", 40(3) *South Texas Law Review* (1999), 555–566; *Id.*, Exploring . . . , 53; Watts, Comparing . . . , 6.

as a broad analytical framework common to a large number of experiences. A clarification of what the meta-theoretical position implies, especially regarding the form-of-government view, comes from a critical volume edited by Gaudreault-DesBiens and Gélinas on the "States and moods of federalism".[44] In their introduction, after having contended that generally "jurists have seemed disinterested, in the last decades, in the *theory* of federalism",[45] they have argued for a study of federalism as a phenomenon, beyond its purely technical realm.[46] This mission statement, which informs all the contributions in the volume, neatly extends the scope of their research to issues barely dealt with by juridical (or political) investigations on federalism.

In particular, the editors indicated why and how the exclusive theorization of federalism as a form of government may be questioned and eventually reevaluated for different purposes, including an analytical one.

The fundamental argument may be summarized as follows. There is simply no reason to exclude the conception of federalism as an autonomous legal concept, a logic and an interpretive lens embedding a set of core elements characterizing it; rather, and most importantly, the suggested use of the concept is thought to provide a valuable practical contribution to the advancement of federal and public law research in a time of increasing complexity, providing a means to free them from the straightjacket of the nation-state.[47]

As indicated by J.-F. Gaudreault-DesBiens and F. Gélinas, this theoretical proposal is capable of challenging the mentioned basic epistemological assumptions underpinning feder(ation)alism and seems particularly worthwhile for the present study. Several recent accounts seem to have endorsed this perspective and sought to overcome the state-centered vision expressed by the

44 Gaudreault-DesBiens and Gélinas (eds.), The States and Moods . . .

45 The majority of them having "directed their efforts towards the strictly technical dimension of the legal relationship that a federal regime implies, or towards the questions of methodology that the comparative study of federalism give rise to", as affirmed by Gaudreault-DesBiens and Gélinas, Opening New Perspectives . . . , 52.

46 It must be noted that they eventually sketched an interpretation of federalism as a concept embedding a set of ethical values: The authors have argued that a normative/prescriptive theory of federalism should be developed; a theory which reveals the deontic content of federalism as a value concept; this framing was further developed by Gaudreault-DesBiens, Towards a Deontic . . . , 93–103; the perspective of the present study is, however, different; it implies seeing federalism as a "neutral" value concept, a set of core elements, a common logic shared by numerous different variously institutionalized manifestations; by doing so, i.e., by considering a set of different arrangements and practices as federal, it will be thus possible to apply federal wisdom in order to frame them, as well as explain and favor their development through their recognition.

47 Borrowing an expression formulated by Lépine, A Journey . . . , 47; *contra*, suggesting that the state remains the natural dimension of federalism as a constitutional concept, see Tierney, The Federal Contract . . . , 287–297, esp. 292.

bulk of the scholarship on federalism,[48] not to reveal its true nature, but to explode its analytical potential and its ability to perform explanatory functions as regards a vast array of phenomena.

In line with the latter accounts, federalism will be here proposed as a theoretical tool that can help frame, understand and explain the functioning of the emerging instruments for the accommodation of diversity – namely, non-orthodox autonomy, legal pluralist autonomous arrangements, and self-governance participatory means – which, as demonstrated in Chapter 5, may all be considered to share autonomous features.

As anticipated, the meta-theoretical dimension of federalism is far from absent in recent research, but it has barely been structured or even recognized as a completely developed theoretical standpoint. The next paragraphs set out to provide an initial attempt to fill this gap, with a review of the relevant literature that has opened up the endorsed perspective and of its (alleged) fathers. This will finally lead to clarifying the proposed meta-theoretical employment of federalism.

Trying to structure the analytical or meta-theoretical perspective of federalism

The "fathers" of the meta-theoretical perspective in the modern literature

The goal of this section is to underscore the seeds of the meta-theoretical perspective in some selected writings. This is to demonstrate that this approach was not unknown to classic authors, but has been somewhat overlooked as the correlation between state and federalism has gained consensus.[49] Therefore, specific attention is drawn to those authors who have been able to a. unveil a broad idea of what can be depicted as federal, and (alternatively or in combination) b. establish the core elements of federalism as a synthetical legal category that unifies such different phenomena as well as c. develop useful analytical tools or expressions to grasp the flexibility of the federal phenomenon.

48 According to Messarra, Antoine, "Principe de territorialité et principe de personnalité en fédéralisme comparé: le cas du Liban et perspectives actuelles pour la gestion du pluralisme", in Gaudreault-DesBiens and Gélinas (eds.), The States and Moods . . . , 227–260, this position is principally due to the fact that most Western scholars are somewhat affected by a nation-state frame of mind or cryptotype. which has led to consideration of territorial polities (regions, provinces, territories) as fundamental elements of "true" federalism.

49 The reasons accounting for the oversight of the meta-theoretical perspective are described by Lépine, Federalism . . . , 39–40; the fact that "federalism is mostly shown through diversity rather than a general definition . . . has to find its roots in the difficulty to combine its essence with the development of the model of the state in the modern epoch" which, linking federalism to the specific models of federation and confederation, did not leave room for "the full expression of the nature of federalism, or at least to consider it as a whole" and for perceiving the federal phenomenon "in its multidimensionality"; therefore, the feder(ation)alist approach has elided the (liberal) state and federalism, and, by doing this, it has discouraged the establishment of a broad notion of federalism since it has promoted its coincidence with a (more or less specific) model of government.

The meta-theoretical conceptualization of federalism appears to be present in several "cutting-edge" strands of classical federal theory. To be clear, they are labeled as "cutting-edge" in the sense that they have introduced either innovative theorizations and models or critical concepts and terms which have opened up new directions of research, even beyond what was originally expected at the time of their creation.

It is possible to identify several "fathers" of the meta-theoretical perspective, namely, C.J. Friedrich, R.S. Davis, and D.J. Elazar. These authors have, to a greater or lesser extent,[50] suggested the existence of a multifaceted federal phenomenon that can be analyzed beyond its strict form-of-government dimension, thus contributing to the development of federalism as an interpretive legal category. To sum up, they have contributed to the expansion of the scope of federalism in a way that appears fruitful for the present inquiry, especially with regard to: the use of federalism as an analytical framework or concept; the idea of the broadness and replicability of federalism even beyond the state and form-of-government dimensions and its historical roots in the pre-modern epoch; the correlated non-essentiality of territory as an element of the analytical notion of federalism; the elaboration of the concepts of federal arrangement or relation (or partnership); the underlying idea that the core of federalism implies a deep structure,[51] an essential logic or method of organization and coexistence common to manifold experiences.

Importantly, inquiring which dimension of federalism or materialization of its principles constitutes the expression of "true federalism" – one of the most ambiguous topics in federal scholarship – is not relevant to this analysis. Rather, the goal is essentially to find elements that support the possibility of building and justifying a meta-theoretical view and wide use of the term.

Some selected passages may help understand the contribution of these authors to the view here proposed.

C.J. Friedrich

The analysis will start with C.J. Friedrich's "*Trends of Federalism in Theory and Practice*".[52] His research related to the widely known concept of the

50 It is indeed necessary to clarify that, of course, the aim is not to suggest that their research only boils down to such contents; in other words, their investigations are also characterized by many other elements that are different from the position of the present work; this section only suggests that their studies have also given decisive insights into the specific perspective endorsed, setting the stage for a meta-theoretical view of federalism.

51 In a way, recalling the concept of "deep unity" of all federal processes described by Zoller, Elisabeth, "Aspects internationaux du droit constitutionnel: Contribution à la théorie de la fédération d'Etats", 294 *Collected Courses of the Hague Academy of International Law* (2002), 39–166, at 51.

52 Friedrich, Carl J., *Trends of Federalism in Theory and Practice* (Pall Mall Press, London, 1968).

"federalizing process" and his dynamic interpretation of federalism[53] hinted at a view of the federal phenomenon that is not far from the meta-theoretical perspective put forward here. Indeed, although Friedrich emphasized several times (especially in other writings) an existing link between federalism and constitutionalism (as a form of democratic government), thus suggesting the former as one of the most important aspects of the latter,[54] in his main research on federalism the concept seems to have a broader scope which goes beyond such an institutional perspective.[55] It thus seems that in his seminal book, much room is left for a wider interpretation of federalism, though, as is to be expected, a significant degree of his attention was drawn to its state expression.[56] Therefore, in reference to Friedrich, it can be said that he offered some important insights regarding the meta-theoretical standpoint, but which were not thoroughly focused on. This corroborates the impression some observers gained about the ambiguity of his thought.[57]

Nevertheless, this sketched view of federalism and the federal phenomenon merits reproduction in this chapter, which is provided in the last chapter of his "*Trends of Federalism in Theory and Practice*". For instance, one could focus on the following quotation: "federalism implies a *process* of federalizing, as well as a pattern or structure. It is the core of such a theory that a federation is a union of groups, united by one or more common objectives, rooted in common values, interests, or beliefs, but retaining their distinctive group character for other purposes. . . . The nature of the particular groups which

53 For an analysis of Friedrich's work, see Burgess, Comparative Federalism . . . and La Pergola, Antonio, "L'empirismo nello studio dei sistemi federali: a proposito di una teoria di Carl Friedrich", in La Pergola, Antonio (ed.), *Tecniche costituzionali e problemi delle autonomie garantite: riflessioni comparatistiche sul federalismo e regionalismo* (CEDAM, Padua, 1987), 123–182.

54 For instance, see Friedrich, Federal Constitutional Theory . . . , 516–529.

55 If one, for example, looked up the term "constitutionalism" in the name index of the book, he or she would not find any voice; the only part that directly addresses the relationships between federalism and constitutionalism is in the chapter "Federalism and Opposition" (58–69), and esp. at 59, where the author set out six hypotheses or reasons supporting the belief that federalism encourages the realization of constitutional democracy; this, however, does not seem to entail that federalism was only seen as a form of constitutional democracy, although, in the article Friedrich, Federal Constitutional Theory . . . – quoted numerous times by Burgess, Comparative Federalism . . . , to sustain the thesis of an ontological connection among federalism as a form of government, liberal democracy and constitutionalism – Friedrich specifically referred to "true federalism" as "the federalizing process under constitutionalism"; on the ambiguity of Friedrich's thought, see La Pergola, L'empirismo . . . , 137–138.

56 Especially if one considers that the second part of the book is dedicated to the analysis of several case studies of federal or federalizing countries; however, the inclusion of the process of European integration should be seen as another confirmation of the author's wide point of view, even if it must be observed that American scholars have always been more apt to framing the evolution of the EC (then EU) in federal terms, as illustrated by Martinico, Giuseppe, "The Federal Language and the European Integration Process: The European Communities viewed from the US", 53(3) *Politique Européenne* (2016), 38–59.

57 On this, see Riker, Six Books . . . , 135–147; La Pergola, L'empirismo . . . , 137–138.

federate will have a decisive impact upon the particular system. Understood as *implying the process of federalizing*, an emergent federal order may be operating in the direction of both integration and differentiation; federalizing being *either* the process by which a number of separate political units, be they states or other associations (churches, trade unions, parties, and so forth), enter into and develop arrangements for working out solutions together . . . making joint decisions and adopting joint policies on common problems, *or* the reverse process through which a hitherto unitary political community, as it becomes differentiated into a number of separate and distinct political subcommunities, achieves a new order in which the differentiated communities become capable of working out separately and on their own decisions and policies on problems they no longer have in common".[58] Afterwards, more clearly, he stated: "The extension of the range of vision that federalism in theory and practice has called for means . . . the inclusion of international federalism"[59] and "It has also meant that the practice of nongovernmental federated entities is being investigated and compared with the realities of federal government".[60] Finally, he affirmed: "the basic insight, now increasingly accepted, is that federations of states and the federal state must be seen as particular applications of a recurrent form of effective organized cooperation between groups. A federal order is a union of groups selves, united by one or more common objectives, a community of communities which retain their distinctive group being. . . . Thus, it is the particular relation which exists in fact that should shape the federal relationship".[61]

From this selection of passages, a meta-theoretical point of view is identifiable, albeit only sketched. Indeed, one can observe that the author (also) used federalism as an analytical tool with potential that is far from being limited to a single dimension. Rather, he recognized that it correlates to a large number of practices and arrangements. In particular, federalism emerges as a common logic that helps the observer frame numerous manifestations, which are thought to involve a relation more than a specific form. It is no accident that he explicitly refers to "states and other associations" or communities while describing the federalizing process, or to the investigation of "nongovernmental federated entities" as part of the current "extension of the range of vision" related to federalism. Similarly, it is not by chance that he defined American federalism as "*a novel, unprecedented concept of federalism*",[62] thus acknowledging the possibility of using this term to describe other models as well as recognizing the historical roots of federalism in several premodern experiences.

58 Friedrich, Trends of Federalism . . . , 177.
59 Ibid.
60 Ibid., 177–178.
61 Ibid., 183.
62 Ibid., 17.

Finally, the described framing recognizes the broad (at least) analytical possibilities of federalism as a tool to explain and understand several phenomena. Indeed, this is something Friedrich had already contended elsewhere when addressing non-territorial forms of federal organization.[63] However, what appears to be missing is an evaluation of the possible implications of such a view, and, in particular, an attempt to define the essential or core elements of federalism as an analytical tool, or a further elaboration of the concept of community[64] and its possible relationships with the state structures.[65]

R.S. Davis

Regarding R.S. Davis, in his seminal book "*The Federal Principle. A Journey Through Time in Quest of a Meaning*",[66] he clearly highlighted the historicity of the federal phenomenon and its ancient roots. Moreover, through the lens of the "federal principle" and its core element, the covenant,[67] he was able to grasp the numerous experiences described in the book – such as the Hellenic experience,[68] Medieval practices,[69] the US model[70] and its replications – and give them a unitary analytical framework.[71]

Besides the chosen connotation of the federal principle, what is also interesting is the very process used to abstract the core analytical – and, in his view, to a certain extent moral[72] – content that characterizes all the described experiences, which reveals the broad perspective endorsed by the author. Having identified the covenant as the primary cell of the federal principle, he then underscored how the concrete implementations of the principle may be

63 Friedrich, Federal Constitutional Theory . . . , 517: "Federalism, as a species of constitutionalism, is oriented toward the specific value of the freedom and security of federally recognized communities. Historically these have been territorially defined communities but this aspect is not necessarily implied in the concept. The now forgotten yet highly imaginative idea of the Austrian socialists Otto Bauer, Herrnitt, and Karl Renner for a solution of the nationality problems of the Austrian empire by organizing it in terms of corporative national bodies without defined boundaries but with defined cultural loyalties . . . is indicative of the broad possibilities of federalism, as was indeed recognized by Althusius, and underlies the practice of many federated associations".

64 As noted by La Pergola, L'empirismo . . . , 129, 137–138 and 147–148.

65 In fact, as observed by La Pergola, L'empirismo . . . , Friedrich considered the federalizing processes within and outside the state structures as two models that do not communicate, while it would seem of interest to look at the interaction between state institutions and non-state ones in terms of federal relationships.

66 Davis, Rufus, *The Federal Principle: A Journey Through Time in Quest of a Meaning* (University of California Press, Berkeley-Los Angeles-London, 1978).

67 Ibid., 3–4.

68 Ibid., 11–34.

69 Ibid., 35–73.

70 Ibid., 75–120.

71 Ibid., 121–154.

72 See Ibid., 2–3.

multiple and varied, but all deserving of equal consideration. In his words, "If *foedus* is there, then no one may choose not only from ten ways of perceiving the subject, but from all the possible variations and combinations of these alternatives Some of these ways have a more recent etymological license than others, some have greater theoretical coherence, some greater empirical verifiability, some more fashionable appeal, some greater coverage than others, some greater operational value. But historically, none has a greater legitimacy than any other. And as descriptive or explanatory modes, all are imperfect"[73] to grasp the "federal galaxy".[74]

Another important insight stemming from Davis's book can be derived from the list of the possible expressions of the federal principle, which indicates the extent to which human organization could be framed as federal from his point of view. It is worth noticing that, among the ways the federal principle is supposed to reveal (and has revealed) itself, a vast array of models is given, shying away from a pure form-of-government point of view. In his view, federalism can thus be employed following "a possible early signification . . . connoting simply *any* cooperative association of groups, whether *territorial or not*"[75]; applied to "any cooperative association of groups . . . but limit the genus by any one or combination of elements: e.g., territoriality, purpose, organization, operation, etc.";[76] retained "for any state formation where "power is divided" following the "US model"" or for other state formation that represents a variation thereof[77]; treated in paradigmatic terms when highlighting its evolution (i.e., Grecian federalism, Roman, Germanic, Western, and so on).[78]

Hence, Davis's contribution to the construction of a meta-theoretical concept of federalism is significant, for it is based on the employment of the term as a common and variable notion to understand a far-reaching universe of legal-constitutional practices, among which the modern form of government

73 Ibid., 216.
74 Ibid., 216.
75 Ibid., 214.
76 Ibid., 214.
77 Specifically, see Davis, The Federal Principle . . . , 215–216, where the author suggested that it may be possible to retain the federal principle for: "state formation where "power is divided" on the lines of any of the existing "federal" or purportedly "federal" systems, and where constitutional/political practice sustains a "significant" measure of "independence" (autonomy" in at least one field of activity"; "any state formation where, though power is divided constitutionally between two or more jurisdictions . . . all "levels" . . . are given "significant" responsibilities in virtually all activities"; any state formation where any "instrumental" or "institutional" recognition is given to any "significant" territorially organized diversity"; "any state formation where "power is divided between two or more levels of authority . . . but there is no presumption of co-equality"; "any state formation where "power is divided" and practiced strictly in accordance with the separatist notions of "twin-stream" or "dual federalism"; "any system where "power is divided", but qualify the term by national categories" (i.e., American federalism, Swiss federalism, etc.).
78 Davis, The Federal Principle . . . , 215.

is but one example. And finally, despite the numerous ways the author defined federalism, the practical analytical usefulness of the concept is strongly acknowledged.[79]

D.J. Elazar

Shifting the focus to Elazar's writings (and, mainly, to "*Exploring Federalism*"[80]) one may find other sources of inspiration for the elaboration of the meta-theoretical standpoint. It should be noted that, not unlike Friedrich, Elazar, while having coined cutting-edge concepts, was much concerned with a specific idea of federalism elevated as a model and inspired by the US experience.[81] For this reason, Elazar is thought to have introduced valuable notions for the development of the perspective endorsed in this study, albeit only partially expanded, given the fact that he was "too much linked to the state model" and to the American form of government.[82]

Despite this, his thought is worthy of analysis, particularly when it comes to recognition of the width of the federal phenomenon through his famous definition of federalism as self-rule plus shared rule.[83] Linking this definition to other parts of the book and subsequent writings, one may realize that it has been employed as a means to highlight the vastness of the federal phenomenon. Federalism was referred to as a "value concept – a term that carries with it an essence, which is interpreted in a variety of ways under different circumstances as long as they adhere to the essentials of the concept so that they serve to allow people to "hone in" on a particular set of deep structural meanings. As a value concept it does not have a once-and-for-all-time scientific definition in the usual scientific sense, although it can be and is defined operationally in well-accepted ways".[84] In addition, in a very

79 Contrary to what seems generally attributed to Davis, by quoting two famous (decontextualized) sentences; see Davis, The Federal Principle . . . , 213–214: "In this condition [the difficulty to find a common understanding of federalism and to link it with a specific meaning], it is tempting to fantasy the possibility of retiring the "federal" concept from active duty, granting it a grace-and-favor residence (in Athens, Rome, or Philadelphia) and declaring a search for its successor. . . . Yet this is the purest fantasy. No one, and perhaps not even a lexicographer Caesar can rule over the domain of etymology. We cannot stem the momentum of two thousand years of usage, nor can we sensibly deny that the longevity of the concept is some testimony to its continuing need, expressive, symbolic, or instrumental. For concepts live, wither, or die as needs must; and over great stretches of time different societies have satisfied their different needs for preferred relations with others through the mutual commitment of *foedus* – a concept that by repeated encounters with different experiences has become interwoven not with one thing, but many things".

80 Elazar, Daniel J., *Exploring Federalism* (The University of Alabama Press, Tuscaloosa, 1987).

81 Lépine, A Journey . . . , 52.

82 Ibid.

83 Elazar, Exploring Federalism . . . , 12.

84 Ibid., 15–16.

famous passage, he argued that federalism "is not to be found in a particular set of institutions but in the institutionalization of particular relationships among the participants in the political life".[85] The latter ideas were further explored and eventually extended in scope in successive writings, trying to grasp the alleged paradigm shift from nationalism to federalism occurring in the post-modern world. He consequently affirmed: "I use the term "federal" here in its larger historical sense, not simply to describe modern federation but all the various federal arrangements including federations, confederation and other confederal arrangements, federacies, associated states, special joint authorities with constitutional standing, and others".[86] Such a use of the adjective "federal" seems consistent with the meta-theoretical perspective proposed here, given the flexible employment he accorded to it. This is confirmed, for instance, in the statement that federalism can be "understood in the broadest political sense as a genus involving combinations of self-rule and shared rule rather than as the one species of federalism accepted in modern times – federation".[87] In other words, the author suggested the underlying logic of federalism is wide in scope, thus replicable in multiple forms besides its state manifestation.

Therefore, the employment of the "self-rule plus shared rule formula" reveals the presence of a meta-theoretical perspective in Elazar's thought. Furthermore, not unlike R.S. Davis, Elazar essentially and historically attempted to investigate and define the deep content of federalism and connect it to the idea of covenant. According to his view, the origin of the federal idea based on covenant is theopolitical and to be traced back to the experience of the Israelite communities in the thirteen century BCE.[88] Afterwards, several ancient expressions of federalism took place, corresponding to what he defined as premodern federal and proto-federal systems,[89] up to the "invention"[90] of modern federalism as a "practical system of government" by the founders of the United States of America.[91] The historical dimension of the federal idea suggests, once more, the breadth of the perspective endorsed by the author – at least to a certain extent – and his search for an inner content of federalism is a source of inspiration for the definition of the core logic underlying the notion.

Yet, the analytical potential of the described formula is narrowed down in Elazar's work, since it appears to be mostly linked to a form-of-government

85 Ibid., 12.

86 See Elazar, From Statism . . . , 428, footnote no. 1, where it is clear that the scope of the use of the term federal is wide and not limited to what is here referred to as the "feder(ation)alist perspective".

87 Elazar, From Statism . . . , 419.

88 Elazar, Exploring Federalism . . . , 117.

89 Ibid., 118–138.

90 Ibid., 49.

91 Ibid., 143.

dimension.[92] Indeed, one should also be aware that, in some sections of his most famous book, Elazar expressed a clear position on modern federalism (considered the genuine expression of the federal idea), correlating it to the division of powers among governments or polities[93] with a fundamentally territorial scope.[94] This reconnects him to the feder(ation)alist thought. Furthermore, it should not be overlooked that while Elazar's account disclosed a broad approach to federalism as self-rule plus shared rule, most of his attention was attracted by a specific and "authentic" archetype, which was tied to modern democratic republicanism numerous times in his seminal book.[95] Indeed, most attention was drawn to the concept of the federal matrix (also) as an analytical (and normative) model. This was built upon the mentioned definition of federalism, with some elements added to its basic contents.

Provided that one keeps this in mind, other ideas and concepts Elazar relied upon, starting from the matrix, are nonetheless interesting for the sake of this work.

The model of the federal matrix was depicted as twofold. The first way this concept was brought forward has to do with its description as the essential scheme of power diffusion[96] typical of federalism (noncentralization), which distinguishes a federal from a non-federal form of political organization or arrangement.[97] Elazar's federal matrix is both a descriptive and a normative/prescriptive model aimed at classifying truly federal experiences. This was built somewhat on the experience of the US form of government, a reading that

92 Immediately after the self-rule plus shared rule formula, Elazar, Exploring Federalism . . . , 12, observed: "federalism . . . involves some kind of contractual linkage of a presumably permanent character that (1) provides for power sharing, (2) cuts around the issue of sovereignty, and (3) supplements but does not seek to replace or diminish prior organic ties where they exist".

93 Elazar, Exploring Federalism . . . , 68–70: "Federalism as a political phenomenon, understood according to the modern meaning of "political", is essentially limited to relations among governments or polities".

94 Moreover, in keeping with his view, to be truly federal, it is said the arrangements should be built upon a "formal agreement between the entities involved that takes on constitutional force (and is often embodied in a constitutional document) as a result of the striking of a bargain that guarantees their respective integrities" (Elazar, Exploring Federalism . . . , 46) and basically reproduce, albeit to different extents, the matrix model which connotes true federalism (Elazar, Exploring Federalism . . . , 34–38).

95 For instance, see Elazar, Exploring Federalism . . . , 25: "Federalism was invented as a means to foster democratic republicanism or popular government in the terminology of the eighteenth century United States"; also, see Elazar, Exploring Federalism . . . , 107: "True federal arrangements must invariably rest upon a popular base"; Elazar, Exploring Federalism . . . , 153: "Thus federalism is a particularly modern device, albeit with ancient roots, inseparable from modern democratic republicanism"; following the same logic, he argued that medieval feudalism cannot be framed as an authentic federal experience (Elazar, Exploring Federalism . . . , 123–126).

96 Elazar, Exploring Federalism . . . , 34.

97 Ibid., 34–38.

does not add much to the construction of a meta-theoretical definition of federalism, given that it equates its core content with a specific scheme of power relations. Nevertheless, the description of the matrix model – which boils down to a network of non-hierarchically organized units and powers, as well as formal and informal relationships[98] – may anyhow offer important insights into what the federal phenomenon could (also) resemble in contemporary times. As has been noted, once freed from the rigidity of a prescriptive/normative aim[99] – and, perhaps, from the state perspective that frequently underpins it – the definition has considerable analytical implications and allows for a significant enlargement of the phenomena that might be seen through a federal lens.[100]

The second "face" of Elazar's federal matrix, less thoroughly addressed, echoes the idea of the replicability of the federal essential logic or scheme. The author stated that it is "as a matrix, almost indefinitely expandable both in scope and in character of the relationship".[101] This view was also specifically expressed in his considerations concerning the contemporary evolution of the state.[102] Notably, the latter representation of the federal matrix appears to be valuable in that it explicitly reveals the analytical potential of federalism and provides a useful explanatory concept.

Another notion that offers a similar contribution to a meta-theoretical perspective – i.e., one that considers federalism as an analytical instrument – is that of *federal arrangement* (or *federal relationship/partnership*).[103] Elazar employed this to describe the existence of relations between polities or entities[104] reproducing a federal logic (the federal matrix) in legal systems whose structures are not completely (or not at all except for that arrangement)

98 Ibid., 225.

99 Which inevitably reduces its reach by excluding what is not authentically federal in the proposed sense, meaning the so-called hierarchical and center-periphery models of organization (Elazar, Exploring Federalism . . . , 34–38).

100 Lépine, A Journey . . . , 21–62.

101 Elazar, Exploring Federalism . . . , 229.

102 Ibid., 223–266.

103 Elazar, Exploring Federalism . . . , 5; subsequently, also Watts, Comparing . . . , 8, resorted to the notion of federal arrangement: "furthermore, other political systems . . . may incorporate some federal arrangements because political leaders and nation-builders are less bound by considerations of theoretical purity than by the pragmatic search of workable arrangements. Such considerations may also lead to hybrids such as the European Union".

104 Indeed, among the federal arrangements were also included, for instance, consociational unions on a non-territorial basis (Elazar, Exploring Federalism . . . , 44 and 49–50), even if the author suggested (Elazar, Exploring Federalism . . . , 18–26 and pp. 49–50) that they are different from a federal organization in that consociations are merely a matter of process, while federalism is a matter of process and structure, the latter assuring stability to the arrangement. Nonetheless, the inclusion of consociations among the federal arrangements appears explicit and justified by the common logic they share with more institutionalized federal relations.

permeated by federal principles.[105] The concept of federal arrangement is a useful concept that contributes to the meta-theoretical employment of federalism. The theorization of the concept of federal arrangement to describe a relation that follows a federal logic is fruitful in that it creates a flexible analytical tool to grasp the variety of federal relationships that may exist regardless of the presence of a federal institutional context.

Additionally, it is not without interest that Elazar (much like the other authors previously referred to) maintained that:

> The federal principle has also been used as the basis for nongovernmental associations, both public and private, that have become characteristic of contemporary world. . . . When these public nongovernmental bodies use federal arrangements, they frequently do so on a functional rather than a territorial basis, thus adding another dimension to the use of federal principles.[106]

He also observed that, while being "particularly common in federal political systems, in which nongovernmental groups must accommodate themselves to a federal distribution of power", these arrangements "are not limited to such political systems . . . but are common in all modern democratic countries", and he suggested that "Liberal democracy with its emphasis on pluralism creates an environment that is highly conducive to such arrangements".[107] Such quotations evoke an idea of federalism which consists of a logic that permeates manifold emergent practices and possibly holds public law relevance. In other words, this passage indicates that a large number of practices may fit into the category of federal arrangement, even if not concerning traditional public governmental bodies.

However, what seems to be missing is a consideration of the public law implications of these arrangements, i.e., on the effects – if any – their existence could have on state organizations and functions, given that some of these associations are thought to perform public law duties. Put differently, whereas attention is paid to the internal reproduction of federal logic within non-government bodies, the same cannot be said of their external relations with state structures and the opportunity to frame them as federal as well. In any case, such a framing is of interest to this work as it shows that federalism may provide a conceptual, analytical framework for the emergent instruments of the "Law of Diversity".

In the end, and leaving aside which version of federalism actually represents the author's definitive position, the insights one can derive from Elazar's work are: he recognized, to a certain extent, that federal phenomena (arrangements,

105 Elazar, Exploring Federalism . . . , 44.
106 Ibid., 63.
107 Ibid.

relations, or partnerships) occur regardless of the presence of a full-fledged federal political system;[108] he developed a broad notion of federalism (with the described limits) and tried to find an essential content of it; he provided some interesting analytical tools, such as the concept of federal arrangement.

Recent accounts dealing with the meta-theoretical perspective explicitly

The precursors: the first explicit use of federalism as an analytical tool to study the European integration process

Besides the suggestions coming from classic federal theory, other authors have also explicitly contributed to a renewal of federal studies and tried to develop a "new conceptual revolution"[109] in this field.

Interestingly, it seems possible to identify a further group of "forerunners", corresponding to the extensive studies that have revolved around the development of the EU by using federalism as a frame for the explanation of its governance dynamics and structures. Particularly notable is that the investigation of the process of European integration has been an object of interest and framed as a federal model[110] from the very beginning by most American scholars, who found themselves more at ease with the use of federal terminology than their European counterparts.[111] This can arguably be regarded as the first example of explicit employment of federalism beyond its well-established state-related models and for analytical purposes. In fact, framing the European experience as a federal phenomenon has surely provided the observers with a

108 Especially if one considers the considerations in Elazar, From Statism . . .

109 Lépine, Federalism . . . , 31.

110 Burgess, Comparative Federalism . . . , 226–248; among others, see Hay, Peter, *Federalism and Supranational Organizations: Patterns for New Legal Structures* (University of Illinois Press, Urbana-London, 1966); *Id.*, "Supremacy of Community Law in National Courts: A Progress Report on Referrals Under the EEC Treaty", 16(4) *American Journal of Comparative Law* (1968), 524–551; Stein, Eric, "Lawyers, Judges and the Making of a Transnational Constitution", 75(1) *American Journal of International Law* (1981), 1–27; Hartley, Trevor C., "Federalism, Courts and Legal Systems: The Emerging Constitution of the European Community", 34(2) *American Journal of Comparative Law* (1986), 229–247; Lenaerts, Koen, "Constitutionalism and the Many Faces of Federalism", 38(2) *The American Journal of Comparative Law* (1990), 205–263; Weiler, Joseph H.H., "The Transformation of Europe", 100(8) *The Yale Law Journal* (1991), 2403–2483; Bermann, George A., "Taking Subsidiarity Seriously: Federalism in the European Community and the United States", 94(2) *Columbia Law Review* (1994), 331–456; Friedrich, Federal Constitutional Theory . . . , 510–533; interestingly, the EU was also studied as a form of state by Caporaso, James A., "The European Union and Forms of State", 34(1) *Journal of Common Market Studies* (1996), 29–52: the analysis compared the EU to three ideal-typical models of state (Westphalian, Regulatory and Post-modern) and assessed the theoretical potential of each one to explain its organization and functioning.

111 On this, see Martinico, Giuseppe, "Comparative Legal Studies and European Integration: Looking at the Origins of the Debate", 41(122) *Boletín Mexicano de Derecho Comparado* (2008), 859–883.

set of useful analytical tools to grasp the characteristics of the European supranational organization.

Yet it should be recognized that the consolidated models of federal theory and practice have been the principal points of reference of these authors; indeed, they have commonly drawn comparisons with the processes and structures of federal states or confederal organizations so as to draw lessons for the development of European institutions in a federal sense. Furthermore, the phenomenon did not distance itself that much from the classic models, somewhat reproducing, albeit in a particular manner, processes and structures that federal scholars are familiar with.

Besides this body of literature, which somewhat concurred with the previous considerations on the meta-theoretical use of federalism, a few more recent accounts have delved further into a reconceptualization of federalism – aimed at expanding its reach and analytical potential.

F. Lépine

Lépine's interpretation of federalism is expressed in two main writings.

In "A Journey through the History of Federalism. Is Multilevel Governance a Form of Federalism?", he investigated the "multilevel governance model" through a federal lens.[112] Accordingly, multilevel governance was theorized as a contemporary form of federalism, the latest version of the federal idea,[113] and the European Union was considered the paradigmatic example of this evolution.[114]

The study entitled "Federalism: Essence, Values and Ideologies" instead specifically described the hermeneutical process of extracting a notion of federalism from the "federal phenomenon" and defined its stages of evolution alongside the increasing complexity of both societies and knowledge.

Following his view, federalism corresponds to a synthetical idea capable of framing the federal phenomenon – which "encompasses federal institutional organizations in different times and places as well as federal thoughts about the diffusion of powers".[115] Thus, the author addressed federalism as an analytical rather than a purely normative or institutional concept.[116] As a result, on the one hand, an inner content of federalism was acknowledged but not identified as a prescriptive doctrine coinciding with a contingent ideology; on the other, the

112 Taking inspiration from the considerations of Hooghe, Liesbet and Marks, Gary, "Unravelling the Central State, But How? Types of Multi-level Governance", 97(2) *American Political Science Review* (2003), 233–243.

113 Lépine, A Journey . . . , 49–63.

114 Ibid., 11.

115 Lépine, Federalism . . . , 34.

116 *Contra*, starting from similar premises, Gaudreault-DesBiens and Gélinas, Opening New Perspectives . . . , have alluded to the existence (or the need to study the existence) of a set of ethical values of federalism; a reasoning further expanded by Gaudreault-DesBiens, Towards a Deontic . . . , 90–91.

federal phenomenon was not reduced to a specific institutional manifestation, highlighting its trans-historical dimension and its continuous evolution.

Hence, federalism, rather than being identified in a particular prescriptive set of principles or institutional features, was mainly described as an analytical framework or an "interpretive paradigm"[117] through which one can observe and explain much more than its closed state-related expression. Specifically, federalism was referred to as a *notion* that

> has to be considered as an elementary abstract mental representation of an object of studies, derived from empirical research and mental induction, allowing the capacity of bringing together a multiplicity of phenomena observed by the selection of some essential features, but not elaborated enough to be used in model or theory building.[118]

As a consequence, as Lépine put it, federalism performs an analytical function leading to practical benefits, for it provides a common ground of understanding for countless practices, generalized enough to get rid of the contingencies that characterize the time and place in which these phenomena take place.[119]

The elaboration of a notion of federalism – albeit rather unclear in some respects[120] – was shown to be a two-step incremental process. The first step consisted of defining a general federal framework or super-code that characterizes and unifies federal practices and studies. In other words, this not only means developing a descriptive concept but also creating a systematic preliminary frame according to which one may understand and explain the observed reality. Accordingly, federalism was taken as a concept that

> Within a defined political space, [it] covers all possible configurations of authority where it is neither possible to concentrate all the power within a single authority, nor to separate that political space into smaller political space ruled by a single authority and closed off from each other.

As a consequence, federalism was considered as a general common framework of a vast "federal phenomenology",[121] which "encompasses all forms

117 An expression employed by Gaudreault-DesBiens and Gélinas, Opening New Perspectives . . . , 71.

118 Lépine, Federalism . . . , 37.

119 Ibid., 36.

120 For instance, see the unclear use of the terms phenomenon and phenomenology, the theoretical difference between the super-code of federalism, and the subsequent definition, the justification of the selected definition.

121 In Lépine, Federalism . . . , 34: "a collection of empirical observations connected to each other through a general framework, which may lead to further abstraction, conceptualization and theorization".

of political organizations that stay irreducible to centralization of power and maintain a form of autonomy, or self-governance, of political authority within a political space composed of several authorities".[122]

The second step aimed to define the notion of federalism in a positive manner. Interestingly, federalism was outlined in its essential elements in slightly different ways in Lépine's two writings. In the first, it is interpreted "in a meta-theoretical perspective, as a general approach of politics, or a paradigm considered in its more general sense", which was made up of some basic elements:

> 1. Federalism is based on a voluntary contract between collective entities (would it be called treaty, constitution, covenant, compact . . .); 2. Thus, it considers the self-governance – or autonomy – of the entities in each level of a two or muti-tier organization; 3. Eventually, federalism considers that the diffusion of power is preferable to its centralization.

In the second, building upon the definition given by D. Karmis and W. Norman, according to whom "federalism is an arrangement in which two or more self-governing communities share the same political space",[123] he stated that:

> a. federalism is to be taken at first as a political phenomenon – overarching on the public realm the multiple dimensions of specific fields as the legal and the economic ones; b. it does not refer to a relation between individuals but between human groups ('communities') that are supposedly already constituted . . . ; c. these 'communities' have self-governing capacity, which supposes that they have established political institutions; d. eventually, the definition of the political space does not refer to a territorial dimension, which allows taking into account (non-territorial) personal and/or functional federal arrangements.[124]

Furthermore, the author illustrated the stages of the evolution of federalism based on the history of federal thought and practices by underscoring the historically-bound, multifaceted, and, finally, continuously evolving manifestations of the federal phenomenon, which mirror the increasing complexity of human interaction and knowledge.[125] In keeping with his view, it is possible to find three "moments of complexity, each linked to the evolution of socio-political structures".[126] First, the "union of polities", which includes

122 Lépine, Federalism . . . , 34.

123 Karmis, Dimitrios and Norman, Wayne, "The Revival of Federalism in Normative Political Theory", in Karmis, Dimitrios and Norman, Wayne (eds.), *Theories of Federalism: A Reader* (Palgrave Macmillan, Basingstoke-New York, 2005), 3–21, at 3.

124 Lépine, Federalism . . . , 37.

125 Ibid., 39 and 40–42: "The diversity of representations of the federal phenomenon is directly issued from the growing complexity of knowledge, partly led by the internal process of complexification and partly led by the growing complexity of social structures".

126 Lépine, Federalism . . . , 40.

the most oldest examples of federal organization;[127] second, the "polity of polities", representing the outcome of the US revolution and constitution, which "just adds a new level of complexity to federal organizations"[128] allowing "the federal idea to fit into the world of sovereign states and to the principles of a democratic republic";[129] third, the "network of functional polities and institutions", a "new moment of complexity in federalism"[130] which reconnects it to the model of multi-level governance, considered as not only the latest expression of federalism,[131] but – as also underlined by the creators of this expression – a

> potential synthesis of most of the approaches of federalism . . . , and mostly the different schools of studies of the analytical approach: it does consider federations and federal states (general jurisdictions) as well as federal institutions created for a specific purpose (task-oriented jurisdictions); it is able to reconcile domestic and international fields; and, eventually, it sets federalism free from the archetype American model and its inherited values.[132]

Finally, Lépine's research represents one of the main structured accounts of a meta-theoretical view of federalism; he provided a strong argument for its plausibility by highlighting the plasticity of federalism as a basic general legal category, and he suggested that some core essential elements of it – at least for analytical purposes – can be found.

As far as the latter issue is concerned, his view – which seems, however, somewhat aimed at reconnecting federalism to multilevel governance[133] – can be complemented by Macdonald's, which implies a major focus on a logic inherent to federalism and its purported widespread diffusion in several *loci* of human life and interaction.

R.A. Macdonald

In his writing "Kaleidoscopic Federalism", R. Macdonald extended the scope of federalism far beyond a classic perspective and suggested that its underlying logic affects people's lives in several dimensions, going as far as conceiving of

127 Ibid., 40–41.
128 Ibid., 41: "there is no historical determinism in the evolution of federal structures, just the adaptation of the federal phenomenon to changing socio-political structures".
129 Lépine, Federalism . . . , 41.
130 Ibid., 41.
131 Ibid., 41.
132 Lépine, A Journey . . . , 58.
133 Not dissimilarly, see Keating, Michael, "Europe as a Multilevel Federation", 24(4) *Journal of European Public Policy* (2017), 615–632: the author underlined that the evolution of the European Union, widely framed through the concept of multilevel governance, may be better understood if studied as a federal phenomenon.

it as a metaphor for the process of self-construction of everyone's identity.[134] Accordingly, he attempted to "move towards an understanding of federalism that is not grounded in republican legal theory" and to demonstrate that, rather, it is "the normal condition of human interaction".[135]

In his view, federalism, therefore, has plural motifs, ambitions, sites, and modes, with this assumption resulting in questioning some generally accepted ideas of classic federal theory[136] and pluralizing its manifestations within and outside the state model.

What is specifically interesting is that, among other things, he argued that federalism (even in the state) essentially embeds a logic of distribution of powers that follows various patterns and is related to the presence of different kinds of fault lines; federalism is an idea whose analytical potential is not limited to its territorial form-of-government expression; the content of this idea relates to the concept of interaction and flexible balance between different layers of authority.

On the first aspect, Macdonald affirmed that each source of law or authority within the state (legislature, executive, jurisdiction, administration, etc.) may be seen as a "distinct site of federalism";[137] and, more importantly, he maintained that these are sites of federalism in the sense that they are *loci* where different sources of authority encounter and interact in a way that does not necessarily result in the reproduction of the territorial distribution of legislative power.

In other words, the idea that federalism implies a unitary pattern of division of powers was relativized and shown as a model that the state and state-related literature have extended to the organization of every kind of public or quasi-public authority. A historical perspective allowed the author to argue that this has not always been the case; for instance, he observed that the provision of many public services and functions by non-governmental institutions at different points in Canadian history did not follow provincial or other kinds

134 Macdonald, Roderick A., "Kaleidoscopic Federalism", in Gaudreault-DesBiens, Jean-F. and Gélinas, Fabien (eds.), *Le fédéralisme dans tous ses états: gouvernance, identité et méthodologie – The States and Moods of Federalism: Governance, Identity and Methodology* (Éditions Yvon Blais-Bruylant, Cowansville-Bruxelles, 2005), 261–284, at 275–276.

135 Ibid., 263; this directly links this author to Althusius's perspective.

136 For what concerns this point, on the one hand, he challenged the belief that federal projects of nation-building are either unifying or disunifying, by proposing that they are all somewhat constitutive in the sense that they always imply the establishment of a new order which both unifies and destroys (Macdonald, Kaleidoscopic Federalism . . . , 264–267); on the other hand, he questioned whether the current study and practice of the logic of division of powers – basically based on how legislative jurisdiction is divided – is refined enough to describe and assess the scope of a complex system in which numerous sources of power and law are intertwined; as a result, he made a strong argument for a deeper focus on the numerous fault lines that characterize a federal system (Macdonald, Kaleidoscopic Federalism . . . , 270–273).

137 Macdonald, Kaleidoscopic Federalism . . . , 270.

of political fault lines, but at the same time included structures and processes which reproduced a federal model of territorial organization.[138] The same goes for the actual functioning of public judicial, executive, and administrative institutions in federal states, which do not always follow the same rationale as the legislature (formally or informally) but nonetheless adhere to federal principles.[139]

A generalization of this way of thinking could lead to the suggestion that, in Macdonald's thought, federalism can (also) be conceived of as a useful explanatory frame and analytical tool for every situation where there are interactions between different sources (or layers) of power in the same space and, as a consequence, a fault line – which may not necessarily be territorial or once-and-for-all set – is present and continuously (re)defined. If, consequently, these situations are considered federal as they share this same essential logic, the possibility of exploring the usefulness of federal theories and tools to explain them and their development is thereby opened up. This is what emerges if one shifts the focus to what Macdonald called "relational non-state federalism" to describe the numerous *loci* of federalism in human life, consisting of "the panoply of voluntary associations and other institutions of civil society that human beings typically join and engage with as part of their sense of self".[140] Federalism firstly informs them internally as a principle of organization because "Most are themselves federated institutions";[141] additionally, it is also thought to have a wider dimension as an interpretive legal category explaining the organization of society into several groupings to which humans owe their loyalties in the same (political or social) space. In this sense, the groupings analyzed through a federal lens are imagined as additional layers of autonomy in a complex organization of powers and authorities or in a complex governance system.[142] Once more, the idea emerges that federalism may work as (at least) an analytical tool to frame institutions and practices outside the strict form-of-government dimension, leading to a far more complex representation of the federal phenomenon.

Therefore, not unlike the previously analyzed accounts, Macdonald did suggest – albeit in a radical way linked to legal pluralist thinking – that federalism is (also) an instrument to grasp the increasing complexity characterizing the governance of diverse societies composed of subjects with multiple

138 Ibid., 267–270.
139 Ibid., 270–273.
140 Ibid., 274.
141 Ibid., 274.
142 This is also recognized by Gaudreault-DesBiens and Gélinas, Opening New Perspectives . . . , 69: "Macdonald maintains that federalism does not lie on in the state. It can be found in the family, in the workplace, in professional associations or in businesses corporations"; they have also pointed out that this perspective is "to a certain extent in the footsteps of Johannes Althusius". The author's perspective is firmly legal pluralist as it conceives of all these layers as different sources of law for they condition human life and agency as much as the political institutions.

identities and sharing multiple loyalties.[143] Such a complex reality implies "shifting boundaries, different and multiple fault lines, and overlapping claims of authority" where "identity cannot be simply fractioned and parcelled out to different institutions in discrete packages" once and for all.[144] However, he did not add to these considerations a thorough investigation of their possible consequences from a public law point of view or the theoretical consequences of framing this reality through federalism.

To sum up, Macdonald proposed a revolutionary vision of federalism which adds interesting insights and analytical instruments to the present inquiry about its meta-theoretical meaning. Besides the extension of the reach of federalism as an interpretive category, one may also notice that he linked federalism to the reconceptualization and pluralization of two core ideas of federal theory, which could be imagined as "symptoms" of the existence of a federal arrangement. These are the correlated concepts of fault lines[145] and (overlapping and not only territorial) sites of human loyalty, allegiance, and identity. Of course, these notions are not unknown to federal theory; quite the opposite, the innovation lies in the plural conceptualization of the two expressions. This allows the observer to identify far more fault lines and sites of federalism – meaning different sites of human allegiances expressing a degree of authority (or autonomy) or voice[146] – than a feder(ation)alist standpoint would. After all, they are thought to reproduce the same logic as a territorial fault line and a territorial form of allegiance: for this reason, examining them in federal terms seems reasonable and may open up interesting theoretical perspectives.

H.K. Gerken

Though Heather K. Gerken's article "Federalism All the Way Down"[147] mainly deals with the US federal political system, it is nevertheless a source of inspiration for the elaboration of the meta-theoretical perspective.

143 A vision also expressed in Macdonald, Roderick A., "Legal Republicanism and Legal Pluralism: Two Takes on Identity and Diversity", in Bussani, Mauro and Graziadei, Michele (eds.), *Human Diversity and the Law: La diversité humaine et le droit* (Stämpfli-Bruylant-Sakkoulas, Berne-Brussels-Athens, 2005), 43–70.

144 Macdonald, Kaleidoscopic Federalism . . . , 277; the author went even further by indicating that psychological federalism is the metaphor for explaining the encounter of "multiple legal subjectivities" within every individual.

145 On another account that studied the concept of the fault line and conceived of it as not necessarily having territorial features, see also Lombardi, Giorgio, "Spazio e frontiera tra eguaglianza e privilegio: problemi costituzionali fra storia e diritto", 1 *Diritto e società* (1985), 477–495.

146 This conceptualization recalls, to a certain extent, Livingstone's vision of federalism, who described the aspects of diversity the society embeds as federal qualities, which, he purported, were to be empowered through a federal structure; see Livingston, William S., "A Note on the Nature of Federalism", 67(1) *Political Science Quarterly* (1952), 81–95, at 83–85.

147 Gerken, Heather K., "Federalism All the Way Down", 124(1) *Harvard Law Review* (2010), 4–74.

In a nutshell, the writing's principal contents boil down to two principal theses.

First, after having argued that the main dimensions of federalism may be framed through the concepts of "voice" and "exit",[148] the author maintained that the former is increasingly critical in our contemporary times. Indeed, given the complexity of tasks that states are meant to perform, the overlap and interconnectedness of jurisdictions among layers of government (present in every kind of state organization to a greater or lesser extent) have become an ordinary condition of the exercise of powers.[149] As a consequence, voice, or shared rule, meaning several types of joint or coordinated regulation, is playing a progressively more central role when it comes to most public decision-making processes.

Second – and this is the most radical thought – she extended the application of a federal analytical lens beyond the federal-state level dichotomy, "all the way down" to numerous functionally defined jurisdictions,[150] basically described as federal layers where numerous forms of (tighter or looser, temporary or stable) aggregation take place.[151] These entities are characterized by the deployment of federal features while at the same time being embedded (or nested) in a defined institutional structure that is not formally modified.[152] In other words, she defined these bodies as "institutional arrangements . . . where minorities rule without sovereignty" – i.e., without expressing a form of exclusive autonomy based on the model of sovereignty – with this "recasting" of federalism implying drawing "attention to the institutions neglected by federalists and their localists counterparts".[153] Examples of such arrangements were identified with "many institutions that constitute states and cities – juries, zoning commissions, local school boards, locally elected prosecutors' offices, state administrative agencies, and the like".[154]

148 Which may be seen as a different way to address the concepts of shared rule and self-rule; voice, in fact, refers to the possibility of influencing the federal decision-making process, while exit was defined by Gerken, Federalism All the Way Down . . . , 7, as "the chance to make policy in accord with their own preferences, separate and apart from the center".

149 On this, see Carrozza, Paolo, "I rapporti centro-periferia: federalismi, regionalismi e autonomie", in Carrozza, Paolo, Di Giovine, Alfonso and Ferrari, Giuseppe F. (eds.), *Diritto costituzionale comparato* (Laterza, Rome-Bari, 2019), 894–951.

150 As defined by Halberstam, Daniel, "Federalism: Theory, Policy, Law", in Rosenfeld, Michel and Sajó, András (eds.), *The Oxford Handbook of Comparative Constitutional Law* (Oxford University Press, Oxford, 2012), 576–608, at 605.

151 Described by Gerken, Federalism All the Way Down . . . , 7, as "the many parts of "Our Federalism" where sovereignty is not to be had"; these forms of aggregation are referred to as minorities, a term that seems to be used in quite general way to describe any form of non-majority form of allegiance; in fact, at 8, she proposes to recast "federalism as minority rule without sovereignty".

152 Notably, this description echoes the framing employed to describe forms of nested federalism in Chapter 5.

153 Gerken, Federalism All the Way Down . . . , 8.

154 Ibid., 8 and 28.

Importantly, the reason why they may be framed as – echoing Lépine – part of the federal phenomenon was clearly stated in the following terms:

> Just as we cast states as sites of political integration because they allow national minorities to rule, so too can we cast cities and juries and school committees as sites of racial and political integration because they allow racial minorities and dissenters to rule.[155]

As Gerken put it, the inclusion of these (layers or actors or) bodies in a federal theoretical framework is not meant to

> deny that there are differences between these governance sites, any more than the existence of federalism theory is meant to deny that states themselves are variegated. The question is simply whether the differences between these institutions are so stark that they preclude discussion of their similarities. Here, at least, we have evidence that the differences are not so stark. Not only have most of the functional accounts for state power been applied all the way down, but there is also a marked similarity in the rules of thumb used to decide who should decide: If there are economies of scale, vest the decision with the centralized decisionmaker. If you want to promote experimentation or choice, let the decentralized units decide. If you care about externalities, look up. If you care about participation, look down.[156]

Importantly, one can certainly notice that the proposed passage reiterates Gaudreault-Desbiens and Gélinas's claims and arguments for the use of federalism as an interpretive paradigm. It does so by highlighting the similarities among the observed institutions and dynamics, which, as a result, justifies the consequent extension of the federal frame and terminology.[157]

In her view, these "parts of federalism where sovereignty is not to be had"[158] are "sites of decentralization"[159] that end up expressing a form of voice in federal terms. Accordingly, they were depicted as bodies where several groups, while not being endowed with "sovereign" autonomy powers, nonetheless have a means of expressing their views and, as a consequence, can considerably

155 Ibid., 9.

156 Ibid., 29.

157 Notably, Gerken, Federalism All the Way Down . . . , 31–33, provided a concrete application of her reasoning through the examination of a jury by explaining how a federal framing may give interesting insights and provide an alternative understanding of its functioning and concrete dynamics; in a nutshell, the jury was theorized as a federal body that puts in place policies and experiences dynamics somewhat comparable to government institutions; although the concrete consequences of this example seem rather US context-oriented, what one can essentially infer is the value and potential of applying a federal lens.

158 Gerken, Federalism All the Way Down . . . , 9.

159 Ibid., 21.

affect the functioning of public decision-making in the (federal) political system as a whole. Put differently, they were referred to as layers of a federal "polyphonic"[160] organization that display self-determination through shared rule, i.e., influence the "classic" governance institutions through their (somewhat autonomous but nested in a wider institutional structure of "sovereign" powers) activity. Indeed,

> in these areas institutional arrangements promote voice, not exit; integration, not autonomy; interdependence, not independence. Minorities do not rule separate and apart from the national system, and the power they wield is not their own. Minorities are instead part of a complex amalgam of state and local actors who administer national policy. And the power minorities wield is that of the servant, not the sovereign; the insider, not the outsider. They enjoy a muscular form of voice – the power not just to complain about national policy, but to help set it. Here power dynamics are fluid; minority rule is contingent, limited, and subject to reversal by the national majority; and rebellious decisions can originate even from banally administrative units.[161]

Furthermore, "[S]pecial purpose institutions, in short, provide minorities with a chance to exercise voice inside the system, not to set policy outside of it",[162] and they

> are servants rather than sovereigns, administrative units integrated into a broader system rather than institutions capable of regulating separate and apart from the center, temporary and contingent sites of minority rule rather than governments capable of commanding the loyalty of a People.[163]

And, interestingly, Gerken also indicated that: "Federalism-all-the-way-down can provide a structural means for achieving goals traditionally associated with rights-protecting amendments like the First and Fourteenth".[164]

160 This expression is borrowed from Shapiro, Robert A., *Polyphonic Federalism: Toward the Protection of Fundamental Rights* (The University of Chicago Press, Chicago-London, 2009).

161 Gerken, Federalism All the Way Down . . . , 7–8.

162 Ibid., 27.

163 Ibid., 29.

164 Ibid., 9, 47–73, and esp. 70–71: "In conventional federalism, the price of state sovereignty is separation from the national sphere. Under the First Amendment, the price of individual autonomy is separation from the public sphere. The First Amendment protects the power of dissenters to act or speak in concert, provided they do so solely on their own behalf. Federalism-all-the-way-down offers a different tradeoff. It allows dissenters to make decisions in the public realm but does not protect them from reversal. It offers dissenters voice, not exit; the status of insiders, not outsiders; the power of the public servant, not the private sovereign".

Therefore, in a way, federalism was put forward as an alternative mechanism to protect rights from an organizational perspective. Such an approach is reminiscent of the accounts that have conceived (minority) rights as a product of the nation-state model and challenged its "inevitability and superiority"[165] by shedding light on alternative or complementary forms of diversity and pluralism management.[166]

To summarize, the analyzed theoretical account suggested a significant extension of the federal discourse to frame a large number of institutions and dynamics beyond the mainstream. Additionally, it upheld the theoretical potential of using a federal lens, as well as the development of federal terminology for phenomena generally overlooked by federal scholarship.[167] The reason for doing so lies in the versatility of the logic and instruments of federalism and its practical-analytical usefulness as a tool to explain the reality of the distribution of powers resulting from "interactions between the center and its variegated periphery".[168] As the author put it, the proposed position should not be regarded as a nominalist claim, for it has a "substantive dimension".[169] Indeed, it makes it possible to have a better and global understanding of phenomena that scholars have acknowledged as expressing federal features but rarely examined through a federal lens.[170] From her account, one can infer that the key to acknowledging the value of federalism as a unique analytical tool is its global analytical reach. Federalism – and the subsequent application of federal terminology – is presented as a valuable mechanism that not only descriptively but also (normatively and) theoretically connects and brings together,

165 Arato, Andrew, Cohen, Jean and von Busekist, Astrid, "Introduction: Forms of Pluralism and Democratic Constitutionalism", in Arato, Andrew, Cohen, Jean and von Busekist, Astrid (eds.), *Forms of Pluralism and Democratic Constitutionalism* (Columbia University Press, New York-Chichester, 2018), 1–30, at 2.

166 Arato, Cohen and von Busekist, Introduction . . . , 5: "This volume considers four principles of organization deemed alternatives to the sovereign nation-state: federation, subsidiarity, status group legal pluralism, and transnational corporate autonomy".

167 The reason why, despite an ongoing extension of the object of analysis, federal scholarship has underestimated the importance of federalism "all the way down" is explained by Gerken, Federalism All the Way Down . . . , 21–22 and 27–28: "The reason for this neglect is the hold that sovereignty continues to exert on our collective imagination – the sense that federalism is designed to promote exit over voice. . . . Special purpose institutions . . . seem like unlikely sites for thinking about "Our Federalism" to anyone influenced by a sovereignty account".

168 Gerken, Federalism All the Way Down . . . , 21; it may be interesting to note that the approach here advocated by Gerken reconnects her to the Elazarian idea of federalism as having to do with the relationships among the differently institutionalized participants of (social and) political life and to Macdonald's pluralization of the concept of site of federalism.

169 Gerken, Federalism All the Way Down . . . , 25.

170 On this, see Gerken, Federalism All the Way Down . . . , 25; furthermore, on the possibility of extending the federal lens to phenomena that share similar features, see also Gerken, Federalism All the Way Down . . . , 29, quoted previously in the text.

through a common ground, all the elements of today's complex structure of power and power relations.[171]

F. Palermo

Palermo's chapter "Regulating Pluralism: Federalism as Decision-Making and New Challenges for Federal Studies"[172] provided further enrichment of the meta-theoretical approach.[173]

In this writing, the author examined the linkages between federalism and innovative forms of decision-making (mainly participatory and deliberative democracy) and made a strong argument for the renewal of federal studies. In particular, he advocated widening their scope, largely for analytical and practical purposes.

His basic assumption might be summarized as follows. Because federalism is "the most tested tool for institutional pluralism" and "the oldest instrument for dividing and diffusing power", it is consequently "the best-suited instrument to serve as a basis for developing governance theories and practices that meet the requirements of contemporary democratic pluralism".[174]

In keeping with his view, in an increasingly complex reality characterized by a trend towards greater pluralism (especially) in constitutional states, "federalism, with its history and its machinery, could be assessed in order to identify how instruments and procedures for accommodating pluralism and participation could be designed and developed". Therefore, "research on federalism needs to be updated to meet the challenges of contemporary societies" and "it is essential that federal studies accompany and support the challenges of today's pluralism with the appropriate methodological and conceptual background" with this endeavor leading to "anticipating trends, and suggesting tools that can provide meaningful and effective responses to the challenges of pluralism".[175]

Importantly, federalism was explicitly suggested as a "conceptual and institutional matrix for contextualizing, proceduralizing, and regulating new forms of participatory decision-making; thus, for regulating governance in addition to government".[176] The present epoch thereby creates the conditions for federalism "to advance and provide theoretical and practical solutions or at least

171 Gerken, Federalism All the Way Down . . . , 29–30; once more, her account echoes Lépine and Keating's considerations on the usefulness of federalism as an analytical tool.

172 Palermo, Regulating Pluralism . . . , 499–513.

173 In the same vein, see Trettel, Martina, *La democrazia partecipativa negli ordinamenti composti: studio di diritto comparato sull'incidenza della tradizione giuridica nelle democratic innovations* (ESI, Naples, 2020), and especially the last chapter.

174 Palermo, Regulating Pluralism . . . , 506–507.

175 Ibid., 507–508.

176 Ibid., 510.

explanations to the mentioned phenomena [new forms of participatory and democratic decision-making]" for no other tool "has more potential than federalism as a conceptual and practical matrix for providing the answers required by contemporary societies, since federalism is the most consolidated and sophisticated tool for regulating institutional and procedural complexity".[177]

Besides echoing the idea of the federal matrix as a model that can be replicated in various ways, most importantly, the author emphasized the connection between federalism and pluralism, leading to the conceptualization of federalism as a descriptive, analytical, and practical tool for the proceduralization of decision-making in plural contexts. Thus, he underscored how federalism can contribute to the development of theories and practices of pluralism and governance.

Taking it a step further, it could be said that this link between pluralism and federalism results in a relativization of the discussion on autonomy and federal institutions in favor of a major focus on the coordination of powers and, more generally, the different voices embodied in society, institutionalized to a greater or lesser extent. Indeed, one may envision that the strict group dimension of federalism, at least from an analytical and practical perspective, gives way to a pluralistic view of the concept, i.e., to the idea that federalism is relevant whenever numerous interests need to be coordinated and respected in a way that takes as many of them as possible into consideration when it comes to public decision-making processes.[178]

J. Tully

To provide an additional justification for the use of federalism as a wide frame of reference for various practices, Tully's account is, once more, particularly helpful. It illustrates how general concepts should not be considered to be set in stone but as dynamic and multifaceted descriptive and analytical means – which are built through dialogic practices that enrich their content. These then reveal their explanatory function when applied to concrete phenomena that show common aspects.

In his *Strange multiplicity*,[179] the author offered a thorough analysis of the use of general theoretical terms based on Wittgenstein's masterpiece *Philosophical Investigations*.[180] He applied this to constitutionalism, but it can essentially work with every general concept in law as in other disciplines.

177 Ibid., 502.

178 This is a perspective that is also adopted in Arena, Gregorio and Cortese, Fulvio (eds.), *Per governare insieme: il federalismo come metodo: verso nuove forme della democrazia* (CEDAM, Padua, 2011).

179 Tully, James, *Strange Multiplicity: Constitutionalism in an Age of Diversity* (Cambridge University Press, Cambridge, 1995).

180 Wittgenstein, Ludwig, *Philosophiscie Untersuschungen-Philosophical Investigations* (Wiley-Blackwell, Oxford, 2009, orig. 1953), translated by Anscombe, Gertrude E.M., Hacker, Peter M.S. and Schulte, Joachim.

The following quotation reveals the standpoint endorsed in this work:

> even if a theorist could provide a theory which specified the exhaustive conditions for the interpretation and application of the general terms of constitutionalism [federalism] in every case . . . this would not enable us to understand constitutionalism [federalism]. For interpretative disagreements would arise over how to apply and follow the conditions, as indeed they do over the interpretation of the classic and contemporary theories . . . . Rather, understanding a general term is *nothing more than the practical activity of being able to use it in various circumstances*: 'there is a way of grasping a rule which is not an interpretation, but which is exhibited in what we call "obeying the rule" and "going against it" in actual cases'. Such a grasp is not the possession of a theory, but *the manifestation of a repertoire of practical, normative abilities, acquired through long use and practice, to use the term and go against customary use in actual cases*. The uses of general terms, he [Wittgenstein] concludes, are intersubjective 'practices' or 'customs', like tennis or the 'practice' of law. *Our understanding of them consists in the 'mastery' of a 'technique' or practical skill 'exhibited' in being proficient players in the particular cases.*[181]

From this, it is possible to maintain a distinction between defining and understanding, where the latter has the most significant theoretical function as it denotes the ability to apply a general concept in a coherent way to describe analogous phenomena. As further affirmed,

> the way to understand a general term is not to look in vain for implicit rules but, like tennis or law, *to acquire the complex abilities to use it correctly in practice by working through and becoming proficient in various examples until one is able to go on oneself*.[182]

In line with Tully's considerations, federalism can thus be considered here as a frame of reference that is employed to understand and explain the functioning of specific emerging instruments for the accommodation of diversity that share common essential federal elements without the need to specify thoroughly what makes a phenomenon truly federal. It is merely necessary that the concept be used coherently. Accordingly, echoing Lépine, it suffices to illustrate what "symptoms" are present in the analyzed phenomena that justify the use of federal framing or semantics. This way, it becomes possible to classify many phenomena in the federal category so that they can communicate and benefit from this theorization.

181 Tully, Strange Multiplicity . . . , 106 (italics added).
182 Ibid., 108 (italics added).

Federalism and the federal phenomenon: why another definition is not needed and how the concept can be theoretically employed

What the literature review presented previously has made clear is that there is room for federalism to be addressed as a general concept implying a logic or a method through which one may be able to frame and explain the functioning of models of governance that do not correspond to full-fledged federal systems. The previous accounts have revealed the potential of federalism as an explanatory concept for an array of phenomena that are essentially connected by the idea of the diffusion of powers and authority in the same space. Each of the previous accounts establishes a pillar of the theoretical proposal here put forward.

In particular, Lépine's work has revealed that federalism can be employed as a frame of understanding that assimilates numerous practices. This moves away from a strict and normative utilization of the concept in favor of a trans-historical and meta-theoretical use.

Macdonald emphasized the potential pluralization of federal concepts, like fault lines and layers of decentralization. This frees them from their narrow state-related meaning and enlarges their explanatory function.

Palermo insisted that the federal wisdom of rules, procedures, and practical developments has very fruitful theoretical potential and that it is time to consider employing it to understand, explain, and foster the evolution of phenomena characterized by governance-related features.

Gerken drew attention to the variety of *loci* in federalism – which include forms of autonomy as well as self-governance participatory bodies beyond the classic "governmental" autonomy.

Tully explained the dynamic discursive process that leads to creating general concepts and the importance of understanding over defining.

In the end, all the accounts provide a basis that justifies using federal concepts – and, consequently, applying a federal semantic – to frame and explain the functioning of phenomena that do not correspond to the classic governmental organization of power but are mostly characterized by governance features.

Based on the previous considerations, it seems that a federal framing can be employed with regard to phenomena that imply a total or partial diffusion of legal authority/power/autonomy in more than one center, having different degrees of public legal relevance (as a result of recognition or tolerance) in the same legal system. In other words, federalism may be considered as a theoretical frame of reference for all those models that imply the expression of a certain degree of (variously institutionalized) pluralism and autonomy and stay irreducible to its annihilation. Therefore, if all the emergent instruments of the "Law of Diversity" can be read as peculiar forms of autonomous arrangements having a major governance dimension, there seems to be room for them to be analyzed through a federal lens.

To this end, one may perhaps use the concept of federal arrangement to describe the particular features that characterize the analyzed tools. This concept has already been used to describe forms of emerging federal structures that do not correspond to classic ones.[183]

Notably, a federal framing is not intended to describe the truly federal nature of these instruments, which seems inconclusive (and useless), but is the conceptual picklock to productively apply federal wisdom to it. In other words, considering a phenomenon as federal is a way to see it that can provide it with a structured set of tools to understand it better. Such a position has a significant practical advantage,[184] which, in turn, represents a further theoretical justification for its use. Indeed, the main reason why this idea of federalism as a common explanatory ground for various phenomena is supported is its overall usefulness. The rules, the processes, and the dynamics of the most structured federal manifestations – the federal states and federal political systems – can help lay the groundwork for the theoretical and practical development of phenomena that share the same core logic. In this sense, once a phenomenon is framed as (to a certain degree) federal, then it becomes possible to apply the "federal (theoretical and practical) toolbox" to understand and explain it, thus creating room for its further refinement and advancement.

In other words, the functioning of federal systems acts as a "vanilla example" of pluralism and governance at work,[185] i.e., a "simple" model of how a plurality of legal authorities and actors can be organized, how they interact, and how their possible conflicts are regulated.

Federalism and the "Law of Diversity": initial thoughts on the theoretical potential of federalism

This last section aims to propose some preliminary thoughts on the possible use of federalism to frame and explain the emergent models for the accommodation of diversity studied in the previous chapters. This is meant to set the stage for further research on this topic. To this end, some themes related to federal theory and practice will be presented that may contribute to a better understanding of the emergent models for the accommodation of diversity.[186] All seek to provide theoretical instruments and practical solutions to foster the evolution of the emergent models for the accommodation of diversity, which all imply a significant governance dimension.

183 For instance, recently, see Keil and Kropp (eds.), Emerging Federal Structures . . .

184 Palermo, Regulating Pluralism . . . , 502.

185 On federalism as a "vanilla example" of managed pluralism, see Ryan, Erin, "Federalism as Legal Pluralism", in Berman, Paul S. (ed.), *The Oxford Handbook of Global Legal Pluralism* (Oxford University Press, Oxford, 2020), e-book version, 491–527.

186 Several indications are drawn from the considerations put forward by Palermo, Regulating Pluralism . . . , 508–513 and extended in their theoretical scope.

Negotiation and asymmetry: a federal model for the "Law of Diversity"

It has been illustrated that the "Law of Diversity" increasingly relies upon instruments based on promoting an active role for diverse groups in the regulation of diversity, i.e., on their self-management through governance means in the framework of a state legal system.

Concerning the organization of complex legal systems, federal theory, and practice have illustrated the centrality of negotiation and compromise as founding elements as well as working instruments for the successful operation and evolution of composite state structures like federal systems.

Consequently, drawing from federal studies, one may presume the concept of negotiation and its operation will take an ever more central role in the evolution of the "Law of Diversity".

Furthermore, the "Law of Diversity" is marked by a great deal of differentiation of legal solutions. Similarly, federal theory has progressively taken into account the evolution of federal structures and acknowledged a trend toward increasing asymmetry. This has, for several authors, always been, albeit to different extents, a feature of federal systems – especially in what are referred to as "holding-together" federal systems.[187]

In this sense, federal studies may be of help in that they provide structured models to regulate the increasing differentiation of legal arrangements while maintaining the unity of the state and help understand all the concrete issues (like, for instance, the financial aspects related to the management of asymmetric systems) that are at stake when dealing with the creation of differentiated solutions for differentiated claims.

Complex decision-making processes

Federal theory and the actual functioning of federal systems may contribute to analyzing the functioning and promoting solutions for the improvement of complex decision-making processes, such as those that are generated by the emerging instruments for the accommodation of diversity. Indeed, all the cases studied in Chapter 4 determine the addition of new layers of governance that continuously and variously interact with different public entities in complex settings. In particular, several of them imply the existence of variously institutionalized self-governance bodies that do not act dissimilarly to traditional governmental or administrative bodies.

In this sense, the variety of the actors and the manifold dynamics that arise from these developments create a complex and intricate system of multilevel

187 Several reasons account for the increasing differentiation in federal organization; on this, see Palermo and Kössler, Comparative federalism . . . , 34–66; Palermo, Francesco, "Asimmetria come forma e formante dei sistemi composti", 2 *Le istituzioni del federalismo* (2018), 255–271; on asymmetry as a feature of multi-tiered systems, and especially the European Union and multinational systems, see also Keating, Michael, "Asymmetrical Government: Multinational States in an Integrating Europe", 29(1) *Publius* (1999), 71–86.

decision-making that may benefit if lessons are drawn from federal studies. The latter could inspire possible further regulation in this area or at least facilitate an understanding of trends in the accommodation of diversity. Indeed, as is evident in federal systems, traditional decision-making processes based on democratic institutions are increasingly complemented by the contribution of various types of governmental, administrative, or hybrid bodies. This is also the case with the "Law of Diversity".

Hence, given that federal theory has traditionally revolved around institutional analysis and intergovernmental cooperation, the rules and mechanisms that have been developed in and for federal systems – aimed at fostering coordination among various authorities – may contribute to identifying dynamics and designing solutions to the problematic issues that can arise in the area of diversity accommodation.

Definition of areas of jurisdiction in complex policy areas: coordination over division

Some recent publications on the functioning of federal systems have moved their focus to the issue of policy analysis from a legal perspective, studying the numerous actors involved in critical areas of regulation – like environment, security, immigration, and fiscal federalism – and their relationships.[188] Accordingly, they have underscored how the reality of policymaking is far more multifaceted and composite than that provided for by constitutional texts that allocate powers to different levels of government.

In a way, the "Law of Diversity" may be seen as another complex policy area,[189] where – especially when it comes to the most recent developments and instruments – a vast array of actors is involved in manifold ways. Thus, an analysis of the operation of federal systems and their trends, such as, for instance, the move towards coordination rather than separation of powers – which reached its peak during the recent coronavirus crisis – offers useful insights for the evolution of the "Law of Diversity" and its governance means. Accordingly, it seems that the more complex and broader (also from a strictly territorial standpoint) the area of management, the greater the need for coordination among the numerous actors involved.[190]

188 For instance, see Palermo and Kössler, Comparative federalism . . . and Palermo and Alber (eds.), Federalism as Decision-Making . . .

189 Palermo, Francesco and Woelk, Jens, "From Minority Protection to a Law of Diversity", 3 *European Yearbook of Minority Issues* (2003–2004), 5–13, at 7.

190 In this sense, coordination may not be limited to the boundaries of the state but also implies a strong role for trans-border cooperation (as well as, as seen, international bodies), especially when it comes to the accommodation of diversity. On the increasing role of trans-border cooperation and the consequent regulation stemming from it, which is emerging as a new independent supra-national area of law, see Palermo, Francesco, "The 'New Nomos' of Cross-Border Cooperation", in Palermo, Francesco, Poggeschi, Giovanni and Woelk, Jens (eds.), *Globalization, Technologies and Legal Revolution: The Impact of Global Changes on Territorial and Cultural Diversities on Supranational Integration and Constitutional Theory* (Nomos, Baden-Baden, 2012), 71–90.

Conflicts of jurisdictions: Trends and tools for their resolution

The approaches of federal systems towards possible conflicts of jurisdiction among different authorities and the tools developed for their resolution are another area that can provide interesting insights to explain and possibly further regulate the emergent instruments for the accommodation of diversity.

In this sense, two main issues arise. The first is a trend in federal systems towards the creation of increasing *loci* and mechanisms of dialogue and coordination among different authorities, especially after the coronavirus crisis.[191] The second is the critical role played by the judiciary when the mechanisms of coordination do not work. Both issues may help analyze the recent developments in the "Law of Diversity": one should expect that the complex systems of governance stemming from its recent evolution would need to foster the creation of stable dialogic and cooperative mechanisms to help the collaborative management of diversity accommodation. If they are not implemented, one should expect an increase in jurisdictional conflict.

Bibliography

Arato, Andrew, Cohen, Jean and von Busekist, Astrid, "Introduction: Forms of Pluralism and Democratic Constitutionalism", in Arato, Andrew, Cohen, Jean and von Busekist, Astrid (eds.), *Forms of Pluralism and Democratic Constitutionalism* (Columbia University Press, New York-Chichester, 2018), 1–30

Arena, Gregorio and Cortese, Fulvio (eds.), *Per governare insieme: il federalismo come metodo: verso nuove forme della democrazia* (CEDAM, Padua, 2011)

Aroney, Nicolas, "The Federal Condition: Towards a Normative Theory", 61(1) *The American Journal of Jurisprudence* (2016), 13–31

Bermann, George A., "Taking Subsidiarity Seriously: Federalism in the European Community and the United States", 94(2) *Columbia Law Review* (1994), 331–456

Berman, Paul S., *Global Legal Pluralism: A Jurisprudence of Law Beyond Borders* (Cambridge University Press, New York, 2012)

Burgess, Michael, *Comparative Federalism: Theory and Practice* (Routledge, London-New York, 2006)

Burgess, Michael, *In Search of the Federal Spirit* (Oxford University Press, Oxford, 2012)

Caporaso, James A., "The European Union and Forms of State", 34(1) *Journal of Common Market Studies* (1996), 29–52

Carrozza, Paolo, "I rapporti centro-periferia: federalismi, regionalismi e autonomie", in Carrozza, Paolo, Di Giovine, Alfonso and Ferrari, Giuseppe F. (eds.), *Diritto costituzionale comparato* (Laterza, Rome-Bari, 2019), 894–951

Chattopadhyay, Rupak, Knüpling, Felix, Chebenova, Diana, Whittington, Liam and Gonzalez, Phillip (eds.), *Federalism and the Response to COVID-19* (Routledge, London-New York, 2022)

Davis, Rufus, *The Federal Principle: A Journey Through Time in Quest of a Meaning* (University of California Press, Berkeley-Los Angeles-London, 1978)

191 On this, see Steytler, Nico (ed.), *Comparative Federalism and Covid-19: Combating the Pandemic* (Routledge, London-New York, 2021); Chattopadhyay, Rupak, Knüpling, Felix, Chebenova, Diana, Whittington, Liam and Gonzalez, Phillip (eds.), *Federalism and the Response to COVID-19* (Routledge, London-New York, 2022).

Elazar, Daniel J., *Exploring Federalism* (The University of Alabama Press, Tuscaloosa, 1987)

Elazar, Daniel J., "From Statism to Federalism: A Paradigm Shift", 17(4) *International Political Science Review / Revue internationale de science politique* (1996), 417–429

Elazar, Daniel J., "The State System + Globalization (Economic plus Human Rights) = Federalism (State Federations plus Regional Confederations)", 40(3) *South Texas Law Review* (1999), 555–566

Friedrich, Carl J., "Federal Constitutional Theory and Emergent Proposals", in Macmahon, Arthur (ed.), *Federalism. Mature and Emergent* (Russell&Russell, New York, 1962), 510–533

Friedrich, Carl J., *Trends of Federalism in Theory and Practice* (Pall Mall Press, London, 1968)

Gamper, Anna, "A 'Global Theory of Federalism': The Nature and Challenges of a Federal State", 6(10) *The German Law Journal* (2005), 1297–1318

Gaudreault-DesBiens, Jean-F., "Towards a Deontic Axiomatic Theory of Federal Adjudication", in Lev, Amnon (ed.), *The Federal Idea* (Hart Publishing, Oxford-Portland, 2017), 75–103

Gaudreault-DesBiens, Jean-F. and Gélinas, Fabien, "Opening New Perspectives on Federalism", in Gaudreault-DesBiens, Jean-F. and Gélinas, Fabien (eds.), *Le fédéralisme dans tous ses états: gouvernance, identité et méthodologie – The States and Moods of Federalism: Governance, Identity and Methodology* (Éditions Yvon Blais-Bruylant, Cowansville-Bruxelles, 2005), 51–96

Gerken, Heather K., "Federalism All the Way Down", 124(1) *Harvard Law Review* (2010), 4–74

Halberstam, Daniel, "Federalism: Theory, Policy, Law", in Rosenfeld, Michel and Sajó, András (eds.), *The Oxford Handbook of Comparative Constitutional Law* (Oxford University Press, Oxford, 2012), 576–608

Hamilton, Alexander, "Federalist No. 28", in Rossiter, Clinton (ed.), *The Federalist Papers* (The New American Library, New York, 1961), 178–182

Hartley, Trevor C., "Federalism, Courts and Legal Systems: The Emerging Constitution of the European Community", 34(2) *American Journal of Comparative Law* (1986), 229–247

Hay, Peter, *Federalism and Supranational Organizations: Patterns for New Legal Structures* (University of Illinois Press, Urbana-London, 1966)

Hay, Peter, "Supremacy of Community Law in National Courts: A Progress Report on Referrals Under the EEC Treaty", 16(4) *American Journal of Comparative Law* (1968), 524–551

Hirschl, Ran, *Comparative Matters: The Renaissance of Comparative Constitutional Law* (Oxford University Press, Oxford, 2014)

Hooghe, Liesbet and Marks, Gary, "Unravelling the Central State, But How? Types of Multi-level Governance", 97(2) *American Political Science Review* (2003), 233–243

Hueglin, Thomas O., *Early Modern Concepts for a Late Modern World: Althusius on Community and Federalism* (Wilfried Laurier University Press, Waterloo, 1999)

Hueglin, Thomas O., "Johannes Althusius: Medieval Constitutionalist or Modern Federalist?", 9(4) *Publius* (1979), 9–41

Karmis, Dimitrios and Norman, Wayne, "The Revival of Federalism in Normative Political Theory", in Karmis, Dimitrios and Norman, Wayne (eds.), *Theories of Federalism: A Reader* (Palgrave Macmillan, Basingstoke-New York, 2005), 3–21

Keating, Michael, "Asymmetrical Government: Multinational States in an Integrating Europe", 29(1) *Publius* (1999), 71–86

Keating, Michael, "Europe as a Multilevel Federation", 24(4) *Journal of European Public Policy* (2017), 615–632

Keil, Soeren and Alber, Elisabeth (eds.), *Federalism as a Tool of Conflict Resolution* (Routledge, London-New York, 2021)

Keil, Soeren and Kropp, Sabine (eds.), *Emerging Federal Structures in the Post-Cold War Era* (Palgrave Macmillan, Cham, 2022)

King, Preston, *Federalism and Federation* (John Hopkins University Press-Croom Helm, Baltimore-London, 1982)

La Pergola, Antonio, "L'empirismo nello studio dei sistemi federali: a proposito di una teoria di Carl Friedrich", in La Pergola, Antonio (ed.), *Tecniche costituzionali e problemi delle autonomie garantite: riflessioni comparatistiche sul federalismo e regionalismo* (CEDAM, Padua, 1987), 123–182

Lenaerts, Koen, "Constitutionalism and the Many Faces of Federalism", 38(2) *The American Journal of Comparative Law* (1990), 205–263

Lépine, Frédéric, "A Journey through the History of Federalism: Is Multilevel Governance a Form of Federalism?", 363(1) *L'Europe en formation* (2012), 21–62

Lépine, Frédéric, "Federalism: Essence, Values and Ideologies", in Gagnon, Alain-G., Keil, Soeren and Mueller, Sean (eds.), *Understanding Federalism and Federation* (Ashgate, Farnham-Burlington, 2015), 31–34

Livingston, William S., "A Note on the Nature of Federalism", 67(1) *Political Science Quarterly* (1952), 81–95

Lombardi, Giorgio, "Spazio e frontiera tra eguaglianza e privilegio: problemi costituzionali fra storia e diritto", 1 *Diritto e società* (1985), 477–495

Macdonald, Roderick A., "Kaleidoscopic Federalism", in Gaudreault-DesBiens, Jean-F. and Gélinas, Fabien (eds.), *Le fédéralisme dans tous ses états: governance, identité et méthodologie – The States and Moods of Federalism: Governance, Identity and Methodology* (Éditions Yvon Blais-Bruylant, Cowansville-Bruxelles, 2005), 261–284

Macdonald, Roderick A., "Legal Republicanism and Legal Pluralism: Two Takes on Identity and Diversity", in Bussani, Mauro and Graziadei, Michele (eds.), *Human Diversity and the Law: La diversité humaine et le droit* (Stämpfli-Bruylant-Sakkoulas, Berne-Brussels-Athens, 2005), 43–70

Martinico, Giuseppe, "Comparative Legal Studies and European Integration: Looking at the Origins of the Debate", 41(122) *Boletín Mexicano de Derecho Comparado* (2008), 859–883

Martinico, Giuseppe, "The Federal Language and the European Integration Process: The European Communities Viewed from the US", 53(3) *Politique Européenne* (2016), 38–59

Messarra, Antoine, "Principe de territorialité et principe de personnalité en fédéralisme comparé: le cas du Liban et perspectives actuelles pour la gestion du pluralisme", in Gaudreault-DesBiens, Jean-F. and Gélinas, Fabien (eds.), *Le fédéralisme dans tous ses états: governance, identité et méthodologie – The States and Moods of Federalism: Governance, Identity and Methodology* (Éditions Yvon Blais-Bruylant, Cowansville-Bruxelles, 2005), 227–260

Neo, Jacklyn L., "State Legal Pluralism and Religious Courts: Semi-Autonomy and Jurisdictional Allocations in Pluri-Legal Arrangements", in Berman, Paul S. (ed.), *The Oxford Handbook of Global Legal Pluralism* (Oxford University Press, Oxford, 2020), e-book version, 1628–1668

Palermo, Francesco, "The 'New Nomos' of Cross-Border Cooperation", in Palermo, Francesco, Poggeschi, Giovanni and Woelk, Jens (eds.), *Globalization, Technologies and Legal Revolution: The Impact of Global Changes on Territorial and Cultural Diversities on Supranational Integration and Constitutional Theory* (Nomos, Baden-Baden, 2012), 71–90

Palermo, Francesco, "Regulating Pluralism: Federalism as Decision-Making and New Challenges for Federal Studies", in Palermo, Francesco and Alber, Elisabeth (eds.), *Federalism as Decision-Making: Changes in Structures, Procedures and Policies* (Brill-Nijhoff, Leiden-Boston, 2015), 499–513

Palermo, Francesco, "Asimmetria come forma e formante dei sistemi composti", 2 *Le istituzioni del federalismo* (2018), 255–271

Palermo, Francesco and Kössler, Karl, *Comparative Federalism: Constitutional Arrangements and Case Law* (Hart Publishing, Oxford-Portland, 2019)

Palermo, Francesco and Woelk, Jens, "From Minority Protection to a Law of Diversity", 3 *European Yearbook of Minority Issues* (2003–2004), 5–13

Popelier, Patricia, *Dynamic Federalism: A New Theory for Cohesion and Regional Autonomy* (Routledge, London-New York, 2021)

Riker, William H., *Federalism: Origin, Operation, Significance* (Little, Brown & Company, Boston, 1964)

Riker, William H., "Six Books in Search of a Subject or Does Federalism Exist and Does It Matter?", 2(1) *Comparative Politics* (1969), 135–146

Ryan, Erin, "Federalism as Legal Pluralism", in Berman, Paul S. (ed.), *The Oxford Handbook of Global Legal Pluralism* (Oxford University Press, Oxford, 2020), e-book version, 491–527

Sahadžić, Maja, *Asymmetry, Multinationalism and Constitutional Law: Managing Legitimacy and Stability in Federalist States* (Routledge, London-New York, 2021)

Shapiro, Robert A., *Polyphonic Federalism: Toward the Protection of Fundamental Rights* (The University of Chicago Press, Chicago-London, 2009)

Stein, Eric, "Lawyers, Judges and the Making of a Transnational Constitution", 75(1) *American Journal of International Law* (1981), 1–27

Stepan, Alfred, "Federalism and Democracy: Beyond the U.S. Model", in Karmis, Dimitrios and Norman, Wayne (eds.), *Theories of Federalism: A Reader* (Palgrave Macmillan, New-York-Basingstoke, 2005), 255–268

Steytler, Nico (ed.), *Comparative Federalism and Covid-19: Combating the Pandemic* (Routledge, London-New York, 2021)

Tierney, Stephen, "Federalism and Constitutional Theory", in Jacobsohn, Gary and Schor, Miguel (eds.), *Comparative Constitutional Theory* (Edward Elgar, Cheltenham-Northampton, 2018), 45–66

Tierney, Stephen, *The Federal Contract: A Constitutional Theory of Federalism* (Oxford University Press, Oxford, 2022)

Trettel, Martina, *La democrazia partecipativa negli ordinamenti composti: studio di diritto comparato sull'incidenza della tradizione giuridica nelle democratic innovations* (ESI, Naples, 2020)

Tully, James, *Strange Multiplicity: Constitutionalism in an Age of Diversity* (Cambridge University Press, Cambridge, 1995)

Watts, Ronald L., *Comparing Federal Systems* (McGill-Queen's University Press, Montréal, 3rd ed., 2008)

Weiler, Joseph H.H., "The Transformation of Europe", 100(8) *The Yale Law Journal* (1991), 2403–2483

Wheare, Kenneth C., *Federal Government* (Oxford University Press, London, 4th ed., 1963)

Wittgenstein, Ludwig, *Philosophiscie Untersuschungen-Philosophical Investigations* (Wiley-Blackwell, Oxford, 2009, orig. 1953), translated by Anscombe, Gertrude E.M., Hacker, Peter M.S. and Schulte, Joachim

Zoller, Elisabeth, "Aspects internationaux du droit constitutionnel: Contribution à la théorie de la fédération d'Etats", 294 *Collected Courses of the Hague Academy of International Law* (2002), 39–166

Conclusions

The path of the study

A global comparative perspective unveils the variety of legal responses to diversity within the constitutional tradition(s)

These final pages will be devoted to weaving together the threads of this study and highlighting its main achievements.

The first aim of this work was to illustrate the vitality of law regarding the management of diversity, both in terms of constitutional approaches and legal instruments put in place in different areas of the world.

Such vitality has revealed that the accommodation of diversity is a multi-faceted legal phenomenon, of which the mainstream practical and theoretical perspective is just one – though doubtlessly significant – dimension.

The latter is tied to the evolution of the treatment of diversity in the Global North and the liberal-democratic tradition.[1] It relies on a rigid distinction between non-discrimination and minority rights' addressees, on the concept of minority (and indigenous peoples) as a homogenous group having specific and "natural" ethno-cultural features that justify differential treatments beyond non-discrimination, on the minority-majority discourse, and on the centrality of rights as the key protective instrument and central discursive-theoretical framing in this area.[2]

Yet, in parallel to the most consolidated tools, the book has also emphasized the existence and theoretical significance of constitutional approaches and legal instruments that complement them within and outside the liberal-constitutional tradition.

First, the South American and Southeast Asian regions host legal systems that have incorporated diversity at the very core of their constitutional structures.[3] The case models of Bolivia and Ecuador represent the most innovative approaches of the South American continent. These add to the global

1 See Chapters 1 and 2.
2 On this, see Chapter 5.
3 See the analysis in Chapter 3.

DOI: 10.4324/9781003493518-8

discourse over diversity accommodation through the establishment of constitutional systems that affirm and variously implement the principles of plurinationality and interculturalism, thus acknowledging the composite nature of their societies. Singapore has been chosen as an example to illustrate the innovations in Southeast Asia, where pluralism is not only a societal reality but also a basic constitutional principle in several countries. Pluralism, pragmatism, flexibility, persuasion, and governance mechanisms over rights attribution are the pillars of its rather government-directed system, which constitutes an interesting alternative to liberal-democratic perspectives to constitutionalism and diversity accommodation.

Secondly, the study has shown how the Global North itself is experiencing notable developments in this area. From a macro-perspective, European international law has tried to update its contents to respond to the challenges that contemporary times pose, especially in European societies. It has done so by proposing a renovated concept of integration and encouraging states to shift their focus from (selected ethno-cultural) minorities to the regulation of diversity as a global societal phenomenon.[4]

Moreover, at the micro-level, several forms of what has been referred to as emergent instruments have been analyzed, all potentially representing very inclusive and flexible forms of accommodation of diversity that heavily rely on bottom-up action and governance means rather than the logic of rights attribution.[5] Notably, their structure makes them particularly conducive to the renewed idea of integration that emerges from the European documents.

Recognizing these developments means validating them from a theoretical standpoint. Though this may be difficult – as it requires moving away from reassuring categories and approaches – recognizing the theoretical dignity of these phenomena creates the conditions for them to be further studied and both their successes and shortcomings assessed.

Especially regarding the emerging instruments, theoretical recognition, and framing appear fundamental. They help the legal scholar to develop a comprehensive grasp of this area of law and how it advances and continuously recalibrates his or her analysis as well as theoretical assumptions based on this. In addition, recognition and validation serve practical functions, as they contribute to defining and classifying legal tools that may help practitioners when looking for practical solutions to diversity issues.

Main theoretical proposals and contributions

This brings the conclusions to the synthesis of the main theoretical contributions – presented in Chapters 5 and 6 – that emerge from the updated state of the art of this area of law provided by the first four chapters.

4 On the European developments, see Chapter 3.

5 On this, see Chapter 4.

What appears to be clear from this study is that the accommodation of diversity is a multifarious legal phenomenon that takes place at several levels.[6] Such complexity requires systematization and a theoretical appraisal based on the relativization of the consolidated mainstream standpoint. Without this, several legal phenomena here analyzed would be overlooked.

This is the main reason that underlies the introduction of the concept "Law of Diversity". This notion is meant to overcome the theoretical limitations one encounters when studying this area of law through the lens of minority (and indigenous peoples') rights categories. The "Law of Diversity" offers the scholar and the practitioner an enabling instrument to comprehensively address the complex legal phenomenon of diversity accommodation and its manifold manifestations within various constitutional traditions.

Furthermore, the classification of instruments and models that follows from the unified perspective offered by the "Law of Diversity" unveils the logic and functioning of the instruments for the accommodation of diversity as well as their evolution alongside societal and constitutional developments. This, once more, is useful for (especially comparative) scholars and practitioners. The former are encouraged by this conceptual tool to extend their perspectives of comparison, which may lead to further reciprocal communication and learning among models in this area. The latter can benefit from a comprehensive classification of models that explains their evolution and process of refinement depending on different societal conditions and constitutional settings.

Complementary to the introduction of the "Law of Diversity" is the meta-theoretical employment of federalism, proposed to frame the emergent instruments for the accommodation of diversity in the Global North, which appear to be the most in need of theoretical recognition, validation, and explanation. As all the instruments analyzed imply forms of decentralization of authority that increase the expression of pluralism and diversity, the connection to federalism as a multifaceted phenomenon that implies the diffusion

6 Palermo, Francesco and Woelk, Jens, "From Minority Protection to a Law of Diversity? Reflections on the Evolution of Minority Rights", 3 *European Yearbook of Minority Issues* (2003–2004), 5–13, at 9, have proposed the "Law of Diversity" as a renewed approach to the issue of minority rights, suggesting that "more sophisticated instruments are needed for realizing the greatest possible expression of each of the different interests at stake in the concrete case, especially in the complex system of multilevel governance in Europe. These instruments shall avoid the domination of one position over the other and guarantee the necessary – permanent but never stable – balance between equality and difference, protection and living together, rights and obligations, autonomy and integration. Due to the continuous need for readjustment, the positions as well as the instruments – including the balances which the latter represent – can never be considered as established once and for all". What the present work has attempted to demonstrate is that the evolution of the instruments and models for the accommodation of diversity predicted by the authors is taking place, and several features of the emergent models and instruments for the accommodation of diversity confirm their outlook.

of powers is, first of all, intuitive.[7] The literature review offered in Chapter 6 has further demonstrated that, besides this intuition, federalism may be seen as a frame of understanding for manifold phenomena of governance (and, especially, for the emergent self-empowered forms analyzed in Chapter 4). Ultimately, these entail the reproduction of the same core logic. Consequently, if federalism is imagined as a meta-theoretical frame so that the phenomena analyzed can be defined as expressing federal features, then one can make use of federal theory and practice to understand and explain them.[8] Given that the emergent tools are undertheorized and still in the process of consolidation, the lens of federal theory – which embeds the most structured set of rules and principles concerning the management of composite legal systems – and federal practice – which shows the evolution and trends of federal systems as "vanilla examples" of the management of pluralism – hold clear potential.[9]

Federalism and the "Law of Diversity": in search of appropriate concepts for contemporary times

What the analysis conducted in this study has attempted to demonstrate is that the time is ripe to complement established categories and approaches of public law to apprehend the complexity of the legal phenomenon (in general as well as) in the area of diversity accommodation.

The introduction of the concept "Law of Diversity" and the meta-theoretical reconsideration of federalism have been put forward as tools for navigating a reality that is complex and multifaceted, where consolidated categories may benefit from being supplemented by new enabling semantics. Without this, this area of law may only be described and studied from a partial standpoint that cannot completely explain how diversity is concretely accommodated beyond top-down public law regulations and structures.

The complexification of human life and organization – which goes along with significant technological developments in the era of information – appears to be a transversal phenomenon that, albeit to different

7 Trettel, Martina, *La democrazia partecipativa negli ordinamenti composti: studio di diritto comparato sull'incidenza della tradizione giuridica nelle* democratic innovations (ESI, Naples, 2020), 232–233; also, see Sonnicksen, Jared, "Federalism and Democracy: A Tense Relationship", in Tudela, José, Kölling, Mario and Reviriego, Fernando (eds.), *Calidad democrática y organización territorial* (Marcial Pons, Madrid-Barcelona-Buenos Aires-São Paulo, 2018), 29–50, at 30: the author underlined the existing "long tradition in political thought of linking federalism and other forms of non-centralism with separation of powers that reinforces rule of the people".

8 Similar proposals have been advanced, as regard democratic innovations, by Trettel, La democrazia partecipativa . . . , 234; see also Palermo, Francesco, "Regulating Pluralism: Federalism as Decision-Making and New Challenges for Federal Studies", in Palermo, Francesco and Alber, Elisabeth (eds.), *Federalism as Decision-Making: Changes in Structures, Procedures and Policies* (Brill-Nijhoff, Leiden-Boston, 2015), 499–513.

9 Ryan, Erin, "Federalism as Legal Pluralism", in Berman, Paul S. (ed.), *The Oxford Handbook of Global Legal Pluralism* (Oxford University Press, Oxford, 2020), e-book version, 491–527.

extents, touches both public law and state organization. From a global perspective, this phenomenon has been described as the emerging paradigm of connection. This increasingly complements forms of human organization tied to the paradigm of homogeneity, which has characterized the modern epoch.[10] The latter originates from and is tied to the Industrial Revolution and represents an era that is informed by the idea of uniformity. Homogeneity and uniformity indeed define every human activity and endeavor, along with state organization and (constitutional) legal systems' principles.[11] The information revolution has been considered the turning point that led to the emergence of the paradigm of connection and the economic and technological transformation that informs the contemporary era. The emergence of the paradigm of connection engenders drastic changes in human life, as it brings the acceptance and interiorization of a great deal of complexity in social and economic activities, as well as in the functioning of legal systems and their instruments.[12]

The present book has attempted to illustrate that, in parallel to these global dynamics, similar developments are affecting the area of interest of this work, where one can observe the concurrence of emerging "plural" and more established "national" paradigms. Concretely, the plural paradigm brings in innovative constitutional concepts and legal instruments. Above all, it implies the rise of governance forms of organizations parallel to the existing and still central public institutions.[13] The previous chapters have shown that governance systems play quite a considerable role as an emerging instrument for the accommodation of diversity – be they manifestations of innovative constitutional principles or forms of bottom-up empowerment.

Hence, against these innovations and complexity, legal theory is called on to maintain its explanatory function. To do so, it is expected to undergo a process of complexification in parallel to those that characterize the legal phenomenon in this area. After all, what the theoretical proposal aims to advance is that legal theory needs updating if it is to remain capable of explaining the evolution of societal and political structures in this area of law. While the state is still undeniably the dominant political structure and the main playing field of constitutionalism and public law,[14] it operates in an increasingly variegated and complex global setting. Several constitutional

10 See Ortino, Sergio, *La struttura delle rivoluzioni economiche* (Cacucci, Bari, 2010), 399–414 and 558–585.

11 Ortino, La struttura . . . , 381–395 and 551–557.

12 Ortino, Ibid., 399–414 and 558–585.

13 On this, see Ortino, La struttura . . .; also, see Morçöl, Göktuğ, *Complex Governance Networks: Foundational Concepts and Practical Implications* (Routledge, London-New York, 2023).

14 Tierney, Stephen, *The Federal Contract: A Constitutional Theory of Federalism* (Oxford University Press, Oxford, 2022), 291–292.

approaches now concur, and a vast range of authorities complement state action from above and below (and aside). Consequently, on the one hand, the liberal-democratic theory of the state and constitutionalism, and the correlated established theoretical categories, retain their fundamental function. However, on the other, if one aspires to have a realistic grasp on the operation of the legal phenomenon in this area (and others), the consolidated categories risk being a limited standpoint, which is why they may need a qualitative leap or an integration.

Furthermore, it seems critical that legal scholars consider those phenomena and add their specific perspectives to those of other disciplines. The public law scholar's standpoint provides a crucial insight into the analysis of governance models since it focuses on their relationships with the structures of representative government and decision-making as provided for by the constitutional framework.[15] Besides reconnecting the legal ideal reality to the concrete operation of legal systems, the systematization of governance within public law theory – for instance, by studying its relationships with the content of constitutional principles, by complementing traditional approaches that heavily rely on the constitutional distribution of powers among state and substate institutions to explain the dynamics of public activity, and by providing solutions for the design of governance procedures to ensure their transparency and legitimacy – can arguably offer a fruitful explanatory standpoint as well as advance evolutionary proposals to address its possible further regulation.[16]

The theoretical proposals in this work aim to lay the foundations for the increased involvement of legal scholars regarding the analysis of these phenomena. The "Law of Diversity" enables the observer to include in his or her examination a multifaceted array of emerging instruments for the accommodation of diversity that have significance in public law. Meanwhile, federalism and federal theory may allow for a better understanding of how they work, as well as how they can evolve and be further developed.

In other words, this book, in light of the updated overview provided of this area, has proposed a revision of diversity accommodation and federalism's conceptual categories to provide them with more complex, less straightforward, and more theoretically productive content, is in line with the complexity

15 On this, see Ferrarese, Maria R., *La governance tra politica e diritto* (Il Mulino, Bologna, 2010); *Id.*, "Governance: A Soft Revolution with Hard Political and Legal Effects", 1(1) *Soft Power* (2014), 35–56.

16 On the need to reconcile the phenomenon of governance and legal theory (that also presents counterarguments based on a more formal reading of law), see Dani, Marco and Palermo, Francesco, "Della governance e di altri demoni (un dialogo)", 4 *Quaderni costituzionali* (2003), 785–794; a study that follows the proposed perspective is Arienzo, Alessandro and Scamardella, Francesca (eds.), *La governance tra legittimazione e vulnerabilità* (Guida editori, Naples, 2020).

marking this epoch.[17] This has meant adding a plural reconceptualization of classic and nation-state-oriented concepts (following what has been called mono- and multi-national paradigms). As seen, as concerns diversity accommodation, such a theoretical operation requires that one departs from exclusively framing this area of law in terms of minority-related concepts to include in the analysis of emergent and less institutionalized models. As for federalism, it implies that one considers its explanatory potential for governance-like phenomena of diffusion of powers, as framing the latter in federal terms is supposed to make it possible to understand them better, explain them, and formulate hypotheses about their development.

As a result, following the proposed perspective, one would notice that federalism and the "Law of Diversity" have deeper connections than those generally studied and theorized (i.e., territorial autonomy and federalism for localized minorities). In other words, traditionally, federalism and the "Law of Diversity" (in the form of minority and indigenous peoples' rights law) have been deemed theoretically separate islands, only occasionally connected. By contrast, the theoretical reconsideration of both unveils deep-rooted relationships. As a result, they can be seen as part of an archipelago, their connections being structural and deep, as increasingly apparent in contemporary times. More evident convergence and overlaps between the revised notions of federalism and the "Law of Diversity" are, therefore, observable since they both increasingly refer, in their plural reconsideration, to the concepts of governance and pluralism. The latter might consequently be regarded as the common theoretical ground for the mentioned areas of research, the stretches of sand that bridge supposedly isolated islands below the surface of the water.

Putting this alleged deep connection into operation may be a critical challenge in years to come, as it improves the understanding of phenomena that are increasingly taking place and contributes to their theoretical framing and consequent progress.

Limitations of the study and points in need of further research

To conclude, it is finally necessary to provide an assessment of the limitations of the work, the possible problems, and the points that may need further research.

First, although the book takes a global perspective, it cannot cover all the diversity accommodation in the world, and many aspects and regions have not been included in the analysis. It might be suggested that other regions or

17 On the need for a qualitative leap in federal studies, see Palermo, Regulating Pluralism . . . , 499–513; as concerns the epistemological limitations of a "minority rights theoretical lens", see Gaudreault-DesBiens, Jean-F., "Introduction to Part II", in Foblets, Marie-Claire, Gaudreault-DesBiens, Jean-F. and Dundes Relteln, Alison (eds.), *Cultural Diversity and the Law: State Responses Around the World* (Bruylant-Yvon-Blais, Bruxelles-Montréal, 2010), 367–380.

countries in the world present innovative models of diversity accommodation that complement the most consolidated ones. For instance, India and South Africa, or Lebanon, have not been thoroughly addressed despite their unequivocally fascinating approaches to diversity management. While this holds true, it should also be said that the selection of the areas of the world and the emergent models was consistent with the specific focus of the analysis, i.e., the most innovative or emergent comprehensive traditions and instruments, and an attempt was made to justify every choice.

Secondly, the work has dealt with several concepts that involve significant definitional hurdles and has deliberately left some of them unresolved. This is the case with the concept of diversity, which is taken as a term encompassing every human differential aspect, be it ethno-cultural or not. Likewise, federalism is only loosely defined, and its framing may be criticized as an instance of conceptual stretching. The reason why these concepts are not defined in detail lies in the fact that their usefulness for the theoretical aims of the work specifically relies on their broad conception. Indeed, the main theoretical goal of the work is not to normatively prescribe how and why different types of diversity should be accorded different treatments – but to open up the study of this area of law with specific regard to the most advanced and potentially inclusive existing instruments. Nor was the intention to define what true federalism is. Rather, it has been used as a way of looking at emergent governance-like phenomena and, consequently, apply principles and rules to them that may be of use for their development. Hence, these concepts have been employed as tools that create the theoretical conditions to capture and understand this evolving area of law. In other words, both terms are theoretical picklocks. Their precise definition is not sought, as diversity serves the function of broadening the scope of observation and avoiding epistemological limitations, while a federal framing allows for consideration of federal theory as a repository of wisdom for better understanding some of the models described in Chapter 4.

The last point concerns the limitations regarding the connections between federalism and the "Law of Diversity", which are only sketched at the end of Chapter 6. This issue will certainly need more time and research to be fully explored. For the time being, the main aim was to underscore the feasibility of this theoretical proposal. Hopefully, further research will be dedicated to this issue, using this work as a starting point.

Bibliography

Arienzo, Alessandro and Scamardella, Francesca (eds.), *La governance tra legittimazione e vulnerabilità* (Guida editori, Naples, 2020)

Dani, Marco and Palermo, Francesco, "Della governance e di altri demoni (un dialogo)", 4 *Quaderni costituzionali* (2003), 785–794

Ferrarese, Maria R., "Governance: A Soft Revolution with Hard Political and Legal Effects", 1(1) *Soft Power* (2014), 35–56

Ferrarese, Maria R., *La governance tra politica e diritto* (Il Mulino, Bologna, 2010)

Gaudreault-DesBiens, Jean-F., "Introduction to Part II", in Foblets, Marie-Claire, Gaudreault-DesBiens, Jean-F. and Dundes Relteln, Alison (eds.), *Cultural*

Diversity and the Law: State Responses Around the World (Bruylant-Yvon-Blais, Bruxelles-Montréal, 2010), 367–380

Morçöl, Göktuğ, *Complex Governance Networks: Foundational Concepts and Practical Implications* (Routledge, London-New York, 2023)

Ortino, Sergio, *La struttura delle rivoluzioni economiche* (Cacucci, Bari, 2010)

Palermo, Francesco, "Regulating Pluralism: Federalism as Decision-Making and New Challenges for Federal Studies", in Palermo, Francesco and Alber, Elisabeth (eds.), *Federalism as Decision-Making: Changes in Structures, Procedures and Policies* (Brill-Nijhoff, Leiden-Boston, 2015), 499–513

Palermo, Francesco and Woelk, Jens, "From Minority Protection to a Law of Diversity? Reflections on the Evolution of Minority Rights", 3 *European Yearbook of Minority Issues* (2003–2004), 5–13

Ryan, Erin, "Federalism as Legal Pluralism", in Berman, Paul S. (ed.), *The Oxford Handbook of Global Legal Pluralism* (Oxford University Press, Oxford, 2020), e-book version, 491–527

Sonnicksen, Jared, "Federalism and Democracy: A Tense Relationship", in Tudela, José, Kölling, Mario and Reviriego, Fernando (eds.), *Calidad democrática y organización territorial* (Marcial Pons, Madrid-Barcelona-Buenos Aires-São Paulo, 2018), 29–50

Tierney, Stephen, *The Federal Contract: A Constitutional Theory of Federalism* (Oxford University Press, Oxford, 2022)

Trettel, Martina, *La democrazia partecipativa negli ordinamenti composti: studio di diritto comparato sull'incidenza della tradizione giuridica nelle democratic innovations* (ESI, Naples, 2020)

Index

For Product Safety Concerns and Information please contact our EU representative GPSR@taylorandfrancis.com
Taylor & Francis Verlag GmbH, Kaufingerstraße 24, 80331 München, Germany

www.ingramcontent.com/pod-product-compliance
Lightning Source LLC
LaVergne TN
LVHW021120300926
849160LV00010B/795
9781032797199